Traditional Micronesian Societies

Traditional Micronesian Societies

Adaptation, Integration, and Political Organization

Glenn Petersen

University of Hawai‘i Press
Honolulu

Library of Congress Cataloging-in-Publication Data
Petersen, Glenn.
  Traditional Micronesian societies : adaptation, integration, and political organization /
Glenn Petersen.
    p. cm.
  Includes bibliographical references and index.
  ISBN 978-0-8248-3248-3 (hard cover : alk. paper)
  1. Ethnology—Micronesia. 2. Matrilineal kinship—Micronesia. 3. Clans—
Micronesia. 4. Social networks—Micronesia. 5. Chiefdoms—Micronesia.
6. Micronesia—History. 7. Micronesia—Politics and government. 8. Micronesia—
Social life and customs. I. Title.
  GN669.P48 2009
  305.8009965—dc22

                                    2008055824

Maps by Manoa Mapworks, Inc.

Designed by University of Hawai'i Press production staff

Printed by The Maple-Vail Book Manufacturing Group

For Damian and Iulihda Primo, who taught me so much
about what it means to be Pohnpeian.
And for Grace, who's been teaching me so much
about what it means to be human.

Contents

Acknowledgments

This book has a very long history, starting as it did over thirty years ago when I first began my own voyaging to Micronesia. I have lived on and off with the family of Damian and Iulihda Primo on the farmstead Otoi, in the community known as Awak on Pohnpei, since 1974. More than anyone else, Damian and Iuli were responsible for drawing me back to the islands, and for all that I have learned about what it means to be Pohnpeian. All the Primos of Otoi and many of the other people of Awak have contributed to my education, but in addition to Damian and Iuli, I especially want to thank Dorip Primo, Lukas Ladore, and Anastasio Dosalwa, each of whom helped me in particularly memorable ways. Among all the many other Micronesians who have aided and taught me, I acknowledge Kikuo Apis' friendship.

A handful of senior scholars first motivated me to undertake this book, and I deeply appreciate their encouragement. Leonard Mason, Ward Goodenough, Douglas Oliver, and Robert Kiste each in his own way helped convince me that I could do this. Francis X. Hezel, SJ, made all the resources of the Micronesian Seminar available to me and has given me boundless encouragement.

Because the gestation period for this book has to be measured in decades, there are far too many people whose work and ideas have influenced me over the years for me to either clearly recall or adequately acknowledge, and far too many will have to go unnamed. But in the course of the five years I spent writing this I called directly upon a number of scholars for specific information, advice, or critical perspective, and I do want to thank them individually: Fran Hezel, John Haglelgam, Kenneth Rehg, Jeff Marck, Nancy Pollock, Karen Nero, Sherwood Lingenfelter, Lawrence Carucci, Michael Rynkiewich, Juliana Flinn, Bernd Lambert, Peter Black, Richard Parmentier, Brian Bender, Paul Rainbird, Anne Chambers, Diane Ragone, Nyree Zerega, and Frantisek Lichtenberk. Dean Myrna Chase of Baruch College's School of Arts and Sciences provided generous financial support for the final stages of this work, and Louisa Moy of the Interlibrary Loan Office at Baruch College's Newman Library tracked down and acquired all the source materials I sought. Emily Pearl did a great deal to polish my prose. I have taught with William Alkire's Lamotrek ethnography for over fifteen years now, and much of what I have come to understand about the nature of Micronesian societies derives from explaining Alkire's account to my students; I thank both him and them. Some of my views here were honed in the course of disagreements about the nature of traditional Micronesian society that I had with the late Per Hage; I am sorry he will not be able to read the work he had so much influence upon, even if he would have agreed with so little of it. David Hanlon and I first met thirty-five years ago in the *nahs* (meetinghouse) at Peinais, in Awak, Pohnpei, and have been disagreeing for much of the time since then about whether Micronesia is something more than a figment of scientists' imaginations. A significant part of what I have written here springs directly from my debates with him; I feel fairly certain that I haven't changed his mind, but in the spirit of sibling rivalry I'd like to think I've convinced him he hasn't won yet.

CHAPTER 1

Introduction

A Perspective on Traditional Micronesian Life

"MICRONESIA" is the name scientists have given to a vast expanse of islands in the central and western Pacific Ocean, and the people who live on these islands have long been called Micronesians. This is not, of course, their traditional name for themselves—indeed, they had none. At least some of them, though, being intrepid voyagers and skilled navigators, have always had a good sense of where all the islands lie, who lives on them, and how to sail among them. The peoples, societies, and cultures of these islands have a great deal in common, and it makes sense to speak of them as a whole. This is a book about them and about the ways in which they have lived their lives. Aspects of their lives have always been changing, and the kinds of changes and the rates at which they have changed have increased since the arrival of outsiders in the nineteenth century. Although much of Micronesian social life continues to reflect these traditional outlooks and practices, so much has changed in recent generations that many young Micronesians today do not clearly understand what their ancestors' lives were like.

I wrote this book as a means of providing a perspective on traditional Micronesian life not only to outsiders who would like to know more about the peoples of these islands, then, but also to help younger Micronesians understand and appreciate the extraordinary achievements of their peoples. While I have tried to be as exact and as accurate as I possibly can in presenting this material, there is little doubt in my own mind that a part of what I am doing is *celebrating* traditional Micronesian societies. The people of Micronesia, and especially of Pohnpei, have been consistently welcoming, hospitable, and open to me for well over three decades now, and this book is a form of homage to them, an expression of gratitude for all they have taught me, both about their own lives and about myself.

MICRONESIA'S ISLANDS are for the most part strikingly beautiful places, and they are, when the weather is good (which is most of the time), very pleasant places to live. But life there, especially on the low-lying atolls, can be difficult in times of drought and when typhoons strike. More than anything else, I believe, it is the social organization of Micronesian communities that has enabled them to survive and even to thrive under these conditions. Micronesians have forged systematic human relations within and between communities, ensuring that everyone works consistently at promoting the general welfare. Virtually everything a Micronesian possesses is shared with family and neighbors, and every family and community is connected by a web of strands to many other islands and communities. In this way, everyone is ensured of being cared for and protected when in need.

The central point of this book, around which all the other themes revolve, is simple: Micronesian societies are organized around interlocking lineages and clans. Lineages are relatively small groups, for the most part located within single communities. Each lineage is a segment of a larger clan, which in turn has numerous lineages dispersed among many different communities and on many separate islands. It is the dispersed character of the clans that provides Micronesians with networks of support, but it is the lineages, with their patterns of face-to-face interaction, that typify the flow of daily life. The lineages possess land and control political titles, regulate marriages, provide the matrix within which child rearing takes place, and in general endow individual Micronesians with a sense of personal identity. Micronesians draw upon their families' lands and the landscapes and seascapes of their home islands for some part of their sense of self, and they draw as well upon their communities. But their personas as members of these communities are formed in the lineages in which they are raised, and as actors in the social dramas of everyday life they are always rooted in their lineages.

In order to describe and explain Micronesian societies, I have broken social life into a number of distinct topics. I make these distinctions purely for purposes of clarity and explanation—in real life all these elements are woven seamlessly into one another. The chapters of this book represent my understandings of how particular aspects of Micronesian societies work. After the present introduction, I begin with a chapter meant to give an overview of just what I think Micronesia is (and a brief consideration of scholars' debates about whether Micronesia actually exists as a genuine or meaningful region) and what it includes. This is followed by an account of how Micronesia was originally settled, how its peoples adapted to conditions there, and how several basic adaptations diffused throughout the islands. I then consider the fundamental matters of descent (ideas about how individuals and groups are bound together through the ties of kinship) and descent groups (that is, the practical organization of the kin groups). Next I take up the closely interlinked subjects of households and families, and land and labor. Two chapters cover sociopolitical life, the first focusing on chieftainship and government, the second on politics and leadership. I then turn to art, religion, and values. Finally, I examine a number of exceptions to the common Micronesian patterns of social life.

Many books have been written about events and societies in Micronesia, but only William Alkire's *An Introduction to the Peoples and Cultures of Micronesia* has attempted to describe at length the nature of traditional Micronesian society and culture. Alkire's book appeared more than thirty years ago and for the most part draws upon the same sources I use here. My approach, however, is quite different from Alkire's. He chose to treat the individual island societies sequentially and discretely, covering, for example, Palau, Chuuk, and the Marshall Islands as separate topics.[1] This approach reflects what has perhaps been the most common way of thinking about Micronesia: that is, that while there are important commonalities among its many societies, each is distinct and deserves to be considered primarily on its own terms. I have decided to write about Micronesia from a quite different perspective. What attracts my attention is not just the similarities among the many societies but my sense that these similarities exist for reasons. It is not simply that the islands are in relative proximity and have influenced one another, but rather that some common patterns of social organization proved to be so useful that they were in time adopted by all these peoples. To this end, then, I have organized my account around themes and explored both the ways in which these themes can be encountered on all the islands and the ways they work themselves out in distinctly different styles on individual islands. That is, while I am by no means suggesting that society and culture are identical throughout Micronesia, I am insisting that the commonalities are far more telling than the differences.

In the best of all worlds a writer has a very clear notion of just whom he or she is writing for. I have written this book, however, with a somewhat ambiguous sense of who my readership is, and that has made it difficult for me to adopt an appropriate and consistent style. I have in fact written this for three different audiences, with different needs and expectations. I would like to think that this will be used in college and university anthropology classes on Pacific islands societies, as an introduction to the peoples of Micronesia and as a systematic exploration of the ways in which traditional Oceanic societies have adapted to the conditions they have faced. To that end, I have tried not to take for granted readers' knowledge about much at all concerning the area. Second, I have hopes that this will be available in Micronesia, and that Micronesians, particularly young people, will turn to it for an accessible, reliable, and respectful account of their ancestors' lives and as a worthwhile attempt to explain why Micronesians do things the way they do them. Finally, I have at the same time written this with my professional colleagues in mind. There is a small but dedicated core of scholars who continue to explore and puzzle over the nature and history of Oceanic societies, of how and why they came to be the way they are. There are points at which I have shied away from trying to explain just why certain aspects of Micronesian social life are the way they are, but I have tried resolutely to demonstrate just how most of these facets are linked with one another, how they function, and, to the extent I am able, how they came to be.

I decided, after much thought, to avoid too much speculation; while there are a few places where I've gone out on a limb, particularly in the matter of what I call the prehistoric "breadfruit revolution," I assume that to the extent that this work will be useful to a wide variety of readers, it will have to be reliable, and that means *not* speculating about too much.

I refer continually to "traditional Micronesian societies." I spend considerable time in chapter 2 discussing what actually constitutes Micronesia, but I should explain right here that I use the term in its historical sense, referring to all the islands and peoples of the region. In recent years there has been a tendency to restrict the term "Micronesian" to just the citizens of the Federated States of Micronesia (that is, the central and eastern Caroline Islands). While the contemporary political scene cannot be ignored, of course, in historical terms the web of connections among all of these island peoples is of much greater importance than the rather restricted definitions of today's nation-states. I use "Micronesian" throughout this book to refer to all the peoples of Palau, the Marianas, the Marshalls, Kiribati, and Nauru as well as the FSM.

I should also take a moment here to explain what I mean by "traditional," a term anthropologists of necessity often use but one about which they do not always agree. I do not for a moment imagine that Micronesia was essentially stable, quiet, and unchanging for millennia. My chapter on island prehistory makes it clear that significant changes have been taking place pretty much throughout the two thousand–plus years that Micronesia has been inhabited. But the very existence of a common framework for organizing social life tells us that a basic pattern proved so successful that it was adopted throughout the area and retained for a very long time. It is this shared pattern, characteristic of all Micronesian societies in the nineteenth century, when most European contact got under way, to which I refer when I speak of "traditional society." It was quickly and dramatically transformed in some places, such as the Marianas (where it was forcibly destroyed by the Spanish) and Kosrae (where epidemics nearly wiped out the entire population). It lasted until quite recently on some of the smaller and more isolated of the Caroline atolls. And it has undergone a gradual and erratic transformation in most of the islands, as a result of trade for commercially manufactured goods, conversion to Christianity, colonialism, and war. I discuss the impact of these changes in the epilogue, linking them directly to the later history of the islands, as the Micronesians have grappled with the forces of colonialism, world war, decolonization, and, most recently, independence.

I have given a great deal of thought to just what tense to write this book in and, quite frankly, have never arrived at an entirely satisfactory conclusion. Much of what I describe here lies squarely in the past, and it is possible that by using the present tense I will confuse some readers into thinking that all these patterns of behavior still exist. I have in the end, however, decided to risk this misunderstanding in order to make the larger, and what I think is the more important, point: that despite the many changes that have taken place, life in Micronesia is still profoundly Micronesian. I write consistently in the present tense (with occasional exceptions) partly as a means of avoiding the confusion that would follow if I were to shift back and forth between past and present, and partly because I want to emphasize the continuities in Micronesian life. Patterns of descent group organization, household composition, and political process are no longer what they once were, to be sure, but they remain much more Micronesian than not.[2]

There are, of course, problematic aspects in this approach. We have very little in the way of reliable ethnographic reporting on any Micronesian societies that were not already appreciably affected by powerful outside influences. There are only a handful of trustworthy accounts of traditional Micronesian belief systems. Likewise, political processes on most Micronesian islands were in some ways already influenced by depopulation and the interference of colonial administrations by the time they were described. And nearly all of them were engaging in some form of trade relations with outsiders, either European of Japanese.

I would like to say something clear and consistent about using early historical sources—that is, the writings of explorers, traders, castaways, and missionaries—but I find that their powers of observation and critical analysis varied enormously. In all honesty, I have no systematic means of evaluating their reliability. To take but one example, the Irish sailor James O'Connell was shipwrecked on Pohnpei in the late 1820s, lived there for several years, and later published a lengthy account of his experiences. Saul Riesenberg produced a critical edition of this work. As the distinguished Pacific historian H. E. Maude (editor of the series in which it appeared) put it in his introduction, the worth of O'Connell's account "as a main ethnographical source on Micronesian culture is largely invalidated if it is accepted uncritically at its face value." Maude says that in his annotations to the edition, Riesenberg describes a "maze of exaggerations, anachronisms, improbabilities, and outright fabrications, commingled with thoroughly accurate and original observations." Some of O'Connell's statements "are flagrantly incorrect," "apparent falsehoods," "far from reality," or "deliberate untruths" (Maude in O'Connell 1972, 5, 18–20). I nevertheless find that O'Connell, because he lacked the ulterior motives of missionaries and administrators (most of whom sought to portray Micronesians as being in dire need of intervention on behalf of European and American civilization) and because he spent vastly more time in one place than any of the explorers, was a remarkably candid observer (although he also, of course, wanted to sell books), and his descriptions of many aspects of daily life are invaluable. I know of no simple, straightforward way to explain how it is that I have decided what parts of his work to distrust and which parts to make use of.

And this in fact holds true for the ways I use all the available sources, including those of trained ethnographers.

In the end, I have to acknowledge that I consider myself able to write this book only because I have spent lengthy periods over the course of more than half my life living on Pohnpei, in Pohnpeian homes, speaking Pohnpeian, and getting to know individual Pohnpeians as they have lived their lives and grown and changed through the years (and I have also traveled throughout the rest of the region). I believe that, as a consequence of these experiences, I have developed a sense of what to believe and what to discount. I have engaged in decades-long conversations about aspects of Micronesian life with a number of others whose judgments I have come to value and trust. I do not assume that what I know about life on Pohnpei today gives me an entirely clear picture of what life was like there 150 years ago or of what other Micronesian societies are like, but it does provide me with an excellent lens through which to view both Pohnpei's past and the rest of Micronesia. How I have chosen to draw upon written sources, then, is of a piece with all that I write here. It is rooted in what I have elsewhere described as the process of struggle that lies at the core of ethnography (Petersen 2005).

Ethnography is not simply the description of cultures; it is also, I think, a necessarily and inherently critical activity. It requires struggle: the ongoing struggle between trying to see what is actually happening and trying to put it into an interpretive framework; the struggle, once one has arrived at tentative conclusions, to then continue paying attention to what is actually going on; and the struggle between seeing patterns of social behavior and losing sight of individual actors engaged in living their own lives. These struggles include the willingness to appreciate tensions between the different aspects of direct observation and interpretation, and between the actions of individuals and collective patterns, and the recognition that a successful attempt to resolve the contradictions in what one sees in and understands about a society should not reconcile them away. This struggle can lead us toward an appreciation of how the countervailing forces and tendencies within societies work to preserve the whole.

This book is at least as much an ethnographic account as it is a work in ethnology. The distinction between ethnography and ethnology, never particularly clear to anyone not immersed in these fields in the first place, is one that has largely disappeared or at least dissipated in recent decades. While "ethnography" has generally referred to the study of individual societies or cultures and to published accounts of them, "ethnology" refers to scientific attempts to explain relations among cultures and the processes of development that shape them. Ethnology today, ironically, is practiced for the most part by archaeologists, whose interests in the patterns of historical development sometimes outweigh their concern with the complexities of what has actually been observed. This book is something of a hybrid. It is ethnographic in outlook, in that it seeks to faithfully describe Micronesian cultures, but it is equally ethnological in intent, because it is meant to explain both how multiple aspects of Micronesian societies are integrated with one another and how these came to be so widely diffused across the islands.

About Micronesia

I discuss the general character of Micronesian societies in chapter 2, and their prehistory in chapter 3, but a brief introduction to the islands themselves and the seas around them—an account of the natural world the Micronesians occupy—is called for.

Micronesia extends across the Western Pacific Ocean from the southwest islands of Palau and the northernmost islands of the Marianas archipelago eastward to the northern outliers of the Marshall Islands' Ratak chain and the southern islands of Kiribati.[3] The latitude at the northern extremity of the Marianas is approximately 20 degrees north and at the southern tip of Kiribati, 2 degrees south, but most of Micronesia lies between 5 and 10 degrees north of the equator. The island of Tobi, at the western edge of Micronesia, lies at 131 degrees east longitude, and Arorae in Kiribati, the easternmost island, lies at 177 degrees east. This is a distance of approximately 3,100 statute miles, that is, roughly the same distance that lies between the east and west coasts of the United States.

There are many different kinds of islands in Micronesia, and diverse ways to count their numbers. Several are relatively large (over one hundred square miles), most are quite small (less than a mile square in area), and some reefs and shoals are barely awash. Many of the atolls include numerous reef islets, and in enumerating islands it is important to distinguish between inhabited, sociologically meaningful units and simple raw numbers of physical units. It is also important to keep in mind that the atolls, though comprising only tiny bits of dry land, often have vast expanses of lagoon, and that it is the marine resources of these lagoons that provide most of the basic subsistence for the atoll populations. In Bruce Karolle's summary (1993, 41) there are 123 island population units (or inhabited islands) and over 2,200 individual islets and reefs, altogether totaling a little more than one thousand square miles of dry land.

The islands have been (and are still being) formed by a variety of processes. In general there are three basic island types: continental and volcanic (known as high islands), and coral (low islands). The continental islands—Palau, Yap, and the Marianas—rest on the eastern edge of the Philippine tectonic plate and are composed of essentially the same archaic geological materials as eastern Asia. The Pacific plate dives beneath the Philippine plate at this point, in a process known as subduction, and this feature marks what is known as the andesite line. To the east

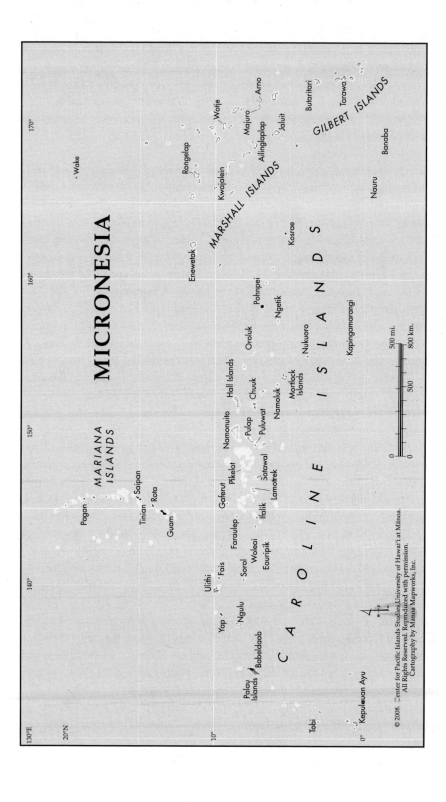

lies the Pacific basin proper, and its seafloor is composed primarily of andesite, a form of basalt. At many points along the sea bottom there are weak spots or cracks through which molten magma flows upward in what are known as plumes, forming undersea volcanoes. Some of these grow so large that they eventually breach the ocean surface, forming the volcanic islands. The intense weathering processes of the equatorial climate erode these islands away. Their soils are fertile but thin; because of the climate they support dense vegetation, and the Micronesians have developed agricultural systems that in many ways mimic the natural vegetation, with a variety of tree and root crops, especially breadfruit, coconut, yams, and taros.

Coral reefs form around all these islands and provide rich habitats for myriad varieties of sea life. As the volcanic islands erode, over the course of millions of years, reefs that were initially joined to the shoreline (fringing reefs) are transformed into freestanding rings that encircle the island (barrier reefs) and are in time left surrounding nothing but open lagoons, thus forming atolls. The relentless battering of currents, storms, and typhoons fragments the reefs, and at points where the shattered coral collects, islets slowly build up. Because of the porous character of the underlying coral, seawater filters in beneath these islets, but freshwater (which has a lower density) from the abundant rains floats atop the salt water in what is known as a lens. By digging down into the sand and coral and fashioning pits that are saturated with this freshwater, atoll dwellers are able to grow several kinds of taro, which serve as the staple crops of nearly all the atolls. The hybrid breadfruit varieties characteristic of Micronesia thrive in the salty atoll soils (unlike most other breadfruit), and while the atolls are not as fertile and productive as the higher islands, they can be fruitful, and many have supported dense populations.

Micronesian populations do not appear ever to have grown as large as those of some Polynesian island chains (e.g., Hawai'i). There are many reasons for this, but tropical diseases do not seem to have been chief among them. It is quite possible that the primary check on Micronesia's population growth has been the climate. In the best of times, the islands are spectacularly bountiful, but weather conditions at times prevail against life there.

Nearly all of Micronesia lies within or along the edge of the Intertropical Convergence Zone, a wide band of low-pressure air that runs along or near the equator. Heavy rainfall and much storm activity are associated with this phenomenon, and its precise location is unstable, tending at times to drift northward or south. This zone is particularly affected by what climatologists call the El Niño–Southern Oscillation (ENSO, more popularly known simply as El Niño). During these El Niño periods the entire climate of the region shifts, and vast areas that normally receive abundant rainfall can experience prolonged droughts. The largest islands, such as Pohnpei, are relatively protected by their deeply saturated surfaces, but smaller islands, and especially the atolls, may be devastated during these periods (which typically last for six months to a year or so).

The solar energy that heats these tropical waters also generates frequent storm activity, powerful typhoons, and occasional super-typhoons of unbelievable intensity. The atolls and smaller islands are often overwhelmed by storms and typhoons, and walls of seawater driven ahead of the winds—storm surges—flow over the atolls and inundate their crops, rendering the gardens sterile. Low islanders must abandon their homes following these depredations and voyage to islands that have escaped the full brunt of the storms. While the high islands are not quite so vulnerable, a direct hit by a major typhoon can destroy most vegetation on even a high island and cause considerable disruption.

The combination of these aspects of the Micronesian climate help explain important aspects of Micronesian social organization and culture. During the best of times the islands are fruitful, pleasant places to live. But they are subject, if not regularly then at least recurrently, to weather-induced destruction. They are far too valuable to abandon, but they can be inhabited only by peoples who have developed means of preserving themselves in the wake of typhoons and droughts. And it is the extraordinary webs of ties binding the individual populations of Micronesian islands that characterize social life there. Micronesia's dispersed matrilineal clans are elegantly adapted to this task. All Micronesians are, through their mothers, members of dispersed clans and, through their fathers, have close ties to additional clans. Each clan has member lineages resident on a number of islands. When extreme hardship visits any given island, its people are able to call upon these connections, journey to other islands, and settle for a time with close relatives while they rehabilitate the damaged gardens.

There are striking differences between the situations of the high and low islanders, and yet their lives are in most ways profoundly similar. The low islanders are above all else focused on the seas that surround them. They derive an overwhelmingly important portion of their subsistence from their lagoons and from the open ocean. For men, deep-sea voyaging skills and esoteric navigational knowledge lie at the pinnacle of all that is deemed worthy. High islanders are more focused on their gardens and on producing foodstuffs that can be given away at feasts, so that individuals and lineages can garner prestige and higher political titles, a pattern that reaches its zenith on Pohnpei.

Environmental and economic conditions for the most part mean that there are larger populations on the larger islands, and the hierarchical politics that organize these larger populations increase in intensity or complexity. Yet the elementary principles that shape how interpersonal relations, social organization, and political process unfold actually vary little between large and small islands. The ties of clanship are virtually identical almost everywhere, and they bind individuals and lineages in distinct communities on the high islands to one another in precisely the same ways that they connect low islanders. And while two of the islands, Kosrae and Nauru, are really quite isolated, they have nevertheless retained all the elements of the matrilineal organization so characteristic of the others. Although Micronesian matrilineal clan and lineage organization probably developed as they did in response to the environmental exigencies of life in the region, these forms have proved so effective in organizing social life *within* communities that they have remained strong and vital even where their primary purpose is no longer linking island populations together.

CHAPTER 2

Micronesia and Micronesians

I WOULD NOT have written an entire book about Micronesia if I did not believe that it existed—obviously, I do. But there are those who doubt Micronesia's existence as a meaningful culture area (that is, a region characterized by a range of similar cultural practices; I discuss this concept at length below). Those who dismiss its validity or usefulness as a conceptual category, however, have for the most part ignored the underlying question of whether it makes sense to speak of culture areas or regions at all. To think cogently about Micronesia, it is worth addressing two questions: Why do we even speak of culture areas? And are there compelling reasons for speaking of a region called Micronesia? Because those reading this book are most interested specifically in Micronesia, let me first address the question of whether Micronesia is a valid concept or category.

Does "Micronesia" Exist?

David Hanlon, a historian who has devoted his career to studies of Pohnpei and Micronesia, has called into question the existence of anything that might be conceived of as Micronesia as a whole. Indeed, he denies that there is something properly called Micronesia. "For the most part," he writes, "Micronesia has existed only in the minds of people from the outside who have sought to create an administrative entity for purposes of control and rule" (1989, 1). He refers to the region as no more than "a figment" of ethnographers' imaginations—"a colonial construct" (1999, 53, 76). "Indicative of only the grossest geographical ordering of the area," Hanlon says, "the term 'Micronesia' actually reveals far more about Euro-American society's concerns for a neat, manageable, efficient, and logical ordering of the world" (1989, 2). He goes on to say that "to speak, then, of Micronesia would seem" to give "credence to a nonentity" (1999, 76). In addition to his resistance to the very notion of an area whose existence has been formulated by people living outside it, Hanlon also argues that "similarities noted by ethnographers in cultural practices or institutions regarding land, kinship, social organization, rank, and political hierarchy do not constitute a culturally homogenous entity" (1989, 2). That is, in his view, any notion of Micronesia implies homogeneity among its peoples, societies, and cultures; the fact that significant differences exist among them means, then, that Micronesia does not truly constitute a culture area. Even after considering much of the evidence I present in this book, he concludes that "it remains difficult to see Micronesia as a whole and unified culture area" (Hanlon 2009, 97).

Hanlon is hardly alone in this—many others question the soundness of recognizing Micronesia as a coherent region. Campbell observes that traditional Micronesia was more culturally "heterogeneous than Polynesia, and generalizations about Micronesian society immediately call to mind a cloud of qualifications and exceptions" (1989, 23). In his comprehensive account of Pacific islands societies, Oliver draws the same conclusion: "The label is more geographic than cultural; while many of the societies in this immense arc share some cultural features, they fall short of the degree of cultural homogeneity that characterized Polynesia" (1989, 967). The question took on pointed political meaning in the 1970s, when the dismantling of the old Trust Territory of the Pacific Islands played a strategic part in the Micronesians' efforts to bring an end to American rule over them. As Leonard Mason put it, "Both Micronesians and Americans have declared that the Trust Territory of the Pacific Islands, commonly referred to as Micronesia, is nothing more than an artificial unit put together and held together by foreigners" (1975, 5), a point to which I shall return in the epilogue.

More recently Paul Rainbird has written that he finds "no cohesive 'Micronesian culture'" but, rather, diversity and "obvious connections with places external to the conceptual construct reified by a line on the map" (1994, 296). He has nevertheless provided a thoughtful, nuanced approach to the question, emphasizing the fluidity of boundaries and the fusion of human types in a region where so much of life entails movement in a sea of islands. He opts to use "Micronesia" as "shorthand for the region, without implying cultural homogeneity" (2004, 40).

Two things seem obvious regarding the debate about whether Micronesia is a coherent region or not and, if it is, how it should be defined. First, the dispute seems to be largely "academic," in the worst sense of the term. Second, issues of both geography and cultural practices have always been near the heart of the matter. The first scientific conceptualization of Micronesia grew out of systematic attempts to map the human populations of the Pacific islands. M. G. L. Domeny de Rienzi proposed a categorization of the peoples of Oceania at a meeting of the Paris Société de Géographie at the end of 1831. J. S. C. Dumont d'Urville then presented his own views at the next meeting (and subsequently shaped nearly all later Pacific islands ethnology). When d'Urville published them in the society's *Bulletin*

(1832), he made it clear that he had developed certain of his views in contradistinction to de Rienzi's, though both men used the terms "Polynesia," "Melanesia," and "Micronesia."

While careful comparison of the two men's work shows significant differences in the criteria they used to define Micronesia, they were in fact overwhelmingly in accord; the rhetorical skirmishing between them was for the most part over academic issues. De Rienzi's "Micronesia" referred to islands lying north of what we now call Micronesia, in particular the groups of islands known as the Bonins and the Volcanoes (de Rienzi 1872, 12, 309–336). He included the islands stretching from Palau to Kiribati (that is, what we now think of as Micronesia) within Polynesia. D'Urville, on the other hand, waffled a bit. He argued first that Polynesians and Micronesians are essentially a single people, and then that they are different enough from one another to be separate, coequal categories (along with the Melanesians). That is, he was attempting to create a taxonomy that was simultaneously inclusive and exclusive. Thus for de Rienzi what we now think of as Micronesia was simply a part of Polynesia, while for d'Urville it both was and was not a part of Polynesia.

The categories the two proposed were grounded in both culture and geography. They spoke unambiguously in terms of divisions framed by the cardinal directions. D'Urville's Polynesia/Polynésie is "eastern Oceania"/"l'Océanie orientale"; Micronesia/Micronésie is "northern Oceania"/"l'Océanie boreal"; Melanesia/Mélanesia is "southern Oceania"/"l'Océanie australe"; and Malaysia/Malaisie is "western Oceania"/"l'Océanie occidental" (1832, 5–6).

Both d'Urville and de Rienzi were dealing with the very issue that still challenges us today: at what point or under what circumstances does one choose between emphasizing the similarities or the differences? (This is of course an epistemological problem; my concern here is only with its relevance to the question of just what constitutes Micronesia.) Both were impressed with the essentially common character of the many Polynesian societies while acknowledging the relatively heterogeneous make-up of the Micronesian societies. But both were equally struck by the high degree of social and cultural resemblance among all the islands extending from Palau to the Marshalls and Kiribati, which both called the Carolines. For de Rienzi the similarities among the Carolines were as important as the similarities among them and Polynesia. D'Urville, on the other hand, judged that although the differences among the peoples of the Carolines were dwarfed by the resemblances, they were nonetheless significant enough to distinguish them from the Polynesian peoples, who were especially notable precisely because of their fundamental uniformity. This is in fact very much where the arguments lie today. Are the differences among Micronesian societies significant enough to conclude that they constitute a coherent region or not? It is, ultimately, a matter of judgment.

I hasten to make two general points. First, all culture areas or regions are intellectual, rather than naturally occurring, categories, and second, issues of homogeneity and heterogeneity are not of primary importance if we keep in mind the dynamics of adaptation and historical development and focus on the ways in which these dynamics result in changes through time and space.

Hanlon believes that the relevance of the culture areas approach (which I explain below) is "increasingly questionable" (2009, 97), but I think it is worth noting that the grouping of distinct entities into categories is a fundamental aspect of human thought. The relevant questions are whether these categories are purely mental constructs or whether they in some measure reflect reality, and how useful they are as we try to make sense of the world around us. We must remember that we are talking about real people, real places, and real behaviors. The ways we group them together and the distinctions we make among them, however, are no more than perspectives we impose upon them. We construct these categories, and make distinctions among them, for specific reasons. In the end, we must keep in mind just what the purposes of these categories are, and judge their validity with these purposes in mind.

We speak of Europe, for instance, or of Latin America or Southeast Asia in the same way that we speak of Oceania. There is nothing homogeneous about the societies and cultures grouped within these regions, but their existence is rarely called into question.[1] Similar processes have been going on since the beginnings of recorded history. Herodotus (1998) wrote of Greece, Persia, and Libya, though what he meant by these terms has little to do with how we use them today. As his "Libya"—North Africa—came to be better known, it was in turn apportioned into the Maghreb, the Sahara, the Sahel, and the Sudan.[2] And as these have more recently been partitioned into nation-states (e.g., Libya, Algeria, Mali, Sudan), most of the older names have grown irrelevant and anachronistic. In time, as the Commonwealth of the Northern Mariana Islands, the Federated States of Micronesia, Kiribati, Nauru, and the republics of Palau and the Marshall Islands further develop their individual political characters and their places on the regional and world stages, the older notion of Micronesia shall perhaps become irrelevant and anachronistic as well. Indeed, the rise of the nation-state has had a way of turning what once were fluid and permeable transitions into abrupt borders. But this should not keep us from appreciating how the peoples who first settled these lands managed to do so with such magnificent success. And they did so largely because of the common adaptations they shared. The issue of whether generalizations about contemporary Micronesia are counterproductive or not is not especially relevant to several thousand years of the region's earlier history.

Hanlon tells us that "anthropology, in the particularism of its ethnographies, has always possessed the power to subvert the idea of Micronesia," and he wonders why "it has not challenged the idea more aggressively and publicly" (1999, 76). In this book I seek to make an entirely contrary point: through adept picking and choosing of workable ways of doing things, pursuit of local adaptations, and the interplay of individual initiatives with broader social innovations, the peoples of these islands have displayed their capacity for changing and developing their lives where necessary and for retaining and preserving their traditions where appropriate. Micronesia exists as a category because, in the dynamism of the historic survival of its peoples, they drew upon a set of shared strategies eminently adapted to the environments in which they lived.

Given the problems that inhere in demarcating Micronesia as a culture area, one might wonder why I have not followed the course taken by Alkire in his Introduction to the Peoples and Cultures of Micronesia (1977) and simply ignored the question. My response is that my own perspective draws on a long tradition in human geography. Because humans do not passively occupy their environments but actively pursue goals within them, they come in time to establish regions that reflect their ways of life. Over time societies and environments mutually influence one another, forming culture areas or regions with unique constellations of natural and cultural elements. Put succinctly, "people create regions" and "regions shape peoples' activities" (Bradshaw 2002, 11–12). One of the central themes of this book is that Micronesian societies have in part been shaped by their active responses to the difficulties of occupying these islands. They have done so through characteristic patterns of social organization, similar in many ways to patterns found throughout the eastern Pacific, but in certain key aspects unique to their own region. At its core this social adaptation hinges on networks of dispersed matrilineal clans and localized lineages. Underlying patterns of household ties, land tenure, and political organization are linked to this matrilineal core. People are afforded enormous mobility through their membership in these widely dispersed clans but are able to manage their own local affairs through their lineages. People and land are readily reallocated as changing demographic and ecological conditions warrant.

Matters of scaling and time are important here as well. In the realm of human cultures, one can identify broad and encompassing culture areas (e.g., sub-Saharan Africa, the Arctic), easily recognizable subvarieties (Chinese and Japanese within Asia), regional or provincial distinctiveness (Normandy and Brittany within France), and local differences (Geneva and Schwyz within Switzerland). Alfred Louis Kroeber wrote, "Human culture is a continuum or continuity, but a continuity gradually changing, and changing equally as it is followed through space and through time" (1948, 262–263). Or as the point has been more recently put, "Places and regions are dynamic, with changing properties and fluid boundaries that are the product of the interplay of a wide variety of environmental and human factors" (Marston et al. 2002, 15).

The problems that we encounter in generalizing about Micronesia as a whole are equally apparent when we look closely at what seem to be discrete local cultures within the broader sweep of the islands. While a continuum of language, culture, and family ties spans the low islands between Yap and Chuuk, for instance, the peoples of the eastern and western islands in Chuuk Lagoon also argue sometimes that they are distinct. The atolls between Pohnpei and Kosrae have been influenced by both of those larger islands, but also by voyagers from the Marshalls and Kiribati, with whom they share similar environments. The Ralik and Radak chains of the Marshalls are distinct enough from one another to have separate names, but the lives of those in the islands in the south of both chains resemble one another more than they do those in the chains' northernmost islands. The peoples of Butaritari and Makin in northern Kiribati are more like their neighbors in the southern Marshalls in their social organization (though not their language) than they are like the southern Kiribati peoples. And then, of course, there are what can be called the outliers. In the same way that Polynesian voyagers occupied islands outside of the area known as Polynesia (including Nukuoro and Kapinga-marangi south of Pohnpei), the low islands to the southwest of Palau are entirely Central Carolinian in their affiliations, while Nui, near the center of Polynesian Tuvalu, is populated by people of Kiribati ancestry.

Micronesians, especially the peoples of the low islands, are mobile, and the region can be understood only in terms of continual interchange, intermixing, and diffusion of linguistic, social, and cultural characteristics. Micronesian languages cannot be understood simply in terms of diverging descent from common roots. Patterns of social interaction produce influences that continually shape languages.

We must bear in mind, as well, the depth of the history we are considering here. Spheres of interaction among islands and island groups change through time, and local regions are thus continually developing, evolving, growing, and contracting. Widely shared legendary accounts tell of past times when there were patterns of interaction among all the central and eastern Carolines. Most locales have multiple, overlapping place-names, reflecting different periods, when given places were identified by specific sets of occupants or events; most communities seem to have continually realigned themselves in constellations with their neighbors. This is even more characteristic of communities *within* any of the larger islands. The notion of a Micronesian culture area, then, should not be taken to imply homogeneity, in either space or time.

Today "the Pacific" is commonly used to describe East Asia and its ties to North America. Traditionally, though, "the Pacific islands" and "the South Pacific" were used interchangeably with each other, and "the Pacific" referred to the islands and island societies extending northeast and east from Indonesia and Australia into the broader ocean basin, a region also known as Oceania. Within this broader region are what nearly everyone familiar with it thinks of as distinct subdivisions—Polynesia, Melanesia, and Micronesia—despite the endless controversies about just what these terms mean.

The definitive mapping of these Pacific culture areas is probably the one sponsored by the University of Hawaiʻi's Center for Pacific Islands Studies and produced by Manoa Mapworks. On it, Polynesia appears as a triangle with its angles at Hawaiʻi, Aotearoa/New Zealand, and Rapa Nui/Easter Island and with an arrow-stem extending into Tuvalu. Melanesia is represented as an oval with its endpoints curving around Fiji and New Guinea. Micronesia is represented as a parallelogram tucked into the angle between the Polynesian triangle's western base and the Melanesian oval's northern curve. The three regions appear in roughly the same way on virtually every other map. With the occasional exception of Fiji, there is little dispute over where the boundaries between them lie. The three culture areas are usually defined in the same terms as they are mapped—that is, spatially. But their origins as concepts are more complex than any map can acknowledge.

The notion of Polynesia is the least controversial, but there is nevertheless an aspect of conceptual confusion regarding the underlying principle that defines it, even if there is little—if any—disagreement regarding its composition. Polynesia is constituted by its peoples, the Polynesians, all of whom speak closely related variants of an ancestral Polynesian language and thus have common historical origins. Most of them live on contiguous, though distantly spaced, islands along the easternmost reaches of the inhabited Pacific basin; it is thus reasonable to speak of Polynesia as a coherent region (even if a few Polynesian societies are physically located in Melanesia and Micronesia). The Polynesian-speaking peoples who established societies on islands far to the west, well within the other two culture areas, are commonly called outliers. Melanesia, on the other hand, is nearly always defined by its location: the islands lying north of Australia and running eastward to Polynesia's westernmost border. Because Melanesia can be seen to lump together societies merely because of their proximity, many maintain that it is not truly a coherent category.

These are, then, the two traditionally contrasting means of defining Pacific culture areas: in terms of common historical descent of the people themselves, as in Polynesia, and in purely geographical or spatial terms, as in Melanesia. Comparing the two is in a sense tantamount to what Gilbert Ryle (1949) called a category mistake; they are different sorts of entities, not different examples of a single conceptual class.

This ambiguity returns us to a fundamental question about Micronesia's status as a culture area: Is it to be defined in the same terms as Polynesia—on a clearly defined cultural, historical, and linguistic basis—or in the same way as

Melanesia—in terms of its geography or location? If it can be defined in terms of the former, then it represents a valid category, most scholars would say. If it is defined in the second sense, however, then it probably does not. It is because of this ambiguity that Micronesia's status as a culture area and its existence as a valid category or construct have been challenged. We must remember, however, that culture areas and regions are by their nature constructs: they are conceived of and spoken of for specific reasons—either for the sake of convenience or for the emphasis of certain points—and there is no inherent, or natural, basis for determining what does or does not constitute such a region.

In reality, Micronesia coincides with neither the Polynesian nor the Melanesian format. If we were to define it simply in residual geographic terms, it might as well be included as part of Melanesia, which to my knowledge no one has ever attempted to do. But to define it in purely historical terms of common language and descent, as Polynesia is, would be to privilege Polynesia as the only appropriate model for delimiting culture areas, which it certainly should not be.

Micronesia

There is in fact a well-established linguistic basis for defining a significant portion of Micronesia: the languages of Kiribati, Nauru, the Marshalls, and eastern and central Carolines (and their outliers) are descended from a common ancestor known as Proto-Nuclear Micronesian and together constitute a language group known as Nuclear Micronesian. Judged by this single criterion, however, the Marianas, Palau, and Yap—which have different origins—would not be reckoned as Micronesian. They are, nevertheless, all Micronesian societies.

My premise in this book is that in terms of their social organization and a general range of cultural practices, all the island societies of Micronesia have much more in common with one another than they do with societies in adjacent areas of the Philippines, Indonesia, Melanesia, and Polynesia. As I will show in the chapter on Micronesian prehistory, this is the result of historical processes of social and cultural diffusion. Fundamental patterns of social organization, in particular the dispersed matrilineal clans with their localized, landowning lineages nested within them, are characteristic not only of all the societies descended from Nuclear Micronesian–speaking ancestors but of all these Micronesian peoples. It is my understanding that a basic set of adaptations—which first developed in the eastern Carolines—provided success in surviving the region's environmental exigencies and patterned relations among communities in a manner that allowed them not simply to endure but to flourish. These adaptations ultimately proved so successful that they were readily adopted by almost all the peoples with whom these easterners came into contact.

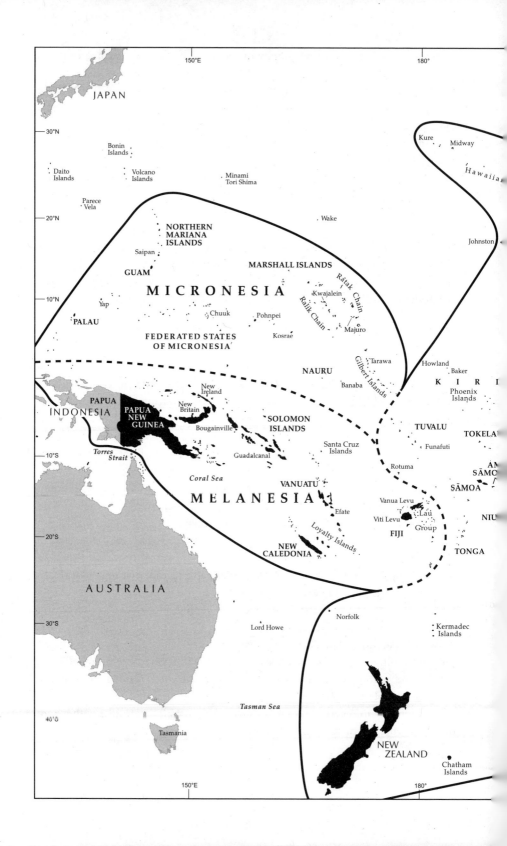

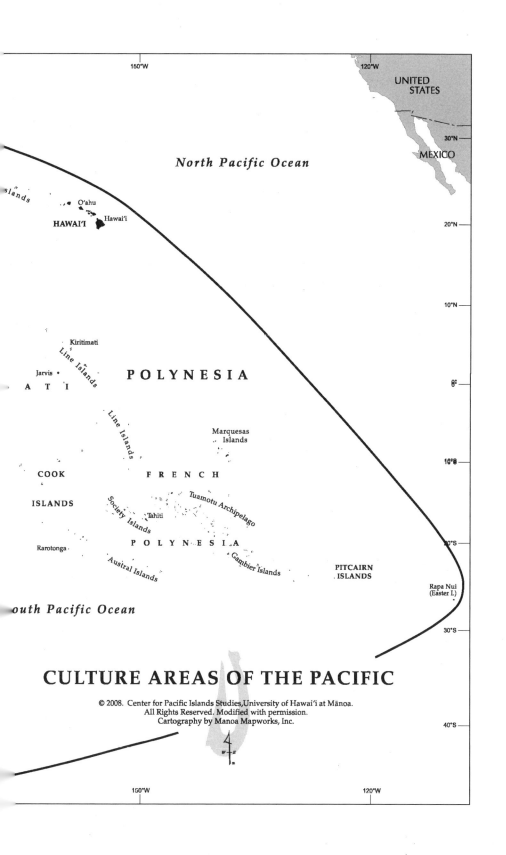

150°W   120°W

UNITED STATES

30°N

North Pacific Ocean

MEXICO

Islands

O'ahu

HAWAI'I   Hawai'i

20°N

10°N

Kiritimati

Line Islands

Jarvis •

P O L Y N E S I A

0°

A T I

Line Islands

Marquesas
Islands

10°S

COOK

F R E N C H

Tuamotu Archipelago

ISLANDS

Society Islands

Tahiti

Rarotonga •

P O L Y N E S I A

20°S

Austral Islands

Gambier Islands

**PITCAIRN
ISLANDS**

Rapa Nui
(Easter I.)

outh Pacific Ocean

30°S

CULTURE AREAS OF THE PACIFIC

© 2008. Center for Pacific Islands Studies, University of Hawai'i at Mānoa.
All Rights Reserved. Modified with permission.
Cartography by Manoa Mapworks, Inc.

40°S

150°W   120°W

Micronesia's peoples did not have a shared sense of themselves as a single people, any more than the Polynesians did, before European navigators and cartographers conferred their respective cognomens upon them. The region is almost impossibly vast, given the available transportation technology, and yet it is clear that there were well-established and commonly used channels of interaction among the islands. This is not to say that each Micronesian island or society was in contact with every other one, but rather that a continuous chain of contacts and connections ultimately linked them all together.[3] It is the *substance* of these connections that in an important sense defines Micronesia.

The inhabitants of virtually every Micronesian island understood themselves to be members of dispersed kin or descent groups, each of which had members in multiple communities or on multiple islands. By virtue of their membership in these groups, which anthropologists call clans, they had well-established rights in other communities and on other islands. This is an important point, and I wish to make it clearly. Most people in most other Pacific islands societies (and in most of the rest of the world) have relatives of one sort or another living outside their own home communities. They can and do, for various reasons—some purely social in character and some having to do with more fundamental requirements for survival—call upon these kinsmen from time to time. But these ties are largely, in both conception and practice, products of specific, individual acts, especially marriages, and are somewhat ephemeral in nature—they must continually be reestablished. But it is in the nature of Micronesian societies that every individual within them is born or adopted into a particular landholding residential group—a lineage—which in turn is, under all but the most unusual conditions, a localized segment of one of these dispersed clans. By virtue of their unchallengeable membership in a lineage within a clan, individuals are free to move elsewhere, to other communities on the same island or group of islands or to more distant islands, find local lineage segments of their clan in this new locale, and claim as their birthright access to the land and labor of their fellow clan mates there.

The significance of this should not be underestimated. Where people occupy environments as tenuous as those of Pacific islands, the potential for disaster—particularly as a consequence of typhoon damage or prolonged drought—preys continuously upon people's minds (Lutz 1988). The possibility of having to pick up and move must always be kept in mind. Other islands or communities, within traveling distance, may be potential safe havens. But there is always the possibility—sometimes the likelihood—that in arriving as supplicants, a group will find itself at a significant disadvantage, and its members may be put to work in an inferior status, as quasi servants. Conversely, people in these societies must always consider the possibility that the inhabitants of other communities or islands within traveling distance, when facing difficult or dangerous circumstances, might conclude that their best recourse would be to attack their neighbors, seize their resources, and either slay them or put them to work as servants. The mythohistories of many Pacific islands peoples bristle with such accounts.

Micronesia's legendary histories record similar events. But more to the point, the fundamental adaptive strategy of the Micronesian peoples precludes the necessity of pursuing either violent or supplicant courses when environmental exigencies arise. Instead, Micronesian sociopolitical systems are organized in such a way that each residential group or extended family—each lineage—is in possession of strong (and nearly unshakable) moral claims to aid from the inhabitants of distant communities. The system is reciprocal, in that at one and the same time it guarantees security both to those finding themselves in danger and to those whose relative good fortunes would be likely to put them in danger of invasion. The traditional Micronesian system of clanship serves very much as modern multilateral treaties do and has proved eminently successful over millennia. Moreover, in the guiding premise of localized lineages operating freely to make the best use of the resources in their respective communities, while simultaneously guaranteeing themselves security via their ties to related lineages in other communities, we can observe a vital example of the contemporary exhortation for the earth's peoples to "think globally, act locally."

As I shall show in the chapter on prehistoric settlement, this pattern of behaviors, group principles, and moral strictures grew out of common practices in the societies of the earliest precursors who first moved into the Pacific islands. The Nuclear Micronesian speakers originated a new variant of this pattern, however, that proved enormously successful, and as they came into increased contact with the inhabitants of previously settled islands to their west—the Marianas, Yap, and Palau—they transmitted some of their adaptive strategies to their neighbors. Micronesian clanship, with its localized lineages, systems of social rank linked to genealogical seniority, and highly flexible guidelines for membership, is not monolithic. It appears in variable formats throughout the region. Related practices and principles—especially in the realms of land tenure and sociopolitical rank—are even more diverse; everywhere, people have worked to modify these patterns to suit particular circumstances, personalities, and historical contingencies. Consequently, no two Micronesian societies are identical, and none have been static through time. They have always been reshaping and reformulating their structures and organizations. They continue, nevertheless, to share so many things that when the circumstances of colonial rule, and their efforts in the middle of the twentieth century to bring it to an end by pursuing political independence, made it expedient, they were able to work together with common understandings of appropriate personal comportment and political process. Micronesia's leaders were largely in agreement with one another in the ways they sought independence from the United States even while there were significant differences in the specific outcomes they sought. In the same way that Micronesians have always stressed the ultimate autonomy of individual lineages, no one was ready to insist that all Micronesians had to govern themselves under a single sovereign government. But their recognition of how much they depended on the quality of their relations with their neighbors ensured that in the end they cooperated closely to achieve the desired results. The Micronesian leaders who negotiated the end of colonial rule over the islands are proud that they achieved sovereign independence without violence. Their ability to do so derived in part from the shared patterns of behaviors and values that have always defined Micronesia.

The Archipelagoes

Micronesia's islands are commonly grouped into a series of archipelagoes: the Carolines, the Marianas, the Marshalls, and Kiribati. For the most part, these names correspond to both cultural and geographical factors, at least as outsiders have perceived them, though only the peoples of Kiribati seem to have had an indigenous name for their islands as a whole: Tungaru. The peoples of the Marshalls conceive of themselves as occupying two island chains—Radak to the east and Ralik in the west. It is possible that in the past the peoples of the Marianas conceived of themselves as constituting a single people, distinct from the people of the atolls to the south, but we have no direct evidence of this.[4]

In some cases, places are referred to by geographical characteristics that set them off from their neighbors. "Chuuk" means "mountains," clearly distinguishing the high islands of Chuuk Lagoon from the surrounding atolls, while in the Pohnpeian language atoll dwellers are known as *mehn namwanamw*, literally, the deep-sea people. The grouping together of all the islands in the Carolines under a single appellation is entirely imposed by foreign geographers and makes far less sense than the broader concept of Micronesia. The peoples of all the islands from Kosrae westward to, but not including, Yap (but including the atolls southwest of Palau) speak closely related Nuclear Micronesian languages and share fundamental social and cultural characteristics, and I will at times refer to these as the eastern and central Carolines. But Palau and Yap, which are sometimes known as the western Carolines, do have different historical origins from the central and eastern islands, and I shall not use that term. Indeed, older sources often referred to "the Palaus" as an entirely separate entity. Yap, lying between Palau and the central Caroline atolls, has a language that has long resisted classification, though recent work suggests that its earliest affinities lie to the south and not to the west or the north (Ross 1996).

Because the islands from Ulithi through the Marshalls have so much more in common, I have tended to draw more heavily on them. The differences characterizing Palau, Yap, the Marianas, Kiribati, and Nauru, however, call for more individual attention.

Kiribati

Kiribati (pronounced "kiribas," the local pronunciation of the archipelago's colonial name, the Gilbert Islands) comprises a chain of islands stretching approximately five hundred miles from northwest to southeast, including Makin, Butaritari, Marakei, Abaiang, Tarawa, Maiana, Abemama, Kuria, Aranuka, Nonouti, Tabiteuea, Beru, Nikunau, Onotoa, Tamana, and Arorae. Also included in this culture area are Banaba, an isolated island several hundred miles to the west, and Nui, long populated by Kiribati-speaking peoples but lying well within adjacent Tuvalu. Tucked between the rest of Micronesia and Polynesia, Kiribati manifests aspects of both. Although Kiribati's people speak a Nuclear Micronesian language, the emphases they place upon the Samoan *fono*-like *maneaba* (meetinghouse) and patrilineal aspects of social organization give a Polynesian cast to their culture. The importance of mobility among the islands, on the other hand, is quintessentially Micronesian. Because Kiribati was administered as a British possession during the colonial period, it tends to get considered separately from the American-held islands north of the equator. Arthur Grimble and Harry Maude, British administrators who did much of the important ethnological work there, however, emphasized many of the Polynesian facets of Kiribati society, and this contributed to the habit of considering it atypical of Micronesia. Yet it was immediately apparent to the early explorers that, for all their similarities, Micronesia and Polynesia represent two different historical patterns and that the Kiribati people are more appropriately grouped with the Micronesians.

It is likely that Kiribati's atolls were still partially submerged when the Micronesians' ancestors first voyaged through the area (a topic I consider in the next chapter). After society was well established there, however, a number of Samoan immigrants arrived (approximately four hundred to six hundred years ago), probably on Beru, and established themselves as part of the population. Because of their proximity to the Polynesian atolls immediately to the south and their ties to Wallis and Futuna islands beyond, the Kiribati peoples had probably been in sporadic contact with Samoa or its influences for centuries. The Kiribati people seem to have readily adopted aspects of Samoan social and political organization. The most obvious manifestation of this are the *maneaba,* the meetinghouses that serve as both a central organizing principle and a primary metaphor for social life. This principle resembles that of the Samoan *fono* (council), with each kin group or community being assigned a specific seat within the building. And while underlying aspects of social life retained the essence of Micronesian clan mobility, the ideology of descent shifted from characteristic Micronesian matriliny to the Polynesians' patrilineal bias.

Because of this cross-fertilization, aspects of Kiribati social and cultural life have consistently been perceived as distinctly different from those found in the rest of eastern Micronesia and treated as somewhat exceptional. By considering them separately for a bit, however, it will become apparent that in most ways they are typically Micronesian. But it will also help us gain a better sense of just what it means to be Micronesian.

The Kiribati chain consists entirely of atolls and reef islands. In this it resembles the adjacent Marshall Islands (as well as Tuvalu), but this also distinguishes it from most of Micronesia, with its complexes of high and low islands. And while its southeastern location makes it less subject than other parts of Micronesia to catastrophic typhoon damage, most of the islands receive significantly less rainfall than Micronesia north of the equator. All but the northernmost islands, which receive enough rainfall to support breadfruit, depend heavily on taro cultivation and giant swamp taro *(Cyrtosperma)* as the premier foodstuff. It is drought, rather than storms, that most threatens human lives in Kiribati, but as in the rest of the region, it is the ability to sail to other islands and take up temporary residence that makes occupation of any of the islands ultimately possible. Without high islands like Yap and Chuuk to fall back on, however, the situation of the Kiribati people is perhaps more tenuous: "The Gilbertese is an inveterate traveler and the traditions are full of accounts which show that from the earliest times he has been accustomed to visit at least the neighbouring islands, and occasionally the entire group" (Maude 1963, 51).

Because of the Polynesian influence, it seems, land inheritance and political succession did not heavily emphasize matrilineal principles in Kiribati. Although a series of groups or units (*boti*/clan, *utu*/kindred, and *kainga*/homestead) parallel and overlap the clans, subclans, and lineages prevailing in the rest of Micronesia, these are organized with strong patrilineal and ambilateral tendencies and thus diverge from common Micronesian matrilineal tendencies. Likewise, in the islands with hereditary chieftainship, there is a strong patrilineal bias in matters of succession.

Nauru

Nauru's language has long puzzled scholars—though it now appears that it is related to Nuclear Micronesian—and for this reason Nauru is commonly treated as particularly exceptional within Micronesia. The island is isolated, even by Micronesian standards, and lies almost directly on the equator. The strong equatorial current makes offshore navigation extremely difficult, and Nauruans rarely venture away from the island. In this they are decidedly atypical of low-island Micronesians. But the same current brings castaways to the island, especially from Kiribati, and although Nauru is perhaps unique as a Micronesian society that does not depend for its survival on well-developed connections with other island societies, its social organization and cultural practices are entirely Micronesian in character.

Nauru is a raised coral island. Rainfall is adequate, but drought must be reckoned with. There is a fringing reef but neither barrier reef nor lagoon; brackish inland ponds are stocked with *ibia* fish *(Chanos chanos)*. The soil is porous and not especially fertile, and the island's primary crops are pandanus and coconut. Men focus mainly on fishing, and women process the pandanus fruits. While Nauruans lack any regular or sustained contacts with other island populations, they maintain a full panoply of local feasts and exchanges among the island's various districts.

The Marshall Islands

The Marshalls consist of two parallel chains of islands, running from the northwest to the southeast and lying just north of Kiribati. The eastern, or windward, chain is known to the Marshallese as Ratak, and the major inhabited atolls include Mili, Majuro, Arno, Aur, Maloelap, Wotje, Likiep, Ailuk, and Utirik; the western, or leeward, chain is known as Ralik and includes Ebon, Namorik, Kili, Jaluit, Ailinglapalap, Namu, Ujae, Lae, Kwajalein, Rongelap, and Bikini. In addition, two isolated

In the Marshall Islands. Spearfishing, circa 1912. Men engage in spearfishing throughout Micronesia. Courtesy of the Micronesian Seminar.

atolls, Eniwetok and Ujelang, lie to the west of the Ralik chain's northern tip. The two chains (not including the isolates) extend over an area of more than 300,000 square miles. Although there are local variations in social organization, language, and culture, there is a strikingly high degree of commonality among them. Many Marshallese are skilled navigators, and while much of their voyaging is from island to island within their respective chains, there is ample travel between the chains, and many sorts of evidence, including widespread legends, archaeological materials, and linguistic influences, make it clear that they sail across several hundred miles of open sea to Kosrae and beyond, as well as to Kiribati.

Unlike the island groups to the west, there are no high islands in the Marshalls; virtually all the traditionally inhabited islands are atolls. Rainfall is substantial in the southern islands, averaging 180 inches per year in Majuro, where the vegetation is lush, but less than half that amount typically falls in the northern atolls, and El Niño can induce droughts when little or no rain falls for months at a time. Along with fish, breadfruit and taro are the primary subsistence crops in the south, with pandanus replacing breadfruit in the north.

Social and political organization in the Marshalls and in the Carolines is for the most part identical, as are most of their material adaptations to atoll life, and lies at the center of the analyses that follow. The highest chiefs in the Marshalls have sometimes been portrayed as exceptionally powerful, and the common people as cowering serfs (Hage 1999a; Lowie 1921), but as I will explain, there is little unequivocal evidence that social stratification was more fully developed there than elsewhere in Micronesia. The relatively early influence of German traders is likely to have resulted in the attribution of exaggerated powers to the chiefs, as a means of promoting commercial coconut production.

The Eastern Carolines

Kosrae

Kosrae (pronounced "ko-shy" and often written as "Kusaie") is the youngest of the volcanic islands. A rugged ridge runs along its length, with the highest point reaching approximately two thousand feet. It covers an area of approximately forty-two square miles. The island is surrounded by a fringing reef rather than a barrier reef and has extensive mangrove flats along its shoreline, where the dispersed hamlets are sited. Rainfall is typical of Micronesia's high islands, averaging approximately two hundred inches per year and varying from one hundred to three hundred inches. Although it is fertile and lies outside the major typhoon belt, the island appears never to have been densely populated. Traditionally the island has been divided into four major regions or districts. Its subsistence economy relies on fish, breadfruit, taro, and yams.

Kosrae is notable for several reasons. Like Nauru, it is especially isolated; there are no other islands within approximately two hundred miles. While it certainly has had contacts with other parts of Micronesia, including the Marshalls, Pohnpei, and the atolls lying between it and Pohnpei, its people are not navigators and engage in interactions with other island societies far less than virtually any other Micronesian community except Nauru. When the Europeans first arrived, it was the only high island in Micronesia entirely organized under the reign of a single paramount chief, whose seat was located among the channels and artificial islets of Lelu, in a bay along the eastern shore. The architectural complex at Lelu resembles a similar complex on Pohnpei and was probably constructed at about the same time, evidence that at an earlier period there was a greater degree of interaction between these societies. Legendary histories of both Kosrae and Pohnpei, as well as adjacent islands, also indicate a fair amount of interchange, although accounts of a Kosrae invasion of Pohnpei should perhaps not be taken literally.

Pohnpei

Pohnpei's area of influence includes Pohnpei (pronounced "pone-pay" and often called Ponape) itself; Mwoakilloa and Pingelap, which are atolls farther to the east, between Pohnpei and Kosrae; and Sapwuahfik, an atoll to the south.[5] (Kapinga-marangi and Nukuoro are atolls with Polynesian populations, lying hundreds of miles to the south of Pohnpei; they are generally included in modern Micronesia as it is politically defined but are not Micronesian as I define it here.)

Pohnpei is approximately 130 square miles in area, with mountains rising to 2,500 feet in the interior, and while average rainfall is reported as approximately two hundred inches per year, the higher areas get significantly more rain than this.[6] Pohnpei's staple crops are breadfruit, yams, taro, and bananas. The island is usually spoken of as having five independent paramount chiefdoms, but this number is deceptive, since its political geography has always been in flux. A vast complex of artificial islets, known as Nan Madol, rests on the fringing reef that brushes up against a portion of Pohnpei's eastern shore. A number of structures were built there out of massive basalt blocks. Local mythohistory describes it as having been the island's capital during an era when the entire island is alleged to have been ruled by a single leader, which would have made it far and away Micronesia's largest single political unit.

Pohnpeian social life includes little interest or concern with the neighboring atolls, unlike Chuuk and Yap, where interactions with the low islands play a greater role in the dynamics of life on the larger islands. For the atoll peoples, on the other hand, having access to Pohnpei's resources has been important enough to keep them actively involved with the high island, although the distances are substantial enough to keep them from visiting frequently. They speak dialects of Pohnpeian, their social, political, and cultural lives are largely patterned after Pohnpei's, and many of their clans are branches of groups found on Pohnpei.[7]

Chuuk

Chuuk (pronounced "chook") has also been known as Truk, Ruk, and Hoguleu. The term "Chuuk" (which means "high island" or "mountain") can refer either to Chuuk Lagoon and the volcanic islands within it or to the general region, including both the lagoon and adjacent atolls. There are few cultural distinctions between the communities of the lagoon islands and those of the surrounding atolls; they interact regularly with one another and speak the same language, with only minor dialectical differences. Islands to the southeast of the lagoon include the Mortlock Islands (Etal, Satawan, Lukunor, Namoluk), Losap, and Nama. Islands to the north include Murilo, Nomwin, and Namonuito. What are now called the Western Islands consist of Puluwat, Pulusuk, and Pulap (including Tamatam, a separate community on the same atoll). Relations among these islands flow almost seamlessly; the only significant physical boundary is the barrier reef enclosing the islands within Chuuk's lagoon. Tensions between the eastern (Nomwoneyas) and western (Faayichuk) areas of the lagoon are probably as marked as are any differences between lagoon islands and outer islands. The populations of many of the lagoon islands are no greater than those of the larger atoll communities; in some ways the societies of the lagoon islands are unlike those of Micronesia's other high islands, despite their volcanic topography. Political life in Chuuk Lagoon societies is much less centralized than on other high islands, and there is significantly less political integration among these groups than is found in many atoll societies. Communities on several of the lagoon islands sometimes coalesce into federations of islands, but these groupings seem to be products of Chuukese coalition-building skills rather than geographic proximity or integration. For the most part, individual small islands and communities on the larger islands run themselves.

Rainfall on the lagoon islands averages over one hundred inches per year and differs little on the atolls. All the islands depend primarily upon fishing, breadfruit, and taro.

The Central Caroline Atolls

Strung out in a long and relatively narrow band between Chuuk and Yap are the low islands (all but Fais and Satawal are atolls) that are probably best termed the central Carolines. The peoples of these islands have long been known collectively as Carolinians in the context of their relations with the Marianas' Chamorros. From west to east the inhabited islands include Ulithi, Fais, Sorol, Woleai,

Eauripik, Ifaluk, Faraulep, Gaferut, Elato, Lamotrek, Satawal, Puluwat, Pulusuk, Pulap, and Namonuito. The latter four atolls are close enough to Chuuk Lagoon to be included within the Chuuk region but have historically maintained active ties with the atolls to their west and participated in traditional voyaging to Yap. There are also a number of uninhabited islets and reefs that provide important resources to the populations of nearby islands. The atoll Ngulu lies between Yap and Palau; its people are Carolinian but have been significantly more influenced by their relations with Yap and Palau.

The atolls lying southwest of Palau (collectively known as the Southwest Islands)—Sonsorol, Pulo Ana, Merir, and Tobi—are inhabited by peoples whose linguistic and cultural affiliations are Carolinian rather than Palauan. The original inhabitants of Mapia, which lies farther south, toward the north coast of New Guinea, were also Carolinians. The traditions of all these islands specifically claim that they were originally settled by people from Ulithi, as a consequence of overpopulation there, and some individuals additionally claim descent from migrants coming from Sorol and other of the central Carolines. They are conscious of their shared origins and identify themselves as closely related peoples (Eilers 1936, 245–246). Their language, social organization, and culture affirm this history. These islands are likely to have served as way stations in occasional interactions between Micronesian societies to the north and the peoples of the islands now known as Indonesia and New Guinea.

The Carolinians are probably Micronesia's most intrepid long-distance voyagers, regularly traversing the hundreds of miles of open sea that separate their islands, and are possibly the world's most skilled navigators. Their readiness to travel and their ability to reach the distant spots they set sail for are limited only by their awareness of the sudden onset of squalls, storms, and typhoons. Their ability to survive at sea following unpredictable storms, and to return home from the Philippines, where the storms sometimes carry them, enables them to be the primary vehicle for much of the interaction that binds Micronesia into a single culture area. While their populations are small relative to those of the larger volcanic islands, their islands were densely settled (unless recovering from recent storm damages), a sign of the highly adaptive qualities of their cultural repertoire, and while they may not have had the numbers to promote significant innovation themselves, it is nevertheless the case that the commonalities that characterize all Micronesian societies, and have allowed them to adapt successfully to their environment, probably owe more to Carolinian voyaging than to any other single factor.

As with all low-island peoples, the Carolinians depend overwhelmingly upon marine resources. Varying with local conditions, their staple crops are breadfruit and taro.

The Mariana Islands

The Marianas differ topographically and physically from much of Micronesia in the size of the islands, their proximity to one another, the origins of the people, and their colonial experiences. There are, however, a number of correspondences with Palau: both include at least several large (by Micronesian standards) islands of limestone composition, located within relatively easy voyaging distance of one another, that were apparently settled by immigrants from island Southeast Asia rather than from Eastern Oceanic stock. But while Palau's peoples are similar enough to those of eastern and central Micronesia for their culture to have been called Carolinian from the outset, the Marianas have often been thought of by outsiders as being somewhat different. Traditionally the Marianas included the four larger islands of Guam, Rota, Tinian, and Saipan, as well as a number of much smaller and only occasionally inhabited islands to the north.

These differences have sometimes been overemphasized, not least by the Marianas' native Chamorro people themselves. Two particular historical circumstances have played important roles in the evolution of these differences. Because of their location along the sailing lanes between the Philippines and Mexico, the islands were occupied by the Spanish long before Europeans systematically intruded into the rest of Micronesia. Much cultural change, both deliberately pursued and acci-

In the Mariana islands. Net fishing, as sketched during Louis de Freycinet's 1819 visit. Fishing with nets is a common communal activity among all the islands. Courtesy of the Northern Mariana Islands Museum.

dental, therefore began long before the era of scientific appreciation for cultural differences that accompanied late nineteenth- and twentieth-century colonial rule. The Spanish imposed religious and social changes along lines, and with a degree of physical force, quite similar to those with which they transformed the Americas and the Philippines. As a consequence, professional ethnographic research did not get under way until centuries after indigenous ways of life there had been much more significantly transformed than in other regions. We are dependent on a handful of the earliest historical reports for our understanding of traditional Chamorro social life and have a much thinner sense of it than we do elsewhere in Micronesia.

Yap

Although Yap (known to its inhabitants as Waab) is technically a group of three large islands, it is in essence a single high island. Its topography is intermediate in a pattern that has Pohnpei and Kosrae at one end (single large islands with smaller islets that have eroded away from the edges), Chuuk at the midpoint (a collection of relatively small islands remaining from a substantially eroded predecessor), and the atolls (only coral reefs remaining) at the other end. Yap lies west of the andesite line, and its geology is continental, but like the Marianas and Palau, it also shows evidence of volcanic activity. As essentially a single high island, though, it has much more in common with the islands that are remnants of volcanic peaks. Its people practice subsistence farming focused primarily on taro. Its central location among the Marianas, Palau, and the Caroline atolls, all of which were apparently settled from entirely distinct sources, is reflected in the problematic nature of its language's origins. Recent analysis suggests that Yapese has an "Eastern Oceanic substrate." This means that prolonged interaction with settlers from several different origins wrought multiple changes on a language spoken by people who originally migrated from the east. Ross (1996) has suggested that it was settled from New Guinea's Admiralty Islands. Whatever its ultimate origins, Yap's language reflects its position as a crossroads. Alkire (1980) maintains that the Yapese were largely dependent on navigators from the neighboring atolls. While there is some contention about this (Hunter-Anderson and Zan 1996), the basic point makes sense: The peoples of the neighboring atolls were more likely to have passed through Yap, or stopped or settled there, than they were to have been visited by voyaging Yapese.

Relations between Yap and the Atolls

"Yap Empire" is a collective term that has been given to a complex of relationships between Yap proper and the atolls lying between it and Chuuk. At intervals of a year or two, up until the late nineteenth century, expeditions originating in the eastern atolls would sail toward Yap, stopping sequentially at each island along the way, gathering canoes, voyagers, and goods, with Ulithi as the final rendezvous point before the last leg into Yap. On Yap, however, only Gatchepar, a village in the Gagil region or district, was directly involved in these relations. Gatchepar's leaders traditionally used the goods they received from the atolls in their political and economic exchange relations with the rest of Yap proper. The islands were organized in a ranked hierarchy that descended generally from west to east, with Ulithi's leaders managing the system. Alkire (1989, 4) lists the constituent islands as Ulithi, Fais, Sorol, Woleai, Eauripik, Ifaluk, Faraulep, Elato, Lamotrek, Satawal, Puluwat, Pulusuk, Pulap, and Namonuito.

Several different strands of relationships linked the atolls with the main island of Yap. As Alkire writes, "All of the outer islands, at specified intervals, were obliged to send objects of tribute *(pitigil tamol)* to the chief of Gagil District on Yap. In addition, outer island representatives presented religious gifts *(mepel)* to the head religious functionary of Gagil, and *sawei* exchange occurred between the peoples of the outer islands and specific Yapese 'overlords'" (1989, 4). For comparative purposes these can all be subsumed into the *sawei*, often referred to as "tribute," and the entire complex is better termed the "*sawei* system" than an empire (Petersen 2000). According to Lingenfelter, "This tribute is generally in the form of woven cloth called *bagiy* (lavalava), coconut rope, coconut oil and candy, coconut syrup, mats from pandanus, and shells of various types. In return these people receive canoes from the Yapese, turmeric, food, flint stone, and other Yapese resources" (1975, 147).

It has been suggested that the so-called empire was established through conquest and that the atolls were "blackmailed" through sorcery and economics: "When the tributary islands show signs of weakening in their obeisance to their overlords, they are visited by magicians from Yap who perform rituals designed to bring on pests, disease, drought, and typhoons" (Lessa 1956, 70–71). Despite Lingenfelter's report that the Yapese claim ownership of atoll lands, Lessa recognized that this was not the way the people of Ulithi viewed the matter, stating that "we should not define ownership of land in the sawei sense too literally." The people he worked with, in fact, spoke of the relationship as meaning "friend" and "never referred to it as implying land ownership" (Lingenfelter 1975, 147; Lessa 1950, 41).

Lessa further explains: "Sawei is not tribute. It is hard to even justify calling it 'rent,' for if the term were to be used in this manner we would be presented with the ludicrous situation of the landlord giving his serf more 'rent' than he receives; for, if anything, the 'child,' in this case Ulithi, gets the better of the bargain, or, at least, comes out even" (1950, 32). He stresses, moreover, that Ulithi and the other atolls were not exploited by Yap, "for what is received from Yap is considered to be more than ample repayment." He concludes, "In fact, taking the greater size and richness of Yap into account, it would seem that the balance is really in favor of the tributary islands" (1950, 43). According to elders who had participated in some of the last *sawei* voyages, "Their relations with Yap used to be felicitous. They did not come out second-best as far as their material wants were concerned" (Lessa 1950, 42). And although Yap claims suzerainty, he concludes, it "has almost nothing to do with internal events" on the outer islands (1950, 35). Lingenfelter, who writes of Yap proper rather than of the atolls, agrees. The Yapese leaders at the apex of this system "gained and maintained political obligations and power, particularly through demonstrations of generosity and the concomitant obligations of reciprocity." As a consequence, the "Carolinians invariably received greater economic benefits from the exchange than the Yapese" (1975, 147).

Although these "tribute relations were a primary source of political capital" for the Yapese involved with them, "ultimate authority" over the *sawei* system is given to a "minor titled estate," not to a high-ranking chief. This makes sense, Lingenfelter says, only "in the context of the Yapese fear of too much centralized power." Careful control over any wealth generated through participation in the *sawei* "places an effective curb on the personal power of any high chief" (1975, 152). Alkire, whose outlook derives from his work among the peoples living on Lamotrek and other islands nearer the eastern terminus of the network, stresses that from their perspective, *sawei* relations with Yap are only one of a nested series of exchange relations.

Palau

Micronesia's easternmost island chains, Kiribati and the Marshalls, adjoin nothing but open expanses of the Central Pacific and neighboring Micronesian and Polynesian islands and are entirely part of the Nuclear Micronesian–speaking heartland. Palau, at the region's western margin, on the other hand, faces the Philippine Sea and edges south toward Indonesia's Molucca islands and the western tip of New Guinea. Although eastern Micronesia manifests Polynesian influences, they are products of shared origins, and the diversity they are responsible for is in fact quite minor. The influences acting upon Palau, on the other hand, derive from an array of sources. Given this distinction, it is striking that from the beginning foreign explorers included Palau not only within Micronesia but within the Carolines. Palauan society and culture differ in significant ways from those of the rest of the Carolines, to be sure, but not nearly so much as many modern ethnologists tend to believe.

The Palauan archipelago is small, extending less than one hundred miles from northeast to southwest. It is a complex checkerboard of volcanic, bedrock limestone, and coral reef islands. The main inhabited islands include Kayangel,

Babeldaob, Oreor (Koror), Peleliu, and Angaur. Palauan farming practices emphasize taro, though breadfruit is of great symbolic importance. Palauans derive much of their living from the seas, but the people are not noted as long-distance voyagers and navigators. The importance of porcelain and glass bead fragments, which were imported from the islands of Southeast Asia in prehistoric times (Francis 2002, 181–192), and are often referred to as "money" in Palauan ceremonial exchanges, suggests that Palau had ancient and well-established ties to distant island regions.

Carolinians from the central atolls who found themselves lost at sea and drifted to the Philippines returned home via Palau and Yap. Palau's ties to the rest of Micronesia were probably first established and then mostly maintained in this manner, but Yapese interest in Palauan resources (particularly limestone for the massive "money" disks) worked in later years to forge ties between Yap and Palau, through voyages that depended heavily on Carolinian navigators. Though it is not a topic about which we have much information, Karen Nero (pers. comm., 2001) reports a wide range of social ties and interactions between Palau and Yap. There is little evidence of anything more than rare interactions with the Philippines or Indonesia in recent centuries; whatever the Palauans' ultimate origins, their primary social and cultural influences and accommodations over the past thousand years or so have been Micronesian rather than Southeast Asian.

DeVerne Reed Smith has described Palau as possessing one of the Pacific region's "most complex and baffling social systems" (1983, 3), but I believe that at least some of this perspective derives from her own deep understanding of all the ways in which Palauan kin groups actually operate (in comparison with the relative paucity of fine-grained ethnographic data from other parts of Micronesia). Palauan clans are geographically dispersed and are composed of localized matrilineages; most have oral histories of migrations that explain their patterns of dispersion and the links among the lineages. To an extent that is perhaps more fully developed than in other parts of Micronesia, however, these Palauan kin groups rely on factors other than descent as a means of recruiting members. There is nothing peculiar, in a pan-Micronesian context, about the fact that "Belauans ally and classify themselves into groups of varying sizes and degrees of exclusivity based on concepts of migration, 'blood,' land, and residence" (Smith 1983, 87), but they may call upon the full range of possibilities more often than the peoples of most other Micronesian societies.

Glass and ceramic bead "money" *(oudud)* plays a significant role in Palauans' prestige exchange economy. Each part of Micronesia has tended to develop some cultural aspect much more intensely than the rest of the islands. In Kiribati it is the emphasis on the meetinghouse; in Pohnpei, the massive stone architecture at Nan Madol; in Yap, patriliny and stone disks; in the Marianas, latte stones on which houses were built. Palau is no less Micronesian for its idiosyncrasy.

CHAPTER 3

The Prehistory of Micronesian Societies

MY INTEREST in the original settlement and prehistory of the islands focuses not so much on what we have learned from potsherds, adzes, and fishhooks (that is, archaeology), on the one hand, or on vocabulary, sound systems or phonology, and syntax (that is, linguistics), on the other, as it does on the development of Micronesian patterns of social organization. As I have said, it is the interwoven strands of matrilineal descent, chieftainship, and linkages among island societies that give Micronesia its special coherence as a culture area. While scholars call into question Micronesia's existence as a meaningful category because it was initially settled from at least two different directions, the west and the southeast, it is the overwhelming commonalities in Micronesian social organization—which long ago spread across linguistic boundaries—that in fact give it consistency as a coherent region. My aim here is to provide an overview of Micronesian prehistory that does justice to what archaeologists and linguists have learned about its settlement while bringing the insights of ethnography and ethnology to bear on these questions in ways that others have not. I do this by first reporting on what has been fairly well established or is reasonably guessed about, and then speculating about what I think might have happened a thousand years or so ago.[1]

An Introduction to the Settlement of Micronesia

The Pacific island peoples have two distinct sets of origins. The first of these is based on a very ancient migration (perhaps fifty thousand years or so ago) out of Southeast Asia and led to the initial occupation of Australia and New Guinea. The islands adjacent to eastern New Guinea—the Bismarck and Solomon archipelagoes—were eventually occupied by descendants of these migrants, perhaps after farming had developed in New Guinea. In a second, much later influx, a gradual expansion of peoples who spoke the closely related tongues of the Austronesian language family led to the settlement of most of the islands of Southeast

Asia, and the islands of eastern Melanesia, Polynesia, and Micronesia. The earliest evidence we have of the Austronesian-speaking peoples comes from Taiwan (although their roots may well have been in mainland China); beginning at about 3000 BC and extending over the course of several thousand years, they moved through what are now the Philippines and Indonesia and then eastward into the Pacific. These two different sets of peoples—from New Guinea and from island Southeast Asia—intermingled along eastern New Guinea's northern shore and in the adjacent islands, mutually influencing one another. Four thousand years or so ago the languages of the Austronesian speakers in this area grew distinct enough from those farther west to become a separate branch of the larger language family, known to linguists as Oceanic.

At about the same time and perhaps continuing long afterwards, a few small, separate groups sailed east from islands in the region, including Sulawesi and the Philippines, into the open Pacific and occupied Palau and the Mariana Islands. And from elsewhere, perhaps the Admiralty Islands off New Guinea's north coast, yet another group settled Yap.

Certain cultural practices (identified by a particular style of pottery) came to be shared by some of the diverse populations living in the Bismarck, Admiralty, and Solomon archipelagoes by approximately 1500 BC. Archaeologists call those who shared these innovations the Lapita peoples, and they soon moved eastward. At about 1200 BC they began crossing the open sea to the east of the Solomons, first to the islands known collectively as the Santa Cruz group, then quickly onward. In doing so they entered and occupied the region prehistorians have come to call Remote Oceania. Various groups of them then headed north and south, while others continued eastward, and within a span of a few hundred years they established numerous settlements. Each of these formed the nucleus of one or another subgroup of the Oceanic branch of the Austronesian language family.

These Lapita peoples, from whom all the inhabitants of Remote Oceania descend, loom large in the history of the Pacific islands because of their bold forays out into the open sea, the vast areas they traversed and inhabited, the rapidity with which they expanded, the range of adaptations to new islands they developed, and the large numbers of pottery fragments they left behind that have enabled archaeologists to identify their settlements. They depended heavily on marine resources and successfully introduced a variety of crops (yams, taros, breadfruit, and bananas, among others) and domestic animals (dogs, pigs, and chickens) that allowed them to exploit the environments of virtually every island they encountered. At the same time, they preserved and promoted trading links with other islands, since many of the islands that they or their descendants occupied were incapable of sustaining habitation unless they maintained some degree of contact and interaction with other islands' populations.

Because the peoples of Remote Oceania share descent from a common set of ancestral cultures and occupy islands that are for the most part quite similar to one another, they remain alike in many ways. They live in hamlets or small villages, make their livings farming and fishing, bind their communities together around the same basic precepts of family and kinship, and usually organize their kin groups and communities through the leadership of chiefs. There are, to be sure, important differences among these island societies, but the peoples of island Melanesia, Polynesia, and Micronesia are far more like one another than they are different. Indeed, they are in some ways nearly indistinguishable from one another.

The Origins of the Eastern Micronesians

Although a great deal of archaeological work has been conducted in Micronesia in the past quarter century or so, the exact origins of the Micronesian peoples remain uncertain. As Irwin notes, "The source of eastern Micronesian settlement, somewhere between eastern Melanesia and West Polynesia, is as vague as that for western Micronesian settlement, somewhere in the Philippines or eastern Indonesia" (1992, 6–7). In what follows I draw a series of my own tentative conclusions based on evidence now available from archaeology, linguistics, and ethnology.[2]

Linguistic evidence suggests to us that the Oceanic languages most likely formed as a consequence of several processes. As the peoples who spoke what would in time evolve into the Oceanic group of languages moved rapidly through Near Oceania and eastward out into Remote Oceania, locating and settling new islands, they continued to maintain connections with their ancestral communities, thereby forging what are known as dialect chains or networks and participating in what are called interaction spheres. That is, these peoples did not simply stop in new locales and engage in lengthy processes of social and linguistic development until some small segment of the population eventually pushed onward toward new horizons. Rather, while some stayed, others moved on. The rapidity of this migration accounts for the lack of clear groupings among the Oceanic languages—linguists have had difficulty demonstrating that one or another branch of these languages is more closely related to any other group or groups (Pawley and Green 1984; Kirch 2000, 98–100). Ultimately, of course, many of these connections were severed, or at least markedly truncated, as the spheres of interaction grew smaller and local languages became distinct and separate.

As the dialect chains broke up, Oceanic diverged into subgroups essentially determined largely by geographical proximity—that is, smaller, residual interaction spheres. In their respective areas these various branches were Southern Vanuatu and New Caledonia, Central Pacific (Fiji and Polynesia), Northern Vanuatu, and Nuclear Micronesia. This entire process unfolded over the course of centuries, from approximately 1500 to perhaps 200 BC, and repeated itself again and again as each of the subgroups in turn diverged into the multiple distinct languages spoken today (although many others formed and disappeared along the way).

We should keep in mind that two somewhat contrary patterns were under way simultaneously. Widespread movements from island to island, accompanied by continuing contacts and connections among islands, were offset by the separation each distinct population experienced as it settled on and adapted to individual islands. Migrating groups carried with them, or were at least familiar with, a range of crops. They narrowed these crop inventories down as they determined what was suitable to their new environments, while at the same time maintaining ties with communities on other islands in order to ensure continuing access to foods, goods, and resources they were no longer able to produce or obtain in their new homes. These island cultures and languages reflect patterns of both divergence, caused by a degree of isolation, and convergence, brought about by continued interaction. Excavations of Lapita-period archaeological sites provide us with fairly clear material evidence that this is just what took place.

At the jumping-off point of this extraordinary radiation lie the Santa Cruz and the Reef islands, often referred to collectively as the Santa Cruz group. They are significant for a variety of reasons. The original settlement of these islands represents what seems to have been the completion of the first successful crossing of truly open seas in these peoples' route eastward into the Remote Pacific. It is likely that until the earlier settler populations reached the southeast corner of the Solomon Islands, they had never had to negotiate any substantial body of water blindly. Because of significantly lower sea levels in the past, lofty mountain ranges on the islands, and relatively short distances between them, they had previously known with some degree of certainty that there were new islands ahead of them. But the Santa Cruz islands lie hundreds of miles beyond the Solomons proper; the first peoples to settle them had traveled well beyond the limits of their knowledge and security. Second, archaeology tells us these islands were settled quite early and served as nodes in exchange networks that linked more distant settlements in Vanuatu and beyond with older communities in the Solomons and westward. Third, and possibly most significant for settlement of Micronesia, they represent a complex of different physical forms. There are both volcanic and atoll types of islands in proximity and well-established patterns of interdependence among their populations (Davenport 1964; Yen 1982; McCoy and Cleghorn 1988). As the sea level dropped and the Reef atolls emerged, residents of the higher Santa Cruz islands would have gained increasing familiarity with the resources to be found on them. Finally, subsistence on Santa Cruz Island itself (known also as Nendo or Ndenu), the largest of the Santa Cruz group, is characterized by its reliance on a wide range of tree crops (Yen 1974), a system resembling that found on Kosrae and

Tamatam islet, Pulap Atoll. An outrigger canoe as sketched during Dumont d'Urville's 1828 visit. Micronesia was settled by voyagers sailing canoes akin to this. Courtesy of the Micronesian Seminar.

Pohnpei and apparently much more developed there than anywhere else in the eastern Lapita range. It is certainly my sense that the Santa Cruz area is one of the key locales from which eastern Micronesia was settled (cf. Kirch 2000, 173–174).[3]

Over the course of several hundred years, roughly 500–100 BC, a number of the different populations that occupied this broader area—collectively representing what is known as late eastern Lapita culture—and were engaged in traveling widely among the islands in Remote Oceania's western reaches must have first explored and later purposefully journeyed northeastward to eastern Micronesia in the same way they had been doing as they moved toward the east and south. Irwin has charted the courses these voyages were likely to have taken, based on a series of computer simulations, and it appears that by using the same sorts of sailing strategies and techniques they employed to settle the rest of the Remote Pacific, early voyagers could have reached eastern Micronesia with no more effort or danger than was entailed in traveling south and east (1992, 121–125).

I stress the point that there is little reason to think that eastern Micronesia was settled from a single island or locale, or even a single circumscribed area, by a single group of people, or at a single point in time. The difficulties linguists and archaeologists have encountered in narrowing down these origins thus reflect not simply the paucity of preserved sites and confusing language data but also the likelihood that in early times conditions themselves were blurred by the high rate of interaction among different peoples. Whatever the precursors of Proto-Nuclear Micronesian speech and culture might have been like, they were a synthesis of at least several sources. As Irwin observes, "The search for single origins and discrete homelands has often proved futile. Eastern Micronesia could have had multiple origins at a time when there was not much difference between the various colonists. They came by cross-wind voyages from already-settled islands perhaps spread over a wider geographical range than envisaged so far" (1992, 130).

Nor is the question of where these populations first settled in eastern Micronesia any more amenable to clear resolution. At that early date the sea level was still falling. This process exposed coral reefs that were in time to become atolls, and it is quite possible that Kiribati's islands, which appear at first glance to be the most obvious stepping-stones, were not yet habitable (Dickinson 2003). Voyagers might well have been familiar with exposed reefs in the region without having actually settled them (Nunn 1994). The low islands could simply have provided convenient wayposts amenable to trial plantings of a few hardy crops able to fend for themselves, as well as access to freshwater, seafood, and safe harbors.[4]

Although Kiribati does lie closer to the general region from which eastern Micronesia's first settlers originated, there is no obvious reason to assume that either atolls or high islands were settled much earlier than the others. What is clear, however, is that the volcanic islands were *not* settled by people who had fully adapted to atoll life: the earliest archaeological sites on Chuuk, Pohnpei, and Kosrae all contain numerous pottery shards, and atoll peoples lack the resources for making ceramics. The high islands' settlers came pretty much directly from high islands. It is my sense that much of eastern Micronesia was settled nearly simultaneously, that is, within a period of two hundred years or so.

Emigrants from the Santa Cruz region would have brought with them a well-established familiarity with the possibilities of interdependent relations among high and low islands, which travelers from the Solomons and Vanuatu might not have had (though they would certainly have been familiar with coral reefs).[5] While we know almost nothing about the subsistence strategies of the earliest atoll settlers, other than that they must have depended heavily on the abundant marine resources (turtles, reef fish, shellfish) that had long thrived in the absence of human exploitation, it appears that from the outset settlers on the high islands possessed the basic sorts of crops that typify the subsistence economies of Melanesia and Polynesia, as well as modern Micronesian farming: coconut, breadfruit, yam, taro, and banana, combined with a variety of subsidiary crops. The new arrivals on the high islands settled along shorelines and reef flats where fishing was optimal and only then moved gradually inland.[6]

It is possible that the early Nuclear Micronesian homeland covered a limited area, but given the essentially simultaneous occupation of Chuuk, Pohnpei, and Kosrae at the end of the first millennium BC, I am inclined instead to think that it extended over a broad area, including most of the islands from the southern Marshalls and northern Kiribati west to Chuuk.[7] This runs against the more common way of envisioning original colonization as proceeding from point A to point B to point C, but Micronesia was settled by highly mobile peoples who voyaged within extended interaction spheres as well as occupying individual islands, and neither the archaeological nor the linguistic evidence suggests otherwise.

In the course of the ensuing centuries, populations occupying the eastern Micronesian islands, as a consequence of changes in both natural and social contexts, came to interact less and less with their southern kin, and their languages increasingly diverged.[8] At the same time, a dialect chain separated out from the multiple variants of the original Oceanic that had been spoken by the immigrants from the Lapita region, and it is this chain that probably best represents the language we call Proto-Nuclear Micronesian. The language "trees" linguists use to diagram relationships among the Nuclear Micronesian languages that diverged from this common tongue may reflect the order in which they separated, but it may also be that they simply mark the relative degrees of isolation and separation of specific island communities (Jackson 1986; Bender and Wang 1985).

Linguistic analysis suggests that Nauruan broke off quite early from a "Greater Micronesian" group of languages, leaving the "Nuclear Micronesian" family (Jackson 1986, 212; Lynch et al. 2002, 117). The languages of Kiribati and Kosrae were apparently the first to diverge within this group, followed by those of the Marshalls; the languages of Chuuk and Pohnpei are more closely related to one another and diverged from one another more recently. We may not be looking at a simple chronological history, however, as much as we are seeing differences in the amounts of contact island populations had with one another, although aspects of both processes are probably relevant here. Some linguists have concluded that the "Nuclear Micronesian homeland" lies in Kiribati or Kosrae (Lynch et al. 2002, 117), but the archaeology thus far available to us consistently confirms that much of eastern Micronesia was settled almost simultaneously, and I doubt that we can point to one specific locale as much more of a homeland than any other.

It is likely, then, that eastern Micronesia was first colonized not by a single, small, relatively homogenous group or population, but rather by a number of loosely connected peoples or populations who brought with them a range of cultural and social practices. Because of this variety of sources, the early settlements would not have been identical but would have been characterized instead by similar but nonetheless distinctive practices. Conclusions regarding differences among high-island pottery styles indicate that this is indeed the case. Kosrae, Pohnpei, and Chuuk ceramics show relationships to what is called late eastern Lapita plain ware, but pots from each island are distinct. Stephen Athens (1990, 29–30) interprets this as evidence that there was little interaction among the high islands at this early date, but it simply could mean that ceramics were not significant trade items.[9]

Patterns of interaction within and between the newly developing Micronesian societies were by no means identical. Prevailing winds and proximity make the Marshalls and Kiribati, at least in some ways, geographical extensions of each other (although this does not explain why there are such significant linguistic and cultural gaps between them). The people of both groups were mobile and engaged in continual interisland navigation within their own archipelagoes; with their skills honed they were more capable of traveling abroad than many other Micronesians.[10] Historical records show substantial extra-archipelago voyaging by both (some undertaken deliberately and some accidental). Kiribati people were carried to Nauru by the strong equatorial current and influenced Nauru language and culture, but there was little if any Nauru influence in the reverse direction, or anywhere else for that matter. Mwoakilloa, on the other hand, was much influenced by ties with the Marshalls (Rehg and Bender 1990).

Relations between Kosrae and Pohnpei are more difficult to comprehend. Linguistics suggest that the two developed separately for a long time. But economic, cultural, and sociopolitical life on the two islands is nevertheless strikingly similar. On the other hand, linguistics also tells us that relations between Pohnpei and Chuuk were much more common than between Kosrae and Pohnpei. And although the people of neither Pohnpei nor Chuuk Lagoon were great travelers during the historical period, the linguistic record suggests that they had substantial interactions during several earlier periods (Rehg 1995, 317–319). The distances from Pohnpei to both Kosrae and Chuuk are nearly equivalent, and in historic times, at least, their peoples rarely navigated the open seas. The atoll populations of the Mortlock Islands and their neighbors to the southeast of Chuuk Lagoon, which lie closer to Pohnpei, however, were able to provide links between Chuuk and Pohnpei in ways that the atoll peoples of Mwoakilloa and Pingelap (who did relatively little open-ocean sailing) did not.

When Nuclear Micronesian–speaking people began moving into the atolls west of Chuuk Lagoon and headed toward Yap, they probably encountered populations, at least in the further islands, whose original ties were to the west, to Yap and perhaps beyond to Palau. Because of sparse archaeological investigations among these low islands, it is difficult to be sure of much about their history, but excavations on Lamotrek and Fais make it clear that although their modern populations speak Nuclear Micronesian languages, their earliest ties were to the west (Takayama 1981; Alkire and Fujimura 1990).

Early Micronesian Social Organization

However vague they may seem, the contributions that linguistics and archaeology have made to our knowledge of Micronesian settlement are more concrete than anything we can derive from ethnology. But in a book about Micronesian societies, it is to social anthropology that we must turn if we want to understand the development of these societies.

We have no way of knowing with certainty much about the kinds of social institutions and organization the original settlers of Micronesia brought with them from the south, but several things do seem rather likely. Modern Melanesian societies in the general region from which the Micronesians' ancestors migrated manifest a great many different kinship and descent systems. Some are characterized by matrilineal beliefs and practices and some by patrilineal systems, some are bilateral, and others combine multiple aspects of these classic types. There is no reason to presume that just because modern Micronesia is overwhelmingly matrilineal, matriliny was the only form initially introduced into the region.[11] Indeed, we should probably assume that in the same way that a number of different peoples or populations made their way into eastern Micronesia some 2,200 to 2,000 years ago, they carried with them a variety of social patterns.

I think it would be helpful at this point to turn for a moment to a central tenet of evolutionary theory, as elaborated by Stephen Jay Gould (2002, 1214ff.), who stressed that the present utility or function of a particular trait does not necessarily tell us much about why or how that trait originally evolved. That is, traits do not originally develop in order to be put to the uses they will later come to serve. The bones that transmit sounds in mammals' ears, for example, are derived from bones in ancestral reptilian jaws, and the precision grip that enables humans to write is derived from a power grip that enabled primates to clamber about high in the trees. As Gould himself noted, this principle is hardly limited to organic evolution— we must keep it in mind as we consider the historical development of social and cultural traits as well. I stress the importance of this notion as we consider a key premise of this book—that modern Micronesian societies are to some extent defined by the matriliny they share—and I hope to explain some of the original reasons why matriliny became a fundamental element of Micronesian life. But we must not lose sight of the simple fact that matriliny has not necessarily served all the same purposes in modern Micronesian societies that it did two thousand years ago. That said, I offer my speculations about Micronesian matriliny's origins.

Few if any attributes of Micronesian matriliny cannot be found in one or another of the island Melanesian societies out of which the ancestral Proto-Nuclear Micronesian speakers came. Moreover, many of the principal elements of Micronesian matriliny are not only shared with Melanesian societies but can in fact be traced back to the earlier roots of Austronesian societies as they expanded through Southeast Asia and into Near Oceania.[12] What is specific to, and perhaps unique about Micronesian matriliny is this: every society in Micronesia employs it as a central organizing principle and is to some extent linked to its neighbors through the bonds of matrilineal clanship. In Melanesia we find societies that are organized around matrilineal, patrilineal, and other patterns interspersed among each another, and the matrilineal clans of adjacent societies are not ordinarily integrated with one another. It truly is quite extraordinary, then, that all of the societies ranging across the entirety of Micronesia's vast expanse share what is in essence a single social institution.

If we look no further than the Solomon Islands, one of the last areas the peoples ancestral to the Nuclear Micronesians occupied before passing out into the Remote Pacific and then on into eastern Micronesia, we can find all these elements, many of them clustered together in the same societies.[13] Oliver (1989, 1038–1042; 1993a; 1993b) describes typical Solomon Islands societies (some Austronesian-speaking and some not) with one or more of the following traits: dispersed matriclans and localized lineages; communities made up of members of multiple different matriclans; matrilineal primacy in land tenure; emphases on primogeniture; and aspects of authority ascribed according to genealogical senior-ity. All of these are central to Micronesian social organization. It is also significant that in at least some, and probably most, of these same matrilineal societies of the Solomons, land could be transmitted through males; descent group membership, even while conceptualized as a birthright, required individuals to play active roles in these groups in order to validate their membership rights; and political leader-ship, though commonly thought of as a product of supernatural status or powers distributed in terms of seniority of birth order, was in fact very much a product of individual political and economic skill and activity. As we shall see, even the excep-tions to the rules that characterize Micronesians' matrilineal practices are shared with their Melanesian cousins.

Because the building blocks of Micronesian societies descend from ances-tral practices and institutions in eastern Melanesia and beyond, the question that needs to be asked here is why matrilineal institutions so overwhelmingly prevailed in Micronesia, when they neither dominated in Melanesia nor were carried east-ward by the Oceanic speakers who settled Polynesia.

Two crucial aspects of social organization seem to underpin matriliny's suc-cess and eventual diffusion throughout Micronesia. These are in fact essentially irrelevant, or at least not directly related to, postmarital residence patterns, wom-en's contributions to subsistence, or men's roles in warfare, the factors ethnologists typically use to explain the presence of matriliny (Ember 1974). The first of these key elements is found in the networks of resilient linkages among widely scattered groups that the system of dispersed clanship promotes; these enable populations residing on generally fruitful islands that are at most times well worth inhabiting, but are nevertheless particularly vulnerable to typhoons and recurring droughts, to persevere in spite of severe climatic drawbacks. The second element is that the matrilineal forms initially introduced into Micronesia were neither simple nor rigid. While they emphasized principles of primogeniture and authority conferred by seniority and birthright, they also incorporated—were crosscut by and infused with—respect for patrilineal and bilateral ties and simultaneously allowed for, indeed required, status to be achieved through superior performances in a variety of roles and competitive practices.

Together these features, which occur sporadically in Melanesia and appear only occasionally as a complete ensemble (as in the Trobriand Islands), evolved into the classic form of Micronesian chiefly societies. Without going into detail just yet, I will explain what the adaptive advantages of these practices seem to have been.[14] Put simply, early eastern Micronesian communities, occupying islands of multiple sizes and types and with access to quite different sorts of resources, and situated within both the unpredictable intertropical convergence zone and the eastern margin of the typhoon belt, continued to engage in long-distance voyaging well after the Lapita people to the south had more or less settled down. Many of these communities remain highly dependent on fairly regular interactions with other islands. What all this means is that while Micronesian islands are far enough apart that most natural disasters are somewhat localized (that is, they strike only some islands), their populations are mobile enough to move efficiently from one island to another when disaster does strike.

These patterns of interaction are complex and entail two crucial and somewhat contradictory elements. It is, on the one hand, extremely useful—perhaps imperative—for populations to maintain well-established ties with other communities, upon which individuals and groups can call in times of need. But it is equally the case that most communities remain continually concerned about the possibilities of being preyed upon by neighboring populations that might at times find themselves in dire need of aid but, either lacking adequate social ties or being unwilling to use them, would be inclined toward hostility and conquest.

As I will explain at length in chapter 4, Micronesia's matriclans each include numerous lineages that are in turn located in multiple adjacent communities and islands. Any given lineage is tied to lineages on other islands not simply through bonds of friendship or patterns of exchange but through deep and permanent kinship connections. It is the broad and supple web of ties linking each of the constituent households or descent groups of any particular community to a substantial number of groups in other communities that enables all the communities of an island or island group to survive. We cannot know exactly how or why this came to be, but it appears that the matrilineal forms that were carried into eastern Micronesia from Melanesia proved considerably more useful to these pioneers than the other sorts of social institutions that arrived with them. Groups with dispersed matrilineal clans thrived under the conditions that prevailed at the time and either expanded at the expense of those who already occupied adjacent locations and islands or were emulated by neighbors who observed and appreciated the effectiveness of their institutions.

This pattern of dispersed clans incorporating multiple localized lineages is especially characteristic of matriliny, although there is no necessary or logical reason why it cannot occur in patrilineal organizations. Because I analyze this matter at length later on, I will not explore it in any depth here. For the moment it is enough to say that while women in these voyaging societies do travel to and settle in new and distant communities, which is how clans come to have multiple dispersed lineages in the first place, most seafaring is done by men. Matrilineal organization means that the individuals who tend to be the most mobile (the males) are not those charged with rooting lineages within specific communities (that is, the females). Within a patrilineal framework, on the other hand, both of the relevant facets of clan organization—dispersion and localization—would be in the hands of the same individuals. This is not an impossibility, but matrilineal organization seems to manage the process much more efficiently and effectively than patriliny can.

Moreover, Micronesians' matrilineal form of organization provides considerably more than just these vital linkages. Within any given community, all or most of the lineages residing there have leaders, that is, chiefs. The leader of one or another of these lineages serves as chief of the entire community. Speaking strictly in terms of ideology or cultural norms, the leader of each individual lineage occupies his (it is almost always a male) position on the basis of birth order (i.e., primogeniture) and birthright, while the leading lineage of the entire community enjoys its status on the basis of its claim to have been the first to settle in the community (i.e., settlement priority). While the leaders of the leading lineage are thought of as having more immediate and thus more effective access to the ancestral spirits of the lineage and the place, the simple fact is that these systems all incorporate enormous flexibility into their actual operations. These patterns are by no means peculiar to matriliny, but they are all deeply embedded in Micronesian matriliny.

This combination of ideological conviction and practical flexibility enables the people of each community to feel reasonably certain about who their leaders are, while simultaneously providing for a degree of ambiguity that, as we shall see in later chapters, helps them select genuinely effective leaders. They are thus able to make fairly clear and unambiguous ritual performances that inform their neighbors and other potential intruders just who those leaders are, in ways that harness supernatural approval and support, even while assuring that particularly competent individuals and strong lineages will be the ones most likely to occupy these key roles and statuses.

Besides being matrilineal, Micronesian clans are also hierarchical. I will explore the nature of this hierarchy in much greater detail in later chapters, but for the moment it is sufficient to say that most Micronesians see a degree of social stratification—the presence of chiefs and chiefly lineages—as critical to maintaining order within their communities and to creating and maintaining linkages between communities. Chiefs serve as highly visible representatives of their lineages and communities; chiefly lineages provide both continuity and a range of eligible candidates from which chiefs can be selected.

Aspects of these social, cultural, and political traits accompanied the first settlers as they migrated north into the Nuclear Micronesian triangle, but it was there that they developed into the comprehensive pattern that characterizes Micronesian life today. Significant differences have of course arisen in the intervening years, but the evolution of most of the patterns we now consider typically Micronesian took place in the islands from Chuuk to the Marshalls and Kiribati approximately two thousand years ago. Because these were voyaging peoples, it seems safe to assume that they had occasional contacts with the societies of Yap, the Marianas, and Palau, but in those early years the intervening atolls may not have had substantial—or indeed any—populations. Enough successful archaeological excavation has been done on Fais and Lamotrek for the evidence of potsherds to tell us that these islands were in regular contact with Yap, and perhaps even Palau, once they were settled, but we are not certain when this was. At the earliest levels thus far excavated, there is no telling whether these atoll peoples had dealings with the Nuclear Micronesian–speaking peoples to the east. But late in the first millennium AD things began to change as a series of developments drastically improved eastern Micronesia's situation and directed its influence westward.

I am hardly the first to suggest that Micronesian matriliny's widespread distribution derives in part from the important role it plays in the maintenance of interisland relations. But even the scholars who have most thoughtfully explored this notion have missed something. Applying a relatively straightforward analysis to the role of matriliny in sustaining these relations, Damas (1979) and Hage and Marck (2002) conclude that when the relative importance of interisland ties declines, matrilineal organization in turn deteriorates.[15] They cite as examples of this process the cases of Pingelap and Mwoakilloa (atolls between Pohnpei and Kosrae), and Eniwetok and Ujelang (isolated atolls in the westernmost Marshalls), where several patrilineal patterns of land inheritance and title succession have come to the fore.

These changes (aspects of which can in fact be seen in many parts of Micronesia) may primarily be consequences of Christianization and colonization, but even if they are largely indigenous in origin, two factors must be taken into account when considering the apparent deterioration of matrilineal relationships. First, the primacy of matriliny in Micronesia, as in Melanesia, in no way precludes the existence of patrilineal or bilateral connections, which are in evidence everywhere. As we shall see in subsequent chapters, matrilineal tendencies in land tenure, residential patterns, political titles, and other arenas all tend to be counterbalanced by ties traced through men. There is not much consistent correlation between emphases on matrilineal ideology and the practical organization of everyday political and economic practices. Second, several Micronesian societies maintain fairly clear-cut dedication to matrilineal clanship despite the long-term absence of voyaging over any significant distances. In recent centuries at least, Pohnpeians rarely participated in overseas voyaging, and Chuukese generally sailed no farther than a few miles to adjacent islands within their lagoon.

I referred earlier to Gould's work in evolutionary theory, and I return to his perspective now in order to address a common misunderstanding about the underpinnings of Micronesian matriliny. Gould and Lewontin (1979) employed an architectural component, the spandrel (the structural area connecting adjacent arches), as a metaphor to describe how features that accompany adaptations but have no direct adaptive value themselves can in time develop adaptive qualities. The relevance of this concept for Micronesian matriclanship is this: Micronesian clans have over the centuries developed characteristics that make matriliny central to the organization of all social life *within* communities. The relevance of the adaptive features that originally led to pan-Micronesian adoption of matriliny as a means of linking communities may have little to do with the preservation of those matrilineal features in later Micronesian history. This is a topic I consider in detail in later chapters.

The Early Micronesian Economy

Although relevant archaeological data from early settlements in the Marshalls and Kiribati are nearly nonexistent, we can surmise that the original atoll settlers supported themselves primarily with pandanus, varieties of giant taro *(Cyrtosperma* and *Alocasia),* and a range of less successful or significant plants and relied heavily upon the waters around them for their subsistence, harvesting shellfish, reef fish, and the deepwater species available to oceangoing peoples. The immediate source of these adaptations was perhaps the Reef Islands. An agricultural inventory much more highly dependent upon tree crops—agroforest composed of coconut, breadfruit, bananas, and other species—was probably carried to the high islands from Santa Cruz, which has a strikingly complex range of tree crops.[16]

We can see at this point one of the most salient consequences of the Micronesian lifeway's continued reliance on relatively frequent and intense interactions among the communities of widely spaced islands. Whereas in Polynesia there was always a degree of interaction among the communities within localized subregions, there was little or no contact between distinct island groups (Kirch and Green 2001, 71–90).[17] In Micronesia, on the other hand, the atoll peoples' wide-ranging journeys, coupled with the integrating dynamics of the Micronesian dispersed clan system, meant that a significant degree of ongoing interaction took place across the region's vast distances. Over the course of several hundred years this resulted in the transmission of a breadfruit species from western Micronesia into eastern Micronesia, where it hybridized with the classic Pacific island breadfruit species carried into the eastern Carolines by the first settlers. Before exploring this theme further, however, we should first turn our attention to the origins and prehistory of the peoples in the western islands.

Western Micronesia

At the outset of this chapter, I quoted Irwin on prehistorians' uncertainty regarding Micronesian origins: "The source of eastern Micronesian settlement, somewhere between eastern Melanesia and West Polynesia, is as vague as that for western Micronesia, somewhere in the Philippines or eastern Indonesia" (1992, 6–7). Prehistorians and linguists agree that Palau and the Marianas were settled by peoples from the Philippines and/or northeastern Indonesia, but on little else. The lives of many modern peoples in the area between Sulawesi and Mindanao are oriented toward the sea (Nimmo 1972), and it is not difficult to conceive of some of their ancestors making their way eastward into the open Pacific. The cultures they brought with them would have been similar to those of the peoples moving along the north New Guinea coast at about the same time, who eventually became the Oceanic speakers who first swung north into eastern Micronesia. Yap seems to have been settled from elsewhere, perhaps the Admiralty Islands off the north New Guinea coast, and its language, which has multiple overlays of Palauan and Nuclear Micronesian influences, appears to be Oceanic in origin (Ross 1996). That is to say, perhaps four thousand years ago the ancestors of both eastern and western Micronesia's populations were essentially the same people, and thus the populations that ultimately settled the opposite ends of Micronesia brought similar cultures with them.

Despite their shared origins in the same general region, there is no evidence that the peoples who first settled the Marianas and Palau were more than distantly related to one another, nor is there evidence that they had much, if any, contact with one another. On the other hand, long-term contact between Yap and Palau, dating back nearly two thousand years, has been established (Intoh 1981, 69). Linguists and archaeologists tend to stress the view that their different immediate origins make the distinctions between western and eastern Micronesian populations much more important than their similarities. Davidson, however, has argued that "we should be wary of wholeheartedly accepting the orthodox model of Micronesian settlement," proposing instead a model that emphasizes "repeated contact across the region, and the passing on of ideas and traits from the margins to the center" (1988, 92, 94).[18]

Early settlers in Palau, Yap, and the Marianas, wherever they came from, crafted pots, fished, and grew primarily taros and yams. Their agricultural practices had significant impacts on their environments, and the continental geology of their islands did not respond in quite the same ways as the geology of the volcanic islands to the east. Open grasslands or savannas, although occasionally encountered in the eastern Carolines, are much more prevalent in the western islands. As Kirch (2000, 172–174) notes, archaeologists working in western Micronesia have encountered significant disparities between evidence (from pollen studies, in particular) of widespread forest clearing (evidently for agricultural purposes) as early as 2500 BC or so and direct evidence from artifacts and residential sites, which dates only to about 1500 BC. They are unsure not only where western Micronesia's settlers came from but also when they arrived.

The Palau and Yap peoples had contact with adjacent atoll populations and with one another, and Palauan and Yapese pottery has been excavated from sites on several of the western and central Caroline atolls (Intoh 1996; Alkire and Fujimura 1990). Archaeological evidence also makes it "virtually certain that the Western Carolinians and the Chamorros had had contact, by design or accident or both," before the first Europeans arrived (Barratt 1988, 5). And while there are notable differences in social organization between each of these societies, to be sure, in recent centuries all were organized around matrilineal clans—that is, they shared fundamental social institutions with eastern Micronesia. Traditional forms of political organization in Yap, Palau, and the Marianas also fall well within the range of variation characteristic of the rest of Micronesia. None of this should come as a surprise when we consider the wealth of early Spanish reports chronicling both the frequent arrivals of Carolinian voyagers who drifted eastward to the Philippines after being driven off course by storms and then sailed home again via Palau and also Carolinian visits to the Marianas (Riesenberg 1965; Lessa 1962).

It is extremely unlikely that matrilineal clanship was carried separately to each of these societies from island Southeast Asia (or New Guinea in Yap's case). Reconstructions of Southeast Asian island prehistory suggest that both kinship and political systems there have much in common with those found in Remote Oceania, as a consequence of their common Austronesian origins. Kinship terms in all Austronesian social systems emphasize generations, gender, and relative age and birth order (Fox 1984, 37). And Bellwood believes that these early Southeast Asian island societies possessed small-scale chiefdoms, or something like them, that were quite similar to those of Micronesia and Polynesia. Rank was based mainly upon settlement priority—what he terms a "founder principle"—and lineages were ranked in terms of their relative seniority within a community but were open as well to constant rearrangement through individual initiative (1985, 146–147).

Historically known societies throughout eastern Indonesia and the Philippines are, however, overwhelmingly bilateral, or cognatic, in organization, that is, they equally recognize or emphasize connections through both paternal and maternal lines.[19] The few that do practice unilineal descent are generally patrilineal (though most of these have been influenced by Islam). The only societies in this general region reported to have matrilineal organization lie scattered among a few islands off the northeast coast of Timor, near the north coast of Australia (LeBar 1972, 1975). Given the absence of matrilineal clanship in the region, there is no compelling reason to think that the peoples who settled western Micronesia from island Southeast Asia were practicing matriliny when they came or, if by some remote chance they did, that it survived in Micronesia any longer than it did in the Philippines or in the general vicinity of Sulawesi.

On the other hand, western Micronesia's matrilineal clans are for the most part identical to the forms that evolved in eastern Micronesia and proved so adaptive that they diffused westward with the Nuclear Micronesian–speaking peoples who inhabit all the Caroline atolls. Western Micronesia was settled before the east, yet a set of traits largely evolved in situ in eastern Micronesia came to typify western Micronesian culture and society. How did this happen? I believe it was a consequence of a significant shift in Micronesian economies, which in turn had tremendous effects on Micronesian social systems. This change might well be called Micronesia's breadfruit revolution.

The Breadfruit Revolution

Prehistorians tell us that much of Micronesia experienced substantial sociocultural transformations in the years between AD 1000 and 1500. These entailed ecological, economic, demographic, social, and political changes in many—perhaps most—of the region's societies. I believe that aspects of this—important aspects—must be attributed to what I call Micronesia's breadfruit revolution, a development in Micronesian agricultural economies that would lead to far-reaching changes in other aspects of life there.[20]

Eastern Micronesia's subsistence economies are overwhelmingly tied to breadfruit (two- to four-pound, very starchy fruits that grow on large, spreading trees). It may be that in the early settlement period only a portion of the Lapita peoples' broader crop inventory was carried northward, but it is at least as likely that in the course of the first millennium of settlement in eastern Micronesia, breadfruit's unprecedented success in the eastern Carolines resulted in the neglect or abandonment of some other crops. It is worth noting that farmers in the Santa Cruz islands have particularly emphasized genetic modification in adapting their subsistence system by producing a wide variety of tree crops, in contrast to the more typical adaptations practiced on the adjacent islands of the main Solomon chain (Yen 1982, 56–57), and that "deliberate selection for crop staple genetic and phenotypic variability seems to be a common practice among Micronesian farmers" (Hunter-Anderson 1991, 42).

Studies of preserved pollen and food remains tell us that from the outset the people who colonized Kosrae and Pohnpei were planting tree crops, along with taros and yams. More important, these studies tell us that the vegetation of the two islands underwent a substantial change in the early years of settlement. As populations grew and their familiarity with their islands' natural environments improved, they increasingly burned the forests along the shores and in the lower elevations and replanted these locales as agroforest. On Kosrae the early settlers planted essentially the same crops as their modern descendants do, a mix of tree and root crops with particular emphasis on breadfruit (J. S. Athens et al. 1996, 837, 843–845); the same holds for Pohnpei (Ayres et al. 1979). In doing so, they were re-creating aspects of the farming systems they had left behind in eastern Melanesia, but the pollen record shows that they were also shifting toward a greater emphasis on breadfruit.

We do not know, unfortunately, much about that breadfruit. This is an important point because recent work on breadfruit by a group of botanists demonstrates that a significant genetic change was taking place at this time in eastern Micronesia. These developments would in turn lead to cultural changes of remarkably vast proportions.

As I have already noted, two crops predominate in modern Micronesian subsistence systems: taros (including the smaller *Colocasia* and the larger *Cyrtosperma* and *Alocasia* plants) and breadfruit. Taros are cultivated everywhere; in some areas—for example, Palau and Kiribati—they are the focus of much of women's labor and provide the greatest share of the staple starchy foods. They are typically crops of Southeast Asia and may have been domesticated either there or in New Guinea; they were introduced into Micronesia both from island Southeast Asia and from eastern Melanesia. Breadfruit is an important food crop nearly everywhere in Micronesia, but in many areas, especially Kosrae, Pohnpei, and Chuuk, it is overwhelmingly the most prevalent foodstuff. It is only in the coral islands at the northern and southern margins, where rainfall is sparse, that breadfruit does not play an important role in islanders' diets and is largely replaced by pandanus. Coconuts are widely planted and are important in islanders' diets, but for the most part they enhance other foods rather than provide staple food value themselves.[21] Bananas also contribute to local diets but are only occasionally considered truly central elements in local cuisines.

Breadfruit is noteworthy for a number of reasons. In addition to being an excellent source of nutrition, it can be prepared in a wide variety of ways, some as simple as roasting the fruit directly on hot coals and others entailing elaborate cooking, pounding, and embellishment with coconut cream (Pollock 1992). Cultivation requires very little labor once new shoots are transplanted. In the eastern high islands one variety or another produces fruit nearly year-round. And in peak season breadfruit trees bear in astonishing abundance, providing surpluses that can be fermented in pits (a process known as ensilage) and preserved for use when the crop is out of season or in diminished availability. When combined with the fish stocks that abound in the reefs and lagoons of most islands, breadfruit provides a healthy, stable, and substantial diet in return for remarkably little effort.[22] A Pohnpeian friend once joked to me that he thought the only way to truly transform his people's relaxed approach to life would be to take chainsaws to the island's breadfruit trees.

This easy way of life is fundamental to so much of modern Micronesian living that it is difficult to imagine it otherwise. And yet it may well have been quite different fifteen hundred to a thousand or so years ago, before the breadfruit revolution. Two key sets of evidence, neither of them particularly well developed as yet, lead me to this conclusion. The first comes from archaeology; the second, botany.

Archaeologists working among the islands of Chuuk Lagoon have been puzzled by what they call "the long gap" in the array of cultural materials they have recovered there. They have uncovered early sites containing pottery shards similar to those found on Pohnpei and Kosrae and dated to approximately the same time period: late in the first millennium BC, circa two thousand years ago. But there is little evidence from succeeding centuries, until about AD 1200–1300, when the population seems to have begun increasing rapidly, in conjunction with artifacts (not appearing in the earlier contexts) that indicate heavy reliance upon breadfruit. King and Parker (1984) observe that this breadfruit-associated efflorescence seems to have appeared almost out of nowhere and that it was accompanied by substantial stone architectural construction, which local people in some cases explain through mythohistorical accounts celebrating connections to the people, deities, and polities of Pohnpei and Kosrae. That is, a major change in Chuukese social life appears to have been associated with both the development of a marked reliance on breadfruit and sociopolitical influences from the east. Archaeologists have noted similar patterns in other parts of Micronesia and described "the great settlement expansion and cultural elaborations of the AD 1000s–1500s" (Hunter-Anderson 1991, 18).

Botanists studying the genetics of breadfruit in the Pacific have shown that two distinct types—one growing wild on Micronesian islands with continental origins, like Palau and the Marianas, and the other found from New Guinea eastward into Polynesia—came into contact with each other somewhere in eastern Micronesia and subsequently produced new hybrid forms eminently suitable to cultivation on atolls. It would appear that the typical eastern Melanesian-Polynesian seedless breadfruit, known generally to scientists as *Artocarpus altilis* and thought to be a domesticate derived from the wild species *A. camansi*, was carried northward by early settlers into eastern Micronesia. At some point it hybridized with the Marianas' wild, seeded *dugdug, A. mariannensis,* then produced a host of varieties that thrive on the Micronesian atolls (Zerega 2003; Zerega et al. 2004; Ragone 2001 and pers. comm. 2001).[23] These botanists have been able to establish the sources of the hybridized Micronesian breadfruit, but they have not yet been able to provide us with any specific insights about precisely where or when this process took place.

This breadfruit hybridization had numerous and far-reaching ramifications. Among them are the following:

1. Hybrid varieties provided the Micronesian atoll populations with a major new food source, one that had not previously been available to them in any significant quantities.
2. The number of varieties (cultivars) of breadfruit historically cultivated on Kosrae, Pohnpei, and Chuuk is nothing short of extraordinary, and as a consequence fresh breadfruit is available on these islands virtually throughout the year. Pohnpeians, for instance, speak of four minor breadfruit seasons in addition to the five-month major season (Lawrence et al. 1964, 47).
3. Because breadfruit requires so little labor input beyond harvesting (which is accomplished using nothing more than a long pole with a fork at its tip), it effectively frees up a good deal of surplus manpower.
4. Breadfruit supplies vast quantities of high-quality carbohydrates in environments where protein is readily available from the sea. In the course of a year, an average acre on Pohnpei can yield more than three tons of breadfruit and in some areas more than five tons (Raynor 1989; Petersen 1975, 1977).[24]
5. The quantities of the fruit available for preservation by pit fermentation (called *mahr* on Pohnpei and known by cognate terms elsewhere) are great enough to feed people in times of drought and following storm damage; preserved breadfruit also serves as a prestige food on some islands. Pohnpeians

report that they have been able to store individual lots of breadfruit in pits for up to fifty years (Lawrence et al. 1964, 55).

6. On Pohnpei at least, breadfruit is extraordinarily resilient. Hambruch, who worked on the island in 1910, was told that within two months of the 1905 typhoon, which by all accounts was the single most powerful storm to strike the island in recorded history, breadfruit trees, which had been left entirely denuded, were fully leaved and bearing young fruits "as large as walnuts" (1932, 348). I have observed trees fruiting within weeks after the end of a rare six-month drought induced by the El Niño–Southern Oscillation.

7. Breadfruit trees are long-lived and continue yielding steadily over the years; on the eastern high islands some trees have been known to bear fruit over periods longer than normal human life spans.

8. These hybrid breadfruit trees provide timber for constructing large seagoing canoes. Wood from the seeded *dugdug* is not nearly as saltwater resistant, and canoes built from it are short-lived.

It is safe to say that the impact of a quantum increase in the availability of fresh and preserved breadfruit revolutionized Micronesian subsistence and thus created conditions for major changes in society as a whole.

Artocarpus altilis breadfruit is quite sensitive to salt and does not grow well, if at all, on atolls.[25] Breadfruit, however, thrives on Micronesian atolls (Stone 1951; Ragone 1988), and it is the *A. mariannensis–A. altilis* crosses that permit this (Ragone 1997, 17–18). Where annual rainfall drops below seventy-five or so inches per year, in the northern Marshalls and southern Kiribati, breadfruit cannot grow and pandanus takes on a much more substantial role, but on wetter atolls such as Arno and Namu, breadfruit is the primary element in diets for half the year, both when it is in season and for months afterwards, when stocks of preserved pit breadfruit are consumed (Stone 1951; Pollock 1974, 109–113).[26] Higher population densities and the relatively marked degree of social stratification in the southern Marshalls are undoubtedly related to the ample food supplies made possible by breadfruit. The greater degree of social stratification in northern Kiribati (in comparison with the southern islands) has long been attributed to the higher rainfall, increased fertility, and abundance of breadfruit there (Wilkes 1845, 73–75; Geddes et al. 1982, 38).

High islands like Pohnpei and Kosrae have remarkably large numbers of named breadfruit varieties. Bascom, working immediately after the Second World War, recorded the names of 78 varieties on Pohnpei (1965, 98), and Lawrence, Hadley, and McKnight reported 80 (1964, 44), while a little more than a generation later Ayres and Haun reported 150 varieties on the island (1990, 214). Farmers there have continued to work at improving their crop inventories.[27] Large, if not quite so overwhelming, numbers of breadfruit varieties are also characteristic of Kosrae and especially Chuuk (Hunter-Anderson 1991; Ayres and Haun 1990). But even among the atolls, where *A. altilis* breadfruit is not ordinarily viable, the hybrids thrive; 24 varieties have been recorded in the Marshalls alone (Mackenzie 1960, 2). It is this incredible variation that makes breadfruit so extraordinarily abundant. Differing varieties are adapted to a range of microclimates and bear at diverse times throughout the year; but all Micronesian cultures make a basic division of the year into two seasons—when breadfruit bears and when it does not.[28]

Botanists, linguists, and archaeologists agree that breadfruit arrived in eastern Micronesia from the south. The Santa Cruz islands, which I have named as a likely source for much of early Nuclear Micronesia's origins, are characterized by dense agroforest that is in many ways similar to that of Pohnpei and Kosrae, although arboriculture there relies on a wider range of tree crops (Yen 1974; J. S. Athens et al. 1996), and "it was probably in the Santa Cruz and possibly the Banks Islands that [seeded] breadfruit was first extensively cultivated and selected" (Ragone 1997, 19). The initial introduction of breadfruit was limited to the *A. camansi*–derived *altilis* varieties. The subsequent introduction of western Micronesian *A. mariannensis* into eastern Micronesia could have been a consequence of voyagers from the west traveling into the east or vice versa, or perhaps some combination of both. It may have happened in a single locale or in a number of different places. It might have been a unique event but is more likely to have been a gradual process. It most certainly happened because the farmers were already deeply committed to working with breadfruit variation and would have both eagerly sought new varieties and recognized the value of the new hybrids when they appeared.

The cultural surge that archaeologists identify in late prehistoric eastern Micronesia is most apparent at Nan Madol, on Pohnpei. On the island's eastern, upwind shore, in the shallows where the barrier reef encircling the island extends landward and becomes a fringing reef abutting the shoreline, a network of constructed channels connects an extensive complex of artificial islets, some capped by imposing structures built of immense basalt blocks. Remains of the earliest human activities at this location have been dated back two thousand years, and it is quite possible that this site is one of the spots the first travelers to Pohnpei originally settled. Initial work on the construction of Nan Madol as a ritual and/or political center of some sort dates to perhaps AD 900–1100, and full-scale construction on the complex has been dated to 1200–1600 (Bath and Athens 1990; Kirch 2000, 197–198). An analogous, though much smaller, complex is located at Lelu, on Kosrae; initial construction there is dated to 1250–1400, with the most extensive work undertaken in 1400–1650 (Cordy 1993; S. Athens 1995; Kirch 2000, 202–204).[29]

Little in the general sweep of Kosraean or Pohnpeian social, cultural, and political beliefs and practices is exceptional or even particularly different from either the rest of Micronesia or Remote Oceania. But aspects of these practices were directed toward the large-scale mobilization of labor, and something out of the ordinary took place to bring about the social conditions that led to the construction of Nan Madol and Lelu. I would not suggest that the hybridization of breadfruit and subsequent rise in the productivity of subsistence systems alone explain this burst of creative energy—Chuuk's subsistence economy is, if it is possible, even more focused on breadfruit than that of the other high islands, but its political economy is much less elaborated than theirs. Yet the emergence of the eastern Carolines breadfruit economy must be reckoned with.[30] I believe that the timing of breadfruit's introduction into Chuuk, combined with an appreciation for the impact of hybridization and its consequences, helps us understand why the peoples of Kosrae and Pohnpei were able to accomplish their magnificent construction feats—they must have experienced an extraordinary rise in available human resources over the course of centuries.

It is possible that Pohnpeians (and Kosraeans) consciously sought to disseminate the fruits of their innovations. A rock outcropping with extensive art incised into it lies in Sapwalap, not far inland from Nan Madol. One of the predominant motifs in this assemblage, an "enveloped cross," resembles patterns found further south in the region of the late Lapita homeland. Noting this site's juxtaposition with the monumental construction at Nan Madol itself, Paul Rainbird argues that "Pohnpei was part of a sea of islands with communities in regular contact over the past thousand years or more," and he goes on to suggest, "One of the conscious consequences of building the structures at Nan Madol was to attract visitors from other islands. This would have brought Pohnpeians notoriety across the western Pacific sea world and the satisfaction that they would be the recipients of such things as knowledge, gifts, trade, and people without having to venture far beyond their own barrier reef" (2002, 142). Nothing is certain about the nature of influences or relations between the complexes at Nan Madol and Lelu, but both their timing and their fundamental similarities suggest that they came as consequences of the breadfruit revolution that took place on Pohnpei and Kosrae.

It is possible, but not likely, that Chuuk was in some way involved in the processes of breadfruit hybridization as well. The juxtaposition of a sudden shift in archaeological deposits, associated with breadfruit processing materials (especially shell peelers), and mythohistorical accounts stressing the influence of Kosrae and Pohnpei suggests that the breadfruit revolution first occurred in the east and was then carried westward into Chuuk, probably by Mortlockese voyagers. King and Parker suggest that it was not until the fourteenth century AD that the new cultural pattern penetrated into Chuuk Lagoon societies, entailing significant population changes, an intensification in breadfruit use, and the spread of a Sou Kachau cult (that is, a set of beliefs and practices venerating deities identified with the high islands to the east); they believe these innovations were in some way related to developments taking place during the same period on Kosrae and Pohnpei (1981, 25).[31] The salt-resistant character of the hybrids may well have enabled them to diffuse to Chuuk through the Mortlock atolls lying between Chuuk and Pohnpei. Hybridized breadfruit varieties were carried eastward and southward into the Marshalls and Kiribati as well, where they served as catalysts for tremendous increases in atoll productivity and population numbers in the wetter islands. A mythohistorical account from Mili tells of a time when there was no breadfruit in the Marshalls and how it was introduced and spread (Mackenzie 1960, 13).

From Chuuk these hybrid varieties traveled relatively quickly, first through the central and western Caroline atolls and then on into the Marianas, Yap, and Palau. They are well established on Palau's Southwestern Islands, which are atolls inhabited by peoples speaking dialects of the central Carolines. The atolls and the Marianas depended heavily upon breadfruit in historic times, and Yap and Palau less so. In the Marianas' Chamorro language breadfruit is *lemai*, a cognate of Nuclear Micronesian *mai/mei*. The Palauan and Yapese names for breadfruit are not related to Nuclear Micronesian. Although breadfruit is an important crop in these latter two groups, it is by no means the preeminent food stuff. Palauans do report that their seedless varieties are more tolerant of salinity, which is of course the reason the *A. altilis* hybrids were able to diffuse there from the east (McKnight 1960, 2–6).

There is a general continuum in the distribution of Micronesian food crops, with yams and taros providing the predominant staples in the west and breadfruit prevailing in the east. There are many reasons for this; at least some of them are environmental. The western high islands all lie inside the andesite line, and their soils are distinctly less robust than those of the younger volcanic islands to the east. And the western islands are subject to a somewhat different climatic regime than those in the east. Palau, Yap, and the Marianas are affected by Southeast Asia's monsoon regime, and rainfall in the west is not only less abundant but also more seasonally distributed (Hunter-Anderson 1991, 47). Although the wild, seeded *dugdug* is native to these islands, the staple varieties cultivated on them are of the same sorts as the *A. altilis–A. mariannensis* hybrids that characterize eastern Micronesia. They were clearly introduced from eastern Micronesia, and in their wake they brought significant sociocultural influences as well.[32]

While the development and spread of the new breadfruit varieties had a major impact on subsistence in Micronesia, it is their influence on social organization throughout the region that is in many ways most remarkable. The archaeological record does not tell us much about interactions between the eastern and western spheres during the early period, but they were certainly taking place. The emergence of what was in many ways a new economic order, however, changed all this. The evidence of this diffusion is of various sorts, but it comes from throughout central and western Micronesia.

The Social and Cultural Consequences of the Breadfruit Revolution

Hybrid breadfruit's suitability to atoll environments, in combination with lagoon fisheries, made it possible for societies to sustain population sizes that were previously inconceivable on these islands. These newer, larger populations were successful enough to produce significant surpluses of a limited range of goods for exchange. They remained, however, vulnerable to the same sporadic climatic exigencies, and their exchange relations with other islands were maintained with an eye toward surviving such recurring crises. The systematic connections linking the islands west of Chuuk to one another and to Yap, in particular, were enhanced (if not originally formed) by these factors. With the development of the hybrid breadfruit varieties, newer and stronger links were added to the already existing ties to Yap and Palau (Intoh 1996; Alkire and Fujimura 1990). A complex pattern of behaviors and values diffused from Nuclear Micronesia. In time the peoples of the eastern and western islands would come to share characteristically pan-Micronesian social and cultural lifeways. It seems that the success of the breadfruit revolution, with all its accompanying social and cultural ramifications that provided impetus for expanding populations, proved so impressive to the peoples of the west that they incorporated aspects of the easterners' social organization into their societies quite quickly, though the sequencing and rate of this diffusion remain far from clear.

Linguists have called attention to what appear to be recurrent rather than continuous connections between Chuuk and Pohnpei (Bender and Wang 1985, 70; Rehg 1995, 317–319). While ties between them may have come and gone over the centuries, clear evidence of Pohnpei's cultural influence on Chuuk is from relatively recent times and quite probably derives directly from the cultural developments spawned by the breadfruit revolution.

People in the islands of Chuuk Lagoon speak in terms of two sorts of clans, those with earlier origins and the later, "immigrant" clans, which claim chiefly status. These latter clans are associated with what Goodenough calls a "cult of Achaw" or Kachaw (Pohnpeian Katau), and "there is evidence to suggest that it was introduced there from Ponape, which may have served as a center of influence from which versions of this cult were carried to other parts of eastern Micronesia," including the Marshalls and possibly Kiribati (1986, 559–560). Variant traditions and mythohistorical accounts from throughout this region reflect a local notion that there once existed a "Kachau Empire" (Nakayama and Ramp 1974).[33] The successes of the high islands may be reflected not simply in their influences in Chuuk Lagoon but also in the transport of basalt slabs to eastern Micronesian atolls for use as shrines (Mason 1947, 32), perhaps in recognition of their role in generating cultural efflorescence throughout the area.

The atolls between Chuuk Lagoon and Yap provide additional evidence. They lie in the very heart of the typhoon belt, and their limited dimensions make them especially subject not merely to immediate, short-term storm damage but also to long-term destruction of their gardens. These islands are productive and densely populated, but their peoples depend utterly and absolutely on preserving close ties with adjacent islands via the webs of matriclanship, and linguistic patterns reflect the magnitude of these connections. As Jeff Marck (1986) has shown, the peoples of islands only an overnight voyage apart speak very similar dialects. The relative rank of lineages and clans is, consequently, a matter of great concern in maintaining the integrity of these linkages. On Ifaluk, for example, "rank is so highly valued and respected that it stands out as one of the master-values of this culture" (Burrows and Spiro 1970, 179). And relative rank is for the most part officially established through settlement priority—the first clan to establish itself in a given island or community is generally recognized as having the right to provide the leading chiefs. But this seemingly straightforward formula is in fact thoroughly complicated by the islanders' awareness of two contrary ways of calculating rank.

The inhabitants of this chain of atolls trace the origins of their communities and their clan histories both directly to Yap in the west and through Chuuk to legendary Kachau in the east (Sudo 1996; Komatsu 1990). Ties to Yap via the *sawei* (tribute) voyaging system linked together all the smaller islands and led westward to Yap, which provided them with critical high-island resources and potential refuge during the worst of times (Lingenfelter 1975; Alkire 1989; D'Arcy 2001). Mythohistorical accounts suggest that the islands were first settled from Yap. At the same time, however, a complementary set of mythohistorical accounts traces the origins of many of the contemporary clans to the spiritually more prestigious Kachau. Islands toward the west are likely to emphasize their ties to Yap, while islands in the east are more likely to stress their Kachau connections.

Because the order of settlement of individual islands in relation to adjacent islands accounts for important aspects of rank among their respective communities, the ancestral migrations out of Kachau and into the atolls are central to the entire system of rank. Micronesian politics are in part organized around competing grounds for legitimizing chiefly status, as we shall see in later chapters. But the critical point here is the islanders' frank recognition that despite the fundamental stress they place on settlement priority, precedence based on settlement from and ties to Yap is on occasion trumped by the status that inheres in later ties to Kachau. The impact attributed to Kachau is almost certainly a consequence of Nuclear Micronesian influences that were set in motion by the breadfruit revolution. Indeed, the most widely distributed descent group in Micronesia is the "Under-the-breadfruit-tree" clan (e.g., Dipwinpahnmei on Pohnpei, Fáánimey on Chuuk, and Féremäü on Pulo Ana), members of which are dispersed from Kosrae in the east (commonly associated with, if not identified as, Kachau) to the Marianas and to Pulo Ana in the far southwest (Marck 2004, 5).

A parallel appears in Palau's mythohistory. According to Palauan accounts, the archipelago's matriclans are relatively late arrivals, having immigrated from Ngeruangel, a small, uninhabited atoll just north of Kayangel atoll (which is larger, inhabited, and an integral part of the Palauan islands); these northern islands provide the best archaeological evidence of interactions with Yap (Intoh 1981, 69). At the heart of Palauan matriclan organization are stories that explain the dispersed nature of each clan's lineages in terms of migration histories, as these newly arrived groups traveled about, establishing themselves throughout Palau (Smith 1983, 41–63; Aoyagi 1982, 20).[34] Palauans believe the five seedless breadfruit varieties to be recent acquisitions (McKnight 1960, 4), and harvesting and processing techniques, particularly fermenting, are essentially identical to those in the central and eastern Carolines. Although breadfruit in Palau has neither much economic importance nor sociopolitical prestige attached to it, a widely recounted and crucially fundamental myth concerns Milad, a dominant cultural heroine associated with, among other things, the rebirth of Palauan society after a particularly destructive era (McKnight 1960; Nero 1992). That is, breadfruit, which Palauans believe to be a relatively recent introduction, derives its importance in Palauan culture from relatively recent social dynamics as well, an indication that its entry into Palau is in some ways associated with the arrival of the matriclans.[35]

In fact, even in the Nuclear Micronesian homeland, in Pohnpei, Kosrae, and the Marshalls, most matriclans have extensive migration myths that explain the ways in which their subclans and lineages came to be dispersed among many islands and archipelagoes. The origins of Marshalls' clans, in local mythohistory, lie on Namu atoll and are associated with a basalt pillar there named Liwantoin-mour ("the one who gives long life") and referred to as "the mother of all clans" (Mason 1947, 32; Pollock 1976, 93–96), which suggests a link between Marshalls' clans and the eastern Caroline high islands, either Pohnpei or Kosrae. It is in the nature of Micronesian matriliny that clans are understood to link together lineages settled in multiple communities on multiple islands; the central Carolinian atoll and Palauan versions I have just cited elaborate on the clans' movements into territory that was already occupied by other populations.

There is no indication of any close connection between the populations that originally settled Palau and the Marianas, and Yap, too, appears to have its own distinctly separate origins. Yap's matriclans are, nevertheless, called *genung,* derived from the Oceanic descent group term *kainanga* and all its Nuclear Micronesian cognates. And although the Palauan and Chamorro languages have entirely different words for clans and lineages, their structure and organization are essentially the same as those of eastern Micronesia's descent groups. There is simply no good case to be made for western Micronesia's matrilineal clans having been introduced from anywhere but eastern Micronesia.

Conclusion

Despite their different historical origins and the different languages spoken in them, the societies occupying all the islands from the atolls southwest of Palau, through Palau, the Marianas, across the central atolls, through the eastern Caroline high islands, and into the Marshalls and Kiribati—that is, the geographic expanse we call Micronesia—were not merely in contact with one another but were connected to one another through a common, shared system of matrilineal clanship by the time Europeans first arrived in their waters. The central tenet of this common system was the maintenance of links among the localized lineages of dispersed clans. While based on elements common to much of Austronesian and Oceanic social organization, the evolution of this system as a composite whole was a specific adaptation to conditions in eastern Micronesia, a fundamental element in an original Nuclear Micronesian lifeway. The system dispersed throughout the Nuclear Micronesian homeland in Chuuk, Pohnpei, Kosrae, the Marshalls, the Kiribati, and Nauru. In later centuries it spread, with the diffusion of hybridized breadfruit, westward and eventually came to characterize all the island societies of western Micronesia as well.[36] We know from other parts of the Pacific that peoples with unrelated languages may be virtually indistinguishable culturally (Ross 1996, 126), and while a number of Micronesia's languages are distinctive as a consequence of their different origins and environments, the similarities among Micronesian cultures far outweigh their differences.

This is of course a simplification of a multitude of complex processes and of a long sweep of history. Although it is grounded in the available evidence, there is not a great deal of hard data available, and I am well aware of criticisms that might be leveled against it. But I am not writing a work on Micronesian prehistory and am not inclined to spin out this thread much further. My point is that social and cultural life in Micronesia, as we know it from foreigners' earliest written accounts as well as more recent ethnographic research, is not the same as it was when the region was first settled. During at least some of the early stages of development, interactions between west and east were probably as important as were the webs of linkages among the Nuclear Micronesian–speaking peoples and their continuing linkages, early on, with the Southeast Solomons–Santa Cruz–Northern Vanuatu sphere and occasional interactions with western Polynesians. But eastern Micronesian societies have become so dependent upon breadfruit that it seems fair to assume the hybridization of the two species that took place in east-central Micronesia was both a product of the peoples' deliberate efforts and a source for profound transformations in their societies. In all of this, the dynamics of the system of matrilineal clans was of the utmost importance.

CHAPTER 4

Descent and Descent Groups

As in all human societies, the various elements of Micronesia's societies—social, cultural, political, economic—are entirely enmeshed in one another, and separating these strands out from one another is really no more than a useful attempt at understanding them. I do have to begin somewhere, of course, and since one of the primary themes of this work is that Micronesia constitutes a coherent region because of the webs of clanship that link its many islands and communities, I have chosen to begin with descent and with the social groups organized by descent—known in general as descent groups and more specifically as clans and lineages.

Lineages are the building blocks of Micronesian communities. Their members hold land in common, tend to work together on that land, often reside together, and act together as political bodies, usually controlling the chiefly titles that are the backbones of island governments. And while lineages derive much of their character from the rounds of group activities in which their members engage each day, their importance derives also from their deeply rooted ties to lineages in other communities, for Micronesian lineages are shaped by their incorporation into the widely dispersed clans as well as by local conditions.

Shared principles of matrilineal descent bind the lineages together into nested hierarchies of subclans and clans. The bonds of clanship, weaving lineages together, permit individual Micronesians and their lineages to depend on the peoples of other communities and islands for aid when calamity strikes. These supple connections are strong enough to have permitted Micronesian societies to thrive for several millennia now. While their purpose—their reason for being—is adaptive, adaptation by itself tells us little about these principles of matrilineal descent.

We must start by acknowledging that no Micronesian community can be considered solely in terms of itself; though each has its own cultural peculiarities and adaptive history, Micronesian communities exist and survive because of the interlocking webs of matriclans and lineages that bind them to other communities.

Within each community are lineages from at least three or four, and usually more, different clans. The clans, in turn, each have member lineages residing in at least several communities and usually on several islands. This pattern creates the fundamental shape of Micronesian social organization: clans are widely dispersed among the island communities, while all communities include lineages from numerous clans. Within each community, one clan or another is recognized as the highest-ranking, and one of its lineages there is charged with supplying the community's chief. At the same time, however, each lineage or group of related lineages has its own leader, often referred to as a chief. Thus the peoples of Micronesian communities are twice-organized. They have their own descent group chiefs and territorial chiefs, who reign over all the people living in the community or its subdivisions.

But it is a single ideological system—matrilineal descent—that underpins both forms of government. Descent groups' chiefs lead their own members, while community chiefs lead the entire community. Although some people will have the same leader serving as both their lineage and their community chief, most are likely to have two distinct chiefs. By the same token, Micronesian political systems are charged with the internal organization of communities made up of separate, autonomous lineages, while simultaneously managing relations with other communities.

This pattern of sociopolitical organization has not merely persisted and thrived but has spread out from the eastern Carolines into all the islands. Only in Kiribati, where Polynesian influences have been strong, has it shown signs of fading. Descent principles shape the form and character of household groups, community leadership, and intercommunity relationships. Because matrilineal descent underlies so many facets of Micronesian civilization, and because it is so profoundly similar from one society to another, it provides us with a place to begin analyzing the tapestry of social, economic, and political life in the islands.

Like the lives of most peoples, the lives of Micronesians for the most part unfold in households. It is within their households that they experience the realities of everyday life, and households could certainly provide a reasonable point of departure for an exploration of life in the islands. But Micronesian households are not isolated, autonomous units. The land they reside on and farm, the workers who labor at farming and fishing, and the patterns of interaction with other households and communities all exist within contexts of much broader social relations. Households are ordinarily embedded within the lineages, which nearly always manage access to both land and labor. In most of Micronesia it is the lineages or their branches that form the most recognizable social groups. In the same sense that an analysis might well begin with households, it could equally well start with lineages. But then lineages are themselves no more than portions of larger-scale units—the clans and subclans—that provide lineages with the support they need to survive the mighty forces the Pacific Ocean arrays against them. There is in fact no entirely appropriate or ideal place to pick up the thread of this analysis. It is for purposes of clear explanation, then, that I choose to begin at the most inclusive level of organization, with the descent principles and the clans. I readily acknowledge, however, that this choice also helps to make my case for recognizing the commonalities that link Micronesian societies.[1]

Principles and Groups

At the core of what is most characteristic of Micronesian societies is the principle of matriliny. Both the matrilineal character and the sheer intensity of the unilineal principles that organize Micronesian societies distinguish them from the Polynesian societies that they resemble in so many other ways.[2] Indeed, by at least one measure, Chuuk is the most matrilineal society in the world (Burton et al. 1996, 101).

The overarching matri-principle has many variants, especially in the west (that is, Yap, Palau, and the Marianas). In Palau, perhaps because of its society's apparent origins in as well as its proximity to the Moluccas, matrilineal ideas and institutions also share elements with patterns common in Indonesia, and DeVerne Reed Smith has described Palau as possessing one of the Pacific region's "most complex and baffling social systems" (1983, 3). Likewise, on Yap, crosscutting notions of patrilineal descent perhaps reflect some of the same historical influences that can be seen in its language (discussed above). It would certainly be possible to approach descent in Palau or Yap as something sui generis and discuss it entirely on its own terms, but in their practical effects Palauan and Yapese clanships are in fact quite similar to those of the rest of Micronesia.

Despite the obvious importance of matriliny, in observable patterns of everyday behavior Micronesian kinship is actually bilateral. That is, Micronesians recognize, honor, and call upon kin ties in both the female (maternal) and male (paternal) lines. In most contexts, they feel equally free to call for help from, or obliged to render it to, any close relative, regardless of what the formal connection between them might be. But the two sets of connections—through the female and male lines—are conceptualized very differently. Matrilineal bonds are inherently enduring, while the important ties among a father, his descent group, and his children, honored in every Micronesian society, are for the most part short-lived; that is, these linkages, which in the technical terminology of ethnologists are referred to as filiation, tend to dissipate after a generation or two. Even in the two realms of life in which the principles of matrilineal descent have their greatest influence—in matters of political and ritual rank and of land tenure and inheritance—Micronesians pay close attention to bilateral ties as part of their pragmatic responses to the exigencies of real life.

In addition to recognizing that descent principles are just that—underlying *principles*—and not what people actually do, we must also keep in mind the substantial range of variation within, and not just between, Micronesian societies. It is easy to believe that the forms and behaviors that ethnographers have come to view as typical or most likely in these societies are the only ones likely to be encountered. But just as each of these societies differs in some significant ways from the others, individual communities, neighborhoods, and households within them also differ from one another. Despite their many similarities and shared histories, each is the product of local developments. Different emphases on different aspects of their descent systems reflect local responses to local events and conditions. Groups on the individual islets of larger atolls or in distant communities on the larger islands may share some aspects of their social organization more closely with groups on other atolls or islands than with groups on their own atoll or island. Attempts to draw generalizations about patterns of social organization on a single island by forcing together seemingly contradictory or anomalous data may in fact cloak not only the existence of real differences but also the reasons for them.

Principles of Descent

Having explained why common descent groups, concepts, and categories are so definitive in describing Micronesia, why it is I begin with them, and why I start with clans rather than lineages, I can now begin to explain and analyze them. The largest, most inclusive form of Micronesian matridescent is represented by categories of people that anthropologists usually call clans. (In much of the early ethnographic writing about Micronesia—in both German and English—these were referred to as "sibs," a term that has largely gone out of fashion in anthropology; for all practical purposes there is no difference between a clan and a sib, and I shall consistently speak of clans.) Most of these clans are not what may be properly called social groups, inasmuch as their members are not necessarily aware of, engaged with, or concerned with one another. They may usefully be thought of as categories, rather than groups, of people. Some Micronesian clans have members spread across vast areas; others are more localized. In general, Micronesians say the ties of clanship weaken with both physical and genealogical distance, but members certainly acknowledge ties to strangers of the same clan even while knowing nothing of the specific history that connects them.

Micronesians conceptualize, or at least speak of, clans as being composed of all the individuals who are descended through their mothers, via an unbroken succession of mothers leading back into ancient times, from the same woman. This woman is known in technical terms as the founding or apical ancestress. The basic Micronesian principle of matrilineal descent (which is a form of the classic ethnological principle of unilineal descent) holds that all the children of that founding ancestress are members of her clan, that all the children of her daughters are members of that same clan, and that likewise, in every subsequent generation, all the children of all the daughters are members of the clan. Membership in the clan is automatically bestowed upon children by their mother, as a fact of birth. By the same token, however, children of the clan's men are automatically members of their own mothers' clans, not their fathers'. The essence of the matrilineal principle, and of Micronesian clanship, is simply that it is a congenital or biological condition, an entirely ascribed status that derives solely from an individual's mother and establishes each and every individual as a member, from birth, of a specific matriclan. This said, it must immediately be acknowledged that there are cases in which people change their clan membership, sometimes as a consequence of their own clan's demise, sometimes because of their long-term residence with and participation in the activities of a household affiliated with another clan. The prevalence of this exception to the rule varies; it is not unusual in Palau and is almost unheard of in Pohnpei.

At its core this Micronesian matri-principle consists of a series of elements, all typical of what ethnologists call clans. I discuss these topics more fully below; here I merely outline the most salient characteristics. Micronesian clans are

Exogamic. Members of the same clan are prohibited from marrying one another. To do so would violate incest taboos. Concerns about violations of these rules often keep adolescent brothers, sisters, and cousins at a distance from one another. Although Micronesians usually speak of these incest prohibitions in unequivocal terms, there are exceptions, which sometimes illustrate the complexities that make the realities of Micronesian social organization considerably more complicated than people claim them to be. Degrees of geographical distance are sometimes thought to lessen the strength of these taboos. Thus Pohnpeians have a saying, *Sohte pel en nan madau,* which literally translates as "There are no taboos across the sea." This reflects an assumption that physical distance is apt to be attended by corresponding genealogical distance and that sexual taboos may thus be relaxed a bit when it comes to relations between individuals from different islands. Some Pohnpeians also express the notion that broader clan taboos, opposed to those of the more immediate lineage, apply more to marriage than to casual sexual activities.

Totemic. Micronesians generally speak of their clans as having originated with ancestors who were part human and part spirit-being. Pohnpei's Lasialap clan, for example, is said to be descended from an eel who gave birth to human children, and the eel is the Lasialap clan's totem. Clan members are expected to observe certain rules as signs of respect for their totems.

Named. Micronesian clans are identified by commonly known names, which for the most part refer to places and/or incidents entailed in their origin stories. Members of a community ordinarily know to which clans their neighbors belong. Subclans and lineages are sometimes named, but knowledge of these names is not so widely shared. Because lineages tend to be closely identified with specific pieces of land, they are sometimes referred to in terms of the places they live or farm.

Dispersed. Ordinarily, a clan's members do not all live together, nor even in the same communities or on the same islands. Unless a clan is on the brink of extinction, with only one or two branches left and very few surviving members, it is highly unlikely that all its members would be acquainted with one another. Subclans and lineages may be more localized, but not necessarily so.

Unilineal. Although there are occasional exceptions to this rule, in general Micronesians become members of only their mothers' clans. It is strict adherence to this unilineal membership rule that allows clans to become dispersed while still retaining their coherence.

Ramified. With only occasional exceptions, clans are branching organizations. Each comprises multiple divisions or subunits. These subdivisions branch in turn into smaller units, which may include even smaller units. In general, clans are composed of subclans, which in turn encompass lineages.

A Few Qualifications

Before I begin exploring this topic systematically, a few qualifications are in order. The first of these is the distinction between descent principles and descent groups. In speaking of descent principles I am referring to a combination of conscious and unconscious patterns in the ways people conceptualize their relations with others. I stress that these patterns and ideas are not necessarily reflected in actual patterns of social activity.

In some cases I will be drawing upon what Micronesians themselves say, with varying degrees of clarity and vagueness, about how their societies are organized. In others, I employ ethnographers' inferences about these patterns of observed behavior and manners of speaking. The nested hierarchy of descent units or categories I am about to describe is not identical to hierarchies of actual government or decision-making processes. Although descent groups are shaped by descent principles, they are by no means the same thing. It is precisely because actual patterns of behavior—in this case, the formation of groups of people—respond to the realities of daily life as well as to underlying principles that I am approaching the matters of descent and of land, labor, and leadership separately.

A great deal of anthropological theory has dealt with concepts of descent and their relations to the organization of actual groups. Marshall Sahlins addressed the problem with typical acuity: "What exactly is the relation between the composition of a group and its ideology of descent?" He pointed out that descent is not simply a rule determining the affiliations of individuals but is also a political ideology. And in addition to relating individuals to one another within groups, "it stipulates the group's relations, or lack of relation, to other groups." Because principles of descent play such a critical role in shaping practices in everyday life, genealogies are sometimes reworked to make them fit into what Sahlins calls "descent dogma" (1968, 54–55). As he describes it, "This capacity of major descent groups to override their own internal discrepancies is one very good reason for choosing to describe the tribal kinship organization from the top down. The greater groups are not the smaller writ large; it is rather the other way around. The 'primary' groups and relationships are shaped by their incorporation in a larger system of a certain type" (1968, 54–55). In terms of the categories I shall be using here, Sahlins is arguing that clans are not built up out of the principles that shape life in Micronesian households and lineages so much as households and lineages are shaped by the nature of the larger clans of which they are a part.

Sahlins says that, in the sorts of tribal societies he examines, the family—what I term the household—is "a little chiefdom within the chiefdom." In other words, "the family order is molded by the tribal order, and even in its most intimate relationships bears the impress of society at large." This means that "from top to bottom the same principles are in play," and thus principles of rank that apply to any level of organization apply to all levels: "The family is thoroughly assimilated to the conical clan in which it is embedded," and "primogeniture holds in the family as in the clan, and the gradations of genealogical seniority it implies hold as well" (Sahlins 1968, 63–64).[3]

In my examination of Micronesian descent and kin groups, I too use a top-down approach (i.e., I begin with the highest order of organization, the clan, and work my way to the household), but for very different reasons and with decidedly different results. I employ this approach for two reasons. First, matrilineal descent is one of the most conspicuous factors Micronesian societies have in common. Second, I wish to demonstrate how a consistent ideological principle works itself out differently in a range of practical situations. Although I start with the descent principle, I try not to privilege it or to assume that it shapes everything. Rather, I start with descent simply because I have to have a starting point and descent principles are more consistent than land and leadership, the two other key variables here. An emphasis on descent draws attention to commonalities and acknowledges that descent principles do double duty, providing not only internal order within groups but also linkages to other communities.

I want to make it clear that I perceive a crucial problem with Sahlins' formulation. His emphasis on top-down diffusion of the political aspects of descent ideology results in two misunderstandings. First, it assumes that the "conical," or hierarchical, principle that plays such a major role in shaping patterns of leadership is of equal importance in organizing relations among groups, whether they are clans or lineages. But as we shall see, this is not the case in Micronesia. Second, it treats the higher-level principle of clan organization as the dominant force in shaping actual groups, while acknowledging flexibility—the reality of responses to actual cases—as no more than an epiphenomenon. But as we shall also see, the flexible aspects of group organization—the exceptions to cultural rules—are as essential to any comprehension of Micronesian social dynamics as are any overarching principles.

The converse of this top-down approach might be described as bottom-up, and it, too, is relevant. In all the range of basic human kin relationships, including ties between parents and children, between spouses, and among brothers and sisters, it is probably the latter that receive the greatest emphasis in the organization of Micronesia's matrilineal societies. Relations between adult members of matrilineages are ordinarily conceived of as ties between siblings. In Chuuk "there is something basic, central, special, and primary about 'sibling' relationships" (Marshall 1979, 202). Marshall concludes, "The truly significant units in Trukese social organization are sibling sets rather than sets of parents and their children. Giving the sibling-sibling tie analytical primacy over the parent-child connection draws attention to sets of persons in the same generation of a descent group as the 'building blocks' of Trukese social organization" (1979, 220). In Palau, too, cross-sibling relationships (as ties between brothers and sisters are called in anthropological terms) are of enormous consequence (Smith 1979).[4] Marshall proposes that an important "element in the conventional Micronesian repertoire is the centrality of sibling relations and their dominance over spousal and parental ties" (1999, 109), and this might be thought of in terms of a bottom-up perspective. It does not appear to me, however, that sibling ties are stressed as strongly in eastern Micronesia, and while they do reflect some of the basic dynamics common to all these matrilineal societies, my focus is directed more toward the composition and organization of groups than toward sibling ties.

It is worth keeping in mind, however, that relations between siblings are reciprocal and thoroughly interdependent. Brothers rely on their sisters to bear and raise the members who will keep their lineages alive, while sisters depend on their brothers to marry into other lineages, thereby gaining access to external resources that will enable their own lineages to thrive. Because nuances of political titles, land tenure, marriage, postmarital residence choices, and the sexual division of labor influence the specific character and intensity of kin relationships as well, the dynamics of sibling and cross-sibling ties are not nearly as consistent across the region as the basic organization of descent groups.

Historical Origins

Perhaps the clearest indication we have that Micronesian descent principles are shared, and not just similar, is found in terminologies referring to descent-based groups.[5] One or the other of two common terms are to be found almost all the way across the region. The first of these is cognate with an ancient and widespread Pacific island term, which appears in Polynesian languages as *kainanga* or some variant form and has a range of related meanings, from "kin group" to "land." In Pohnpei this term appears as *keinek* (lineage); in Chuuk and the central Carolines it is *eyinang, ainang, kainang, hailang,* or some closely related variant meaning "clan" or "lineage"; and in Yap it is *genung* or *ganong* (clan). The second of these terms appears in Pohnpei as *sou* (clan), in the Marshalls as *jou* or *jowi* (clan), in Kosrae as *sucu* or *sou* (clan), and in Chuuk and the central Carolines as variants of *sowu* (clan).[6] There are also a number of local terms, including Pohnpeian *dipw* and Kosraean *sruf* (clan), Chuukese *eterekes* (lineage), Chuukese and central Carolines' *tettel* or *tetten* (branch), and Namoluk *futuk* (which Marshall [1976] glosses as "subclan").[7] Palau's *kebliil* and *klebliil* (for comparative purposes, "clan" and "superclan") do not appear to be linked linguistically with these other terms, but the groups they refer to are organized in essentially similar ways.[8]

Terminologies, social structures, and patterns of activity reflect underlying principles of three levels of descent group organization found throughout Micronesia: clan, subclan, and lineage.[9] But variation among Micronesian societies, not simply in the number of levels of organization but in the ways people categorize these elements, makes it impossible simply to set down lists of comparable concepts from each Micronesian society (for other than historical linguistic purposes). Nor would it be particularly useful at this point to raise questions concerning the principles through which these units go about recruiting their membership. Instead, I begin by merely examining aspects of the variation in the ways these units are conceptualized or categorized.

Although this nested triad of categories exists in nearly all Micronesian societies, it is not always immediately apparent. I am especially aware of the three levels because Pohnpeians, at least those who are familiar with the nuances of Pohnpeian social organization, distinguish between *sou* (clan), *keimw* (subclan), and *keinek* (lineage). Having distinct terms for all three levels is unusual in Micronesia, and in fact, even here, where technical usage carefully distinguishes between these categories, people in casual conversation sometimes use them interchangeably.

John Fischer, for instance, observed, "Native words are of little help in making the distinction between lineage and extended family. Both Trukese and Ponapean have words which depending on context can mean either" (1966, 128). Even though the analytical categories ethnographers use to describe specific Micronesian societies have been fairly consistent, Micronesian languages only rarely possess specific terms for all these categories. Goodenough (1951), for instance, describes five different sorts of matrilineally organized descent categories or levels in Chuukese society, although the Chuukese language provides only two basic terms. In Palau, on the other hand, five terms are in common use for what Smith (1983) reduces to perhaps three categories. Because of the varying linkages between descent categories and actual patterns of behavior, on the one hand, and the terms used for them within societies on the other, language can only hint at historical connections among Micronesian societies.

It is common, then, for the terms (as opposed to the senses in which people use them) that refer to descent groups to be imprecise. On Namoluk, in the Mortlocks, people speak in terms of "one people" (i.e., clan), "one flesh and blood" (subclan), and "one line of people" (lineage), but they ordinarily employ only a single word, *ainang*, to refer to all three. As Marshall explains, "When Namoluk people use the word *ainang*, the particular context indicates to which of the above three categories of matrilineal kin it refers" (1972, 55).[10] Probably most common is the use of just two distinct terms—one for clan, one for lineage. In Ulul, on Namonuito atoll, for example, people speak of *aynang* (clan) and *tettel* (line), but "*aynang* represents a continuum of meaning" that is shaped by geographic and social distance; Ulul's people recognize these differences in meaning (J. Thomas 1978, 42, 52–53.). That is, a single term includes what others would recognize as clan and subclan, while a separate word denotes the lineage.

These terms (and the concepts that underlie them) did not develop independently on each island or island group, but they have certainly tended to diverge from one another.[11] What is more important in this context, however, is the actual operation of Micronesian clanship. I return to the point that Micronesian descent groups function not only as a framework for ongoing social life within communities but also as a means of linking neighboring communities to one another. Accounts of ancestors' origins and migrations demonstrate that Micronesians are not simply aware of neighboring societies but think of their own local histories as bound up in the histories of other communities, islands, and island groups. And although the local-level descent groups—the lineages—are most frequently involved in land ownership and governing activities, the overarching structural principles of clanship are tremendously significant in binding the societies of Micronesia into a whole.

In this, Micronesia differs significantly from Polynesia. For although Polynesia's languages are closely related to one another, and its mythologies tend to share a common sense of migration from legendary origins somewhere in the west (the legendary Hawaiki), the ties that link island communities together do not flow seamlessly across the breadth of Polynesia. While eastern Fiji, Tonga, and Samoa were linked by Tongan navigators, for instance, and populations in the Society Islands (Tahiti and its neighbors) had relations with the peoples of adjacent islands, there appears to have been no web of relations linking all of Polynesia together.[12] Regular voyaging among the Micronesian islands, on the other hand, keeps people involved with one another, aware of one another, and conscious of links, no matter how sporadic, to peoples living long distances away from them. And it was the principles of matridescent that underpinned these relations.

It is worth pointing out that relations among Micronesian societies provide us with important examples for the comparative study of international relations. Traditionally, the study of political relations among states, particularly in light of the norms established in the wake of the Treaty of Westphalia (1648) and codified by Hugo Grotius, holds that whatever the forms of government within specific countries might be—monarchical, republican, or otherwise—relations between sovereign states are inherently anarchic. That is, the sovereignty of states ends at their respective borders, and nothing that governs them at home carries over to the governance of relations among them (see, e.g., Morgenthau 1993; and Waltz 1979).

Micronesian practices stand out in marked contrast to this theoretical perspective. A single overarching set of principles organizes both the lineages, which manage land and livelihood within individual societies, and the clans, which shape relations between societies. Micronesian communities have their own forms of sovereignty and of effective foreign relations among them, to be sure. Although Micronesian societies did indeed fight with one another in the past, the fact remains that most Micronesians, most of the time, were overwhelmingly more likely to visit, trade, and intermarry with their neighbors than to attack them.

Clans

Because matridescent at its most inclusive—the level of the clan—entails virtually no corporate activities (that is, actions undertaken by the group as a whole), it is easy to overlook its importance. But through its absolutely fundamental role in regulating marriage by requiring people to marry outside their clans, it plays a crucial role in organizing interisland relations. Migration stories play key roles in many clan and subclan histories. Because the members of clans are dispersed over large areas, ancestral figures are thought of as having traveled from place to place. In some cases this entails movement from distant places; for example, Pohnpei's Sounmaraki clan purports to have come originally from Marakei in Kiribati, and Liarkatau is said to descend from a woman *(li)* who traveled to Pohnpei from Katau, the legendary site often associated with Kosrae. In some cases these stories refer primarily to movement within island chains—from one part of the Marshalls to another, for instance (Pollock 1976). Within Chuuk Lagoon, relations among some of the clans and their branches are summed up in the phrase *fatanin Weene, sefaunin Weene* (the migration of Moen, the return of Moen); that is, "the history of Moen is one of repeated emigration and immigration by the clans that originated" there (Parker 1985, 125). John Fischer points out that membership in the same clans occurs throughout the eastern Carolines (1966, 130). And ethnographies of the atolls between Yap and Chuuk stress the distribution of the same clans throughout the islands and the general awareness of the importance of clan ties in linking island to island. The Under-the-breadfruit-tree clan is dispersed from Kosrae in the east all the way to Tobi and the adjacent atolls southwest of Palau, a distance of two thousand miles. Shared migration histories form part of the substance of clanship in Palau (Smith 1983). It is the movement of women, who pass on matridescent, that results in the dispersal of the clans and the subclans that form in consequence of this movement.

While clans are dispersed and rarely have any corporate functions, lineages are localized groups with intense involvement in land and titles—and are relatively easy to describe. Subclans, on the other hand, are much more complexly and subtly ordered and need more careful explication. Though simple logic suggests that I discuss subclans between clans and lineages, which is where they exist in terms of hierarchical progression, they are better understood after lineages have been considered.

Lineages

Lineages differ from clans and subclans in several important ways. They are much more likely to be directly associated with specific places and plots of land. The situation is more complex in Yap, but both Lingenfelter (1975, 33) and Labby (1976, 114) have explained that, in the past, localized lineages were corporate landholding groups, as in the rest of Micronesia, although they no longer function in quite this manner. Lineages are often actual residential groups, made up of people living together on the same plot of land and essentially undistinguishable from households, and I discuss many of their attributes in chapter 5. Lineages commonly serve as the basic units owning land, and they are usually the social units that possess or control political titles. Although genealogies are rarely remembered (or at least publicly discussed) for more than three or four generations, lineages are usually small enough to permit most members to specify just how—that is, through whom—they are related to one another. And the number of members in any given lineage is substantially smaller than that of clans and subclans. Moreover, in common usage, "lineage" often refers to a group of people residing together; lineages may thus include members who were not born into them and the act of changing one's membership in a clan, which happens with varying frequencies in different Micronesian societies, actually takes place through the process of joining a lineage, rather than at a higher level. This process seems to occur occasionally in Palau and very rarely in Pohnpei.[13]

Within a clan or subclan, lineages are commonly ranked in terms of the birth orders of the women who are thought to have founded them. Thus people descended from the eldest of a set of sisters constitute a lineage that is deemed senior to the lineages descended from her younger sisters. Because the genealogical depth of lineages tends to be limited, it is more likely that the birth orders of the women who found them are known and remembered, but in actual practice it is not unusual to find that these birth orders are confused or deliberately transposed or have simply been forgotten within several generations. While the most important aspects of most lineages' activities are tied up in the management and inheritance of land, and with the mobilization of the labor that extracts a living from the land and its resources, it is also the case that political titles play a crucial role in the operations of a few selected lineages in each community. Disputes over rights to land and to titles are, as we shall see, a fundamental aspect of life in Micronesia's lineages.

Subclans

Least understood and discussed by anthropologists are what are generally called subclans; these are also the most vaguely defined of Micronesian descent units. The simplest way to describe them is to say that they are the highest-order divisions of clans, but this hardly does justice to their importance. Only a few Micronesian societies possess distinct terms for subclans; on Pohnpei it is *keimw* (which also means "corner"), and on Namoluk it is *futuk* (Marshall 1976, 183). Subclans seem to exist in all Micronesian societies, but even though clan and lineage are concepts likely to be employed by most of the people in a given society, clearly articulated notions of subclans may be familiar only to individuals who are particularly concerned with genealogies or the intricacies of political process.

Although they are often only vaguely conceived, subclans have particular significance. They serve as points at which the two opposing pulls of Micronesian descent principles—dispersed clan ties and intense, corporate lineage bonds—intersect and interact. Micronesian clans are by their nature dispersed. They serve to link particular people within communities, and sometimes entire communities, to people in other communities. Alkire, for instance, describes in considerable detail the perpetual flow of gifts between clan mates on Lamotrek and Satawal (1989, 138–142). Micronesian lineages, on the other hand, are ordinarily localized—they control particular tracts of land. The essence of subclans is to be found both in the vaguely specified or unknown genealogical connections that are believed to forge ties of dependence or reliance between groups of people residing at a distance from one another, and in notions about localization, the phenomenon of Micronesians experiencing themselves as rooted in specific places

In the Mortlock Islands. The wife and daughter of a chief. Mothers and their daughters form the core of Micronesian descent groups. Courtesy of the Micronesian Seminar.

on specific landholdings. The relative intensity of Micronesian descent relations is to some extent tied to distance, both geographical and genealogical. It is assumed that fellow clan members who live far apart from one another (absent any specific knowledge to the contrary) are only distantly related. Subclans are not ordinarily corporate landholding groups, nor do they usually control political titles, but when a land- or title-holding lineage's population begins declining, other lineages from the same subclan are eligible to assume its rights and duties.

Lineages and subclans shade into one another. Marshall observes that on Namoluk "members of certain matrilineages may believe themselves closely related genealogically, although the exact ties have been forgotten," and that "such sets of closely related matrilineages form what will be called subclans" (1976, 182). On Romonum, in Chuuk Lagoon, a subclan is composed of "the members of a [clan] who share a *definite tradition* of common ancestry in the female line, though it is not traceable genealogically" (Goodenough 1951, 65, my emphasis).

Subclans are often spoken of, or described, as having been established by the daughters of their clan's founding ancestress; they are sometimes ranked relative to one another in accordance with the birth order of the sisters thought to have established them. They are frequently named either after the women who founded them or after events that figured in their origin stories. The rankings of the subclans tend to derive from these mythohistorical events and are almost always phrased in terms of birth order.

As a general rule the larger the membership of a clan, or the wider its geographical distribution, the more subclans it is likely to include. Subclans of clans that possess no political titles, as well as subclans that are too junior or low-ranking to lay claim to their own clan's titles, are often unranked relative to one another (or at least most of their members are unaware of any ranking). In general, a single subclan's members are likely to have no better knowledge of the genealogical specifics of their relationships with one another than are members of a clan; the details of these ties have been lost in the past. For our purposes here, their most obvious distinguishing feature derives from the ways in which they represent spatial arrangements: subclans are commonly conceptualized in terms of their places of origin during the course of the movements of the ancestral figures who founded them. These events may have occurred in legendary times or within times still lodged in the early memories of a community's eldest members.

Subclans are also the points at which flux in demographic histories of clans are most noticeable. Subclans grow into separate and distinct clans under some circumstances, hiving off from their antecedents as they increase in size. Ethnographers frequently recount examples where there is debate or discussion concerning the status of a descent group: is it a full-fledged clan, as some of its members are likely to claim, or merely a large subclan, as members of other subclans may maintain? There is, in fact, no clear-cut means of distinguishing between these categories. Smith recounts how she attempted to follow up on earlier ethnographic reports on Palau that differentiated between "two distinct groups termed *kebliil* ('clan') and *klebliil* ('supersib')": "One day I visited the home of an elder and asked him to tell me the difference between a *kebliil* and *klebliil*. He leaned close and whispered, 'The difference is that there is no difference'" (1983, 38). Mason regards some Marshalls' clans as actually being subgroups of more inclusive clans (1947, 23–25). Ritter and Ritter describe Kosrae's four clans as "superclans or phratries" (1982, 35). On Pohnpei a number of what are ordinarily spoken of as clans are sometimes described as branches of larger clans (e.g., some believe the Sounroi and Sounmaraki clans were originally divisions of the Dipwenmen clan), and Goodenough describes essentially similar processes in Chuuk (2002, 41–42). In reverse fashion, shrinking subclans may eventually merge into a single undivided clan. Indeed, the very existence of subclans reflects the organizational potential of clans to expand and contract as well as the ability of descent groups to discharge tasks of redistributing members according to the availability of resources—that is, they manage both land and laborers.

And in the same manner, successful lineages with growing membership may in time expand geographically, moving to adjoining communities or adjacent islands and thus evolve into subclans; it is likely that within a few generations they will be perceived as equivalent to other subclans, though initially of low rank. This is the way, in fact, that many—perhaps most—subclans arise over the course of centuries.

In Chuuk, Parker notes, "subclans are usually localized in more than one community, and usually on more than one island, often including atolls outside the lagoon." Parker explains that they "are formed by virilocal marriages of women from one community to another" and cites as an example groups on Iras island that trace their ancestry to the Paata district on Toon island, via marriages on Romonum island (Parker 1985, 127–128).[14] Their children retain ties to their mothers' matriclans but also create newly established, localized subclans. Pohnpei's Lasialap clan, which traces its origins to an ancestral eel-mother, is divided into subclans conceptualized in terms of both the birth order of the ancestress' daughters and the places or points at which each was born in the course of a migratory journey their mother undertook. Migration stories are also fundamental historical elements of Palau's *klebliil*. In the course of its travels a group stops for a time as a woman gives birth; continuing on, it splits into opposing branches, a process known as " 'one leg and the other leg' *(bital oach ma bital oach).*" As Smith notes, "The ideology of a *bital oach* is that each leg is formed by descendants from one of two sisters" (1983, 60). In the Marshalls, too, subclans are associated with places visited in the course of the larger clan's dispersal throughout the archipelagoes (Pollock 1976, 85, 96). This continual flux between clan and subclan and between subclan and lineage is in part responsible for the terminological and conceptual vagueness, and apparent confusion, that characterize relations among the various levels of descent groups.

In short, subclans tend to be localized branches of clans—linking groups of lineages within a given area. The consistent appearance of subclans throughout Micronesia seems to suggest that societies everywhere in the region have found that subclans allow a single overarching system to accomplish two very different tasks simultaneously: to organize connections between people residing at a distance from one another and to organize daily living arrangements within and among the smaller groups.

How is it possible that the very immediate, face-to-face relationships that characterize lineage life are so thoroughly integrated into the extremely vague relations characteristic of clan ties? Subclans accomplish this by marking the movements of remote ancestral figures to specific, local places, linking people and place together.

Seniority and Ethnological Theories of Rank

Clans are not, then, about specific places (although their origins often are); rather, they are about connecting people who live in very different places. Lineages, on the other hand, for the most part *are* about the intense relations of people to very specific places, and subclans link these two different sets of concerns to one another. Even though clans and lineages draw upon the same matridescent ideology, they are very different sorts of entities. And these differences raise some fundamental questions. Despite similar appearances, when we look at how clans, subclans, and lineages actually work, we find significant differences. The lowest-order divisions of clans are not, as Sahlins suggested, simply smaller-scale replicas of the larger descent groups. While all draw upon the same organizing ideology, in practical terms each operates quite distinctly.

Why are these two very different practical tasks integrated via a single ideological system? Aspects of this pattern are found throughout most of Oceania, but the specific manner in which societies that are dispersed over such vast areas are integrated with one another via the same ideological constructs that organize them internally seems not only typical of Micronesia but atypical of societies in other Pacific regions. And while Polynesia's clans are comparable in many respects, they tend not to share the intense unilineal character of Micronesian descent. They are both more bilateral and much less likely to be dispersed over broad geographical areas.

Ultimately, we have to recognize that discussion of Micronesian clanship is complicated by the fact that the concepts and behaviors entailed in it spill across boundaries implied by English-language terms and concepts. While the threads that define how people are tied together via descent principles are overwhelmingly biological in conceptualization, the attitudes and behaviors that characterize relations among those who consider themselves to share the substance of descent consistently challenge any preconceived notions that English-speakers might have about them. Principles of Micronesian clanship are not exclusively, nor even predominantly, about what most English-speakers would think of as kinship—that is, relations among people ordered largely by notions of biological and sentimental connection and obligation. Instead, they range across a variety of existential domains, including economics, politics, and religion. Smith's evocation of the situation in Palau aptly captures the situation in Micronesia in general: "[There are] major organizational principles by which Belauans ally and classify themselves into groups of varying sizes and degrees of exclusivity based on concepts of migration, 'blood,' land, and residence. Each Belauan unit utilizes several different principles to determine membership. Furthermore, the unit expands or contracts in size and nature depending upon which principles are being emphasized for a specific purpose" (Smith 1983, 37).

With a few possible exceptions, Micronesian clans in the abstract are all equal and autonomous; that is, because clans are so widely dispersed, they are not ranked relative to one another. At the same time, however, in the concrete realm of politics, relative ranking of clans does hold a limited but nonetheless fundamental position in Micronesian life, because ranking is important in specific cases and places. Clan rank—not in terms of individuals but in terms of groups—exists in two contexts: among the multiple branches or subclans that make up clans, and among the multiple clans that occupy a specific locality. That is, in any given locale at least some of the clans present are ranked according to local beliefs regarding their order of settlement.[15] But in all cases, whether regarding individuals or groups, rank is always a product of both practical political processes and the descent ideology of seniority.

I have written at length about technical and theoretical aspects of seniority and clanship as they can be observed in Micronesian societies (Petersen 1999b), and I discuss questions about the meanings of seniority in chapter 6, on chieftainship. Here I want to consider only a few aspects relevant to a broader understanding of Micronesian social life itself.

While both Micronesian and Polynesian descent systems have been used as primary examples of what anthropologists call conical clans (which are characterized by internal, hierarchical ranking, and which I discuss at length in chapter 6), for a variety of reasons Polynesia has much more frequently been drawn upon to illustrate them. It may in fact be that some aspects of Polynesian societies are better understood via the lens of Micronesian social organization. In dissecting Polynesian sociopolitical organization, conical clans, and succession to chiefly office, Patrick Kirch explains, "Typically, the senior male in direct line of patrilineal succession from the group ancestor claims the position of highest rank in the conical clan" (1984, 32). Although he is focusing entirely on Polynesian societies, I am prepared to suggest, using what we know about the dynamics of Micronesian social organization, that the reality is considerably more complex than Kirch's sentence acknowledges. As we shall see in later chapters, the so-called ideal form of succession (what Kirch [1984, 34], terms a "strong ideological bias") may not be very typical of what actually takes place. There is often uncertainty in establishing which of several meanings of "senior" is in effect in any given case—the term does not necessarily imply a strictly direct genealogical line. It may well be deemed inappropriate for a man to "claim" a position of rank. There are important differences between asserting a claim and actually achieving office. Which person holds highest rank in a given clan is often a matter of some dispute. And it is hardly the case that rank—even when it is publicly acknowledged—necessarily brings automatic succession to office.

"Seniority," which is on the one hand so important to the social order, is on the other hand a quite ambiguous concept, a matter to which we shall return in chapter 6. Here I simply explain, for purposes of clarity, that this ambiguity arises largely because "senior" tends to have two meanings that are sometimes at odds with one another: both those who are chronologically older and those who are closer to the line of firstborn children can legitimately claim to be senior. Irving Goldman called attention to the problem of "status ambiguity" in Polynesian societies: "Primogeniture establishes an *ideal* of descent, whereas simple seniority, which gives some equivalence to all children of first-born, offers a line to fall back on when birth and personal qualities do not coincide" (1970, 14). I would describe this ambiguity a bit differently as it applies to Micronesia, but it is nevertheless entirely relevant. A fundamental characteristic of leadership and status in all Micronesian societies is a contradiction growing out of the simple facts of social life: Younger brothers of elder sisters are chronologically senior to (that is, older than) their elder sisters' sons, even as they are, in terms of the pure ideology of primogeniture, junior in ritual and genealogical status to these same elder sisters' sons. This ambiguity is a central dynamic permeating many facets of sociopolitical life.

What this means for Micronesian social life is that if we take a single facet of Micronesian clan organization—the purely primogeniture-based hierarchy of access to political titles—and assume that this form is imposed upon or characterizes all aspects of clan organization, we then keep ourselves from understanding that other facets are equally important. We should instead recognize that Micronesian clans use a wide range of possibilities when organizing responses to a variety of tasks, from highly localized problems of land tenure and labor recruitment to the forging of linkages among groups of people spread out across scattered archipelagoes.[16]

CHAPTER 5

Household and Family, Land and Labor

THE SHARED PRECEPTS of clanship linking Micronesia's far-flung societies are offset by the roots that individuals and small groups have sunk into specific places. Micronesians' ties to fellow clan members are matched in importance by their attachments to the lands they live on and farm, the communities in which they reside, and the islands they call home. It is no exaggeration to say that Micronesians identify deeply with their land. It provides them with places to live and food to eat, with important elements of their political status, and with symbolic and emotional aspects of simply being alive. To fully grasp the character of Micronesian social life, one must first appreciate the degree to which Micronesians consider people and their land as complementary facets of a single body, the lineage. On Lamotrek, for instance, so intertwined are people and their land that a single term, *bwogat,* means not only the lineage that lives and works together on the land but also the land on which the lineage lives and works (Alkire 1989, 46–47). On Pulap, "sharing food demonstrates kinship and symbolizes the sharing of land, which also is essential to identity" (Flinn 1992, 5). In this chapter I consider Micronesian societies in terms of groups of people living in particular places, focusing on the households in which people live, the lands from which they earn their livelihoods, and the organization of their labor.[1]

Households and Families

The simplest place to begin is with a group of people residing together on a specific plot of land, which can, for our purposes, be called a household. These people generally conceive of themselves as being related to one another and form what might also be called a family. At least some of the members of this residential unit are usually members of a core descent group—a lineage—and the homesite is ordinarily on lands belonging to or claimed by this lineage.

Micronesian climates are characteristically hot and humid, and traditional Micronesian housing is not meant to enclose daytime activities but is instead intended primarily to provide sleeping accommodations and shelter from rain and storm. A typical homesite contains several structures, including sleeping quarters; a small shed for cooking fires and the stone oven, which must be covered because of the frequent rains; and sometimes larger buildings for canoe storage and/or ceremonies. Because the atolls have limited land area, homesites there tend to cluster together into something like villages, though structures are usually built on individual lineage land and shielded from one another by trees and other food crops. On most of the larger islands, however, households are more likely to be scattered about, and the term "village" refers more to a social community than to the physical layout of homes. Because most households consist of multiple buildings and the settlements are scattered, it is not always self-evident just where one family's residence leaves off and another begins. Given the dense vegetation, especially on the larger islands, it is often impossible even to see more than a single homesite at a time, and only the smoke of cooking fires rising up from among the trees may give clues to where people live. Pohnpeians say they prefer this dispersed fashion both because it makes it impossible for an invader to attack the entire community simultaneously and because they do not like to live close to one another. As a young man once explained it to me, "Mehn Pohnpei sohte kin mwahuki dokpene" (Pohnpeians don't like bumping into each other).

Kosrae. Houses, as sketched during Feodor Lütke's 1827 visit. Their high roof peaks are typically Kosraean, but these houses are otherwise much like residences throughout the eastern Caroline Islands. Courtesy of the Micronesian Seminar.

To make these patterns easier to grasp, I begin by describing typical physical layouts of settlements and households in several parts of Micronesia, although there is little variation among the islands. In all four of these cases—Bikini, Chuuk, Ulithi, and Palau—matrilineal descent and matrilineages are of primary importance in determining land tenure and access to political titles, but the actual organization of households—of where people choose to live and raise their children—is quite flexible. The heads of matrilineages, who usually are (or are thought of as) mother's brothers to the lineage members, need to participate actively in the lives of their lineages, but they often live in the households where they grew up with their fathers. Even though the households tend to be scattered, the communities themselves are small, people move about among residences easily, and adult men are able to fully engage in the activities of several of them.

Bikini. A Marshalls' lineage *(bwij)* normally possesses a number of plots of land, each of which is a narrow strip *(waeto)* running across the width of an atoll islet from the lagoon shore to the ocean reef. On some islands, matrilineages are more likely to dwell on one of their own plots (Mason 1947, 41), but on Bikini most households are organized around a lineage head *(alab)* living on a *waeto* where he inherited rights from his father. Bikini's residences are widely dispersed along the lagoon shore, and as in the rest of the Marshalls, a household typically includes two or three sleeping houses (for each of its component married couples and their children) along with a shared cookhouse. The makeup of these households is flexible, with younger married couples moving from time to time between the households of their respective parents. A man who has become head of a household raises his own children there, and as adults they will have rights to their father's land as well as to the lands of their mother's matrilineage (Kiste 1974, 54–55, 68–70).

Chuuk. Chuukese communities, like those on the other high islands, are quite dispersed. As Goodenough noted, "The houses were usually located well back from the shore, up on the mountain slopes, as a defense against a surprise night attack from the sea." A map of Romonum island in 1900 shows "that the houses were scattered about the island on the high ground after the manner of a loose neighborhood, each house with its extended family forming a hamlet" (Goodenough 1951, 132–135). On a plot of lineage land lies a dwelling house, occupied by the lineage's women and their husbands and children, and partitioned-off sleeping compartments for each married woman (Goodenough 1951, 68). Large, important lineages have their own *wuut*, a combination men's house and meetinghouse. These provide sleeping quarters for the lineage's young unmarried men and are often built along the shore so they can also serve as canoe houses. Every lineage has its "hearth" or cookhouse *(fanag)*, where members work together preparing its meals. And each lineage estate has a menstrual house for its women.[2] The land and the buildings on it are named, and a "lineage may be referred to by the name of its past or present house or meeting house as well as by its territorial name," as John Fischer noted. He concluded that on at least the larger islands there is "considerable freedom in where a couple will live and no very clear rule can now be given for the formation of extended families" (J. Fischer 1966, 132). While a household might well include several married sisters and their families, it is likely to be headed either by a man living on his own matrilineage's land (that is, with his sisters) or by a man who has opted to stay with his father on land made available to him by his father's lineage.

Ulithi. On Ulithi's densely populated atoll islets, homes are built close to one another and together they form settlements that look like villages. As Lessa says of Ulithi, the households are nearly side by side: "This is no place for families who like to be by themselves." Still, the land surrounding each dwelling is planted in flowers and food crops. "Women sit outside their houses, usually in groups, and perform most of their household chores there in the shade" of a breadfruit tree, their small children beside them. Cookhouses are adjacent to each dwelling. Canoe houses "line the shore and provide not only shelter for their canoes but a club-house for the men of the lineages that own them." Men do some of their chores there, while children dart in and out, and at night the men often sleep among the canoes (Lessa 1966, 16–17). Young couples move freely among the households of their parents, often sleeping in a separate dwelling, but tend ultimately to settle in a household of the husband's kin. As Lessa notes, "it is futile, then, to discover rules of residence from a static census of houses alone" (1966, 22).

Palau. In contrast to the dispersed homesteads and isolated hamlets found elsewhere on Micronesia's larger islands, "the Belauan village is a concentrated group of residential houses *(blai)* and club and chiefly meetinghouses *(bai)*, all built upon elaborate stone foundations and linked together by elevated stone pathways which fan out from a central paved square" (Parmentier 1987, 56). Each community has a number of clubhouses, where the men of different age groups spend a great deal of their time working and socializing (Barnett 1949, 32). Most villages have carefully tended taro patches, watered by small streams, on one side and the lagoon and its reef resources on the other. Paths paved with stones lead from the village to the taro patches and connect a series of smaller hamlets with the central village. Houses are built at intervals along either side of these paths. Smith describes a household as a unit that cooks together and sleeps in one building: "Therefore, if there are three such independent structures on one piece of mutually held land, I consider them to be three households, although to a Palauan they are one 'house'" (1983, 19). While land is largely thought of as being held by matrilineal groups, children are likely to grow up in households headed by their fathers, and Palauans are given to emphasizing the importance of their ties to fathers (Barnett 1949, 33–36). It is difficult in Palau, as in many other parts of Micronesia, to find any consistent relationship between where people actually live, how they inherit their land, and how they ultimately establish and maintain their clan and lineage ties.

We can see, as we compare patterns from these different islands, that the similarities are striking. Whether households are dispersed, clustered, or strung out along paths, they are separated by trees and other vegetation, screening them off from one another. They are built on land that is for the most part owned and controlled by matrilineages, but young married couples and their children move about without a great deal of constraint. As couples mature, they may settle on the land of either the wife's or her husband's lineage or on land made available to the husband by his own father and his father's lineage. There are often multiple dwelling houses but always a common hearth or cookhouse, where the lineage or household's food is prepared and shared. Almost everywhere there are larger structures, some owned by individual households or lineages, some the property of the community at large, which serve multiple purposes; these are variously described as club-, meeting-, or canoe houses. Despite the enormous emphasis Micronesians place on matrilineages, matrilineal descent, and matrilineal inheritance of land, then, there is in fact a great deal of flexibility in most of the key arrangements of their lives. Mothers are always said to be crucial figures, but so are fathers, mothers' brothers, and brothers and sisters. While Micronesian societies are obviously characterized by their shared matriliny, they may in some ways be better understood in terms of individuals' active engagement in the lives of the many people they interact with each day.

Some Qualifications

Before I begin analyzing the complex intertwining of Micronesian households, families, lineages, and their lands, let me first note several exceptions to the generalizations I will be making.

Micronesian households, like households and families everywhere, pass through what are called domestic cycles. Put in simplest terms, the domestic cycle refers to universal processes beginning with the marriage of a man and a woman, expanding as the couple bear children, contracting as grown children leave, and ending when both members of the couple die or when they divorce. Because Micronesian households often include numerous adults, along with their children, and because they remain settled on collectively owned plots of land, they are not nearly as ephemeral as this description suggests, but they do grow and contract in size as children are born or adopted, new spouses move in, members take up residence elsewhere, and people die. There is, therefore, no normal or typical household—all are continually passing through the stages of the domestic cycle.

While every Micronesian is, by definition, born into a matrilineage, there are many reasons why some individuals deliberately leave or gradually drift away from their homes and families. Women with children to care for are likely to be less mobile, but men—especially young men, but some older men as well—are not always as rooted to places or connected to people as Micronesian culture would seem to dictate. For a variety of reasons, individuals sometimes attach themselves to households where they have no immediate or obvious ties, and may move from household to household over the course of time. It is also common for entire families—that is, wife, husband, and children—to move for a time to a new household or community.

What is more, it is quite customary for Micronesian children to be adopted, often by relatives residing in other households, before they are even born. Ordinarily they remain with their birth families as infants; as they grow, they begin to spend time in their adoptive households; and as they mature, they decide just where they will take up residence. I shall explore this pattern later, but it must be kept in mind that until they make these decisions, they are effectively members of two households, and many remain closely tied to both throughout their lives.

Young people spend much of their time in one another's company and at night are likely to sleep together at the household of one of their number. There may be a cluster of teenagers sleeping in a home for weeks at a time, though only one of them might actually call it home. Indeed, it may happen that none of those sleeping in a household on a given night are technically residents there. This of course adds to the continual variation in the composition of the group of people who spend their time in any given household.

Sleeping arrangements are typically affected by the strict observation of incest taboos. While the details vary among societies, Micronesians in general go to considerable effort to keep sexually active, but not fully mature, young men and women of the same clan out of situations where they might be sexually tempted by one another. On the other hand, social obligations among brothers and sisters are of great consequence in Micronesian societies and seem to be especially important in Chuuk and Palau (Marshall 1979, 1999; Smith 1979).

Put simply, in matrilineal societies brothers have what appear to be inherently contradictory interests in their sisters' sexuality. That is, sisters bear children who are members of their brothers' matrilineages and who will be responsible for the lineage's stability and success in succeeding generations; brothers care about who will father their sisters' children, children upon whom they shall, in time, come to depend. This preoccupation has been considered by some to pose a threat to a core principle of matriliny, exogamy—the insistence upon marriage outside the lineage and clan. Exogamy, moreover, forbids not just marriage but also sexual relations between fellow clan members.[3] As a consequence, a range of formal behaviors characterizes relations among brothers and sisters and matrilateral parallel cousins (i.e., the sons and daughters of sisters, who are members of the same lineage). From the onset of puberty, these youngsters should not sleep near one another, should engage only in restrained interactions, and should behave in ways that allow them to avoid one another (Labby 1976, 172; Fischer et al. 1976, 200). Thus, sleeping arrangements in households are such that, despite the tendency for most children and adults to sleep in a common chamber, the older boys and young men, or occasionally the girls and women, must find somewhere else to spend their nights. Canoe houses and feast houses often become de facto men's clubhouses. This is another reason why it can be difficult to specify clearly just what constitutes a household or lineage: it is well-nigh impossible to speak with any certainty about the membership of a given household when some spend very little time there.

Finally, in many of these societies, adults, particularly men but sometimes women, spend a great deal of their time together in club-, meeting-, or canoe houses. Undoubtedly the most celebrated instances of this are Palau's *blolobel* or *mengol,* Yap's *mispel,* and the Marianas' *uritao* (or *maulitao*) practices, in which young women (often referred to as concubines) are placed by their families or communities in men's houses, where they serve its residents in a variety of ways. Sexual aspects of these services have sometimes shocked outsiders, but in island societies where premarital sexual activities are usually thought of as a normal part of human development, the focus is largely on the opportunities provided to the young women and their families to accrue valuables and prestige (Parmentier 1987, 93–96; Lingenfelter 1975, 82; Russell 1998, 148–149).

Physical Conditions of Homesites and Households

Micronesia's tropical climates dictate that many of the materials used to construct dwellings, mainly palm fronds and reeds, deteriorate quickly, although the extensive mangrove stands on the high islands provide relatively long-lasting timbers. New structures are continually being erected and old ones abandoned, making it difficult to be sure just what is occupied and what is not. Even on the high islands, where runoff from often torrential rains and the resulting mud lead people to build on permanent stone platforms, it is not always clear just which of these footings are actually in use and which have been temporarily abandoned.

Social Conditions

Most early socialization of children takes place in and around the households in which they grow up, and their important social interactions are with the adults and other children who reside with them. Households organize the most cohesive work groups; nearly all tasks in Micronesian communities are performed by groups of people, and it is the members of a household who are most likely to work together. Because of the importance of household labor organization, as well as ideologies of land tenure and ownership, the day-to-day, practical control of land—that is, decisions about who will do what on which plots of land—is largely in the hands of a household's mature adults, male and female. Households, then, are centers for most productive activities. They are also the points at which most consumption takes place. With occasional exceptions, influenced by age or gender (especially on Yap), whatever is produced or received by a household is available for consumption by all its members. And although feasting and ritual exchange commonly involve communities as wholes rather than single households, informal exchanges among households are constantly under way. On Pohnpei, for example, as breadfruit (or other foods) are pulled hot from a stone oven and placed into hastily plaited palm-leaf carrying baskets, a passing child is likely to be handed a basketful and told to carry it home. The child, absorbed in his or her own preoccupations, simply drops the basket off at the household's cookhouse and continues on. The freshly baked breadfruit is eaten by the first hungry household members to spy it. Goodenough (2002, 53) describes much the same sort of phenomenon on Chuuk. Food thus passes continually from household to household in ways that even the members are only partly aware of.

Significant variations in household composition and organization occur not only among different Micronesian societies but also within them. John Fischer's census work in the islands of Chuuk Lagoon in the years shortly after World War II led him to conclude that "considerable differences in land tenure, incidence of residence forms, and some other aspects of social structure might be found among the various islands, in spite of linguistic similarity and native feeling of cultural unity" (1958, 509). Even within communities differences in the makeup of family units can be significant. Alexander Spoehr, who studied Majuro in those same postwar years, emphasized that Marshallese household composition "does not conform to rigid principles of formation." Despite the formal recognition of matrilineal principles, he explained, "there is also a feeling for bilaterality." Indeed, "like the people themselves," Marshallese social organization "has a casual quality . . . and is flexible and varying" (Spoehr 1949, 113). And on nearby Arno, Akitoshi Shimizu found that individuals choose among "multiple alternatives" when deciding where to reside and earn their living and that household composition is a result of "a dynamic process in which" many "factors interact" (1987, 26), while Michael Rynkiewich concludes that "the household is not an important ideational group" (i.e., conceptual category) but rather "an important action group" (1976, 108).

Among the factors that shape decisions about who lives with whom, two are particularly important. One is the overarching Micronesian emphasis on ties through the female line. For purposes of acquiring land and managing access to political titles, there is a shared bias toward matrilineal patterns. At the same time, however, the actual organization of subsistence labor—primarily the work of farming and fishing—also seems to have an impact on residence decisions (Alkire 1960).

A well-known episode in the history of anthropological theory, the so-called postmarital "residence rules" debate of the 1950s between John Fischer and Ward Goodenough—that is, the question of where a man and woman are likely to settle after they marry each other—largely turned on how to interpret and explain the composition of Chuukese household groups in the years immediately following the war. Using essentially identical census data reporting on where couples took up residence following marriage, these two accomplished scholars thoroughly disagreed on how to interpret the data (Goodenough 1956; J. Fischer 1958; Kronenfeld 1992). Their differences stemmed largely from the importance each attributed to descent ideology and to the organization of labor, and hinged on a number of ambiguous cases in which men remained in the households where they were raised. In terms of traditional Chuukese social patterns, these men were living on the lands of their matrilineages, and Goodenough interpreted them as cases of matrilocal residence. Fischer, on the other hand, pointed out that "matrilocal" commonly meant that a husband settled with the family or lineage into which the wife was born, and thus he did not classify these cases as matrilocal. Fischer's suggestion that anthropologists employ the terms "virilocal" (residence with the husband's natal household) and "uxorilocal" (with the wife's natal household) has been subsequently adopted by a great many anthropologists; it grew out of the confusing character of these residential decisions. When viewed in the larger context of Micronesian social life, however, it can be seen that this Chuukese pattern, of young men opting to live with their fathers rather than in the households of their new wives, is not in the least unusual.

When a man and woman marry, each brings rights and attachments to the lineages, lands, and households of his or her mother and father and perhaps of adoptive parents as well. Continual variation in the composition of households, changes in the landholdings of the relevant groups, and environmental fluctuations make it difficult for anyone to predict where the best place to make a living is likely to be a few years in the future, and the dynamics of personal relations between spouses and between them and their respective families shift often enough to make each household's history unique. Leonard Mason noted that "post-marital residence seems to possess little significance" in most of Micronesia. Despite various reports of consistent residence patterns, he observes, "adherence to the ideal is not strongly supported by quantitative observation" (Mason 1968, 285–286). There are clearly tendencies in most Micronesian societies, but the notion of residence "rules" does not adequately describe how people decide on where they are going to live.

There is still the problem of explaining interconnections between the ideology of descent and the practical issues of organizing the work of daily subsistence. Individuals' actions and motivations are often ambiguous. It can be difficult to distinguish among decisions made on the bases of descent principles, emotional ties to individuals or groups, and practical access to usable land, given that the same term or terms may be employed to refer to all of these. On Lamotrek, where the term *bwogat* refers both to groups of people and to their lands, what constitutes family, domestic unit, residential group, homestead, or landholdings cannot always be determined with certainty (Alkire 1989, 46–47).

Though social and economic changes have reorganized much of Micronesian life in recent years, I have no reason to doubt the existence of much of this diversity in earlier times. Most of what we know about Micronesian households tells us of their important adaptive functions, and this variability played a crucial part in assuring survival.

Anthropologists have also attempted to explain the evolution of Micronesia's matrilineal clanship itself in terms of residence rules and household composition, based on a range of hypothetical influences, including, among other factors, organization of the labor requirements for farming and fishing (Alkire 1960, 1977; Goodenough 1956; Murdock 1948, 1949; Knudson 1970) and the composition of war parties (Divale and Harris 1976). But basic matrilineal principles are a given in Micronesia, while the nature of households is not.

While matri-principles alone do not determine most important decisions, they do influence the composition of households and systems of land tenure. But if land is seen as a source of both survival and identity everywhere in Micronesia, it is still viewed within the overall outlook of Micronesian culture, which recognizes that survival and identity depend ultimately on the quality of relations one maintains with others. Like everything else in Micronesia, including people, land can be and is transferred among individuals and groups. In every Micronesian society, land is continually being given to others, either for temporary use or in permanent conveyance.

What Households Look Like

Typical Micronesian households are, first of all, multigenerational. It would be impractical for newly married couples to set up housekeeping on their own—everyone requires land to live and work on and other people to work with—and the domestic cycles of parents and children overlap. Under ordinary circumstances a young couple is likely to reside with either the wife's or the husband's parents. Because of the matri-bias, in many Micronesian societies there is a greater tendency for couples to choose the wife's mother's household (since the wife's father may well have moved into his own wife's mother's household), but as we have seen, this is only a tendency. A household generally includes mature parents, along with one or more of their aged parents; one or more of their adult, married children, their unmarried children; and their resident children's children. A typical household *might* look something like the one described in the following chart.

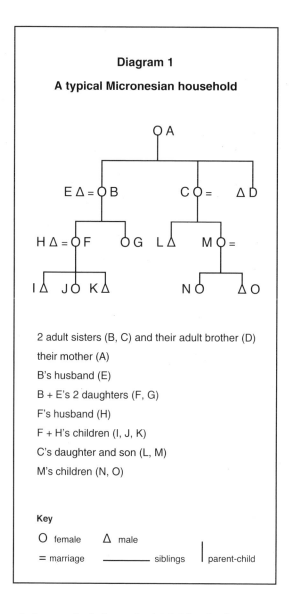

Diagram 1

A typical Micronesian household

2 adult sisters (B, C) and their adult brother (D)

their mother (A)

B's husband (E)

B + E's 2 daughters (F, G)

F's husband (H)

F + H's children (I, J, K)

C's daughter and son (L, M)

M's children (N, O)

Key

O female   Δ male

= marriage   ——— siblings | parent-child

In some societies, particularly on the high islands, there seems to be a somewhat greater likelihood that a group of brothers will stay with their father. But as I have said, there is considerable variation in the composition of households, and there may well be no typical form at all in some societies.

In addition to variations based on the idiosyncrasies of individual families, the size and composition of households influence and are in turn influenced by social status. This works in several ways. A larger household may well be able to draw on a greater range of resources. A household with an ample supply of adults has a generous supply of skilled labor available to it, while large numbers of healthy children are indications not only of a household's future potential but also of the virility, fertility, and productivity of its current members. It can mobilize more labor than its neighbors, for both basic domestic needs and for participation in community life. There is certainly no linear relationship between a household's size and its ability to affect the course of social events, but in the process of choosing who is to represent a lineage as its chief, the head of a productive, active household is likely to be a leading candidate. Conversely, a leader of a prominent lineage—a chief—is in need of people to work with and for him and is likely to try to attract members to his household.

Gender Roles

Men and women bring different, but essentially equal, assets to their households. Because of the fundamental precepts of matriliny, among other factors (including Micronesians' general respect for each other), nowhere in the islands are women formally or officially denigrated. They are regarded and treated respectfully. In Palauan society, for example, women are clearly acknowledged to be central to every aspect of life, and Pohnpeians sometimes say that in their society women used to have more important roles than they do now (Petersen 1982b). At the same time, however, there are recurring reports of women being beaten or overworked. These may be consequences of relatively recent forms of socially induced stresses (Hezel 1999, 320–323), since earlier writers (e.g., A. Fischer 1957, 185–186; Gladwin and Sarason 1953) specifically commented on the equality of and support for women. And of course these are not mutually exclusive alternatives—Micronesians are as capable as any other peoples of saying one thing and doing another.

In Yapese society, "a man and a woman were said to be like the two halves of a palm frond, fitting together at all points to make a unity" (Labby 1976, 28), and I have heard Pohnpeians refer to a man's wife as his outrigger—she stabilizes him. It is difficult, however, to generalize much about the specific contributions of the sexes, because these roles vary so much from one Micronesian society to another. On some islands women do the bulk of the farming, whereas on others this is primarily men's work. And though most fishing is viewed as men's work, in fact much of the marine resource base is in the shallow reef and shoreline waters harvested by women. In the islands of Chuuk Lagoon the most productive fisheries are the women's province while the men not only cultivate the gardens but also do most of the heavy work entailed in cooking (Goodenough 1951, 24).

Although men's and women's contributions to their households' larders vary, there is a consistent pattern in the sexual division of the more social aspects of labor. In general, Micronesian men are thought of as being responsible for discharging their households' more visibly public roles. Men ordinarily act as leaders and spokespersons both at meetings dealing with their communities' internal affairs and in proceedings concerned primarily with visitors from other islands and abroad. But in the organization of a household's domestic tasks and in decisions regarding its participation in community events, women are clearly leaders (Kihleng 1996). Because outsiders (at least Americans and Europeans) are prone to viewing visible, formal, public performances, especially those entailing speechmaking, as the principle elements of leadership, it is possible to interpret Micronesian patterns of gender relations as patriarchal or at least characterized by a strong emphasis on male authority. But Micronesians themselves greatly admire planning skills and organizational competence and are fully conscious of those who display these capabilities, assume domestic responsibilities, and manage household life, all without calling much attention to themselves. Diligence and humility, too, are much admired in most Micronesian societies, and women are recognized as men's equals if not superiors in all these character traits.

In the division of domestic labor, as in most aspects of Micronesian life, there are few hard-and-fast rules. While there are clear tendencies, patterns, and habits distinguishing the tasks normally assigned to men and to women (and sometimes to young and to old), women can and do take on jobs and roles normally done or held by men, and vice versa. Women do not ordinarily climb trees to harvest breadfruit or coconuts, but when circumstances warrant it, some do. On Pohnpei the preparation of kava is an overwhelmingly male preserve and responsibility, but women occasionally engage in this work and evoke no comments. A woman paramount chief reigned on Lamotrek when William Alkire was conducting his research there in the early 1960s. He heard occasional doubts expressed about her abilities, but this would probably have been the case with any chief (Alkire 1989). And in Palau and the Marshalls it is not unusual for women to fully occupy and perform the duties of chiefly titles. In the Marshalls this is so common that the words for "woman," *li*, and "chief," *iroj*, have been contracted into a single term, *liroj*, a female chief.

Throughout Micronesia men are in charge of cooking in stone ovens and certain ritual food preparations, such as Pohnpei's pounded breadfruit and coconut pudding *(lihli)*, and sometimes help with everyday food processing that ordinarily falls to women. They take on child care responsibilities when necessary. In my experience, most Micronesian men are quite comfortable handling babies and are doting fathers. Indeed, Micronesian notions of chieftainship draw heavily on the warm and supportive roles fathers are generally thought to play in peoples' lives. Although chiefs occupy the role of mother's brother within their own lineages and derive much of their authority from this position, in the community at large chiefs are commonly spoken of in terms that reflect expectations that they should nurture their people. Chiefs are widely expected to "take care of" their people in ways that are best understood as fathering (Marshall 1972, 29; Wilson 1976, 88; Hughes 1969).[4]

Micronesian patterns of clanship and household organization have been thought to represent exemplary cases of what anthropologists have called the matrilineal puzzle (Richards 1950; Gough and Schneider 1961; cf. Petersen 1982b). Ethnological theory has long struggled with the dynamics of matrilineal descent: how is it possible, scholars have wondered, for men to be attached simultaneously to two different households or families, that of the lineage into which they are born and that of their wife and children? This situation has been assumed to create stresses and tensions that make matriliny inherently unstable and brittle. In the course of Micronesia's long history, however, matriliny has proved to be quite the opposite. John Thomas specifically challenged the relevance of the matrilineal puzzle to life on Namonuito, where "it is women, not men, who make the descent group a unit of primary social orientation and loyalties . . . thus vesting the adult females of the descent group with authority of the most crucial sort" (1980, 176–177).

While David Schneider suggested that matrilineal descent groups are inherently subject to stress because they retain control of both their male and female members (1961, 8–10), Mary Douglas, using African cases, argued that there is another way of viewing this situation. She believed the crosscutting ties that resulted from males marrying into their wives' groups made for "a criss-cross of reciprocal obligations" and could "explain the resilience and strength of matriliny." She concluded, "If there is any advantage in a descent system that overrides exclusive, local loyalties, matriliny has it" (Douglas 1971, 128, 130).

In many ways, then, Micronesian households tend to be organized around women. Even when a matrilineage is not at a household's core, women discharge a range of duties that keep households viable. At the same time, men—because of their public political roles, their navigational skills and responsibilities, and the ties they forge between descent groups—are very much involved in the operations of Micronesian matriliny. Divisions of responsibility between male and female to some extent reflect distinctions between the related but distinctly different tasks of lineages and clans. Women are in some ways more involved in the internal workings of lineages, while men are charged more directly with maintaining links within the larger clan's localized lineages. This generalization cannot be pushed too far, of course, because of the flexibility of Micronesian residence patterns. And in the end it remains the case that matriclans are dispersed because women, as well as men, move from place to place and island to island.

Dynamics of Household and Lineage Organization

Close to the core of each Micronesian's being is his or her membership in a matrilineage. In whatever manner this lineage is shaped or organized, it gives the individual an identity that is powerfully rooted in the knowledge that belonging to this group confers real economic security: It provides nearly unassailable access to land and to a web of personal ties that are rarely broken. Moreover, Micronesian children are raised not just by their parents, nor simply within their nuclear families, but are instead cared for, looked after, nurtured, and taught by grandparents, aunts, uncles, a range of older siblings and cousins, and neighbors.

Whatever uncertainties and stresses the natural and social environments visit upon them, Micronesians do not deal with them alone. Whatever any individual might lack in his or her ability to be what has been called "a good enough parent" is more than compensated for by a broad net of lineage attachments. Under most normal circumstances Micronesian households provide ample emotional support for those who live in them. Precisely because the lineage plays such a fundamental role in the shaping of each individual's essence, healthy lineage members are inclined to make sure their lineage mates are secure enough and strong enough to contribute fully and successfully to their lineage's, as well as their respective household's, survival.

At the same time, however, Micronesians' ties to their fathers and to their fathers' lineages are carefully cultivated and maintained. There is a passage in E. E. Evans-Pritchard's classic work (1940) on the Nuer (a people of Sudan), flagged by Schneider (1965) and by Murphy (1971), in which Evans-Pritchard comments that the very strength of Nuer patrilineal ideology allows people to honor matrilateral ties without compromising their sense of patriliny's overriding authority. Schneider objected to this as a contradiction in terms, while Murphy celebrated it as precisely the sort of contradiction that makes social life possible. It seems to me that Micronesian matriliny might be understood in much the same way. Nothing shakes or threatens it. It simply exists at the core of Micronesian social relations. And thus Micronesians are in no way compromised when they turn to their fathers in search of personal connections, affection, and land and for a range of other needs they seek to have met. Fathers tend to be looked on as nurturing, supportive, interested, and indulgent figures. Chiefs, though they are in fact mothers' brothers to the men of their lineages, are frequently spoken of as father figures who must be obeyed, to be sure, but who are expected to love and care for their people above all other responsibilities. And chiefs must set aside the parochial concerns of their own lineages to assume responsibility for their entire communities (all of which I shall discuss in later chapters).

Micronesians pour a great deal of their selves into their relations with all their kin. Most people are related in one way or another to nearly everyone else in their community, and in many ways Micronesian kinship is genuinely bilateral—ties extend broadly, establishing connections through both male and female lines. In this sense it is necessary to reiterate that matriliny is a form of descent, a principle that emphasizes the importance of one particular sort of connection. The larger sweep of Micronesian kin relations includes matrilineal descent within its scope, but it is only a principle, no more than a guide to what might actually be done. This principle marks out certain limited aspects of the broader web of ties and is used as much to restrict access to resources—land and people—as it is to guarantee ties to other groups and their resources. But households, as opposed to lineages, draw on bilateral ties in recruiting members. Households and lineages may in some cases be identical, but there is no requirement that they be; given the requirements of exogamy, it would be unusual to find households consisting only of lineage members.

Micronesian children are commonly raised in households organized around lineages of which they are members and to which they are closely attached, and as they grow, they establish firm stakes in their societies. When they live in households where their most immediate connections are traced through their fathers, however, they have not only these immediate relations but also their matrilineages to call upon should they find paternal ties lacking in strength or depth. That is, an individual can always fall back on lineage ties. At the same time, though, survival in traditional Micronesian societies depends not merely on one's membership in a descent group, with its broader clan linkages, but also on these bilateral connections. A Pohnpeian whose wife is American, but who remains deeply enmeshed in his community, once confided to me that he would have liked to have defied his lineage's position during a dispute over a political matter. But he could not, he said, because his wife had no kin of her own on Pohnpei—no one he could turn to as an alternative to his own direct relations. He found himself too reliant on his own lineage. Bilateral ties forged through marriage and patrifiliation, then, provide flexibility and alternative sources of support but, in doing so, may furnish individuals with a sense that they can, when they feel it absolutely necessary, disagree with lineage authority.

In the absence of government welfare institutions, pensions, and insurance programs, individuals and households can be certain of weathering personal disabilities or misfortunes only to the extent that they are embedded in a web of social and emotional ties to others who feel, and honor, their responsibilities to provide them with support. Certainly, one's lineage comes first, but in fact marriage, children, neighborly propinquity, and personal friendships all provide alternative sources of support. Individuals and households may find the expectations and demands their lineages place on them burdensome, but while possibilities for resisting these exist, they are few. Alternate sources of support, then, provide at least a minor degree of flexibility and freedom. The larger community, too, provides alternatives to lineages, in the same way that being under the umbrella of a strong, successful lineage's autonomy assures individuals and households a degree of latitude within their communities.

Households and lineages are expected—if not required—to play active roles within their larger communities. Thoughtful people in most Micronesian societies see themselves as vigorously creating society, not merely participating in it. But this dynamism creates certain contradictions for more devoted members. Micronesian households are in fact quite malleable. I repeat, for the sake of emphasis, some of what I have already quoted from Spoehr's work: "Marshallese social organization as a whole is not highly formalized. Like the people themselves, it has a casual quality. The composition of the household is not rigidly defined by custom and is flexible and varying" (1949, 113). Rules concerning where one is expected to live are, in the end, ideas about what is appropriate; they are not hard-and-fast rules about how people actually behave. As a consequence, many individuals and groups of individuals find themselves pulled between the overlapping groupings to which they belong. This is not necessarily the same as the matrilineal puzzle, but it is a related phenomenon.

Siblings can find themselves trying to make difficult, often inherently controversial, allocations of resources—labor, land, and goods—between competing sets of ties and obligations. In matrilineal societies, sisters owe allegiance to one another and to their brothers, and yet some of them may also have significant investments in the lives and careers of their husbands or in a specific child. A group of brothers may be torn between their obligations to one another as members of a single lineage and their obligations to their spouses and households. Because people grow up with these sorts of competing demands and contradictory tensions, they are likely to be adept at handling them. But it sometimes happens that individuals and households find themselves unable to satisfy all the competing demands made on them and in the unsatisfactory situation of having to say no to—and thus alienating—some of those on whom they rely. Precisely because emphases on loyalty to one's lineage and household are so pervasive, this can come at a substantial emotional or psychic cost. Leo Tolstoy wrote in *Anna Karenina,* "All happy families resemble one another, but each unhappy family is unhappy in its own way." Micronesian households certainly resemble one another, but each may be privately cultivating its own particular source of unhappiness.

An individual's or household's status in the community is affected by the character and reputation of his or her lineage, which means that people are expected to pursue courses of behavior and participation that enhance their lineages' reputations. At the same time, however, individuals' personal successes and standing in their communities can and do provide them with a degree of leverage within their lineages. Households and lineages are simultaneously, then, the building blocks of communities and themselves shaped by the nature and composition of the communities in which they are located.

Micronesians embed themselves in webs of relationships and experience them as simultaneously liberating and oppressive. A Pohnpeian of long acquaintance once explained to me that his society was not likely to develop its economy along American lines if its social system remained the same, for as long as a few people continue to farm traditional crops, their relatives know there will always be food for them and may not be inclined to make choices in keeping with Western precepts of economics. His remark hauntingly echoes that of the nineteenth-century missionary Albert Sturges (1873), who despaired of instilling in the Pohnpeians any desire to pursue personal wealth, a commentary to which I shall return shortly.

In another context, and years earlier, this same Pohnpeian spoke to me of the demands his kin placed on him. Because they are family (*peneinei*, a Pohnpeian word referring to a wide range of kin), he explained, he cannot honorably refuse the requests they make of him. And because nearly everyone in his community can make a claim to be family, it is difficult for him to hold on to anything except house and land for very long. But it must also be pointed out that precisely because virtually everyone in small communities is related to everyone else, any explanation of an interaction between two individuals that depends on the simple assertion that it took place because they are kin is not entirely straightforward; since virtually everyone is kin to everyone else, claims about the demands of kinship do not necessarily explain the specifics of particular interactions. Given the enormous cultural emphasis placed on generosity in Micronesian societies, most people find it difficult to refuse any request, and yet the dynamics of political life require that people make decisions about just which requests they will honor and which they will refuse or ignore.

Dealing with conflicting obligations, demands, and requests is of course not much of a problem for those who are not especially hardworking, ambitious, or particularly dedicated to serving their communities (and each community is likely to have a few such slackers). But for leaders in Micronesian societies, it is an absolute requirement. The households of successful men and women—of community leaders—are notable for the relatively large numbers of people who reside in them and for their industriousness and active participation in the life of the community. An individual cannot pursue an active political role in the community without the cooperation of his or her household and lineage. By the same token, however, a household or lineage needs to identify those of its members who are thoughtful, diligent, and charismatic enough to represent the group in public, and to then groom them for future service.

Because Micronesian sociopolitical life is organized around the complementary premises of lineage/clan and household/community, lineages and households depend on specific individuals to represent their interests in the larger community effectively. Communities in turn depend on the representatives of their constituent groups to be effective enough to guide the individual households and lineages toward consensus and solidarity. And thus the pairings both of communities and households and of households and individuals are in continuous streams of interrelationships with one another.

These observations are, of course, normative; they are views and wishes about how things *should* be. Micronesian societies are not without occasional sociopathic members. There are those who are cruel, self-aggrandizing, selfish, uncaring, lazy, or incompetent. But precisely because Micronesians are familiar with these aberrant specimens, they work hard at crafting rules to prevent them from abusing others, and at keeping their worst proclivities in check. It is in the ideal possibilities of the healthy household and the healthy community that Micronesians find the models they use for political leadership; it is in experiencing aberrations that they are motivated to construct the political forms and practices that ordinarily prevent deviant individuals and behaviors from taking over their societies.

Material Aspects of Households

Another useful way of viewing Micronesian households is through the roles they play in their societies' economic organization. Here I draw on a traditional formulation that distinguishes between land, labor, and the technology—the skills and tools—that enable people to invest their labor into their land and its resources. I deal with land and labor in subsequent sections. Here I consider the household as a productive unit characterized by its possessions: its equipment, tools, techniques, knowledge, and aptitudes.

In general, the humidity of Micronesian climates, in combination with local crop inventories that lack grains that can be dried, mean that with occasional important exceptions, households are not places where foodstuffs can be stored. Crops are harvested and fish caught as needed; food is prepared, sometimes in large quantities, and then distributed not only to members of the immediate household but also to nearby kin and neighbors. What are stored in Micronesian households are some of the items people use to make their livings. The steeply pitched, high roofs characteristic of most Micronesian dwellings are meant not only to shed rain and improve interior air circulation but also to provide for storage. Household equipment and personal possessions are cached up among the beams and rafters, semihidden in the darkness. On Pohnpei this area is called a *mweleng* (essentially an attic), and a local aphorism, *Mweleng ehu ohl* (A man is an attic), means that men should be inscrutable and able to conceal their thoughts and feelings as if they were hidden beneath the roof peak.

The largest portable item any Micronesian household is likely to possess is a canoe. These vessels vary greatly in size, from small paddling canoes carrying one or more individuals and used within lagoons, to the great oceangoing sailing canoes. Paddling canoes are carved out of a single log and stabilized by a simple outrigger boom. The big oceangoing canoes sailed on interisland voyages are built of hewn planks, fitted with elaborate outriggers, and mounted with platforms and occasionally shelters. They are likely to be considered lineage property. Because of their great value, canoes are usually stored in canoe houses, the largest of which can hold several canoes. As mentioned earlier, these structures also serve as club-houses, meetinghouses, and sometimes as dormitories for visiting travelers as well as members of the lineage and community.

While canoes are commonly stored in their own shelters, other materials used for fishing can be stored in either a dwelling or a canoe house. These include nets, spears, hooks, lines, and traps. The same is true for farming and food processing equipment, including mangrove-wood digging sticks, long breadfruit-picking poles, shell peelers and graters, and wooden, coral, and basalt pounders.

Equipment for a variety of other tasks also constitutes part of a household's property. This includes shell adzes and axes for woodworking; wooden bowls for food processing and serving; sennit (coconut husk fiber) twine for a variety of lashing tasks; tools for making bark cloth; ornaments; and exchange valuables or "money" (in the case of Palau and Yap). Pottery was made and used on the high islands when they were first settled, but it eventually disappeared everywhere except in the Marianas and the westernmost Carolines. Perhaps most noteworthy are the looms: Micronesian women (and, on Yap, men) in the islands from Yap and Kosrae use backstrap looms to weave delicately colored and textured cloth from a variety of fibers, especially banana leaf and hibiscus bark, employing weaving practices originally brought to Micronesia from eastern Indonesia (Riesenberg and Gayton 1952; Rubinstein 1986).

Many Micronesians raise dogs for food, but because these are also treated as household pets or watchdogs, they can hardly be considered livestock. Chickens are kept, but there were no other domesticated animals before Europeans arrived (though wild birds are sometimes kept as pets). Pigs were avidly adopted and incorporated into the exchange economy once Europeans introduced them. For the most part, Micronesians get their animal protein from fish (or in some places, large fruit bats). With the exception of a few small communities in the remotest interiors of the high islands, everyone lives within easy distance of the lagoons and sea, and virtually everyone fishes.

A Micronesian household's greatest productive assets are in its members' collective knowledge and skills. Lineages and their members possess specialized proprietary knowledge about where to plant certain crops, how to cultivate them, how to perform rites to improve their chances of success, and how best to process them. The same holds true for fishing; individuals know where and when to seek out specific forms of marine life, and how to catch them.

While there is not a great deal of craft specialization in Micronesian societies and although most people are capable of doing well at most tasks, there are people known for their exceptional abilities. Medical practices—including massage techniques (what might now be called physical therapy), the use of herbs and other forms of naturally occurring products, and religious/psychological performances by those able to go into trance (what would now be termed psy-chotherapeutic techniques)—are certainly better-known and -practiced by some individuals; aspects of the ritual knowledge possessed by Chuuk's specialists have been explored by Goodenough (2002). Some people are regarded as particularly skilled or successful farmers and fishers; others, for example, have reputations as proficient canoe builders. And navigation, especially, is a field of knowledge in which men train long and hard to gain expertise; among the atolls the status of a skilled and intrepid navigator *(pelu)* can be greater than that of a chief (Alkire 1989, 127–129).

Land

In the sense that we humans tend to take for granted the air we breathe, or that fish seem oblivious to water, people who inhabit large land masses assume the existence of land as a matter of course. This is not the case in Micronesia's island societies, where the seas occupy an overwhelmingly huge proportion of the natural world. Land is valuable not merely for the livings it allows islanders to earn from it, but because they are so keenly aware that it makes human life possible in the first place. To be sure, Micronesians' attachments to their land in many ways resemble those characteristic of any agricultural society. But their consciousness of it as a fundamental condition of existence gives land an added dimension and immediacy; it bears hypercharged symbolic and emotional meaning and force.

As a consequence Micronesians are, despite their many and varied ties to the seas around them, even more intensely attached to their lands than to the sea and, despite their tendencies toward restraint and understatement, speak eloquently about these ties. The exigencies of making a living on the islands have always shaped Micronesians' experiences and thus their societies and cultures; these in turn have enormous influence on how islanders perceive and inhabit their homelands.

Another way of saying this is that, in Micronesian lives, land is not simply about resources and survival but about much, much more. Micronesians (like other peoples) occasionally go to war over land, but they have a wide and effective array of ways to deal with land that fall far short of war. Land is about creating and maintaining relations with others as much as it is about simple survival, but then of course relations with others are as much about survival as they are about anything else.

It follows, then, that there is a fundamental contradiction, or at least a duality, in relations between people and land in Micronesia. Although lineages hold on to land closely and carefully, their possession of it is also constantly in flux; as land passes between individuals and groups, it serves as a medium—almost a currency—through which social relations are transacted. Micronesians are always seeking to add to their holdings, but they accumulate land in the same manner in which they accumulate anything else. The underlying motive is to be able to give it away. But then the point of giving land away is to forge ties that enable one to gain access to even more of it. Thus land not only provides the basis for life in Micronesia but also serves as a metaphor—perhaps the key metaphor—in Micronesians' considerations of their own lives. Much of Micronesians' objection to American rule over their islands in the decades following World War II was a product of their fears about losing their land, a point to which I shall return in the conclusion.

Land and Differences among Island Societies

Although Micronesia is obviously named for the small size of its islands, the most salient thing about land there is probably not its limited supply. Given the productivity of the seas around them and the abundant rains that water the gardens on most islands, Micronesians on all but a few of the most marginal islands, or during droughts or following major typhoons, seem rarely to have been near the edge of starvation. And while ecological variations result in some notable differences between societies on the atolls and those on high islands, the similarities are much more striking. People on the high islands, where land is significantly more abundant than on the atolls, are not noticeably less concerned about it than the atoll peoples.

The sociopolitical structures of Micronesian societies are essentially the same whether we speak of a small atoll like Lamotrek, with a population of less than two hundred people, or a high island like Pohnpei, with as many as thirty thousand inhabitants.[5] The intensity of people's interests in the possession, cultivation, and inheritance of land varies little from Palau to Chuuk to the Marshalls. In this, Micronesia offers interesting comparisons for theories about social evolution in Polynesia. In his pioneering work *Social Stratification in Polynesia,* Marshall Sahlins attempted to distinguish among different types of Polynesian societies in terms of the technological and ecological adaptations they made to different sorts of island environments. He believed his findings demonstrated that the greater the productivity of an island society, "the greater the distributive activities of the chief, and the greater his powers," thus leading to a greater degree of social stratification (Sahlins 1958, xi). Others have concluded that the key factor determining the degree of stratification in these societies is simply population size. That is, the larger the island and its population, the larger its economy and the greater the roles its leaders undertake (Orans 1966). Comparing atolls within Micronesia, Leonard Mason concluded that "chieftainship is elaborated most in the very culture best supported by economic abundance" and that chieftainship and authority are "directly related to the production of surplus food" (1968, 328). Or as Martin

Orans phrased it, among the Polynesian islands "there is a perfect correspondence between population [size] and degree of stratification" (1966, 31). Irving Goldman, on the other hand, argued that while such models of social organization were rooted primarily in assumptions about the role of political power, it was not power but status and rivalries for status that were the driving factors in the development of Polynesian social life (1970, 22–23).

With the notable exception of a few of the Marshall and Kiribati atolls at the respective northern and southern extremities of these archipelagoes, Micronesian islands in normal years receive plentiful rainfall and are fertile, productive, and comfortable. Although the range of food types on some of the atolls is limited in comparison to the abundance available on high islands, there is little evidence to indicate that peoples on the atolls have much difficulty feeding themselves. Lutz speaks of Ifaluk anxieties about being without food but then explains that this is experienced as a consequence of not having kin, of having "no one to care of them," rather than from specific fears about natural shortages (1988, 128–129). Schneider (1957) came to similar conclusions regarding the social impacts of typhoons on Yap.

Early accounts reported quite large populations on some of the atolls. Whether these were a consequence of internal population dynamics, of an influx of people from neighboring typhoon-ravaged atolls, or merely exaggeration is not clear. Kosrae, on the other hand, seems always to have had a relatively small population (P. Ritter 1978; S. Athens 2007). But there is not much indication of overcrowding or severe population pressure anywhere. The absence of such problems appears to have been due to typhoons and periodic droughts on the one hand, and, perhaps, of deliberate cultural practices on the other.

I find it impractical to generalize about land and social stratification in Micronesia beyond making the simple observation that there tends to be more stratification on high islands and less on low islands. This is not a matter of population densities—most atolls have much denser populations. Nor is it a matter of natural resource distribution, with chiefs managing the flow of goods and crops among different environmental zones, a suggestion Sahlins had put forward. In general, differences in the degree of social stratification among Micronesian societies seem largely to be a direct consequence of population size, which is in turn primarily a corollary of land area (and perhaps exposure to typhoons). The high islands are generally more stratified than most of the atolls. On the other hand, some societies on the Marshall atolls appear to be more stratified than those in the volcanic islands of Chuuk Lagoon.

The most significant element in all of this, however, at least to my mind, is that the basic systems of land tenure, descent and kinship, and formal (as opposed to practical) political organization are essentially the same across the region.

Population sizes—and not other factors—generally shape no more than limited aspects of social hierarchy. Land tenure practices differ little, whether the islands are high or low, big or small. And where land tenure does differ significantly, as in the Marshalls, this appears to be as much a product of colonial and commercial influences as it is a matter of indigenous practices.

It has also been suggested that differences in staple food crops on Micronesian islands might correlate with local forms of social organization, but Alkire (1960) found that this seems not to have been the case. Most Micronesians are not slash-and-burn farmers; they do not cultivate extensive tracts of land for a season or two and then let them lie fallow or abandoned. Rather, their ties tend to be to relatively small plots of land under continual use. On the Caroline atolls and Palau and Yap, taro (both *Colocasia* and *Cyrtosperma*) tends to be the primary starch crop; on most other islands breadfruit—and, in the drier parts of the Marshalls and Kiribati, pandanus—is the primary staple. The work of cultivating these root and tree crops is quite different, to be sure, but in either case what is most significant is that people rely on work performed by earlier generations, whether in digging and improving the taro pits or in planting the trees. Everywhere we encounter a similar phenomenon: the legacies of the ancestors' improvements. In cultivating the same land year in and year out and eating the food it provides, subsequent generations continuously reconnect themselves to it. Undertaking practical activities on land that is imbued with symbolic significance means these activities take on great symbolic weight. Farming is not merely a means of survival; it is a deeply social and spiritual task as well.

Land Tenure

The English-language term "land tenure" is appropriate to the discussion of Micronesian lands. It signifies something different from simple ownership, deriving as it does from a Latin root meaning "to hold," and originally evolved largely in concert with concepts of rights and duties. It is useful for comparisons inasmuch as Micronesians quite consciously hold their lands within webs of social rights and duties.

Despite land's utter centrality to Micronesian identities, access to and possession of it are inherently contingent. The histories of Micronesian communities are studded with disputes over land; indeed, daily life is freighted with the residues of unresolved disputes. Access to land comes ultimately through relationships with individuals and groups, and the quality of these relationships and the individual characteristics of those party to them have an enormous influence on this access. While Micronesian cultures specify sets of rules defining how land is to be distributed and held, we shall see that practical and interpersonal aspects of everyday life shape the actual transfer of landholdings. Everyone has his or her own interpretation of what the local culture calls for and how the facts of a particular case fit into that interpretation. I thus use "land tenure" as an overarching, encompassing term, entailing several prime concepts, including the composition of lineages and other sorts of kin groups' rights to work land and to transfer access to land away from the group.

Precisely because land is of such significance in Micronesians' lives, scholars tend to explore the nature of land tenure in specific Micronesian societies and have largely overlooked the similarities among them. Three key aspects emerge. First, rights to land (and to certain other sorts of property) may be vested in groups, in individuals, or in both. Second, rights to land are of several kinds or degrees, summed up most simply as residual and provisional.[6] Third, distinct plots of land are merged into joint estates held by corporate lineages or household groups. These plots, or particular sorts of rights of access to them, are added to or removed from estates through a variety of transactions.

Micronesians live in small-scale societies, and their neighbors are also their kinsmen and -women. In the daily flow of life they deal with people with whom they share a multitude of close historical and emotional connections, and the precise ways in which these connections were initially forged are not always remembered or relevant. Matriliny becomes of real relevance in only a few explicit contexts. Land is one of these. Access to and control over land is framed in matrilineal terms, and it is easy to mistakenly assume that the emphasis on unilineality means that, in land matters, matriliny is practiced exclusively. It is not. Instead, individual claims to land cut across the grain of matrilineage control in such a way that the nature of Micronesian land tenure can really be understood only as a conjunction of both lineage interests and individual prerogatives.

Because land is of little immediate use without labor to work it, and because Micronesian lives are so thoroughly embedded in lineage and household groups, it can at times be difficult to see how land tenure is relevant to individuals. At any given moment, land tenure may appear to be fully encompassed by descent and/or residential groups. But the processes that work to constitute an estate—a group's holdings—are continually adding and subtracting plots and rights and obligations; these processes engage the entire spectrum of kin ties of the individuals who together make up lineages and households.

Matrilineages serve as corporate groups that ordinarily hold land and derive important aspects of their social status from their land; they hold on to it tenaciously. Nevertheless, these groups, through a variety of means, are continually adding and subtracting both parcels of land and members who claim rights in the group's land. In the Marshalls, individuals inherit use rights *(ninnin)* from their fathers. These rights entitle those who hold them to live and work on the land, but they are contingent on contribution of adequate labor to the lineage; that is, these rights are provisional. They are inherited in the male line by succeeding generations and are important enough that the specific rights of each subsequent generation have their own terms (Tobin 1956, 16–17). A similar pattern occurs in Chuuk Lagoon, where Goodenough (1951, 92–96) refers to it as *jefekyr*, and in Namoluk in the Mortlocks, where Marshall reports that it is called *afukur* (1972, 37). Palauan children are raised on their father's land and in many cases "are permitted continued land use and conditional membership" in his lineage; as a group his children "seek to earn land from him" (Smith 1979, 266–268). While in some societies customs of inheritance from fathers are highly institutionalized, in others they are less formal though equally important.

I have been distinguishing between matrilineal descent and bilateral kinship. Micronesians stress the importance of cultivating a wide range of ties to others, most of which are couched in the idiom of biological relations—that is, they are spoken of as kin. Some of these ties are thought to be formed in the act of procreation and can be conceptualized in essentially the same terms as Western notions about genetics. Others come about through the course of a child's raising or an adult's marriage. Still others stem from long-term residence with a group. But in every case these ties, once forged, can be passed along to succeeding generations. That is, although a child is almost without exception born into its mother's lineage and clan, its relation to its father (in technical terms, "filiation") means that the child recognizes close kinship ties with its father's kin, on both the father's mother's and father's father's sides. And the child is related to its mother's father and all *his* kin on both his mother's and father's sides. Each individual is at the center of what anthropologists call a kindred, an informal category composed of all those with whom he or she recognizes kin ties.

Matrilineal descent emphasizes a single strand out of all these many ties, but it in no way erases or denies the rest. Political titles, land, and, most tellingly, marriage possibilities stand out from the general web of kin ties and draw our attention to matrilineality, but they by no means define the full extent of kin ties. And thus it is that individuals can and do inherit land, rights to use land, and in some cases access to political titles from a range of relatives. Only in the rarest cases are Micronesians restricted to calling upon or relying on just their own matridescent group.

Under ordinary circumstances an individual is born with certain rights in land as a member of a landholding matridescent group. But it is almost as common for individuals to be given land or certain rights to land by their fathers. And since their fathers may have received portions of that land (or those rights) from *their* fathers, individuals are likely to receive land that originates with neither their mother's nor their father's descent group. These extensive chains of connections mean that, despite the emphasis on matrilineal corporate landholding, access to land is in fact not especially matrilineal, even if the corporate descent groups that manage the land stress their matrilineal roots.

Although each member of a matrigroup shares equally in rights to the group's land, each individual also has access to land that is not the group's. Ordinarily, members of the lineage have use rights to, or at least the right to request the use of, any land that a co-member has rights to use. But the individual ordinarily retains the privilege of determining whether that land becomes the joint property of the lineage or is to be passed on in some other way. Because land itself can realize its full value only if it is cultivated, individuals are able to make proper use of their land only as long as they share it with kin who will help them work it. And thus individual tenure of land or rights to it is almost always blurred or modified by this habit of granting others rights to it and its produce.

Residual and Provisional Titles

> Land is fast;
> land floats;
> land is stable;
> land moves—
> land and its fellowship,
> food and its people.
> —*Chuukese poem transcribed and translated*
> *by Ward Goodenough (in Parker 1985)*

Micronesians conceptualize land as being both immobile and in constant motion, passing from individual to group, group to group, group to individual, and individual to individual. It is common for a newborn's placenta to be buried under a newly planted tree, symbolically tying the child to the place where he or she is born. On larger islands family members are buried on a household's land. People feed from breadfruit trees planted by their elders and plant taro in pits dug by their ancestors. In the 1970s an older Pohnpeian of my acquaintance occasionally pointed to a breadfruit tree growing in front of his door, fondly recalling how his deceased mother had planted it when she was young, perhaps in 1900 or so. I once heard another Pohnpeian speak of how much he "loved" a particular coconut palm and how it pained him when he was required to fell the tree in order to provide a clearly visible basemark for the aerial photography being used to complete a cadastral survey. Peoples' ties to their land and its products run deep.

At the same time, however, titles to land flow freely in a continuous current of personal relations. Yapese liken women to the navigators of canoes, guiding their lineages to satisfactory landholdings, but in the Yapese view of things the land itself moves too, from lineage to lineage (Labby 1976, 16). And Smith observes that "the Yapese phrase, 'The people exchanged land, and the land exchanged people' (Labby 1976, 32) also is appropriate to the Palauan situation" (1979, 267). Embedded in each plot of land, then, is not simply a material source of survival but a specific history of personal relationships. Land represents lineage and family, ties to fathers and grandparents, marriages and adoptions, friendships and obligations. A challenge to an individual's or group's possession of a plot of land is so much more than a threat to the group's ability to earn a livelihood. It is simultaneously a threat to the group's social existence and to its status as part of the community, society, and culture that bestow identity on individuals and groups.

Rights and obligations inhere in the well-established relations that channel this transfer of land, as well as in the relations that are newly created by these transfers. In transferring land to others, individuals and groups see themselves as retaining certain rights in the land and in their relationships with those to whom they transfer land. Anyone receiving land is expected to acknowledge certain obligations and duties toward those who initially gave it. If these obligations are not properly discharged, there are presumptions about the rights of those who previously held it to reclaim this land. In describing these webs of contingencies, Goodenough (1951) describes two basic types of tenure or title to land: "residual," referring to the rights retained by those who transfer land to others, and "provisional," referring to the conditional character of ownership by those who receive the land.

This basic pattern appears in many manifestations. Several are of significance here, foremost among them being the absolutely fundamental practice of providing what are known as first fruits offerings to leaders. These are presentations of the first crops harvested at the beginning of a new season, along with further offerings as certain crops, especially breadfruit, progress through their seasonal stages. The underlying rationale for these gifts is what is most important in this context. They are meant to acknowledge, in a formal manner, the ancient and deeply embedded rights that the lineage purported to have first settled a community or island holds to all the land within its purview. Failure to discharge one's obligations to this senior or chiefly lineage is tantamount to denying its residual title and rights and thus its leader's legitimacy and oversight. First fruits are not taxes in the sense that they can be construed as important sources of chiefly revenue. Although those who provide these gifts to their leaders sometimes speak of how chiefs "eat" their titles (that is, that chiefs depend for their livelihood on these contributions), the fact is that outside of the Marshalls, where German colonial influence on the cash income from coconut production seems to have significantly transformed the system, those who receive first fruits tend not to profit substantially from them—at least in a material sense. This is because chiefly households tend to have adequate labor for their own production needs (indeed, they are frequently more productive than other households) and because leaders are expected to be generous and to redistribute substantial portions of what they receive. Leaders who did not give away much of what they receive would be perceived as having failed to discharge their own obligations and thus having morally forfeited their rights to collect first fruits.

Even on Nauru, where stress is laid on individual rather than lineage control, ownership is complemented, according to Wedgwood, by equal emphases on generosity and institutionalized giving; under certain circumstances almost any personal property is expected to be given up to anyone asking for it (1937, 15–17). Likewise, land rights are commonly divided into several categories. In Goodenough's "residual" and "provisional" senses, on Nauru "one person will claim to be the owner of a block of land and another will claim to be the 'caretaker,' tending, collecting, and using the crops upon it" (Wedgwood 1937, 17).

A second significant aspect of the residual/provisional dichotomy in land titles is the relations between elderly parents and their children. We still find today, throughout Micronesia, cases being brought to court in hopes of resolving disputes that have grown out of expectations grounded in these old and well-established practices. Despite the enormous emphases all Micronesian societies place on family responsibilities, in both emotional and practical terms, and on the resulting closeness of family relationships, the fact is that such sentiments serve to some extent to assuage, or at least to cover over, fears and anxieties about the potential failure of individuals to behave according to the accepted rules and practices.

Traditionally, in Micronesian societies, as in other agricultural societies, when people reach an age and physical condition where they can no longer support themselves, they rely on their children or other younger relatives to care for them. The popular idea, of course, is that children will readily provide this care out of both love and a sense of duty. But it sometimes happens that parents are not entirely certain that their children will indeed behave according to the culture's norms. For this reason, it is a widely accepted principle that parents, and indeed adults in general, can transfer land titles with the explicit qualification that the transfer's ultimate validity is contingent on the behavior of the ones who receive the land—that is, that the recipients will provide adequate and continuous care to the elderly person or persons who gave them the land. Legal systems introduced by foreign powers, with their notions of fee simple land (which means that title comes without obligation), have, in many Micronesian societies, wrought significant changes in land inheritance, in many cases quite deliberately.[7] But land is often still deeded away with the expectation or understanding that the recipients will care for the one from whom they receive it. If this care is not forthcoming or is provided at a level the elder party thinks inadequate, a legal action to reverse the transfer may ensue. Depending on the specifics of the case and local legal precedents, the transfer may indeed be rescinded.

In later chapters, when I discuss the nature of chieftainship, I will return to this point. Chiefly lineages' claims over land grow out of precisely the same moral code that establishes the rights of a parent over land he or she has transferred to a child. As long as duties and obligations are appropriately discharged, the transfer of title over the land should not be challenged (which does not mean, of course, that it never is). The identical notion applies whether the land's title is a political matter, relating to chieftainship, or a family matter.

The crucial point here is that the origins of this sort of dispute lie not in colonial- and postcolonial-era legalities but in traditional Micronesian notions of residual and provisional rights and titles. To the extent that land serves as a means of keeping score in the flow of social relations, it is important to Micronesians not only because of its role in the present (it can be farmed) and the ways it draws upon the past (it plays a significant part in establishing one's identity) but also because it provides a means of planning for the future (it serves as insurance, pension, and investment portfolio).

Having pointed out the practical significance of land, I must immediately stress that the symbolic meanings that grow from this context permeate every aspect of Micronesian life. Land is cognitively and emotionally important at every turn, in every aspect of Micronesian life, whether economic issues are at hand or not. Land symbolizes the social relations that make survival—moral and emotional as well as physical—possible. Relations embedded in the possession of, responsibility to cultivate, and right to inherit land pervade interpersonal interactions of every sort. Most Micronesian families experience, for example, slowly simmering disputes among siblings over the inheritance of their parents' land; these sometimes flare up into more intense quarrels.

Alkire (1974) draws attention to the lingering antagonisms of land disputes in the Woleai. These disputes are about relations both within and between families and are freighted with all the hopes, hurts, and fears that characterize family relations in any society. By analogy, we might note that in the United States it is sometimes said that, in the end, divorce proceedings are "all about the money." To the extent that this is true, it is because Americans keep score—track the courses of their lives—in terms of money, and the dynamics of interpersonal relations are to a considerable extent conceptualized in the language of accounting—profit and loss. In Micronesia, land is the visible currency of relations; life is by no means all about land, but it is quite easy to mistakenly conclude that it is.

Labor

Micronesians typically work communally, often in groups shaped by age or gender, though at other times these groups are thoroughly mixed. It is common for work parties to be so casual in their composition and so heartily engaged in social banter and ancillary activities (such as meal preparation) that it can be difficult for an outsider to gauge just how much work is actually being accomplished. It is equally the case, however, that some tasks, especially in esoteric occupations such as navigation, are tinged with sacred qualities and are undertaken only within the strictest sorts of guidelines. The knowledge, skills, and personal fortitude required of navigators are held in the highest regard, given that interisland voyaging is what makes life in most of the islands possible in the first place. In what follows, though, I focus on aspects of labor entailed in the more mundane realms of farming and fishing.

Recruiting People

A recurring theme in Micronesian life is the basic problem of imbalances in the ratios of people to land among a community's lineages and households. For Micronesians themselves the problem is clear and has two facets. A lineage with a growing membership faces a dilemma that can be interpreted, depending on how one looks at the matter, as either having too many people for the amount of available land or too little land for the number of people drawing their subsistence from it. A growing lineage needs either to acquire more land or to decrease the size of its membership. Other lineages, with declining numbers, face the converse problem. They need either to attract new co-resident members or to divest themselves of some of their landholdings. A group with too much land and too few people is liable to invite envy, antagonism, and, eventually, open hostility and possibly violence. The historical record suggests that although Micronesian societies have seen a fair amount of fighting, most of it has not been over land, undoubtedly because of their effective mechanisms for redistributing land when its allocation becomes unbalanced.[8]

Micronesian societies redress these imbalances in several ways, including adoption, inheritance through the male line, the making of gifts, and reallocation by chiefs.

For all the practical, social, symbolic, and emotional importance Micronesians attach to land, many aspects of social life there are predicated on the underlying notion that without people—or, more specifically, their labor—land is unproductive and therefore not especially useful. Lineages and households are as much in need of adequate sources of labor as they are in need of land, and sometimes more so. There are inextricable links between people, food, and land. The source of these linkages is particularly evident in Chuuk: "Anything that has acquired a productive or practical value as the result of human labor is owned as property, whereas ownership is less likely with things directly consumable from nature" (Goodenough 1951, 30). An equivalent concept exists in Yap: "The concept of invested labor or effort, of *magar*, was pervasive in Yapese culture." The authority of the ancestors is embedded in land because people recognize that "it was they who had made the land what it was, had developed its resources, built its gardens, its taro patches, and its fishing equipment, and it was they who had earned for it the social position that its occupants represented" (Labby 1976, 18–19). It has also been observed that in Yap "land would be neglected and valueless without people to maintain it [and] people would starve without the land to support them" (Kirkpatrick and Broder 1976, 203). That is, the support that individuals draw from their land is perceived to be the product of what they and others have put into it. The land's value is realized via the food that comes from it, and this food in turn has been cultivated by the people who inhabit, inherit, and protect the land. Without the people, the land loses significant aspects of its value; without their land, the people can neither survive nor reproduce.

In Palauan communities, Smith tells us, land "is used to attract people as kinsmen." As one Palauan explained to her, "Giving land is to tie people. . . . If we give them land, we know they will stay with us" (Smith 1983, 121). In the Marshalls it is a chief's title to land that allows him to attract people to his community. Marshallese believe that land equals people; that is, people are drawn to land. But they are also convinced that a chief's real status derives not from the land but from the people on it. The Marshallese word *kajur*, glossed as "people" (as opposed to "chiefs"), also means "power" (Rynkiewich 1972, 81–82). A Marshallese chief's status and authority are believed to be products of the people he can mobilize and how effectively he can mobilize them, and his strength thus comes directly from the people.

Because of particular family histories and aspects of individual personalities (or both), people occasionally find themselves without claims to land or unable to press their claims successfully. They may have failed to participate in lineage affairs or to discharge the duties and obligations entailed in provisional land rights; they may have transgressed important mores or taboos and thereby offended someone in overarching authority (i.e., a lineage head or chief); they could be children of those who have for some reason forfeited access to land; they may have engaged in stupid or reckless behavior that caused them to relinquish or simply abandon title; or they may merely be lazy and without initiative or a desire to accept personal responsibility.[9] In any case, even here, where land plays so large a part in personal identity, some people find themselves without it. These are likely to be the sort of people whom Goodenough describes as "client" members of lineages, who perform services to a lineage in order to gain full membership. In the past, he reports, certain clients occupied positions that might elsewhere be termed domestic employees; these individuals provided labor in return for the privilege of access to a living (Goodenough 1951, 73). On Pohnpei, such people are known as *lidu*, a term that has been translated as both "servant" and "slave."

There is nothing in the larger pattern of Micronesian social life that suggests to me that slavery as an institution—that is, the systematic exploitation of a class of people who are deemed inherently inferior and are without rights to personal freedom—has ever existed there. Precisely because every Micronesian, with only occasional, idiosyncratic exceptions, is born into a landholding lineage, no landless class or inherently servile population exists.[10] Nevertheless, there are historical and personal circumstances that render some people vulnerable or indifferent. Others simply find life with their families stifling or otherwise unbearable and are willing to give up whatever might be necessary in order to pursue personal freedom away from home. It is precisely those who find themselves in this predicament, and then must subordinate themselves to others in order to survive, who set examples that spur others to avoid the consequences of irresponsible behaviors that might lead them to become similarly landless and vulnerable. Micronesians recognize differences between those who are in reduced circumstances because of random or impersonal misfortune and those who occupy such a status because of their own fecklessness. The latter category draws disdain, while the former is more likely to elicit compassion. And the Pohnpeian term *lidu* aptly illustrates this. It may denote either derision or commiseration, depending upon circumstances.

It is also the case that there are in Micronesian societies occasional mean-spirited and malignant, or extremely demanding, men and women who treat their families badly. Such a person (ordinarily a man) may be said to treat his dependents as *lidu,* as servants or slaves. Thus both the concept and observable cases of what might be termed slavery exist, but such cases are exceptions that serve as reminders to the rest of society and cannot be said to be typical of Micronesian social life.

Micronesian conceptions of land tenure ensure that under normal circumstances everyone has access to land. Still, doubts about access to it remain. Because people do worry about access to land, it is used as a means of attracting others to and keeping them working on land. There are always groups and leaders hoping to increase the number of people residing and working on their lands, since it is not the land itself but the people working on it who make it produce. Precisely because groups are eager to gain new members and thus access to their labor, none can be entirely certain of all of their own members' fidelity.[11] This need for labor, along with the relative inability to command it and the consequent imperative to attract it, places continual checks on the abuse of authority in Micronesian societies. Nearly everyone has multiple routes along which to trace claims to land and thus possesses a range of residential alternatives and stands ready to abandon an abusive leader.

Early missionaries found this mobility of Micronesians and their families disconcerting and experienced it as confounding all their efforts to convert them. I have long been bemused by a letter the Reverend Albert Sturges sent to his mission's Boston headquarters in 1873, after he had spent two decades working on Pohnpei: "Want of authority and ownership greatly hinders our work in reconstructing [society] here. Everybody owns and does everything in general but nothing in particular—wives, children, lands, property belong to everybody and nobody. . . . Our chief, rather noted for inefficiency, even among our imbecile rulers, is so kind hearted that punishment is his 'strange work'" (1873, 6).[12] At Sturges' nagging insistence, a council, which he was instrumental in establishing, "passed a few laws, among others, one giving a homestead to every man, on condition he build a house on it, and he can own but one. This law is the most radical of any they need, as it strikes at the root of the great evil here—a sort of socialism, quite destroying all our efforts to fix them as to place or property" (1873, 8).

In the Marshalls, where chiefs have been especially assertive regarding their rights over land, when the people of Arno atoll employ the *kajur* term for people or strength, they do so "in ways which explicitly indicate that the power or strength of the paramount chief was dependent directly on the amount of 'strength' (i.e. commoners) he had. If the chief wanted to carry on any activities other than subsistence, he had to have the economic support of the commoners" (Rynkiewich 1972, 81–82). "Although the chiefs were said to 'own the people' as well as everything else, the commoners could, and did leave the jurisdiction of their hereditary ruler for that of another, if they felt they were being treated unjustly or perhaps, if they could obtain greater benefits elsewhere" (Tobin 1967, 81). Earlier I raised questions about the existence of residence rules. It is just this sort of mobility that plays such an important part in making postmarital residential choices much less predictable than cultural norms would seem to indicate.

Anthropologists interested in relationships between land tenure and the rest of social life in the Pacific islands have often focused on the importance of access to land—of both having and restricting access to it. Some have focused on adoption, fosterage, and other forms of transferring people among lineages and households. Because Micronesians conceive of the labor necessary to work land as being of essentially the same importance as access to land itself, the reality is that individuals and groups are continually concerned about both the land and the labor available to them. And because lineages and households vary in size through time, their leaders sometimes worry about gaining access to more land in order to retain members, as their numbers increase beyond the group's ability to provide everyone with enough land; and at other times they fear that that membership has shrunken below the point at which they can effectively utilize and thus hold on to their land. Any understanding of the dynamics of Micronesian societies, then, has to recognize that the availability of adequate supplies of labor presents as much of a challenge to survival as does the problem of sufficient land.

Adoption

In every Micronesian society, the vagaries of population history—in response to random natural and social phenomena—result in imbalances in the numbers of people belonging to, and the amounts of land available to, lineages and households. There are a great many ways these differences can be addressed, including marriage, gift giving, and conquest. Marriage is the most obvious means of extending the webs of kinship that provide access to land and labor. Older family members typically arrange young people's first marriages, in expectation that alliances with successful families will be forged. But it seems that in most of Micronesia marriages tend to be somewhat ephemeral. Though nearly everyone is monogamous, individuals are likely to marry several times in the course of their lives. As a consequence, marriage cannot be relied on as a certain means of acquiring and retaining labor. Instead, Micronesians depend heavily on the practice of adoption. Smith, for example, found that in the Palauan community she studied, 58 percent of the population had been adopted and that households averaged five adoptions apiece (1983, 205). Adopted children live in 54 percent of Arno's households (Rynkiewich 1976), while on Lamotrek over one-half and on Satawal more than three-quarters of the population had been adopted when Alkire worked there in the 1960s (Alkire 1989, 60). Marshall thus concluded that "adoption is a very common transaction in Micronesia, with typically half or more of all children being adopted" (1999, 120).

Adoption in Micronesia has many forms and meanings and includes a range of emotional aspects, but its extraordinary prevalence is largely due to the ways in which it functions to provide flexibility and alternatives in the lives of individuals, as well as assurances of land and labor availability to kin groups. Micronesian adoption is not in the main intended to ensure care for orphaned children, since their lineage mates would automatically assume responsibility for them. Rather, it is viewed as a means of both forging closer ties between the families involved and providing those who are adopted with a second set of rights and claims as well as duties and responsibilities. Adoptions ordinarily occur at about the time of a child's birth, sometimes shortly before it, sometimes several years later. An adopted child may or may not move immediately to the residence of the adoptive household, and the child may well move back and forth between its birth and adoptive households. As a matter of practical, as opposed to emotional, decision making, the crux of adoption comes as the child matures and begins to consider establishing him- or herself as an adult member of society. Throughout Micronesia, one who is adopted usually has the option of choosing to activate ties as a member of the household and lineage of either the birth family or the adoptive family. Once the individual has made a decision and taken up residence, however, he or she is ordinarily expected to make this a permanent commitment.

Rynkiewich's discussion of adoption on Arno might be applied to almost any other Micronesian community:

> Adoption, as a process of kinship affiliation, serves as a contingency strategy in the realm of social action. Once an adoption has occurred, for any of a variety of reasons, the adoptive relationship can be extended to include coresidence or inheritance. Whether or not this will happen depends not so much on the context of the adoption event itself as it does on the subsequent social situations that develop relative to the wants and needs of the adopter, the adoptee, and the adoptee's natural parents. An adoption negotiated for one reason may be transformed to serve other needs at a later date, Adoption on Arno can only be understood as an institution with many sources, many functions, and a flexibility that allows for transformation of relationships over time (1976, 94–95).

Marshall's analysis of Namoluk adoptions is equally applicable: "Adoption and fosterage also lead to the maximum utilization and optimum distribution of available human resources. Couples without children may adopt children. Whenever an extra person is needed (for whatever purpose), a foster child may be taken. Large families with insufficient resources may relieve some of the economic burden by giving one or more children in adoption or fosterage." Namoluk adoption works as well to transfer land and rights in land and "thereby plays a role in the recurrent redistribution of land resources" (Marshal 1972, 43).

What this means is that throughout Micronesia individuals who have been adopted are endowed with options about where and with whom they will take up residence. While these relationships are complex and imbued with emotional undertones, they can be summarized in this way: individuals born into households or lineages that turn out to have, by the time they are ready to make decisions about where to reside, an abundance of land relative to the available amount of labor are likely to remain with their birth households. On the other hand, individuals born into households with a shortage of land relative to the amount of labor available are likely to activate their adoptive ties.

Because changes in the amount of land a group possesses, the number of members whose labor can be called upon, and ratio of labor to land are difficult to predict very far in advance, adoption allows young adults to make decisions at the time the labor they are going to be contributing to a household and the land they feel they are going to need access to can be more appropriately judged. Despite the importance of matridescent in all Micronesian societies, then, some members of any Micronesian population opt to settle with their adoptive families rather than with the lineages into which they are born. This flexibility in honoring descent principles in matters of residence and day-to-day survival is paralleled in the matter of succession to chieftainship, where principles of matrilineal primogeniture serve more as a starting point in the selection process than as rules to be strictly observed and implemented.

Land and Political Theory

A complex web of ideas, assumptions, and historical traditions shape relations among Micronesian land tenure, lineages, chieftainship, and political life in general. But this richly textured fabric does not, in fact, differ all that much from aspects of European and American political traditions. I turn for a moment to Western political thought in order to provide a context for understanding some of the subtleties of Micronesian life. The era of the English Revolution provides modern political theory with much of its basis for considering relations between property—or more specifically, land—and political life. In *Two Treatises of Government*, John Locke provided not only his contemporaries but also subsequent generations of thinkers with some convincing arguments regarding the appropriate nature of government. In his first treatise Locke challenged arguments, put forward most notably by Robert Filmer, in support of what is now known as "the divine right of kings." This notion held that the legitimacy of the king's rule derived from his authority over all the realm's lands as a consequence of his succession from Adam, to whom God had granted dominion over all the earth. Rather than directly disputing the king's antecedents, Locke instead denied that "*Property* in Land gives a Man Power over the Life of another" and reasoned that "no Man could ever have a just Power over the Life of another, by Right of property in Land or Possessions" (Locke 1960, 205–206, I.iv.41–42). In the second treatise, Locke went on to develop one of political philosophy's better-known premises: "Every Man has a *Property* in his own *Person*. . . . The *Labour* of his Body, and the *Work* of his Hands, we may say, are properly his. Whatsoever he then removes out of the State that Nature hath provided, and left it in, he hath mixed his *Labour* with, and joyned it to something that is his own, and thereby makes it his *Property*" (1960, 328–329, II.v.27). That is, humans create property by conjoining their own labor with nature.

The second treatise is much better known, inasmuch as it lays groundwork for precepts arguing that the legitimacy of government lies in its defense of property, while the first treatise is largely viewed as being of primarily academic, rather than political or practical, interest. But the effort and skill Locke put into the first work should remind us that principles underlying conceptions of the divine right of kings were widely subscribed to in that era, which helps explain the intensity of the English Civil War, the Restoration, and the Glorious Revolution. It was the ultimate victory of the republican cause, as much as the force of his logic, that has given Locke his preeminent place in the modern canon.

But the point I want to stress here is that there have been periods—eras, in fact—when republican and monarchical principles coexisted. As Pocock's

Machiavellian Moment (1975) fully demonstrates, aspects of both these contrasting outlooks informed Western political discourse for centuries.

I use Locke and the context in which he thought and wrote because this is the most useful analytical language available to me to explain successfully the dynamics of Micronesian political life to those who have learned to think about these questions in ways that are rooted in English-language political and philosophical traditions, rather than through ethnographic perspectives. That is, I am interpreting Micronesian political thought in terms of a philosophical tradition that is foreign to it. I do not suggest that in what follows I am precisely representing how Micronesians conceptualize these matters; I instead use aspects of the Western intellectual tradition as a means of rendering a very different perspective on things comprehensible to Western readers.

Micronesians express what are in Western terms contradictory views of chiefs' powers over land. Each view is sometimes used to confute the other, but my intent here is to show instead how they fit together as aspects of a larger conceptualization. In its seventeenth-century English milieu, divine-right theory maintained that the legitimacy of kings derived from the intersection of (a) descent from a line of rulers who traced their origins to Adam's dominion, (b) the rights over all the lands in the realm that came as a consequence of this descent, and (c) the authority over all those inhabiting these lands that came as a consequence of the king's proprietorship over the lands from which the people made their livings.

Similar precepts inform traditional Micronesian society. While the authority and the rights of chiefs are sometimes attributed to conquest (especially in the Marshalls), in general the authority that inheres in a Micronesian chief by virtue of his office is ascribed to his descent from ancestors who were the first to occupy or settle an island or place. Almost everywhere we find that the leading lineage or clan claims that its legitimacy as the preeminent group comes as a consequence of this settlement priority. The chief of a place is chief by virtue of being the leader of its premier descent group. And the concept of residual title bears this out. What is owed to a chief—first fruits, respect, and, in some circumstances, obedience—is owed to him because of his group's precedence. The chief's eminence comes because of his status as a (or the) senior member of the senior group. Both the importance of seniority of descent and the importance of residual title over the land because of settlement priority are referred to by nearly every Micronesian when discussing why a chief is a chief, what privileges a chief is due, and what responsibilities encumber him. Whatever disagreements Micronesians may have about what constitutes chieftainship and which individual should occupy the office, they all know intuitively how and why one is supposed to become a chief.

At the same time, we can see that there is a shared notion that the descent groups that occupy land—the people who work it, improve it, and derive their identities from it—are also its rightful proprietors. And there is a common notion that the land derives its value from the work that a lineage and, more important, its ancestors, have put into developing and improving it, making it productive farmland, making it capable of yielding a living to those who continue to cultivate it. While the chiefly lineage's claims over land derive from priority of settlement and descent, the claims of the lineages residing upon this same land derive from the labor they have put into it. And although Micronesians readily attest to the chief's authority over the land, they are equally vocal about the lineage's rights over it. A chief cannot alienate a lineage's land—remove it from them or drive them off it—unless there is an overriding consensus within the community that the lineage has done something socially unacceptable or reprehensible to bring this upon itself or has clearly and repeatedly failed to discharge its acknowledged duties to the chief. As Goodenough notes, in Chuuk there may arise "a situation in which powerful persons and lineages could take advantage of weaker ones." He adds, "While this has happened, the entire community is likely to unite against a too frequent offender" (1951, 60).

In short, there are two differing Micronesian concepts regarding land rights. And the nature of Micronesian political thought cannot be understood unless both of these viewpoints are comprehended simultaneously. Unfortunately, most of those who have reported on Micronesian chieftainship and land tenure have assumed that the Micronesian statements about chiefly authority and dominion that resonate with European conceptions of the divine rights of kings constitute the totality of the Micronesian perspective. And thus Micronesian chiefs are commonly portrayed as being in possession of rather awesome authority. But closer examination of the dynamics of Micronesian sociopolitical life tends to belie this stereotype. The only way to make sense of this disparity is to recognize the simultaneous existence of these two contrary notions.

Locke's notion in the second treatise was that land became property—was separated out from nature—by the labor of those who worked it and that property was thus imbued with the personality of those who created it. Land belonged to those who cultivated it, and it could not rightly or justly be taken from them. To prevent the unjust taking of land by those who were stronger, individual property owners joined together to create governments, the original purpose of which was to protect the property of those who consented to join together and thus founded the government. His logic lies at the heart of subsequent theories of the "social contract"—that is, that people consent to government and can therefore withdraw their consent, thereby acting to change the government.

James Harrington, writing in the same era and drawing from Machiavelli's point that it was the possession of arms that assured people their rights as political actors, insisted that the right to bear arms was in turn dependent upon individuals' secure status as owners of their own land.[13] A monarch exercises limited sway over landholding people, and they are not obliged to fight for him—their arms are their own. Government roughly approximating democracy was possible only where people held land in relative equality. Under these circumstances, citizens possessed the human resources needed to distribute political authority in a diversified and balanced way and were thereby able to establish and preserve a stable polity. This in turn assured security of tenure for landholders; they could pass their land on to their descendants, who were in turn assured not only of a place in political life but also of the means through which to participate actively in it (Harrington 1992; Pocock 1975, 386–390).

In a preindustrial society based on a subsistence economy, property rights cannot be used to threaten individuals or to deny them opportunities to provide for themselves. Instead, it is the rights of each lineage over its own land that enable its members to function as political actors. Under normal circumstances, lineages' relationships with chiefs are defined by their tenure over their land and by their possession of their own arms. In Micronesian societies, every adult male is a potential warrior, as well as a freeholder. Chiefs are obliged to listen and to heed. Throughout Micronesia public politics are conducted via councils composed of the heads of all the local lineages. Freedom of speech seems to be the norm, inasmuch as these councils engage in consideration of public business until all have expressed what they wish to say, and then the councils pursue consensus before any action can be taken.

Finally, and most significantly, the overlapping of these two seemingly opposing political themes—chiefly rights based on hereditary authority over land, and lineage rights based on who works on the land—appears to reflect another central aspect of republican theory. By acknowledging the chief's authority over their land, lineages assure themselves that he will be responsible for protecting it. And because the chief is the leader of the entire community, and everyone in it acknowledges his authority, a threat to any one lineage's land means the potential mobilization, via the chief, of the entire community to defend it. In readily acknowledging the chief's ultimate authority over their land, Micronesians are not denying their own proprietary rights but instead assuring themselves of their government's protection of their lands. This is very much, if not precisely, the way Locke explained the nature of government.

As I said, I cannot be certain that an interpretation based in Western political theory adequately represents Micronesians' understandings of their own political systems. But I believe that it does capture the underlying tension between the honor and deference chiefs receive, on the one hand, and the sense of individual and lineage autonomy, on the other, that together characterize Micronesian political dynamics.

CHAPTER 6

Chieftainship and Government

THIS AND THE FOLLOWING chapter are about the broad sweep of political life in Micronesia. I have divided the topic in two primarily to make it more manageable. In this chapter I deal with what I am calling government, while in the next chapter I treat the overlapping spheres of political dynamics and leadership. The grounds upon which I distinguish between these grow out of my own experience; they reflect the ways in which I have come to understand Micronesian societies, not any preexisting disciplinary or philosophical models. I want to make it clear, however, that my approach is informed by classical Western political thought. As I explained in the preceding chapter, ideas long debated by some of the Western tradition's most influential thinkers have helped me think about how best to explain Micronesian sociopolitical life to non-Micronesians, while remaining as faithful as I can to Micronesian conceptions. I have tried hard to avoid forcing Micronesian social life into Western models; I use them to elucidate rather than to categorize.

For analytical purposes I use "politics" in a sense I have drawn from Aristotle. In this context, "politics" refers to what people want their communities to do for them and how they set about achieving these goals. This includes the formal structures or constitutional grounds of governance, the ways in which people actually participate in political life, and some of the ways in which individuals, groups, and institutions interact.

When I speak of "government," I refer primarily to the formal structures of political life. In Micronesia this entails the institutions of chieftainship, including ritual responsibilities, linkages between land and political titles, external or foreign relations, checks and balances among different facets of government, and the nature of sociopolitical rank. To avoid confusion, I will be explicit: In what follows I treat government as one basic element within the overarching umbrella of political life. Some aspects of politics thus lie outside the formal realm of government (and are sometimes referred to as "civil society"), while others determine how governments operate and how well they function.

By "leadership" I mean what the most active and/or effective members of society—and these are not necessarily the chiefs—do in the public realm, as well as how they do it and why they do it. I also include matters of who becomes a leader and how one does so. Given my starting presumption that politics are directed toward achieving certain communal goals (as well as individual ambitions), leadership entails a range of means by which individuals and groups pursue these goals.

I should also say something here about power, which is commonly conflated with or mistaken for politics—that is, taken to be much the same thing as politics—in a great deal of contemporary political thought. Both Micronesian mythohistory and historical accounts tell of battles between communities, but only some of these represent true struggles for power. Occasional but significant acts of raw violence occur within communities, but it is difficult to find much unambiguous evidence of individuals or groups relying habitually on straightforward physical coercion or threats of it in Micronesia, which is how I understand normal usages of the term "power." Micronesians understand the possibilities of power and fear it; because they fear it, they have devised political systems that provide built-in checks and balances to counter potential abuses of power. It is unusual to see genuine manifestations of power, and however much people may be aware of its potential, they in fact spend very little time actually fretting about it.

Chiefs: Place and People, Territory and Lineage

Micronesian concepts of chieftainship for the most part define the character of government in the islands. To be sure, there are many kinds of "chiefs" in Micronesia. Each society has its own forms of government, organized around its own sorts of formal leadership roles. But the underlying principles are very much the same everywhere, and these principles entail two related and overlapping but nonetheless quite distinct categories of chiefs. These are what I call lineage chiefs and territorial chiefs.[1]

Lineage chiefs are heads of descent groups. They are ordinarily mature men who have some claim to a degree of genealogical seniority within the group, whether this is reckoned in terms of being a member of the group's senior line or a senior member of any line within the group. Women sometimes serve as chiefs, but even though they are often important political actors, women in most cases do not take on the public roles of chieftainship unless there are no eligible males competent to do the job. The authority and responsibility of lineage chiefs is in most cases limited to the membership of their lineages and those who reside in households identified with them.

The relative importance of lineage chieftainship varies throughout Micronesia. In some areas (e.g., Chuuk) basically every lineage or localized descent group has its own chief. In other areas (e.g., Lamotrek) only a few leading groups have chiefs. And in others (e.g., the Marshalls and Pohnpei) it is common that only the ruling lineage has a formally recognized chief.

Territorial chiefs are leaders of what are ordinarily well-recognized, geographically demarcated places, whether they are islands (or clusters of islands), districts or portions of islands, or subsidiary divisions of larger polities. They are the official leaders of all the people living within this territory. Their authority is generally much more substantial than that of lineage chiefs. On Palau and Pohnpei, among other places, people sometimes consider themselves members of a territorial chiefdom other than the one in which they reside, and it might thus be argued that local chiefdoms are not entirely geographic in nature; they are, nevertheless, spoken of, conceived of, and for most purposes organized as territorial entities.

Paramount chiefs lead the most extensive and inclusive polities. They have local or district chiefs below them and no one above them. The territories over which they reign—paramount chiefdoms—are autonomous and effectively sovereign. Smaller atolls are likely to have a single paramount chief reigning over the entire atoll; most larger islands have several paramount chiefdoms. Kosrae is the only high island with a single paramount chief wielding authority over the entire island. In the Marshalls paramount chiefs sometimes reign over portions of several islands; individual islands or atolls may be divided into portions that recognize different paramount chiefs, but it seems likely that this is primarily a postcontact pattern.[2]

Everywhere in Micronesia territorial chiefs occupy their positions because they are the lineage chiefs of the senior lineages in the places over which they reign. Put another way, some lineage chiefs, because the respective groups they head are the senior groups on the island or in the district, are charged with a second and usually more important position: they also serve as leader of all the people in that place. That is, no one is simply or merely a territorial chief, a leader of a place rather than of a group of people. This phenomenon is by no means peculiar to Micronesia—it is encountered in other parts of the Pacific islands—but its ubiquity in Micronesia seems to make it a particularly definitive Micronesian practice.

Land and Chieftainship

As we have already seen, virtually all Micronesians recognize a degree of chiefly authority over land. But in and of itself this tells us very little. Simply being chief does not give an individual much active control over land. Rather, a chief symbolizes his lineage's residual authority over land, conceptualized in terms of priority of settlement or of conquest. When a group possesses the largest share of land in a given place, it is likely to justify its prominence by asserting that it was the first to settle the area. The group with the largest landholdings portrays itself, then, as having priority and as therefore being preeminent. There are frequent disagreements about this. The true seniority of the officially recognized senior lineage is often questioned, though rarely in public. The simple fact is that most people want their community to have a prestigious leader (why have one who is not prestigious?), and it is the senior lineage's leader who personifies all of his lineage's seniority and authority over land. The chief's authority over the land does not inhere in him as an individual so much as it derives from his role as head of the ruling lineage, which by definition has the most substantial ties to the spirits of the locale. This means, then, that it is a mistake to interpret a chief's authority over land as being lodged in or reflecting the power of the individual.

Moreover, the chiefly lineage's residual title over the community's land, whatever the nature of its claims may be, is balanced or limited by the other lineages' provisional titles. Lineages possessing estates—that is, currently working and occupying them—see themselves as investing their labor and thus themselves into their land, thereby making it at least as much their own property as it is the senior lineage's. This is not an either-or situation; both sorts of lineages have legitimate claims. Their provisional title to land underlies the nonchiefly lineages' sense that if necessary they can resist or oppose the chiefly lineage. But it is the actual occupation and working of the land that gives them the strength to do this. Their provisional title and their actual strength together make it unlikely that a chiefly lineage will abuse its authority. Micronesians readily acknowledge that failure to render first fruits to the chiefs may result in various sorts of retribution, but it is equally the case that members of nonchiefly lineages say that once they have made the requisite gifts, they have fully discharged their duties and responsibilities and thus possess essentially complete rights to their land. As long as the "contractual" requirements are met, then, lineages are certain that they possess sufficient rights to their land.

In cases of conquest the system of authority seems to be much the same. Ordinarily, when one group is overthrown as the chiefly lineage in a given locale, the basic structures of chieftainship and land tenure remain unchanged; residual title simply shifts to a new lineage. Over the course of years or generations, the lineage that has gained chieftainship via conquest eventually transforms the nature of its claims to seniority—it comes to be understood to be the leading group by virtue of settlement priority. There are cases where conquest remains rooted in long-term memory (especially in the Marshalls), but not many. In most of Micronesia legitimacy is more comfortably grounded in priority of settlement, and that is how it is most commonly portrayed. Because of the many environmental exigencies Micronesia's island societies are subject to—and this is especially true on the atolls most exposed to typhoons, where cycles of settlement and abandonment have been recurring for millennia—there is rarely, if ever, a clear record or account of who first settled an island, nor of when they did so.

In the Marshalls, German-sponsored copra production in the last third of the nineteenth century apparently enabled paramount chiefs to advance their claims to overweening titles more dramatically than elsewhere in Micronesia.[3] When Spoehr wrote of "rigid class structure" there, he also acknowledged exceptions to this, supposing that an older class system was in the process of breaking down (1949, 74, 78). But others have interpreted the evidence differently. Tobin describes a more widespread concept of "joint ownership of land rights" with chiefs and people each possessing specific rights. He reports that at the 1951 Marshalls Congress, while the chiefs asserted their ownership of all land, the majority of the people's representatives disagreed, insisting that land was owned by everyone (1952, 6). In a similar vein, Rynkiewich argues that the depth of individual lineages' associations with specific landholdings, combined with the centrality of lineages to the Marshalls' political organization, can be understood only if lineage tenure has been significantly more secure than some (including Spoehr) have suggested (1972, 81; cf. Tobin 1952, 22; Yanaihara 1940, 41; and Mason 1986, 51). Luther Gulick, among the first and one of the most observant of the Boston missionaries, recognized this seeming contradiction: even where authority is the most potent in the Marshalls, he wrote, it is not palpable (1862, 302).

Chiefs and Communities

The twin themes of descent and land underpin Micronesian politics. Because of precepts about authority over land, the person recognized by the leading descent group as its senior member is thus the senior person—that is, the chief—over the entire place. Several important corollaries follow from this.

First, members of the descent group that controls a territorial chief's title must be conscious that their ability to retain possession of the title depends to some degree on their ability to provide leaders who are acceptable to the community at large. This seems especially important in the Marshalls, where the influence and authority of a paramount chief are consciously reckoned in terms of the people over whom he presides; that is the *kajur*—both "people" and "power" (Rynkiewich 1974, 144–148). If a chiefly descent group allows itself to be headed by leaders who are ineffective, abusive, or deeply disliked, it will in time see its credibility diminish and its legitimacy challenged. It needs to choose skilled, or at least competent, leaders if the rest of the community is to continue willingly recognizing it as the chiefly descent group.

Second, precisely because the community as a whole depends on the senior lineage's head as its leader, community members may well become involved in the senior lineage's internal affairs, playing some part in making decisions about who is to be its leader and thus the community's chief. On Yap, for example, where the legitimacy of clan leadership is a matter for concern, "a chief who is out of harmony with the village and code of right conduct is in serious trouble," and an "incompetent, tyrannical, or deceitful" chief can be removed and a new leader chosen from the pool of legitimate heirs. It is a district chiefdom's council, and not the lineage itself, that selects an individual from the members of the lineage owning the land that provides the chief—that is, the individual who will succeed to the paramount chief's title (Lingenfelter 1975, 75, 114, 118, 123–124).

Because these overlapping precepts of territoriality and descent are shared by all Micronesian societies, Micronesians hold in common a tacit understanding of what constitutes a chief in terms of intercommunity or interisland relations. He is the leader of a place and of all the people living in it, but his status is not his own. Rather, he holds his title because of his position in the senior descent group in that place. He thus carries with him not merely the authority of the title but also the authority that inheres in his descent group's status as the first settlers or conquerors there. As senior member of the senior group, he also bears the authority, established by his ancestors and their spirits, that inheres in that place. And because Micronesians generally assume that a chief is not likely to be selected by his own descent group if he is not viewed as a legitimate, competent leader by the rest of their community, they are willing to assume that a chief from another community or island is as legitimate a leader of his community as their own chief is of their community.

In most of Micronesia, chiefs are imbued with what anthropologists call "mana," a term with ancient Oceanic roots. I discuss this phenomenon at length in the following chapter; for the moment I will simply describe it as a supernatural or spiritual force, originating with ancestors, that underlies the sacred character of political authority and may also be channeled by other especially talented or effective individuals. While a chief's authority within his community is tied to the mana of his ancestors, it is the addition of foreign-affairs responsibilities—representing the island or community in its relations with other communities—that produces the characteristic form of Micronesian chieftainship. Communities want, or believe they need, leaders for a variety of reasons, but there is no inherent reason why the form of leadership should be so similar from one society to another. The common form of Micronesian chieftainship is a product of shared origins, of course, but it has been maintained over the centuries by the roles that all chiefs play in organizing and focusing relations between communities. Micronesian chieftainship, then, is complex—it constitutes the government. It simultaneously entails the internal management of descent groups, management of relations among descent groups within a community, management of the community as a whole, and management of relationships between different communities. And because survival in Micronesia depends so completely on relations with other communities and islands, government is very much shaped by the dynamics of these foreign relations.

A Basic Model of Traditional Micronesian Governments

In the context of this book, I use "government" to mean specific patterns of behavior and social institutions that organize communities that are territorially based or defined, rather than individual lineages or households. And while territorial communities often have porous or ambiguous boundaries (sometimes not even delimited by an island's shoreline), they exist everywhere in Micronesia.

Having made this generalization, I must immediately qualify it. Although chieftainship is the most visible aspect of Micronesian governments, Micronesian government cannot be understood by asserting that it is based entirely on chieftainship, which is what sometimes happens when Micronesian political institutions are described summarily. In providing Micronesian societies with the effective leadership that has enabled them to occupy their islands so successfully for the past two millennia, chieftainship draws as much on members of the community who are not chiefs as it does on the chiefs themselves. This is because Micronesian governments are organized around the reality of full-scale communal participation much more than upon the ideology of the centralized rule of a single leader. Micronesians want and, as nearly as I can tell, believe they need chiefs; this institution would not typify every Micronesian society (as indeed it does) if people did not find it both enormously effective and emotionally satisfying. What is more, even though every Micronesian community relies on essentially the same principles of chieftainship, chiefs are not all charged with the same sorts of duties and responsibilities. In general, on the smaller islands chiefs work to ensure their society's survival, while on the larger islands chiefs are concerned more with managing the consequences (and dangers) of abundance.

Let me make this clear: chieftainship is not identical in all Micronesian societies. Variations in political organization exist not only in different parts of Micronesia but even among different communities on the same islands; there are also marked variations over the course of time within communities. My point is not that the shared origins of Micronesian chieftainship mean that there is a single political dynamic or form in Micronesia, but that for the most part the many similarities that do exist derive from shared origins and have remained so similar for so long because of their highly adaptive character.

There are problems with the term "chief." Micronesians in some societies use a single, interchangeable term to refer to holders of specific leadership positions or titles, people of high genealogical rank, indigenous religious leaders or priests, elderly or other particularly respected individuals, and occasionally other categories of people. In Palau, for example, *rubak* can refer to "an adult male, a foreigner, an elder, or a chief" (Palau Society of Historians 1997, 1), and on Yap, *pilung* refers to a wide variety of leadership statuses (Lingenfelter 1975, 99–108).[4] More important, however, is that most Micronesian societies have multiple categories of chiefs beyond the basic dichotomy of lineage and territorial chiefs already discussed.

Excluding the lineage chiefs for the moment, the first of these additional categories concerns levels of political integration. There can be, depending on the specific society and variations within it, village or community chiefs (which I also call local chiefs), chiefs of divisions within villages, paramount chiefs of portions of larger islands or entire small islands, and chiefs of divisions of paramount chiefdoms. Micronesian political organization has a federal character that entails a hierarchical web of chiefs leading discrete communities or neighborhoods (discussed further in the section "Centralization and Decentralization," below).

Another category of chiefs includes the holders of the multiple kinds of titles that complement or parallel one another within communities or are in some cases simply ranked relative to one another. On Pohnpei each community has three different sorts of leaders. At the level of the paramount chiefdoms *(wehi)* these are the Nahnmwarki (a more or less sacred title), the Nahnken (a more or less secular title), and the *samworo* category of priestly titles (today replaced by the *koanoat*, an honorary title); similar divisions exist at the level of local communities *(kousapw)*. In Yapese villages three statuses "stand out above all others: *pilung ko binaw* 'voice of the village,' *pilung ko pagael* 'voice of the young men,' *pilung ni pilbithir* 'ancient voice,'" and, as Lingenfelter observes, "These are the highest-ranking statuses in any village and carry the greatest power. They are the village chiefs" (1975, 99).

A range of offices characterizes Chuuk as well, although its society is commonly spoken of as being among Micronesia's least hierarchical. Varying types and degrees of rights over land are organized in political terms. The individual with authority over a lineage's land is the *sowupwpwun*, or "lord of the soil"; a group of siblings holding land that they have received from their father recognizes the head of his lineage as *somwoonum fenu*, or "chief of land"; and the leader of a district's senior line is *somw soopw*, or "chief of district" (Goodenough 2002, 33–35). Within a lineage there can be both an executive head or chief of talk, *somwoonum kkapas*, who is the lineage's oldest competent male member, and the chief of food, *somwoonum mwenge*, who is the genealogically senior male in the senior female line (Goodenough 2002, 37). And then there are the *itang*, or "political priests," who are the "most prestigious and awesome members of Chuukese society" (Goodenough 2002, 290).

On Kosrae there are ranked chiefs; the highest, Tokosra and Kanka, appear to be of nearly equivalent rank. The Tokosra has sometimes been described as a sacred chief, and the Kanka as a secular chief (Sarfert 1920, 55; J. Fischer 1966, 178). On Lamotrek there is the *tamol*, who is the chief proper, but there is also a second-ranking title, the *tela* (Alkire 1989, 32).

In the Marshalls, people speak of categories that have sometimes been called social classes. The *iroij lapalap* is a paramount chief; the *iroij erik* are lesser chiefs; and the *bwirak* are children of chiefs. The *iroij* have been termed "royalty" (as have members of Pohnpei's Nahnmwarki line), and the *bwirak* called "nobility" (like Pohnpei's Nahnken line). Another status is the honorary *atok* title, conferred upon men of special ability or notable accomplishment, much like Pohnpei's *koanoat* titles (Spoehr 1949, 74–76).

Any attempt to describe this multiplicity of titles is further complicated by the sequences of ranked titles that characterize a number of these systems of government. In Palauan, Pohnpeian, Kosraean, and to some extent Yapese societies—that is, the larger islands with bigger populations and more developed hierarchies—the numbers of chiefly titles are swelled by this phenomenon of ranked sequences of titles. In some places these titles run in ranked series along which individuals endeavor to work upward, step by step; these can be likened to stairs or ladder rungs that individuals endeavor to ascend, although on Pohnpei the notion of a path of titles *(ahl en mwar)* is the explicit metaphor. The pattern on Kosrae seems to have been quite similar. In Palau men might also move upward through the ranks of titles (Useem 1946, 117, 121–123). In Yap men advance through ranked grades of increasing ritual purity known as eating classes, though this may be a relatively recent development within the traditional system (Lingenfelter 1979).

This widely distributed pattern is significant for many reasons. Political systems with ranked titles effectively accomplish two contrasting tasks at once. On the one hand, they demonstrate hierarchy and difference: higher titles confer higher status. At the same time, those with lower-ranked titles gain status by their association with the highest titles and in many cases are able to demonstrate their leadership potential as they seek to progress toward the highest titles. Ranked sequences of titles illustrate the intersection of achieved and ascribed status. The lines of titles generally belong to specific lineages or subclans, and most of those who hold these titles are members of these descent groups. Advancement upward through the ranks requires not only some claim to genealogical seniority (which as we shall see is subject to manipulation) but also a degree of political participation and merit. It is by virtue of particular individuals' displays of these practical skills that the group controlling the title line manages to prove to the rest of the community that it is properly discharging its chiefly responsibilities. And inasmuch as communities commonly have some say in who is to become chief, the line of titles provides a venue that enables them to make informed judgments.

This pattern also makes it clear that titles belong to descent groups and not just to specific households or individuals. The authority of chiefs, even when exercised over territorial communities, is rooted in their own descent groups and is ordinarily established, maintained, enhanced, and exercised by the group at least as much as by the chief. Moreover, the possibility of access to the highest titles via upward progression through the ranks of titles, along with the multiple titles themselves, promotes lineage solidarity; subdivisions or branches can be persuaded to participate and support the lineage as a whole by rewarding their members with titles (J. Fischer 1966, 177). And finally, it should be stressed that in their capacities as community organizers and as mediators with the supernatural world, chiefs perform an array of services for their people. In the wider community, individuals and households expect leaders to officiate at a variety of life crisis and life cycle events, especially funerals. A ranked sequence of titles means that if the chief is unavailable because of commitments elsewhere (or in some cases because of the infirmities of advanced age), some other titleholder in the sequence can, because he shares in the chief's mana, effectively serve in the chief's stead. Thus a viable substitute is always available.

Because complementary sets of titles are usually repeated at each level of territorial government, in both the paramount chiefdom and the local communities, Micronesian societies with larger populations incorporate a great many people into their structures of government. In Palau and Pohnpei it sometimes seems as though nearly any adult male can in one context or another be reckoned a chief. In addition, women are in many cases included in this nomenclature. Most male political titles, for example, feature female equivalents (as in European patterns of, e.g., king/queen, duke/duchess), usually occupied by the titleholder's wife but in some cases possessed by other women in their own right.

The ranked nature of titles intersects with conceptions about seniority, both within and between lineages and clans, to create status differences that can be ambiguous and easily misinterpreted. High or paramount chiefs have sometimes been called kings, and it is not unusual to find the terms "royalty" and "nobility" used in accounts of Micronesian societies, especially regarding the Marshalls and Pohnpei. Local terminologies do sometimes distinguish between the relative ranks of certain high-status groups, and there is certainly room to argue that Micronesian patterns of leadership deserve the same sorts of recognition accorded to traditional European forms of government. Paternal connections are important in all these matrilineal societies, and children of chiefs or of senior members of chiefly lineages are known in the Marshalls as *bwirak* and in Pohnpei as *serihso;* these terms have often been translated as "nobility," inasmuch as their status is exalted but does not permit them to hold the highest chiefly titles. By a process that is similar to what etymologists call back-formation, their parents are then termed "royalty." But even in Chuuk and its nearby atolls, where there are minimal formal status differences, children of a lineage's male members are its *jefekyr* (Goodenough 1951, 33), and more specifically, Hall and Pelzer (1946, 22) described a status group, *öföker samon* (chief's people), comprising the "sons of chiefs, sons of chiefs' brothers, and their children."[5] In the Marshalls *ninnin* refers to the land that passes to the children of a lineage's males (Tobin 1956, 23ff.). In Palau *ulechell* are the children of a lineage's men (Palau Society of Historians 1997, 2, 37), and in the same vein Pohnpeians use the term *ipwieng* to denote paternal descent. That is, concepts of a distinct category marking the children of male lineage members are widespread; chiefs' children are often specially singled out, but it is difficult to say that they constitute a discrete social class.

Indeed, it is in some ways inaccurate to suggest that there is even a true chiefly class in any Micronesian society, because of the vague boundaries between the status of the chief as an individual and as a member of a chiefly lineage. Because a significant number of mature male members of chiefly lineages are ordinarily eligible to succeed to the chieftainship, any of them, along with the group's senior females, can potentially be termed "chief" or spoken of as possessing chiefly status in certain circumstances. This has as much to do with their personal characteristics and qualities as it does with ascribed status. The majority of members of a chiefly lineage are not in fact usually referred to as "chiefs" (though there may be contexts in which they are). While people in these societies share concepts or categories that can be rendered as "chiefly," this does not mean that there exists a class of people who unambiguously or unequivocally occupy chiefly status.[6]

This is not, however, the way in which Micronesia has long been portrayed. Robert Lowie (one of the founders of the American ethnological tradition), basing his ethnology on German sources, described Marshallese commoners as "degraded serfs cringing before the select class," a "body of pariahs" locked in a "relationship, doubtless fostered for ages, [that] engendered a servile frame of mind on the part of the oppressed caste" (1921, 351–352). Saul Riesenberg described Pohnpei's paramount chiefdoms as having been "organized on a feudal basis." They were ruled by "royal and noble classes" while the local chiefs "held their fiefs as vassals under the principal tribal chiefs" (Riesenberg 1968, 8,14). And George Peter Murdock found that "small feudal states with an elaborate class structure" were nearly everywhere in Micronesia and were in the process of evolving in Chuuk and nearby islands. He said he had seen there, "'on the hoof,' so to speak, a process of state development and class formation" (Murdock 1965, 245–247).

It is easy to infer from such portrayals that there are deeply significant class differences of an economic character in Micronesia. This is not the case. There are ritual and political differences—that is, differences in status and authority—but because of the degree to which chieftainship is achieved, a chief who acts forcefully probably derives his commanding presence from his own personal character, not from his lineage's status. And because of the importance of councils, even strong chiefs do not ordinarily wield a great deal of personal political clout. The closest Micronesia actually comes to manifesting anything like class as it is known in Western societies lies in the social realm. The extent of rank's influence is limited, but within its province it is of real significance.

Political Process

More reliable descriptions of actual political process contrast with the older perspective. I am not suggesting that differences in rank and status are absent, but rather that the quality of interactions among the people and their leaders does not reflect anything remotely resembling rigid class distinctions. To the extent that these differences do exist, they should instead be understood as vague, ambiguous, nuanced, and equivocal in practice, if not in local Micronesian theories. Most political decision making is in fact done in council, by leaders of the communities' descent groups representing their lineages' views and interests, and not by a small cadre of hereditary leaders.

In order to convey a more detailed sense of the roles of chiefs in a range of Micronesian societies, I quote several accounts at length here. Andrew Cheyne's description of 1840s Pohnpei (echoing Charles Wilkes' account from Kiribati) provides an apt illustration:[7]

> When a meeting is deemed necessary, messengers are sent to the different chiefs to request their attendance.... The chiefs having assembled, the object of the meeting is laid before them by the King or head chief, and everyone is at liberty to give his opinion. These discussions are at times very animated, especially when they have indulged freely in Kava; and on several of these occasions, I have witnessed violent quarrels between different speakers, which were only prevented from terminating in blows by the interference of the other chiefs. The opinion of the majority on the subject under consideration having been ascertained, the discussion is terminated. (Cheyne 1971, 182–183)

For matters of great importance on Lamotrek,

> where there may be disagreement concerning the proper course of action, a meeting will usually be called of the men on the island.... When the meeting convenes the senior chief will either present the problem or waive this duty to one of the other chiefs. After the opening remarks each of the remaining clans chiefs will discuss his position, then call upon the next senior men to state their feelings.... Each of these individuals will either comment on his position or, if he has none, pass without discussion. Any man of lesser status, save in the face of violent feelings, would leave his representation to one of the senior clan or lineage heads. At the end of the meeting a decision depends on implied unanimity of opinion. If any disagreement remained such a decision would be postponed until a later meeting. (Alkire 1989, 35–36)

The qualities of chiefs on Lamotrek have also been described:

> Day-to-day and year-to-year living on Lamotrek, or any similar island, is consistent enough so that most decision-making situations have been met before in the lives of the individuals involved. A particular course of action, depending on the relevant circumstances, is recognized as the proper course of action by chiefs and most of the inhabitants. The measure of a "good" or "bad" chief, then, is not in his ability to provide novel or unusual solutions to old problems, but rather in his ability to initiate and supervise at the proper time those responses which are well

known among the inhabitants. The "bad" chief is the individual who delays such action or who hedges in decision-making. (Alkire 1989, 70–71)

And on Yap the political process is much the same:

Decision-making on Yap is rarely, if ever, a one-man affair. The power of a chief is tempered always by the power of the *puruy* "council" of important leaders in the village.... Depending upon the subject of the discussion, word is carried to the village sections and subsections where additional councils are held and decisions are passed on and executed.

In a public council all members of the village may come and listen, but only the ranking estate leaders of the village may talk.... Decisions of the council are reached by consensus. Issues are discussed until public consensus is reached, or until a consensus is deemed impossible and the issue is dropped. (Lingenfelter 1975, 114–115)

In Chuuk, "one of the functions of the clan chief was that of people's representative before the village chief and as a link between the people and the village chief," and therefore "it was highly important to have an able, impartial and intelligent man in this role." An ineffectual clan chief could be replaced at the request of the village chief, but only upon the action of the clan members, who would "elect a new representative": "In the clan chief, one finds the seeds of representation on the part of the people" (Hall and Pelzer 1946, 24). As Goodenough observes, "The powers of chiefs, as such, in community affairs were limited," and "disputes and offenses to which the chief and his lineage were not party, were private matters to be resolved by individuals and lineages concerned." Furthermore, "a chief who meddled too much in disputes between lineages in his district could find them uniting in an effort to kill him" (Goodenough 2002, 298–299). Goodenough quotes an "*itang* teaching" by Kintoki, which in part explains the following:

The authority of chiefs is realized by people's coming together in assembly with humbleness and with circumspection and deference and with all carrying out their duties in accordance with "Under Bow." The working of "Under Bow" is not a matter of choice, but a matter to be woven together by explaining it and making it evident to one another. It is not something by which to create boundaries between people or cause people to be divided. (Kintoki 1986 in Goodenough 2002, 307)[8]

Useem reports his observations in Palau: "Although power was distributed unequally and along hierarchical lines, it was not linear but circular. While chiefs outranked other title-holders, their right to rule was circumscribed" (1950, 144). At every turn, according to Useem, Palau's leaders are checked by their communities.

No titleholder could act without the approval of the others; individual and clan ranks, the latter theoretically immutable, were continually undergoing change; rules that apparently ordered succession did not, in fact, guarantee anyone a position of authority (1952, 268). In some areas even low-ranking clans and villages had the right to argue in councils and to exercise a veto. Though criticism of the elite was supposedly a grave offense, people were likely to "acquiesce to any orders given but actually…evade their execution while verbally simulating compliance" (Useem 1950, 144–145). Parmentier adds, "A chief rules in respectful recognition of the council of which he is the leader and in the knowledge that ultimately the support of the people contributed to his own status" (1987, 75).

Much the same principle held in the Marshalls: "In the Marshalls language, 'kajur' means not only commoner as a social rank but also translates as 'power, force, strength.' This implies that an Iroij Lablab is only as strong or powerful as the continued loyalty of his subjects allows" (Mason 1986, 5). German reports of Marshallese chiefs often portrayed them as autocratic, but Rynkiewich finds these appraisals "suspect," both because of a tendency to see the islanders as "slaves to custom" and because most of the available information came from chiefs eager to convince the Germans that they individually owned all the land and the people. He notes, "The data from Arno, mainly oral history, imply that the paramount chief did not control all rights and could not act capriciously" (Rynkiewich 1972, 80; see also Carucci 1988, 36–39; and Spoehr 1949, 77). And Carucci points out, "Tight constraints on chiefly power were likely on all of the northern atolls" (1988, 38).

What flows inexorably from these observations is the absolutely central importance of political participation of all the descent groups living in a community. Chiefs preside rather than rule, and do so carefully because they are charged with ensuring that the community's lineages support their government. The primary point of government—that is, of chiefs—in these communities is to coordinate and focus the participation of the lineages. Basic survival in Micronesian societies requires both the effective management of land and labor by local descent groups (the task of lineage leaders) and effective relations with other communities and islands (the responsibility of territorial leaders). Communities need to be well organized both for domestic reasons, which entail, in particular, spiritual and economic aspects of feasting along with farming and fishing rituals, and for external reasons, primarily foreign relations and warfare. In principle at least, Micronesian government channels the mana of the chiefs in ways that make it available to the entire community.

Territorial Organization and Structure

Accounts of Micronesian sociopolitical organization have tended to pay particular attention to descent, but much of Micronesian government is actually structured around forms of territorial organization. Simply describing the hierarchical structures of local and paramount chieftainships, however, tells us little more than does calling political systems in other parts of the world "feudal" or "federal." The organization of feudal societies can in fact be focused on the power and authority of the king or highest-ranking liege lord or can instead emphasize the prerogatives of local vassals. Federal systems likewise can either be focused on the dominance of the centralized national government or stress the preeminence of the local entities (commonly called states). That is, the dynamics of centralized and decentralized power are not inherent in these forms; they are instead aspects of particular cases. In the same way, the nature of chieftainship in particular Micronesian societies is neither inherently centralized nor decentralized. In practice, however, consistent emphases are placed on dynamics and relationships that preserve the relative autonomy of local communities.

Feudalism and federalism refer to ways of arranging and separating powers— not simply within governments but among different hierarchically organized levels or branches of them. Different responsibilities and forms of authority are wielded by different organizational levels of government; that is, there are larger and more inclusive centralized levels and smaller, less inclusive decentralized or local levels. In the American federal system, for instance, there are the government of the country as a whole (often called the national or federal government), state governments, county governments, local or municipal governments, and often wards or council districts. There also exist a great diversity of other entities, including school districts, utility districts, and regional authorities. American history has in part been defined by tensions and struggles between higher and lower levels of political authority. Likewise, under European feudal conditions kings, princes, dukes, earls, marquises, counts, barons, and knights (among others) were charged with responsibilities and authority in their respective spheres, but the nature of their responsibilities and authority varied greatly. While "feudal institutions [were] fundamentally inclined to decentralization," in specific historical instances centralizing political trends "transcended the original nature" of these institutions (Cantor 1991, 272).

In Micronesia, too, there are hierarchically ordered levels of authority. These ordinarily include paramount or high chiefs; local, district, or village chiefs; and lineage or clan chiefs. All three levels are not always well defined and named, but almost everywhere we find notions of household group leaders, local chiefs, and paramount or high chiefs. Their relative authority and respective responsibilities vary widely, but as in feudal and federal systems, their realms are generally conceptualized in terms of homesteads or estates, villages or districts, and autonomous or paramount chiefdoms. There are sometimes intermediate levels of organization as well.

In Palau, in addition to villages (*beluu*, a term that can refer to political units of almost any size), there are also village complexes, subdistricts, districts, and federations, the latter two both termed *renged* (Parmentier 1987, 56–66). On Lamotrek there are the *tamollihailang* (clan chief), the *tamolnitabw* (district chief), and the *tamolufalu* (paramount chief) (Alkire 1989, 66). On Pohnpei there are the *meseni en keinek* (lineage chief), the *soumas en kousapw* (local chief), and the Nahnmwarki (paramount chief). In the Marshalls there are the *alab* (lineage chief), the *iroij tikitik* (minor chief), and the *iroij lapalap* (paramount chief). In Chuuk there is less emphasis on the concept of a paramount chief or district, but in the past there were regional confederations or leagues of local groups and islands that constituted a third level of organization in addition to lineages and villages (Goodenough 2002, 38). These different levels of leadership are by no means entirely parallel or identical across all the island groups, but the underlying principles of hierarchically nested authority and responsibility are essentially the same.

On the smallest atolls, it is common for there to be a single paramount chief over the entire island, while some of the larger atolls have several entirely separate and autonomous communities. On Pulap atoll, for instance, the communities of Pulap and Tamatam islets are thought of, and function as, entirely distinct and autonomous polities. The atolls east of Yap acknowledge the authority of Yap's Gatchepar village over them, as well as a chain of authority running eastward through the atolls from Ulithi, but the *sawei* system of which this authority is a part is not integrated in the political sense that regular decisions are made and imposed from above. The paramount chief of Lamotrek, likewise, is recognized as chief of Elato and Satawal but is not involved in their day-to-day political activities. In the Marshalls paramount chiefs do not necessarily reign over entire atolls but instead may have claims over portions of several atolls. Among the high islands, only on the smallest, Kosrae, is there a paramount chief of the entire island. Pohnpei's mythohistory tells of a dynasty, the Sau Deleurs, who ruled over all the island, but I am not convinced that this was ever truly the case (Petersen 1990). In the Carolines people sometimes talk of an ancient Katau Empire that linked together all the islands between Yap and Pohnpei (Nakayama and Ramp 1974; Goodenough 2002, 123–132), but to the extent that these linkages existed, they were social and economic, not political, in nature (Petersen 2000).

Centralization and Decentralization

What is most striking here is the division of powers and responsibilities among the levels of chieftainship. As a rule, most of the people in any Micronesian society do not see themselves as particularly concerned with the paramount chief and affairs that relate to him. The people (*kajur* in the Marshalls, variations of the term *aramas* in the eastern and central Carolines) emphasize their direct ties to their lineage and local chiefs. It is these leaders who ordinarily deal with the paramount chiefs, not the people themselves. On Etal in the Mortlocks, for example, a clan chief is expected to behave in an especially respectful fashion precisely because he is the group's representative to the atoll's district and paramount chiefs (Nason 1974, 124–125).

Societies on Pohnpei, Yap, Palau, and the Marshalls each in their own way exemplify different aspects of these divisions of power. Let me begin with Pohnpei, where I first began to grasp this pattern. It is easy to assume that the concentrated, sacred authority of Pohnpei's paramount chiefs is evidence of a high degree of political centralization, but in Pohnpeian political theory, ironically, the existence of the paramount chiefs is actually intended to assure decentralization. According to Pohnpeian mythohistory, the island was for a time under the rule of a single dynasty, the Sau Deleurs. But the power they exercised eventually corrupted them and turned the Sau Deleur chiefs into tyrants. As one indigenous Pohnpeian historian, Silten, who was born in the mid-nineteenth century, explained it, their arrogant behavior became increasingly offensive to the humans and the gods until "the high gods of Pohnpei and the high men of Pohnpei, and the sacred men of Pohnpei and the spirit mediums got angry and brought by magic the destruction of Pohnpei" (Petersen 1990, 32). The instrument of the tyrants' downfall was the culture hero Isokelekel. Following a great battle in which the last of the Sau Deleurs was overthrown and then destroyed, Isokelekel sent

> for the rulers of the towns, the high men of the districts, high men of the great islands around Pohnpei and all the people to come.... It was they who knew what was right for Pohnpei and what was to be done in Pohnpei.... He then appointed some men to rule the five centers of the land which form Pohnpei. They then assembled and came to him. He told them, "Pohnpei will not be the same as in the former regime which had only one ruler...." The Pohnpeians then rejoiced at [his] kindness to Pohnpei, and presented some men to join him in making rules for Pohnpei. (Petersen 1990, 42)

Luelen Bernart, another Pohnpeian historian born at about the same time, described the consequences of this change: "All the people were free to do their own will, for the ruler of the state [paramount chief, *kaun en wehi*] gave them permission for all their wishes" (Petersen 1990, 45). In the era that followed this great change, according to Pohnpeian historian Masao Hadley, the local chiefs *(kaun en kousapw)* "were responsible for the local chiefdoms (sections, *kousapw*), for the people, and for the movement of tribute *(uhpa)* to the high chiefs *(soupeidi)*" (Petersen 1990, 44). In other words, the underpinnings of the modern Pohnpeian polity, according to Pohnpeian political thought, lie in a reaction to overcentralization.

As local chiefdoms *(kousapw)* grow in population, they break apart, preventing local leaders from becoming too distant from their people. In the past, Pohnpei's Awak region was organized into as many as six local chiefdoms. Following the depopulation of the nineteenth century, Awak gradually became a single chiefdom, but in the twentieth century, as the population steadily grew again, new chiefdoms hived off, prompting one old and thoughtful local chief to tell me, by way of explanation, "One man cannot rule a thousand" (Petersen 1982a).

Yapese liken their highest leadership to the three stones used to support cooking pots over a fire. In this central metaphor, all of Yapese society rests on the three highest-ranking villages. If one should fail, the pot falls. "This is the basic philosophy of Yapese politics," Lingenfelter explains. The three paramount chiefs and their villages are equally important: "None should become so strong as to cause another to fall" (Lingenfelter 1975, 122.). The *'tha,* ritual relationships that form lines of communication between Yap's geographical and political units, limit and balance the power of the paramount chiefs, who are required to conduct their affairs through subordinate chiefs (Lingenfelter 1975, 133). The relationship between Yap proper and the atolls linked to it through the *sawei* plays a significant part as well. "In the context of the Yapese fear of too much centralized power," Lingenfelter finds, it makes sense for the apex of the exchange system to lie in a relatively minor village, Gatchepar. The exchange goods that flow in from the outer islands are channeled through a village council, forcing the high chiefs to depend on the council for support and thus placing "an effective curb on the personal power of any high chief" (Lingenfelter 1975, 152). According to Lingenfelter, "Together the chiefs and their supporting villages maintain a balance of power in Yap politics. Each struggles in his particular sphere to gain advantage over the other, but each is controlled in turn by the other two. The symbol of the pillars for the cooking pots illustrates the interrelatedness of all three. If one fails or becomes weak, the whole system collapses" (1975, 126).

In Palau, "while chiefs outranked other title-holders, their right to rule was circumscribed" since titleholders were unable to act without the approval of the other leaders (Useem 1950, 144). Even low-ranking clans and villages in some areas held rights to argue in councils and to exercise a veto (Useem 1952, 268).

In the Marshalls paramount chiefs were particularly thought of in terms of their ability to protect atolls from outside attack. As Rynkiewich makes clear, in order to assume the paramount title successfully, a claimant had to gain the support of the people—his source of strength. Only then would he be strong enough to assure the atoll's defense (1972, 64; 1974, 144). While modern paramounts in the Marshalls extend their authority over, or at least onto, multiple atolls, before the arrival of steel tools and firearms most, if not all, of the atolls were more or less autonomous (Mason and Nagler 1943, 6; Mason 1986, 48; Carucci 1988, 35). As

Carucci explains, Europeans attributed to Marshallese chiefs the powers of European feudal organizations and then treated them as if they indeed possessed these powers (1988, 36).

In part these hierarchies of organization work something like federal systems, as I have noted.[9] At any given level, the units—villages, sections, and so on—have their own political organizations and leaders. Yapese communities are divided into sections and subsections, which frequently compete against one another. Although the divisions are hierarchically ranked, they also serve to offset and counterbalance one another; they are dependent on one another. Furthermore, the relative rank of villages and sections is offset by the authority of individual chiefs. That is, an ordinary person from a high-ranking village has greater rank than a chief from a lower-ranking village, but the chief has much greater authority. As Lingenfelter puts it, "Rank, then, gives prestige, but titled land gives power" (1975, 92–93, 107). By the same token, however, a chief does not exercise authority on his own. Rather, he "is always expected to work in consultation with or through a *puruy* 'council'"; should he act alone and lose the council's support, "he may be removed from office, or, as happened in the past, the other chiefs might arrange to kill him" (Lingenfelter 1975, 100).

In addition, villages and their subdivisions possess many different sorts of leadership positions, three of which—occupied respectively by a mature man, a young man, and an elder—Lingenfelter calls the village chiefs (1975, 99). Other important statuses include overseers, priests, magicians, and gardening, fishing, and war leaders (Lingenfelter 1975, 103–110). There are in Yapese communities, then, numerous sorts of formally recognized leadership statuses; many of these are called *pilung*. *Pilung* is often translated as "chief," yet not everyone who is called *pilung* is a chief; for comparative purposes, however, we must understand that there are leaders in Yap whom any Micronesian would recognize as chiefs.[10]

Much the same sort of complexity exists on Pohnpei, where there are a plethora of titles and no clear-cut notions about which of them should properly be translated as "chief." The Irish sailor James O'Connell, who was shipwrecked on the island in the 1830s, found it "difficult to determine where the title *chief* ceases, as every landholder takes the title of his property." So many people were referred to as *aroche tikitik* (small chief) that "aroche might as well be translated freeman as chief; but then there would be no word in the language signifying chief" (O'Connell 1972, 124).[11]

Pohnpeians view their island's modern political system as simply the most recent in a series of historically evolving political formats. The island now comprises five independent paramount chiefdoms, called *wehi,* each of which is divided into multiple *kousapw,* which I call local chiefdoms (but which are often referred to as sections). In the past there also seem to have been a number of somewhat smaller autonomous territories that were also called *wehi* but did not have quite the same status as the paramount chiefdoms. The status of a chiefly title derives in part, then, from the size of the chiefdom itself.

In Pohnpei's paramount chiefdoms there are actually two parallel lines of titles of ascending rank, each surmounted by a high chief. One of these lines is charged with more sacred, ritual responsibilities, and at its pinnacle is the Nahnmwarki, the paramount chief. The second line has a more secular and administrative quality to it, and at its head is the Nahnken, whose position has sometimes been likened to that of a prime minister (or Samoan talking chief). The local chiefdoms are organized in a similar fashion. Without going into detail about who has access to these titles or how individuals advance upward through their ranks, I will simply note here that the Pohnpeian term now translated as "chief," *soupeidi* (which has replaced the earlier terms *aroche* and *samol*), includes a generalized notion of leadership and can refer, depending on context, to only those with the highest title in each line; to the top three or so titleholders in each line; to all the titleholders in both lines; to all the titleholders in only the paramount chief's line; to all members of the paramount chief's clan, subclan, or lineage; or to several other possible categories. A third line, called *samworo* (priestly) titles, fell into disuse following the Pohnpeians' conversion to Christianity in the late nineteenth century and has been replaced by a line of *koanoat,* or honorary, titles, and those who hold them may also be called *soupeidi.* The inherent ambiguity of Pohnpei's *soupeidi* concept reflects the somewhat ambiguous nature of Micronesian chieftainship in general.

The Nahnmwarkis are recognized as having the highest rank and political authority. But the sacred character of their status tends to keep them from playing an active role in most day-to-day affairs. The status of the Nahnken, while not quite so exalted as that of the Nahnmwarki, in most cases confers considerably more practical authority. The holders of the titles just below the apex of each line are also imbued with much of the supernatural power of the high chiefs and can act in their stead. The same is true for titleholders within the local communities. And together the higher titleholders of all three lines in the paramount chiefdoms, along with the local community chiefs and other well-respected men, constitute a council, the *pwihn en wahu,* which is in theory advisory to the Nahnmwarki but in fact wields considerable authority. I repeat Cheyne's description of council meetings at which all had an opportunity to speak out, often with great animation: "The opinion of the majority upon the subject under consideration having been ascertained, the discussion terminated" (Cheyne 1971, 182–183).

There is a good deal of variation in the degree of political centralization in Kiribati, between the northern and southern islands, as well as historical ebb and flow. While a village council model of politics organized around the meetinghouse (*maneaba*) prevails, it is also accompanied by a widely dispersed chiefly clan, the

Karongoa n Uea. Butaritari and Makin, where there is a relatively dominant high chief, lack the *maneaba* system. A traditional account tells of Butaritari occupying Beru and establishing a "tyrannical" regime there; this included the very Carolinian-like use of a raised platform for the chief. Ten Tanentoa, a warrior from nearby Nonouti, was then recruited to overthrow the despot and burn down his *maneaba*. In doing so Ten Tanentoa reestablished a much less centralized polity over which he reigned (rather than ruled) as high chief (Maude 1963, 17–18). This episode in important ways echoes the downfall of Pohnpei's tyrannical Sau Deleurs at the hands of the culture hero Isokelekel, who is credited with reestablishing its much less centralized polity.

According to the shipwrecked sailor Kirby, who lived three years on Kuria and whom the American explorers Wilkes and Hale judged fluent and reliable, the grandfather of Abemama's high chief (in the late 1830s) had first established himself a sole ruler of Abemama, while the current chief had extended his rule over Nonouti and Kuria as well (Wilkes 1845, 83). This chief, Tem Binoka, inspired terror in the people and ran roughshod over customs in order to establish his clan as supreme; in doing so, he nearly obliterated the role of most other social groupings (Grimble 1989, 217).

Kiribati thus manifests several crucial themes in Micronesian social life. One of these is the simple, rough association between the fertility and size of the resource base, the size of the population, the degree of social stratification, and the degree of political centralization, a relationship I discuss in the next chapter. A second reflects the typical dynamics of conquest: A new chiefly line is installed, instead of the original occupants being slaughtered or exiled. We see here the characteristic tensions between having an interest in strong leaders because of fears of invasion and conquest, on the one hand, and insisting on an effective council form of government and the relatively egalitarian ethos that accompanies it as a means of preventing abuse of chiefly power, on the other.

The Palauan term *rubak* is often taken to mean "chief," but as in other parts of Micronesia its meanings actually depend on context. According to the Palau Society of Historians' official *Belau Ethnography* (1997, 1), "*Rubak* refers to an adult male, a foreigner, an elder or a chief" (cf. Barnett 1960, 58). While each of a community's titles belongs to specific lineages *(kebliil)*, rights to appoint individuals to these titles are laden with checks and balances. The initial selection is made by the lineage's elder females, but it can be made only with the consent of its *rubak*s. Once the lineage as a whole has confirmed its choice, it goes before the entire community's council of chiefs *(klobak)* for final approval. Although each title is the property of a particular lineage, the top ten or eleven titleholders, who constitute the council, rule over the entire community, and it is therefore the stated Palauan view that half the authority over each title "is held by the public."

If the council disapproves of its candidate, the lineage must repeat the process and choose another to represent it on the council (Palau Society of Historians 1997, 4–5).

On Lamotrek, clan and territorial chiefs are assisted by subchiefs known as *tela* (adze) and administrators called *ochang*. Nonchiefly clans are represented in council by their *telalïhailang* (adze of the clan), "whose power is *theoretically* less than that" of a chief or adze (Alkire 1989, 32–33). I emphasize Alkire's qualification that a nonchiefly clan's leader "theoretically" has less authority, because it affirms my point that, in the end, leadership depends at least as much on the abilities of individual leaders as it does on the structure of government. Throughout Micronesia, individuals without the highest rank or titles may in fact be the most influential figures in their communities. At meetings of Lamotrek's entire male population each lineage is represented by its leader. Men of lesser status speak only if they disagree significantly with their leader: "At the end of the meeting a decision depends on implied unanimity of opinion. If any disagreement remained such a decision would be postponed until a later meeting; thus, ample time is given for tempers to cool (if the argument has been heated) and for the general public opinion to express itself, which any single individual or kin group would find difficult to oppose" (Alkire 1989, 35–36).

In the Marshalls leadership consists of multiple categories, including those that Mason (1947, 53–54) listed as *iroij lapalap* (paramount chief), *iroij elap* (chief), *iroij erik* (minor chief), *iroij in til* (leader), *bwirak elap* (noble), *bwirak* (lesser noble), and *jib* (fringe of nobility). Both Mason and Spoehr suggest that vagueness about the specific qualities and duties of these ranks was the consequence of a recent process of simplification (Mason 1947, 54; Spoehr 1949, 75–77), but Micronesian status systems in general seem to have built in heightened ambiguity as they grew increasingly elaborate.

I again stress my sense both that because Micronesian polities are so similar to one another and because they have survived and thrived for so long, I cannot conceive of their formats as being simply accidental or random adaptations. Everything I have learned about Micronesia tells me its peoples have reflected thoughtfully on how their political systems work. And I find that these conceptual frameworks resonate with the ideas of some of the world's most influential political thinkers, specifically Machiavelli, Hobbes, Locke, and Rousseau.[12] In his work on the nature of republics, *The Discourses on Livy,* as well as in the much more celebrated *The Prince,* Machiavelli consistently treated the ultimate point of leadership, whether by the people themselves or by a single man, as providing the community with good government and held that the primary purpose of good government was to preserve the community's autonomy. This could to some extent be accomplished, he argued, by reflecting on human character and social dynamics and then establishing rules for conduct that deal with things as they are, not as we should like them to be. Hobbes, in *Leviathan*, approached the development of government with a similar emphasis on the importance of reason, holding that people sought to find ways of bettering their lives through improved security. To the extent that they were able to accomplish this, they did so by means of consent, agreeing to place authority in the hands of one who could effectively exercise it. Locke emphasized the importance of privately held property both in providing people with the ability to restrain the authority of those to whose leadership they had consented, and in providing them with the leverage that enabled them to withdraw their consent. Rousseau saw that consent was most effectively achieved in small, face-to-face communities.

In my efforts to understand Micronesian political systems and to say something useful about them, I have come to see that Micronesians can be understood to apply similar principles in their own lives. They are concerned with constituting effective governments guided by responsible political systems. But they are conscious of how easily leaders and governments can be corrupted by the authority invested in them, and thus take essentially equal and simultaneous steps to restrain, constrain, and limit their leaders. They do this in a great many ways. They disperse power and responsibility among different levels of political organization. High chiefs are checked or counterbalanced by local chiefs. Territorial chiefs are offset by lineage chiefs. Chiefs, as executives, are limited by councils. Chiefly offices are often paired, so that those with sacred status are offset by those with secular authority. And in their personal demeanors and patterns of social interaction, Micronesians cultivate habits of rectitude and concealment that make it difficult, if not impossible, for leaders to assert their authority in ways that would allow them to convince their people that chiefs hold greater powers or are able to exercise them more effectively than they actually do (Petersen 1993). The sacred aura with which chiefs are imbued is counterposed both by the overwhelming familiarity and intimacy of interpersonal relations inherent in small-scale communities and by the fabric of respect that is due (and routinely shown) to anyone who is advanced in years or genealogically senior. Several thousand years of Micronesian chieftainship have not convinced Micronesians that their chiefs are divinities who must be unquestioningly obeyed. This is not happenstance; it is a consequence of deliberate political architecture.

Warfare

Thus far my account of Micronesian political life has minimized the significance of violence. It has done so for at least two reasons. First, I believe the political skills Micronesians marshal in order to resolve conflict without resort to armed violence have been seriously underestimated by many scholars. And second, I believe that at least some Micronesians clearly understood what they were doing as they created institutions and pursued actions intended to curtail violence. To be sure, however, armed conflict has played a notable part in a wide range of Micronesian social activities; in many ways Micronesians are a martial people. But of much greater significance, I think, is the role that their awareness of the possibilities of violence has played in stimulating them to pursue means of avoiding the open outbreak of hostilities, both within and between communities.

Warfare—that is, organized hostilities and violence—is a dynamic aspect of Micronesian governments. Though by no means conducted solely by the governments of territorial chiefdoms (as opposed to lineages and their chiefs), the management of military activities is certainly among their primary functions. I use the term "war" here to refer to organized hostilities between communities, rather than conflicts between descent groups within communities. Because every mature male is expected to be able to participate in armed conflict (and most are apparently eager to do so), personal bravery is an important aspect of Micronesian cultural expectations; it is especially evident in celebrations of the warrior ethos, attributions of mana, and the recognition of special abilities. For these reasons combat is deemed the task of mature men, not youths. Warfare is steeped into the fiber of Micronesian social and cultural life, although it is not as prevalent as oral accounts often make it appear, nor is it always as violent as it is made out to be when it does take place. But always there is the potential for real havoc.

Although my own preference is to limit use of the terms "war" and "warfare" to activities organized by communities' governments (that is, the purview of territorially based leadership), this is not how Micronesians generally conceptualize them. In the Pohnpeian language, which I take as reasonably representative of the rest of Micronesia, several words commonly refer to combat. *Pei* (fight) is used to speak of both individual encounters and those between larger groups. *Mahwin* refers to larger-scale hostilities and can mean either "battle" or "war." But no distinction is made between armed conflict among descent groups and among communities. Past conflicts are frequently spoken of in terms of an invasion by one descent group or another, but this may simply refer to the chiefly descent group that led an attack by one community on another. Because so much of war's everyday relevance comes from mythohistorical conquests of communities, in which one leading descent group is replaced by another, it is difficult, if not impossible, to distinguish between conflicts fought between communities and those fought between lineages.

It is equally important to understand that in using the terms "war" and "warfare," I am not implying that Micronesians fight in ways that are in any significant way comparable to the waging of armed conflict between large nation-states with standing armies. However well-organized Micronesian military affairs might be, they are of necessity small-scale, rarely including more than a hundred or so combatants on either side. What Micronesians speak of as "wars" are most often what modern historians would refer to as battles; their "battles" would be termed raids or skirmishes. Pohnpeians tell stories of how in at least some of these engagements the combatants faced off against one another, doing no more than exchanging insults and abuse and hurling occasional spears and sling-stones. On Yap the outcomes of combat are sometimes prearranged. This is not to say that there are no episodes of genuine homicide, but precisely because of the emphasis on warrior codes of honor, noncombatants are rarely endangered, except in specific, individual acts of vengeance.

The causes for fighting in Chuuk (as described by Goodenough) are probably representative of those in all Micronesian societies. They include men's anger at too-frequent courting of their community's women by men from another area; a chief's desire to extend his domain; desire for control over resources, especially fishing grounds; desire for goods and land as the price of peace; chiefs' rivalry for fame; disputes over land; desire for revenge; and competition for possession of a chiefly title (Goodenough 2002, 273).

Because of the distance separating so many of the island populations, warfare can in fact be quite difficult to pursue. When it does take place, it is likely to require a good deal of planning and organization. Chuuk's military specialists (itang) are celebrated for their strategic acumen, not their fighting skills. But there are significant accounts of attacks being launched across considerable stretches of open sea, and these are of necessity planned, organized, and implemented with great care.

Because most Micronesian warfare is conducted in the form of skirmishes, raids, and small-scale battles, and there are no standing armies to threaten either their own or neighboring communities, there is little need for defensive fortifications. Hilltop redoubts were at some point constructed in Palau and Chuuk and appear occasionally elsewhere, but in at least some cases these are more likely to serve as shrines or temples than actual forts. Pohnpei has extensive stoneworks at the inland site of Sapwtakai (whose name means "stony ground"), where they are linked to a major, locally celebrated conflict known as the War at Sapwtakai, and also at Nan Madol, the vast complex of artificial islets on the island's eastern fringing reef, some of which are surmounted by massive stoneworks. Nan Dowas, the largest structure there, is without peer in the island Pacific and has often been described as a fortress, but it is in fact a tomb site. Similar construction, on a somewhat smaller scale, was also undertaken at a site known as Lelu in Kosrae. Channels and canals in both Nan Madol and Lelu indicate that neither was built to resist invasion; indeed, both were in use as ceremonial and/or residential centers when Europeans first arrived.

The most visually arresting evidence of Micronesian warfare comes from Kiribati. The American naval explorer Charles Wilkes, published an extensive account of his travels in the islands, including his lengthy interviews with two shipwrecked sailors who had long been stranded there. His report on the islands includes several striking engravings of sennit armor and shark-tooth–studded weapons made and worn by men of Tabiteuea, and he describes the men there as marked with scars, evidently from battles. From this evidence he concludes, "War seems to be one of the principal employments of these people" (Wilkes 1845, 47). The Wilkes engravings have been widely reproduced, and in later years a photographer in Fiji also posed a Kiribati man in his studio, wearing a set of this armor (d'Ozouville 1997). As the full text of Wilkes' report makes clear, however, the weapons and armor were recent adoptions, in response to the depredations of foreign whaling ships' crews. The weapons and armor were in fact observed only on the island most affected by these experiences; in most of the other islands Wilkes saw neither war implements nor many scars (1845, 66, 72).

John Kirby, an English whaler who had been shipwrecked on Kuria for three years and whom Wilkes described as intelligent, fluent in the language, and observant of local customs, told Wilkes that "armour has been only a short time introduced or in use on the islands, and is not yet common in all of them" (Wilkes 1845, 93). In fact, Kirby described the people he knew as quite peaceful; there had been no war on any of the three islands where he had lived during his three years there (Wilkes 1845, 90). The second castaway, Robert Wood, told Wilkes that in his seven years on Makin he saw only one man put to death and that there had been no wars there for one hundred years (Wilkes 1845, 93). It is likely, then, that this most striking example of Micronesian warfare represents a response to foreign influences rather than traditional practices.[13]

Warfare and Chieftainship

Although the ultimate origins of chieftainship are irretrievably lost in the era of the ancient societies that first moved out of insular Southeast Asia, through the island Pacific, and onward into Micronesia, most Pacific island societies have retained the basic notion of chieftainship. One reason for this is that chiefs provide communities with the appearance of effective military organization. The role of chief (as opposed to the actions of specific individuals) is meant to enlist and channel the aid of the supernatural world (including deities and ancestral spirits) in protecting the community from natural hazards and to provide it simultaneously with the appearance of a sociopolitical hierarchy effective enough militarily to defend the community successfully from invaders. The ranked sequences of titles and the emphasis on descent from spiritually charged, and sometimes divine, ancestors create the appearance of both effective organization and leaders possessing supernatural powers.

The appearance of order is intended especially to convince potential invaders to reconsider their intentions. It has many internal or domestic purposes as well (such as organizing competitive dance performances and feasts), but these are generally subordinate to the larger purpose of generating propaganda for external consumption. Virtually every fine-grained ethnography of Micronesian societies provides evidence that although people readily speak of their leaders' potency, they are often given to ignoring those with whom they disagree or whose strictures they find burdensome. Most Micronesians are quite capable of insisting on the sacred character of their leaders, and on their own readiness to obey their chiefs without hesitation, even while nonchalantly going on to do exactly as they choose.[14]

With a few important exceptions, everything we know about traditional Micronesian societies comes from the reports of outsiders, representing powerful and potentially disruptive forces; these include explorers, traders, missionaries, the military, colonial administrators, and anthropologists. Micronesians find it in their interests to portray their communities to these outsiders as well organized and capable of defending their interests.[15] As a consequence, much of the data available to us emphasizes the strength and authority of chiefs. There are repeated assertions that the word or the rule of the chief is "absolute" in early ethnological accounts of Micronesian societies, especially those of the Germans, who for the most part were writing at a time when notions about ancient Teutonic feudal rights and obligations were dueling with the liberal and imperial ideologies entailed in the rise of the modern German nation-state.[16]

But Micronesians have largely been quite prepared to hail their chiefs' authority even as they continue to do pretty much as they themselves deem appropriate. Some people steer away from dealing with chiefs whenever possible in order to avoid having to conform publicly to the etiquette of obedience. Others simply say one thing and do another. Moreover, as I have explained, the autonomy provided by land tenure systems that place most direct control over lands in the descent groups that occupy them assures that these groups retain access to resources, enabling them to disregard or even defy the territorial chief. And because of the importance of the warrior ethos in Micronesian cultures, nearly every adult male is in a position to act—that is, to fight—not only in support of the community but, if need be, in opposition to its chief.

Despite the key roles chiefs play in the defense of their communities, they are not necessarily warriors or war leaders. In the Marshalls, where in the early contact period several paramount chiefs engaged in expanding their realms by incorporating neighboring atolls into them, special war leaders *(leatoktok)* apparently played a significant part in a victorious chief's successes (Rynkiewich 1972, 147).

Although Pohnpei's semidivine culture hero, Isokelekel, legendarily conquered the island by driving out the despotic Sau Deleur dynasty before he established the modern Nahnmwarki system of paramount chiefs, these men are sacred and usually quite elderly; they are not warriors. Before competitive feasting took on its great significance in contemporary Pohnpeian culture, participation in combat was looked on as one of the primary ways in which men achieved status, but there does not seem to be a special category of war leaders (Petersen 1982b). In Chuuk the war specialists, *itang*, are charged with much of the organization that goes into preparing for battle, and while chiefs can serve as war leaders, there is a preference for the *itang* to do so (Goodenough 2002, 275); it was not the chief who led his people to war. On Yap there is a *tagac*, or "renowned warrior," in each village, and these warriors lead "in warfare with the approval of the chief." War is commonly "a method of political maneuvering" used by leaders to consolidate political power and providing "chiefs powers that the ideology of Yapese culture denies." Thus chiefs do not themselves commonly engage in combat but instead "prearrange" the war's outcome (Lingenfelter 1975, 110, 171, 175). Kosrae's chiefs are uniformly described as elderly men, hardly active warriors.

Although warrior qualities and abilities are important in achieving status and can be interpreted as manifestations of an individual's mana almost everywhere in Micronesia, there seems to be no Micronesia-wide pattern of chiefly behavior in war: chieftainship per se depends more on the image of effective organization it projects than on the specific actions of chiefs. Given the prevalence of storms and droughts, life is already precarious enough on all but the big islands east of the typhoon belt—Pohnpei and Kosrae. Communities require the organizational talents of leaders not only to spur them on to production levels that can help them weather these trials but also to protect them from populations displaced by environmental calamities and seeking new homes or at least temporary access to resources. Though Yapese warfare plays a major role in local political life, the fact that the outcomes of wars are sometimes prearranged suggests that it is the threat and appearance of war, and not the actual destruction of resources or displacement of populations, that is most important. Given the tenuous nature of existence on so many of these islands, Micronesians do not deem it a good idea either to kill those on whom they might later need to depend, nor to lose potential allies who might in time help defend them. Instead, cultivating warlike demeanors coupled with effective means of defusing and preventing, or at least limiting, war seems more effective. This does not mean, of course, that such strategies always succeed or are unfailingly pursued.

The implications of all this for the nature of Micronesian politics and government should be obvious. Despite differences in symbolic aspects and in the numbers of layers or levels of chiefly organization, the underlying principles remain much the same across the many islands and societies in the region. But even though chieftainship depends so thoroughly on a chief's channeling of mana and his general ability to protect the community, it is not ultimately about leading the community in war or waging war on its behalf. In addition to the societies that have specified war leaders who are not chiefs, there are others where, because of the gerontocratic aspects of government (e.g., in Kosrae and Pohnpei, where men work their way upward through a ranked sequence of titles, or Ulithi, which Lessa describes as "mildly gerontocratic" [1966, 31]), men do not ordinarily become high-ranking chiefs until they are elderly. Although able performance in war can play a part in the process of working one's way upward toward a chiefly title, especially since succession to chieftainship is somewhat ambiguous in most of these societies, it is not a shared aspect of chieftainship. Micronesian chieftainship does not seem to rest on physical force or violence either in its origins or for its continued salience and success. Any theory attempting to explain chieftainship by emphasizing its violent or physically forceful aspects runs into a stumbling block. While coercive authority is commonly attributed to chiefs, their actual ability or propensity to compel obedience is idiosyncratic—it does not fully inhere in the roles themselves but is largely a product of individual personalities.

Micronesia nevertheless abounds with examples of institutionalized, culturally esteemed warfare. Mythohistorical legends of great battles, invasions, and extraordinarily heroic warriors are recounted everywhere. Many of the mythohistorical charters for chiefly descent groups are rooted in conquest. And perhaps most tellingly, dance performances from all over Micronesia rely extensively on martial themes. Among the earliest accounts we have of the Carolinian atolls are detailed descriptions of elaborate spear and stick dances (Barratt 1984, 71). In some communities these war dances provide one of the readiest forms of release for pent-up or repressed emotions. In societies where a great premium is placed on disguising or concealing hostility and other negatively charged emotions, which most Micronesian societies do, occasional frays or more frequent dance practices and performances provide an important emotional outlet.[17] Indeed, it might be argued that some of the emphasis laid on the warrior ethos is intended to accomplish precisely this—to allow a channel for suppressed interpersonal conflict.

The fact is that Micronesian societies have placed enormous emphasis on concealing and harnessing conflict and on channeling hostility into positive forms. Pohnpei's formal apology ritual, *tohmw*, amply illustrates this process. When an injury, physical or otherwise, is incurred by one party, whether by accident or intention, the community's leaders act quickly to bear a kava plant in front of the leader of the injured descent group or family, prepare the kava, and, by means of

Yap. Young men performing a war dance, during the 1910 German ethnographic expedition. Micronesians throughout the islands perform similar martial dances. Courtesy of the Micronesian Seminar.

proffered cups of kava and repeated requests for forgiveness, render both an apology from the offending party and its acceptance by the injured party. In Pohnpeian theory, at least, the use of kava, which has enormous spiritual force, in this context means that no one, not even a paramount chief, can refuse to accept an apology so offered; this in turn means that revenge can be ruled out. And it is indeed unusual for such an apology to be refused.

Pohnpeians, like other Micronesians, also possess spells meant to bind up ruptured social relations and restore calm, even where injured sensibilities still remain. Perhaps most significantly in this context, Pohnpeians today maintain that in the past, when a community member was killed by someone from another community or part of the island, the culturally approved practice was to determine the clan membership of the perpetrator, select someone from the victim's community of this same clan, and then have him avenge the killing by taking the culprit's life. This was done deliberately in order to have the act of vengeance carried out between members of the same clan, thus bringing the dispute swiftly and directly to closure.

While Micronesian governments are to some extent organized around warfare and related activities, then, and Micronesian culture celebrates the warrior's role, we can see that Micronesian societies possess a full repertory of ways in which violence and open warfare may be staved off. The extensive means of avoiding open hostilities at their disposal, coupled with the elaborate cultural emphases on warrior roles, make it clear that violence is always perceived as possible and not always avoidable, but it must be understood that force is not the primary manner through which governments conduct their community's political affairs.

Foreign Relations

To the extent that war, as Clausewitz wrote, is the continuation of politics by other means, chiefs are responsible for that which warfare continues: foreign relations. This is not the sort of terminology that is ordinarily applied to the political practices in small island societies, but there is no good reason to deny them the respect due their diplomatic skills. In Micronesia, foreign relations are almost by definition as much the province of descent groups and their leaders as they are the mandate of territorial chiefs. The very nature of Micronesian societies, organized as they are around lineages nested hierarchically within clans and subclans, hinges on the notion that organizing interactions among groups of people living in different places is simultaneously the task of both dispersed branches of descent groups and territorial leadership. When these relations are managed by members of different branches of the same extended descent group, we tend to speak of them in terms of kinship; when they are dealt with by territorial leaders, we lump them with politics. Both sorts of interactions, however, are crucial to survival in the islands, and both can rightly be referred to as foreign relations.

At the core of everything I have been portraying as typically or essentially Micronesian is the web of ties between and among communities and societies spread across this vast expanse of the Central Pacific. That is, relations linking together dispersed branches of descent groups assure individuals, families, and lineages that they will be able to obtain aid from kin residing in areas less affected by storms, droughts, and other sorts of trials, whether visited upon them by natural or social forces. On the other hand, foreign relations in the charge of the chiefs of places—of communities or islands—are focused more on defense of the entire community; they are intended to demonstrate that a community or island is capable of coordinating the efforts of all its localized descent groups effectively enough to repel outside attempts at invasion or conquest. These responsibilities are by no means mutually exclusive; as in all realms of social activity in Micronesia, distinctions among categories of people and groups—whether based on gender, age, descent, or other criteria—are rarely hard-and-fast.

In dealing with these foreign relations—relatively large-scale, formalized interactions between communities or islands—chiefs are not viewed as the heads of specific descent groups. Rather, they are spoken of and treated as the leaders of the entire community or place. They represent not just one or another of the constituent elements of the place's population, but the entire populace. They are, in the technical terms of international relations theorists, sovereigns and are treated as such in the course of interactions between island societies. On many islands paramount chiefs are charged with the conduct of external or foreign relations as their principal responsibility. Two examples are Etal (Nason 1974, 126) and Ulithi (Lessa 1966, 34; Figirliyong 1977, 12). Palauans have what Useem termed a system of "in-facing" and "out-facing" chiefs; that is, "some group-arrived-at decisions are not communicated to non-members, and some social functions are not performed in front of outsiders," whereas other sets of behavior are intended expressly for outsiders (1945, 586–587). Similarly, Lamotrek has a "chief for for-eigners" (Alkire 1989, 163). Although some of these forms have evolved partly in response to colonial pressures, they have largely grown out of indigenous practices and institutions.

Such relations can be quite complex, inasmuch as members of one or another of a community's localized descent groups may find themselves in a position of being expected to defend the community from an invasion by distant relations, that is, members of their own clan. But it is precisely this interweaving of mul-tiple sorts of ties that provides Micronesian societies with bonds strong enough to ensure survival in often-tenuous environments. By having two complementary sets or sorts of social organization, one based on co-residence in a specific place and the other on kin ties among people residing in widely separated places, they provide themselves with enhanced opportunities both to reach out to communi-ties in other places when in need and to defend themselves from other communi-ties when they are threatened.

What is more, these two discrete but relatively complete and competent sets of sociopolitical relations serve equally to establish checks against any who might seek to abuse their authority. As Alkire points out in his discussion of Lamotrek's complementary chiefly systems, "Even though the rights of a chief derived from the multiple sources of kinship and territoriality, the decision of one chief would not often come into conflict with that of another" (1989, 68). The dual systems do not ordinarily overlap but instead enable individuals and lineages to play one off against another when they believe it to be in their interest.

Nearly every aspect of Micronesian leadership involves some degree of dual-ity or multiplicity of chieftainship. Despite the hereditary aspects of chiefly suc-cession and the powers ascribed to the chiefs, Micronesians have managed at every turn to place checks in the way of anyone who would abuse his authority. Foreign relations are likewise conducted along these two tracks. Much of what needs to be done is accomplished by localized lineages maintaining relations with members of the same clan or subclan residing elsewhere. The entire community benefits from these relations because goods and services circulate constantly through communities. At the same time, however, all the localized descent groups in a community, in recognizing a common chief of the place, guarantee themselves the means of mounting a coordinated defense in times of danger.

CHAPTER 7

Politics and Leadership

I AM DISTINGUISHING between government and politics because even though Micronesian chiefs occupy reasonably well-defined offices, which can be appropriately viewed as island governments, politics permeate nearly every aspect of island lives. Micronesian political life is characterized by opposing pulls between quite inclusive participation in a community's decision making, on the one hand, and the hierarchical organization of authority and responsibility, on the other. Within lineages, most individuals actually have relatively equal rights and responsibilities; within communities, most lineages have well-established rights and responsibilities. Hierarchy and rank are fundamental to Micronesian political life but exist within a participatory context, recognizing that every individual and group possesses legitimate interests in the community's continued success. Competition for social status is a fundamental aspect of Micronesian politics precisely because there is a significant degree of social mobility among individuals and groups. Politics and leadership in Micronesian societies can be understood only as growing out of this continual interplay between hierarchy and equality. Although hierarchy and equality are often treated as if they are opposite poles, in Micronesia they are complementary aspects of an essentially common political culture.

Feasting and Competition

Everywhere in Micronesia, as in the rest of Oceania, people engage regularly in ritual and celebratory feast making. There are many sorts of feasts and many occasions for them, but in general, feasts are occasions when groups of people—from as few as two households to the entire populations of several communities—come together and ceremonially exchange food and often other sorts of goods. Many feasts include singing, dancing, speech making, praying, mourning, or rejoicing; most entail good fellowship, generosity, kindness, and earnest competition to see who can provide the most. "First fruits" feasts and rituals are among the most common. They may be elaborate or quite minimal, but in essence they all reflect the same underlying assumptions: at the beginning of harvest seasons for all important crops, a portion of the first food harvested by each household or lineage is presented to the chief, in recognition of his authority over the land and his lineage's residual rights over it.

Micronesians organize and make feasts to mark a wide range of events or relationships, including, most prominently, first fruits and other seasonal subsistence activities; life-cycle events such as weddings and funerals; and the acknowledgment of political relations. Feasts—though manifestly made to mark specific occurrences—are commonly intended as means of demonstrating an individual's, household's, lineage's, or community's productive abilities, generosity, and commitment to the common good. They also provide ways of establishing, acknowledging, or enhancing relationships, and in time they will entail repayment, either in kind—that is, a reciprocal feast—or in some other form of compensation.

Because of their diverse functions, feasts are means to a multiplicity of ends. While chieftainship personifies Micronesian government, it is through feasting that the public flow of political activity is channeled. In particular, first fruits and related rites both recognize the authority of the chiefly group and propitiate its ancestral spirits. This lies at the heart of chieftainship's ritual character. The ruling descent group bases its authority on its having first settled the place over which it reigns or else on its having achieved some form of conquest; in either case there is a clear notion that its ancestral spirits are the ones most closely and effectively engaged in assuring the place's security and bounty. There is an expectation—or perhaps a hope—that when people ritually honor their chief, his descent group's ancestral spirits will be persuaded to bestow rewards on the entire community or at least allow them to survive comfortably. It is in feasting practices, along with councils, that Micronesian political life becomes fully participatory and at least partly meritocratic.

When the harvest season begins in Chuuk, "the people pay homage with offerings and are reminded of the protection from the supernatural and enemies on earth that the chief affords them." These chief's feasts *(umwi samon)* are both economically and socially beneficial in that they have "a tendency to build social solidarity and identity with the group in a society where cohesive forces are constant at the family level only." What is more, "the additional production of food required by the chief's feast provides a surplus to be used during lean years" (Hall and Pelzer 1946, 25–26). Although the scale of Chuuk's political institutions is somewhat smaller than that of other high-island societies, massive wooden bowls *(uunong)*, which constitute a substantial portion of a lineage's possessions, are used to present prepared breadfruit to the chiefs, and communities participate in "competitive races" with one another (LeBar 1964, 14–15; Hall and Pelzer 1946, 24). Competing with food, Goodenough observes, enables a lineage or a community simultaneously to provide hospitality to others and to compete with them, and the great chiefs of the legendary past were celebrated for the size and numbers of feasts they gave (2002, 265).

In the Marshalls, feasting promotes island-wide solidarity as lineages and other sorts of social groups exchange food with one another, forging "an interdependent and sustainable community" while at the same time competing for status "by giving more and more highly ranked valuables, thereby increasing one's rank through indebtedness." At the same time, these gifts are also offered to the ancient deities or spirits "with the intention of creating indebtedness"—that is, assuring that nature and natural resources are beneficent (Carucci 1997, 36, 67, 78–79, 179).

In Yap's competitive feasts *(mitmit)*, village chiefs serve as leaders. They engage in ceremonial exchanges, first accumulating great quantities of food and valuables and then presenting them to other communities. As Lingenfelter notes, "The chiefs do not collect for the sake of collecting. Collections are made for ritual or political ends, to assure the good of the people through religious observances or to achieve some political goal. This is not to say that the chiefs are not self-seeking, but rather that the desire to remain in power curbs any self-seeking tendencies" (1975, 145). Ultimately, "rank and jurisdiction of political power are demonstrated" through these exchanges (Lingenfelter 1975, 181). And even on the adjacent atolls, where the resource base is markedly smaller than on the high island, people engage in competitive feasting (Lessa 1966, 19).

In Palau the status of a district is determined by the ability of its capital village to stage elaborate ceremonial feasts *(mur, mulbekl, ruk)* attended by dignitaries from allied villages (Parmentier 1987, 90). At large *mur el beluu* (village feasts), one-half of the village fetes the other half (Palau Society of Historians 1997, 62–63).

Much of Pohnpeian life revolves around an elaborate cycle of feasts that are known collectively as *kamadipw*, which translates as "to beat the brush," in reference to the lengths to which people go to make their land yield up sufficient quantities of foodstuffs so that they may excel in the island's highly competitive political economy. Some of these feasts specifically honor chiefs; some are first-fruits offerings; some mark events in the life cycles of individuals; and some are straightforward competitions between descent groups, communities, or individuals. Enormous quantities of Pohnpeian feast goods—yams, kava, and pigs (a post-contact replacement for dogs)—are presented, prepared, and distributed at these feasts, and the status of men and women and their families is very much influenced by their abilities to make and contribute to feasts.

In Kiribati, where food surpluses are less pronounced than in most of Micronesia (and where droughts in the southernmost islands make for one of the least habitable environments in the region), in order for an individual or family to be deemed worthy of respect, it must have an ample variety of prestige foods (Geddes et al. 1982, 43). The explorer Wilkes wrote that feasting and dancing were more important here than war (1845, 99).

Although Kosrae is more centralized than other parts of Micronesia, feasts nevertheless play a significant role in political advancement as well as marking life-cycle events. As Phillip Ritter observed there, "Considerable effort was spent in competitive feasting" (1978, 20; cf. Lewis 1967, 13).

It is in the competitive aspects of feasting that we are able to observe fully the degree to which achievement and participation are absolutely central to the composition of government. Groups possess leadership positions at least as much because of their members' abilities as because of their genealogies. The extent of the resources available to them—in terms of both land and labor—determines how well they can continue to demonstrate their right to reign. This is not to say that control of leadership positions is based simply or largely upon material achievement; it most certainly is not. But a group must be able to manifest its mana in order to retain its legitimacy, and in Micronesia this is done through acts that entail mobilizing resources, giving away goods, and accruing honor. Individuals prove themselves, and thus their right to lead their respective descent groups, in the same way. They must demonstrate these qualities to both their lineage mates and to the community at large. In other words, Micronesian feasting is *potlatching*, to use a term anthropologists have borrowed from the competitive feasts of the Native American societies of North America's northwest coast.

Political Ability and Style

Micronesian chiefs are not simply leaders; they are officeholders. Those who hold the highest titles are generally believed to possess special ties to ancestral and supernatural beings and forces. Their genealogies and abilities together justify and legitimize both the offices themselves and their rights to them. Chiefs are under continual scrutiny and must be responsive to public opinion and pressure. It is rare, though it does happen, for individuals to succeed to chiefly titles before they are fully mature, if not middle-aged or elderly. Their behavior and personal qualities have been observed by the entire community for decades. Their participation in social activities, many of them competitive, and in the ordinary flow of daily social life has been closely monitored. By the time they become full-fledged holders of important titles, their leadership abilities and styles are already well known.

Age thus plays a significant part in Micronesian politics. Several qualifications, however, should be kept in mind. First, though the elderly are universally respected in Micronesian societies, respect in and of itself does not translate into authority, especially when it is so widely accorded. Second, the advanced ages of those wielding authority, in combination with the general familiarity everyone in a community has with every other member, mean that those who ultimately do

Chuuk. A man with a frigate-bird feather and a comb in his hair, during the 1910 German ethnographic expedition. His ornaments are typical symbols of leadership in societies of the central Caroline Islands. Courtesy of the Micronesian Seminar.

achieve high office have been carefully vetted by their constituencies. And third, because of their physical limitations, the highest-ranking leaders are often those least likely to be able to physically compel obedience—they are able to lead through the prestige of their office, through their character, and by example, rather than by brute force.

Because chiefs everywhere in Micronesia govern through councils, they are generally unable to dictate. If they are to execute their duties, they must remain modest, respectful, thoughtful, and generous. Arrogance and arbitrariness are likely to get them nowhere, although these traits are sometimes encountered. Barnett described a Palauan "obsession" with ambition, but he also wrote that in Palau "everyone is humble, poor and unimportant" (1960, 15). Even the most capable leaders are likely to downplay their abilities. To the extent that Micronesian leadership qualities can be directly observed at all, they are multiple, nuanced, ambiguous, and complex. But for our purposes here I will point to three key aspects of these qualities.

Chiefs must first be able to listen to what the members of their communities are saying and to interpret what they mean. This requires enormous sensitivity, something Micronesians are trained in as a matter of course while they are children. In most cases such sensitivity depends on a capacity to sit quietly and pay attention, which in part accounts for a fundamental aspect of Micronesian political style: it is, above all else, low-key. Palauan leaders, for example, are especially quiet (Useem 1946, 64), and Palauans call politics the "way of whispers" (Parmentier 1987, 72). People who are given to speaking a great deal are not usually much listened to. On Pohnpei they may be gently derided. I have heard individuals described as "skilled at talking, unskilled at doing."

Second, chiefs are expected to be generous. Generosity is by itself a practice or personal attribute Micronesians value immensely and is looked upon as a sign of worthiness in its own right. But in societies where so much of social interaction and interpersonal relations is based on exchange of food and other goods, generosity is also essential to the cultivation of successful political relations. One who is merely skillful enough to be productive is respected for his or her abilities. But one who produces and then gives away what is produced is not merely garnering respect but also earning social credit, investing in the community, as it were, and reaping benefits in terms of support when it is needed to influence community opinion. From this habitual generosity flows the common notion, already noted, that, like fathers, chiefs and other leaders should "take care of" the community and its people (Marshall 1972, 29; Wilson 1976, 188).

Third, the most effective leaders are those able to combine wisdom, intuition, and social skills with an ability to listen in such a way that they can put forward a program that is simultaneously responsive to what the community is willing to do and thoughtful enough to provide the community with competent direction. Some Micronesian leaders are more forceful or emphatic; others, much less so. There is no single model or style. Useem pointed specifically to competing Palauan stereotypes of chiefs: one strong and ruthless, the other devoted to using authority as a means of advancing conditions for the entire community (1948, 24). Alkire noted that on Lamotrek different personalities among chiefs result in different degrees of authority (1974, 47), and Lessa observed much the same thing on Ulithi (1966, 32). Chuuk's *itang* (war priests) were expected to use their supernatural powers both to make the chiefs they served be feared and authoritative and to encourage public harmony and respect (Goodenough 2002, 314–315).

It is certainly fair to say that communities do not always have effective chiefs, of course. Communities sometimes require little more than a figure around whom to organize, one who can simply keep things moving. As Alkire points out, the measure of a chief is "in his ability to initiate and supervise at the proper time those responses which are well known among the inhabitants" (1989, 70–71). To be sure, it is not always easy to recognize ineffectual leaders. Chiefs who are intellectually gifted may actually disguise their abilities to some extent and rely on others to voice their ideas. In doing so they not only gain the respect that Micronesians pay to the self-effacing but also promote communal participation and thus generate commitment and loyalty.

In the end, what is important is that the well-being of the community is lodged with the collective leadership of all its descent groups and their representatives to the council; in the multiple, ranked titles that enable lower-ranking but politically astute individuals to speak, to guide, and to act; and in institutions that encourage the community's members, or at least a sufficient portion of them, to produce and exchange goods, not simply within the community but also with other communities and islands. This Micronesian emphasis on exchange and redistribution of every sort of goods and possessions results in a most complex interweaving of equality and hierarchy.

Equality and Hierarchy

Despite the many aspects of participation, competition, and achievement entailed in the concept of chieftainship, it depends fundamentally on notions of social rank. Some groups and individuals have more of it than others. Those who are chiefs ostensibly hold their positions because of the status of their lineages and because of their ranks within their lineages. An individual does not ordinarily become chief without some preexisting social rank or the capacity to make effective claims to it, but in the end one's personal rank, as well as the rank of one's lineage, is enhanced by the effective exercise of chiefly duties and prerogatives. At the same time, however, Micronesian emphasis on keeping leaders and government effectively in check, as well as an underlying philosophical outlook that views government as being both charged with the community's well-being and inherently threatening to it, promotes a pervasive sense of equality.

Micronesians consider it the task of their chiefly governments to serve them, and in some contexts they have high expectations of their leaders. As I have already pointed out, in addition to the many other qualities chiefs are expected to demonstrate (e.g., compassion, intelligence, respect, bravery), they must also be generous. A Pohnpeian once questioned my suggestion that people in his society engage in elaborate feast-making practices largely in order to gain prestige and thus advance in political rank (Petersen 1987). Pohnpeians, he said, hold generosity *(sapan)* in high regard for its own sake. This is true, but there are nevertheless differences between simply being seen as an intrinsically good person and pursuing a reputation as one able to give munificently. As another Pohnpeian confided to me, the people of the community wanted her husband, who was one of a group of brothers eligible to become the next chief, to be the one who succeeded to the chieftainship because he was the most productive and generous among them. "We Pohnpeians like our chiefs to give us things," she said. In the overall organization of Micronesian political life, it is not merely a generous spirit that counts, but also the actual transfer of goods from those who have to those who do not. If Micronesian politics can to some extent be characterized by the importance attributed to differences in rank, Micronesian economics can to a similar extent be characterized by the equality that results from what might be called leveling behavior.

Because people expect generosity from their chiefs, the legitimacy and success of these leaders depend on their willingness to redistribute portions of the gifts they receive by virtue of their residual rights over land—that is, the presentations made to them as first fruits and tribute. In this there are differences between high and low islands. On the high islands the natural environments permit economies of abundance. Competitive feasts motivate households' productive activities. Those with good land, ample labor, aspirations for chiefly titles, and sufficient ambition engage in a great deal of work in agriculture, fishing, and crafts. They are able to accumulate goods at a significantly higher rate than other households. But the point of this accumulation is to be able to engage in competitive generosity—to give away more than others. This serves multiple purposes. It demonstrates their inherent generosity; it creates obligations on the part of those who receive goods from them; and it clearly manifests their mana, the spiritual powers of their ancestors—that is, it demonstrates that they are in good standing with their ancestral spirits and that these spirits are potent and engaged.

On atolls, environmental limitations are more likely to weigh against the superabundance that figures in the competitive feasting characteristic of the higher islands. Nevertheless, the bountiful character of an atoll such as Pingelap enables its people to mirror much of the feasting behavior of neighboring Pohnpei: "The ability to display and distribute large quantities of taro and pigs serves to affirm the affluence of given family units. Prestige is an important element in Pingelapese society, and displaying and awarding important food products provides tangible evidence of material eminence" (Damas 1994, 155). Atoll chiefs, too, are expected to be paragons of generosity. Chiefs in the Marshalls must be generous, fair, and supportive (Rynkiewich 1972, 65; Pollock 1974, 110). On Ifaluk chiefs in general are expected to be generous, and the island's highest chief must give the most lavish gifts (Burrows and Spiro 1970, 126–127). Kiribati is in general characterized by its "staunchly democratic society" and its ethic of absolute egalitarianism (Geddes et al. 1982, 83, 121). Chiefs are expected to immediately redistribute whatever goods they receive from their people (Lambert 1966, 156), and even where chieftainship takes on its most elaborate forms, as in Butaritari, equality is still pervasive (Geddes et al. 1982, 84).

Chieftainship can be best understood in terms of these contrasting pulls. Chiefs and their households engage in accumulation. Certainly they are on the receiving end of so-called tribute payments. And yet they are rarely able to amass much more economic wealth than anyone else in the community—precisely because of all the expectations of generosity on their part. Leading households receive continual requests for aid, gifts, and contributions. Indeed, high-ranking households may in some cases actually appear poorer than others both because of the demands placed on them and because of emphases on modesty and humility. This point helps us understand Barnett's comment that in Palau, despite the ambition of its leaders, "everyone is humble, poor and unimportant" (1960, 15), The European voyagers who visited Kosrae in the 1820s wrote of what they interpreted as an aristocracy, but in fact all their accounts indicate that there was little distinction between the chiefs and the rest of the populace. Feodor Lütke was especially clear about this in his description of the paramount chief, the Tokosra:

> If he had been recognized as supreme chief by all the other chiefs, what in the other islands the Europeans call *King*, he would probably have a little more power than the others, some sign that could distinguish him from them—and at least, he would not have been poor. We saw nothing of this. No one, outside of his presence, concerned himself with Tokosra, and it was only by chance that we learned of his existence. The wealth that he has on the island is of less importance than almost all of the others. (1982, 111–112)

In other words, Micronesian chiefs, despite their rank, are not likely to be significantly wealthier than other members of their communities. Obviously, there are qualifications to this. First and foremost is that chiefly lineages and households do owe some portion of their social status to their political and economic statuses. A large, successful lineage with extensive claims to landholdings is much more likely to be able to establish itself effectively as the ruling lineage. It is more likely than other lineages or households to attract individuals who find themselves landless for one reason or another and are willing to take on roles as retainers or domestic helpers. The group's status is likely to attract in-marrying spouses from prominent lineages or households who bring with them substantial landholdings and who are capable, active workers who make substantial contributions to the household's productivity. Continued successes may enable them to hold on to certain prestige objects or goods over the course of succeeding generations and thus accumulate a few valuable heirlooms, such as woven belts on Pohnpei, large stone disks on Yap, or the ceramic pieces known as money on Palau. And there are the equivalent of sumptuary rules in some Micronesian societies. High-ranking or chiefly families may be permitted to wear certain items of clothing or jewelry or engage in certain actions that others cannot. But these differences are relatively limited in their scope and overall effect on social standing.

All Micronesian societies exhibit some notion of hereditary status. But these inherited status differences do not confer economic benefits of the sort that would allow us to characterize those who possess them as constituting a ruling socioeconomic class. As I have explained, the seniority of certain lineages confers on all their members a degree of social status or rank, and the notion of seniority of descent within the senior lineage is important in determining who will become its leader and thus the community's chief. In this sense, there is something in Micronesia akin to social class. But it is limited by the larger social and cultural contexts. There is in Micronesian societies a clear sense of contractual agreement, or, as classic social theory puts it, consent. As long as first fruits and related ritual presentations are made to chiefs, then the lineages that render them have theoretically unassailable rights to the land they occupy. This means there are virtually no significant economic class differences—and certainly no mutually exclusive classes of landlords and landless workers.

I am not suggesting there are no abuses related to land tenure, but it would be viewed as inappropriate and beyond the chief's legitimate prerogatives if he were to appropriate land from a group that has adequately discharged its responsibilities. That is, senior lineages' residual rights over land are more than counterbalanced by the rights and privileges of the lineages that actually occupy and work the land. The ideologies and rhetoric of seniority and chieftainship can, however, sometimes mask the fact that nonchiefly lineages perceive themselves as quite secure in their tenure and able to resist unwarranted demands placed on them.

To be sure, an expanding lineage can sometimes successfully make what are considered illegitimate claims upon land, but to do so is ordinarily impractical, inasmuch as it is likely to be self-defeating; that is, whatever it stood to gain in economic advantages it might lose in moral authority. As we have seen, the entire organization of lineage-land relations in Micronesian societies is designed to shift land to groups that have an abundance of labor, without requiring conquest or expropriation. And because senior groups are unable to accumulate much wealth, the long-term, self-reproducing character of social class as it is understood elsewhere does not genuinely apply to social differences in Micronesia. As Lessa observed, despite the great importance of rank on Ulithi there is "virtually no social stratification," and "wealth is evenly distributed" (1976, 62).

We can see that there are multiple aspects to the offsetting or counterbalancing tensions between hierarchy and equality. It is important to realize, though, that Micronesians themselves tend to conceptualize this differently. I do not mean that Micronesians would not recognize these descriptions, but that this is not how they are given to formulating their own understandings. Instead, Micronesians practice and believe in what I shall call the reciprocity of respect. What is missing in many ethnological (comparative and theoretical), as opposed to ethnographic (descriptive), accounts of Micronesian politics is recognition that respect does not flow only upwards from people to chiefs. Although Micronesian political principles and practices require that a variety of respect behaviors be shown to chiefs, it is equally the case that respect must also be shown to a variety of other people, including parents, older people in general, certain kinds of siblings and cousins, and even strangers. Respect behaviors do not necessarily imply the existence of political authority. Moreover, one who receives respect is expected to return it—that is, to act in a respectful manner toward those who have shown him or her respect. Even those who exercise political authority are expected to do so respectfully.

The leading principles of political practice *(keluláu)* with which Palauan councils *(klobak)* are charged are respect and honor *(omengull ma omeluu)* (Palau Society of Historians 1997, 11). The Pohnpeian concept *wahu* can be translated as both "respect" and "honor." Pohnpeians have told me that while respect is directed upward from the people to the chiefs and from the chiefs to their ancestors, it equally flows down from on high toward the people. One who is honored is expected to act honorably, a concept hardly unique to Micronesians. John Haglelgam, from Eauripik, in the central Carolines, once discussed with me an extreme form of respect behavior common to many islands in his region, in which a sister lowers herself to the ground, in a posture that sometimes is likened to groveling. This public performance is obvious and has been much remarked upon. But a brother must honor and respect his sister in a variety of everyday forms, some of which are less obvious but nonetheless significant, to the extent that the brother's respect obligations may be greater than his sister's.

On Pohnpei the only persons allowed to raise themselves above a chief, and hence the individuals responsible for managing feasts because only they may walk freely about on the raised platform in a feast house, are the sons of men in the chiefly lineage. No one would suggest that chiefs' sons do not owe their fathers respect and obedience—they are merely indulged a bit more than most people are.

The physical calculus of high and low occurs in culturally distinct forms in different parts of Micronesia, but as a general principle it is pan Micronesian. In and of itself, of course, this tells us nothing more than that respect is due. It does not tell us about the reciprocal respect that flows in the opposite direction. On Ifaluk, along with rank and kindliness, respectful speech is among the most important values. To act in a chiefly manner, a chief must speak respectfully (Burrows and Spiro 1970, 133). The people of Arno "emphasize the reciprocity in relations between chiefs and people" (Rynkiewich 1972, 81). In the Marshalls in general "there is a reciprocal relationship which concerns rights as well as obligations between the chiefly family and those families of commoner status who live on the lands over which the Iroij Lablab exercises authority" (Mason 1986, 3). And in Kiribati it is expected that those who are entitled to respect will earn it (Lambert 1981, 158).

Goodenough describes the expectations on Chuuk:

It was expected of a good chief that he would be *mosonoson* (a person of humility) in his dealings with others and not display *namanam tekija* (arrogant behavior).

For example, it was bad form for a chief personally to express displeasure with people, to scold them publicly, or personally to order them to prepare for one of the regular feasts which were his due. When dealing authoritatively with his people, he was expected to do so indirectly....A chief who orders people around directly is likely to be unpopular (1951, 143)

It is also expected that in the same way that people demonstrate the etiquette of respect toward those of higher status, they show respectful behavior toward those of lower status (Caughey 1977, 29). It may be the case that the low-key demeanor expected of a Chuukese chief is deliberately offset by the tougher approach of the war leader.[1]

Yapese chiefs achieve legitimacy not only through genealogy and land but also through personal characteristics. They must cultivate the support of councils of older men. As Lingenfelter observes, "One of the primary means of gaining such support is through demonstrations of generosity and an attitude of humility. While aggressive behavior is necessary for a chief, it ideally should be covert, and accompanied by an outward manifestation of humility" (1975, 166).

Although Micronesians customarily exalt their leaders when speaking about them in public contexts, especially situations in which outsiders are involved, and act respectfully toward them, in private conversations people often express considerable skepticism about the qualities, character, and powers of the chiefs. That is, while the formal rules of social practice tell us to expect that because chiefs are honored they are honorable, people know that because chiefs are human they are prone to a full array of human weaknesses and foibles. Precisely because they are supposed to exhibit respectable behavior, any failure on their part occasions animated gossip. This pattern is so thoroughly instituted on Pohnpei that there is even a term for it: *pil en pahn mweli*, or "the water under the boulders," refers to the trickling of water under a loose talus of stones (a common phenomenon on an island that receives as much rainfall as Pohnpei), which makes noise but has no effect on anything. It refers to the continual criticisms softly spoken about the behavior of chiefs—this one is lecherous, that one is greedy—that are almost never openly acknowledged or acted on.

It would be easy to conclude mistakenly that public demonstrations of respect and expressions of loyalty accurately reflect the sum total of Micronesians' attitudes toward their chiefs. They do not. Nonetheless, these behaviors have commonly been employed by outsiders to demonstrate the "absolute" and arbitrary powers of chiefs over their people (e.g., Mason 1947, 44; Grimble 1989, 148). But respect postures, forms, and behaviors are as prevalent among the small populations of the Caroline atolls, where chiefs exercise little real potency, as they are in the more densely populated high islands with their much more influential chiefs.

Vastly more telling is the widespread Micronesian sense that power has the potential to corrupt. Lord Acton famously commented, "Power tends to corrupt, and absolute power corrupts absolutely." So completely do Micronesians grasp this principle that absolute power exists nowhere outside their mythologies. I have already cited Useem's explanation that power in Palau is "circular" because title-holders are unable to act without the approval of the other leaders. But an effective system of checks and balances is by no means peculiar to Palauan societies. The multiple categories of chieftainship present in every Micronesian society provide an array of checks and balances.[2]

Mana and Legitimacy

Mana is an important aspect of Micronesian chieftainship, but it does not play as central a role as it seems to do in Polynesia. As discussed briefly in the preceding chapter, mana is a concept (or a phenomenon) widespread in the Pacific islands; it has many aspects and many local variants, but its overarching sense is of a supernatural or spiritual force with which certain individuals, usually people of senior social rank or high political position, are especially imbued. Raymond Firth (1967/1940) long ago pointed out that mana's presence is made known by its manifestation in material activity; that is, the cause is revealed by its effects. High-ranking or high-titled persons are normally expected to act in ways that suggest they possess mana. Access to it is thought to be to some extent inherited, and the passing of mana from one generation to the next plays a key part in both Micronesian theories of descent and the dynamics of primogeniture: Elder siblings ordinarily inherit more of it than their younger sisters and brothers: "To be consistently effective was to be manaman or to have *feyiyeech* ('go right'). This attribute or quality came to people from the spirit world and constituted what we may call spirit power" (Goodenough 2002, 72).

Precisely because mana's presence is manifested through performance, it can also be observed to reside in or be channeled through individuals who are not necessarily the most senior. Individuals who are successful in their endeavors—such as those who are particularly skilled in, for instance, farming, fishing, combat, or healing or adept in the use of esoteric knowledge—are thought likely to possess mana. In most of Micronesia, mana is especially demonstrated by the production of abundant quantities of prestige goods, by excelling at combat, or by a high order of navigational prowess.

In the eastern and central Carolines it is known as *manaman;* in the Marshalls it is *menmen;* in Kiribati, *maka*. In Palau and Yap, where Nuclear Micronesian languages are not spoken, there are related, but not entirely identical, concepts. Yapese *tabgul* refers to "ritual or sacred purity" and *macmac* to "power or dangerous power" (Lingenfelter 1977, 333; pers. comm., 2001). Palauan *meang* connotes "sacredness," and *klisiich* "power" (Parmentier 1987, 68). But Parmentier also suggests, "Belau seems to be missing the notion of 'sacredness' as an active, effective, or performative force; chiefly power in Belau seems rather to be passive, positioned, and stable" (pers. comm., 2001). Karen Nero indicates that Palauan *chedaol* is more likely to connote the sacredness of the chiefs while *klisiich* derives from a sense of "strong and healthy" rather than a supernatural source (pers. comm., 2001).

It is possible to overestimate the hereditary aspects of mana in Micronesia. The prevalence of offices and titles—of multiples sorts and ranks of chiefs—would seem to suggest that hereditary mana plays the single most important role in people's access to political status. If mana and related concepts were in and of themselves of preeminent importance, however, then hierarchical aspects of social organization would depend almost entirely on simple genealogical social rank, which is in fact the case almost nowhere in Micronesia. Rather, everywhere in Micronesia genealogies provide a range or category of individuals deemed eligible to accede to chiefly office. Pure genealogical seniority is given its due, but it is rarely decisive.[3]

Still, legitimacy is commonly framed in terms of lineage and primogeniture, and one of the primary reasons—if not the main reason—for this is mana. Micronesians want their leaders to possess it. It is, after all, viewed as the source of the efficacy that people hope to see their leaders put to use on their behalf.

Clear evidence of this belief is found in the ubiquitous practices of respect postures and positioning. I spoke of these practices in the previous section, but here I want to explore them more fully. On ceremonial occasions chiefs and others of high rank occupy positions above others. This is ordinarily done in one or the other of two ways. First, in ritual and ceremonial contexts, chiefs and others occupying important political offices are usually seated in special ways or special places, often on raised platforms, requiring others to look up toward them. So fully developed is this pattern on Pohnpei that although two shared Nuclear Micronesian terms for chiefs occur in Pohnpeian as *samol* and *aroche*, they have been almost entirely abandoned for the generic *soupeidi*, that is, "one who customarily or conventionally looks downward," a specific reference to the places chiefs and others of high rank take on the raised platforms within Pohnpeian feast houses. In Palau the leading council members are known by the rank of the seats they take in the meetinghouse. On Yap, sitting is the posture of authority, while standing is the position of service and work (Lingenfelter 1975, 108). Among the earliest Spanish accounts of the central Caroline atolls appears an account of a chief sitting upon a raised platform (Cantova 1722, 235). In "a large communal house" at Lelu in Kosrae in the 1830s, "five aged chiefs sat on widely separate mats" (Lesson 1982,

54). In most of Kiribati, political life is organized around the meetinghouse, and the literal meaning of *boti*, Kiribati's primary descent groups, is the group's ranked seat in the meetinghouse (Maude 1963, 11). In the Marshalls "special places of honor are reserved for the paramount chiefs" (Spoehr 1949, 79).

The second set of forms includes stooping, squatting, and even crawling in the presence of high-ranking persons. These displays of respect have often been misinterpreted as marks of obeisance or utter and abject submission but must be understood within a larger context. Nearly every one of the early accounts reporting on Kosrae comments on the postures of respect assumed before the Tokosra, the island's paramount chief, and the other chiefs. Duperrey, for example, described common people "respectfully squatting at a distance" from chiefs and remaining "reflective and silent and uncommunicative" (1982, 10). Lesson, who commented on the advanced age of nearly all the chiefs and the paramount as "groaning under the weight of his years," described people falling on their knees and crawling as a chief approached (1982, 50). And while Lütke reported little in the way of visible subordination before most leaders, this was not the case with the paramount chief, "in front of whom the common people and the urosse [chiefs] prostrated themselves equally." But he also asserted that there was little beyond this respect behavior that distinguished the paramount from the rest of the people, who did not concern themselves with him at all when he was not present. Indeed, Lütke seemed puzzled to find the paramount's wealth "of less importance than that of almost all of the others" and that his house "has nothing distinguishing about it" (1982, 111). That is, these respect behaviors do not necessarily indicate that those toward whom they are directed either possess material wealth or exercise much in the way of physical force or power.[4]

It is also important to recognize that similar forms of behavior can be observed in other contexts. While postures of respect toward chiefs are encountered throughout Micronesia, similar forms of deference are directed toward individuals occupying other social categories as well. In Chuuk, where chiefly status is probably less elaborate than anywhere else in Micronesia, Goodenough, who has analyzed the contexts in which "a person is 'taboo from setting himself above another,'" notes, "*Jii meji pin wöön* (he is forbidden from above-him) is given as the reason for a number of prescriptions of behavior." He continues:

> There are persons to whom crouching or crawling behavior, known as *föpwörö*, is exhibited. It is shown only to certain people whom one is "taboo from above." It is not permitted to be physically higher than they are. If such a person is seated, one must crouch or crawl in passing by or in coming into his presence. Persons to whom this behavior must be shown are chiefs and *jitag* [*itang*] by persons of lower status, brothers by their sisters, and daughters by their fathers. (Goodenough 1951, 111; cf. Goodenough 2002, 56, 298)

Most of the behaviors associated with this pattern, which include not only respect postures but also avoidance behaviors, disinclination to initiate interactions, and reluctance to refuse requests, are in fact observed toward a significant range of relations, a number of whom are women and/or younger people. They are nearly identical to the behaviors Duperrey described on Kosrae.

These behavior patterns are, in other words, practiced in relationships other than those between chiefs and their people, so we cannot conclude from the simple existence of these postures that people are doing anything more than showing respect for their chiefs when they lower themselves in their presence. These behaviors do not ipso facto indicate that people practicing them live in abject terror or suffer utter subservience, subjection, or domination. Lütke reported that Kosraeans speak softly in the presence of chiefs, but he also observed that in general "the usual custom is to speak softly" (1982, 13, 125). Chuukese chiefs are expected to practice humility and refrain from arrogance (Goodenough 1951, 143–145). This is what I have been calling the reciprocity of respect.

Laurence Carucci's account of Kurijmoj (Christmas) on Eniwetok and Ujelang atolls provides not only one of the most detailed and fully developed analyses we have of Micronesian feasting but also a highly specific account of the relationship between mana and chieftainship. While Christmas is obviously an introduced concept, the ways in which these Marshallese peoples celebrate it illustrate traditional Micronesian precepts regarding the underlying purposes and expectations of seasonal feasting. Chiefs fully imbued with sacred or supernatural power *(menmen)*, along with indigenous deities (and since conversion, the Christian God), are in Marshallese cosmology associated with unlimited access to abundance and prosperity. Supplying bounty, especially food, is a characteristic activity of a beneficent chief, while food itself is the prototypical symbol of nurturance—of being well taken care of. When people make feasts, they expend "huge amounts" of energy and deplete the available resources. In doing so, they accomplish several tasks. In addition to promoting island-wide solidarity and reinforcing and enhancing social status, people offer gifts to the ancient deities "with the intention of creating indebtedness"; because the deities (including the Christian God) "are inherently more highly ranked than are mortal humans, they must reciprocate in greater measure than any gift they receive." Feasting is thus intended as "a ritual tool to guarantee that renewal and regeneration will be forthcoming" (Carucci 1997, 36, 67, 78–79, 179).

Everywhere in Micronesia, with the apparent exception of Palau, the term *ani* or *eni* or one of its close cognates refers to ancestral spirits, who are to a degree conceptually merged with deities. This includes Yap and the Marianas, where the Nuclear Micronesian term has been borrowed. Respect for and worship of the spirits of the ancestors lie at the center of all Micronesian religious belief. It is they who are the source of mana. But it is important to recognize here the underlying notion that mana is not ordinarily conceptualized as representing the will of those spiritual entities with whom it originates or those spiritually charged humans who channel it. In the sense of Emile Durkheim's classic notion that human societies create their gods in their own image, Micronesians expect that the deities, like fellow members of their own societies, will honor the norms of reciprocity. Mana is capable of influencing, and even directing, the supernatural realm and through it the natural world to behave in ways that benefit human communities. Thus, properly propitiated, the spirit world will both protect the human world from impending catastrophes—especially typhoons and droughts—and promote bountiful harvests. In Yap and the atolls to its east in particular, but elsewhere as well, people assume that sorcerers endowed with or able to channel mana are capable of directing destructive storms to specific locales as punishment or retaliation. Indeed, much (but by no means all) of indigenous explanation for the *sawei* system linking the atolls to Yap is explained in terms of fears of retribution if these duties are not performed (Lessa 1964; Schneider 1957).

Goodenough has explored the conception in Chuuk that "everything that was especially efficacious (manaman) came from the spirit world" (1986, 558). Spirits migrating westward from Kachaw or Katau ("sky-world") "served as patron deities of particular lineages, clans, and their associated localities" and in time transformed into "legendary founding chiefs." This in turn

> explains why clan ancestors and the founders of chiefly lines who come from elsewhere are invariably described in terms that make them, too, *énúúyaramas* [*enúú*/ spirit, *aramas*/human]. It explains, also, why those who wish to bolster their political power with magical power, which itself derives from the spirit world, should claim clan ancestry from Kachaw. It follows, moreover, that those who held powerful chiefly titles should, themselves, be treated in legend as *énúúyaramas* (Goodenough 1986, 558–559; cf. Goodenough 2002, 83–84).

In a similar vein, David Hanlon has described the brothers who, according to legend, undertook the massive construction project at Pohnpei's Nan Madol (and thus paved the way for the evolution of the island's first hierarchical political format) as "stranger-kings" (1988, 9).[5]

These arguments are cogent but overlook several crucial points. First, nearly all of Micronesian mythohistory recounts tales of visitors from distant, partially known places; only some of them are ascribed spirit or divine status. Second, on Pohnpei at least, from whence Goodenough (1986) believes this pattern diffused as part of what he calls a "Kachaw cult," what are known as *eni aramas* are by no means all viewed as possessing foreign roots or as being chiefly ancestors; many of them seem to be no more than ancient figures with superhuman powers or status. Third, and most telling, the sacred character of Micronesian chiefs—that is, the aspects of their status that derive from the possession of mana—appears to be something the earliest settlers brought with them: chiefs everywhere in the Nuclear Micronesian–speaking societies are imbued with mana, whether their immediate ancestors specifically traveled from abroad or not.

The mythohistories of some islands explain that virtually every significant historical development was in some way prompted by influences or travelers from abroad. In Chuuk and the surrounding atolls there are competing influences from the west (Yap) and the east (Kachaw) (Goodenough 2002, 123–132). An ancient name for the region of Pohnpei now known as Sokehs is Pwapwalik, which can be translated as the place of "speech from outside" and refers to the tradition that this region was populated by many people from abroad, speaking a multitude of tongues. A few, but no means all, of them had spiritual or semidivine status. I think it makes more sense to say that while a common explanation or charter for hereditary rights to chiefly status draws on notions of spiritual force or efficacy that are in turn based on origins in the spirit or sky world, it is equally the case that such status is also attributed both to priority of settlement and to conquest. These are by no means exclusive categories, but neither are they synonymous.

Rank, status, and political office are of profound importance in these societies and draw upon a variety of distinct sources. Any of these elements can be used individually, but more often they are braided together to enhance their strength and resiliency. It is not just on Ifaluk that "rank is so highly valued and respected that it stands out as one of the master-values of this culture" (Burrows and Spiro 1970, 179). It is the case everywhere in Micronesia and applies to chieftainship as well. The underpinnings of these phenomena can be attributed neither to particular, local histories nor to single historical processes. They form irreducible, foundational elements of Micronesian society.

Succession to Chieftainship

Community chiefs and paramount chiefs hold their positions because they are heads of the premier or senior localized descent groups in the places where they reign. The question of who becomes a community or paramount chief, then, is primarily the domain of the leading descent group. Nevertheless, the people of these communities, however much respect they hold for their chiefs, are rarely inclined to follow them blindly or to suffer abuses of authority interminably. For this reason, the leading descent group—the lineage providing the chief—must take the rest of the community's outlook and interests into consideration when deciding who should succeed to the office on the death of their chief. Although in theory they can act unilaterally, to do so runs the risk of alienating those upon whom the chief actually depends for his support. As I have noted, in those cases where a descent group does not root its claims to leadership in settlement priority, it ordinarily grounds them in conquest. But military upsets do not always come from abroad; lineages have been overthrown by their neighbors too.

To preserve its status, then, a chiefly descent group must choose its leader wisely. It does so in much the same way any descent group selects its chief, but it is likely to exercise more than average care in making its decision. Essential to any understanding of succession is the recognition that despite the consistent emphases on genealogical seniority, the Micronesian system of matrilineal primogeniture works as well as it does, and has lasted as long as it has, because primogeniture is viewed only as a rough guideline for actual practice, not as an absolute rule or requirement. In reality, almost any male able to claim matridescent from a senior woman in a chiefly lineage can under some circumstances be considered for succession to the chieftainship. Decisions about succession are typically made either by the dying chief or by consensus of the lineage's elder men and women, but in either case, genealogy is only one—albeit an important one—among a number of factors they take into account.

What is more, the genealogical aspects of succession are not themselves especially clear. Micronesians tend to speak of succession in ways that make it seem predetermined and exact, and outsiders are given to interpreting the process in their own terms. Thus patterns of succession to European thrones have tended to influence outsiders' grasp of what takes place in Micronesia. But the scrupulous, predetermined order of succession to the British throne, for example, is in fact a modern phenomenon. Over the course of many centuries succession to the throne underwent a slow transformation, during a process in which hereditary rights grew from being only of marginal importance to achieving rough equality with other factors entailed in election of the king. Not until the Act of Settlement of 1701, which firmly placed "succession in the disposal of parliament," was there "presumption of a hereditary descent of the crown, but a presumption that was subject to modification or abrogation by the parliament's will" (Nenner 1995, 5–6). Something similar has perhaps been happening in contemporary Micronesia, but traditionally this was not the case.

Micronesian systems of matrilineal primogeniture in most cases do no more than establish a range of individuals eligible to claim a title—or to have a case made on their behalf, since modesty often keeps people from openly pursuing titles. This is very much the same sort of phenomenon Irving Goldman pointed to in Polynesia: "Seniority of descent is derived from primogeniture, but it is not identical with it since a title holder need not always be the actual first-born but only a descendant of a line of first born" (1970, 21, 14). Indeed, many Micronesians acknowledge that their political systems work as well as they do precisely because of the range of choices provided to them as they go about selecting their leaders. Throughout Micronesia a degree of ambiguity is built into the formal order of succession.[6]

Two closely related but distinct patterns are commonly put forward as ideals. In the first, the line of succession runs through a chief's younger brothers and only then to his sisters' sons. In the second, a chief's eldest sister's sons should immediately succeed him. On Pohnpei the two competing norms are slightly different: While the chief's eldest sister's eldest son is acknowledged to be genealogically senior, the holder of the second-ranked title in the relevant line of chiefly titles has an equally valid claim to succeed a deceased chief (Petersen 1982a). On Yap, the only one of these societies where patrilineal principles are formally preeminent, chieftainship is supposed to pass from the chief to his eldest son (Lingenfelter 1975, 112–113).

The process is complicated everywhere, however, by a less clearly stated principle acknowledging that there are always alternative interpretations of seniority. Although seniority of descent is important, seniority in terms of absolute age also weighs heavily in succession decisions. In Micronesia advanced age is always considered worthy of respect. And thus it is that an older man with junior genealogical status may well be reckoned a better candidate than a younger man with a more senior genealogy. In some sense, it is the existence of these dual concepts of seniority that provides the ambiguity. In different ways, both an older but genealogically junior male member of the lineage and a younger man more closely descended from the lineage ancestress are senior. While people are quite aware of this ambiguity as they consider who might next become chief, they are not given to expressing it when discussing with outsiders just how an orderly succession to authority takes place. Diagram 2 (p. 178) illustrates this situation in its simplest form.

Barnett was especially struck by this dynamic in Palau, where both advanced age and political and economic success command respect. Although there is an expectation that as men grow older their political status will increase, "it must inevitably happen that some men with high-ranking titles are younger than some other men either with or without titles" (Barnett 1960, 59). Roland Force, too, observed that in Palau age and rank are in perpetual competition with each other (1960). As Barnett notes, "The Belauan theory of social existence does not fit the facts of life. The theory is that with advancing age a man assumes a title and engages in the praiseworthy manipulation of his family's wealth. This does happen, but obviously it cannot happen to every man" (1960, 58–60). Though both age and titles are meant to carry with them prestige, a high-titled but relatively young man would do well to keep quiet in councils and heed the words of his elders (and thereby gain credibility), while an aged man without a significant title *(wogel sahal)* is in a somewhat pathetic position and would do well not to draw

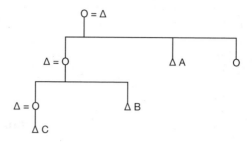

Diagram 2

The following diagram illustrates this succession conflict in its simplest form.

When this lineage's chief, A, dies, he might in theory be succeeded either by B, who is a full generation older than C, or by C, who (as the son of B's elder sister) is genealogically senior to B.

Key

○ female   △ male

= marriage   ——— siblings | parent-child

attention to himself. Palauans clearly recognize the gap between the stated norms and the actual patterns of real lives.

On Yap, both relative and absolute age are critical in succession. Although a chief's elder son has a claim to the authority lodged in his father's land, "if his absolute age has not yet placed him in the category of mature man, he may not act as chief." Instead, one of his father's brothers assumes the position of "estate father" and speaks for "the authority of the land." Once he has acceded to this position, the estate father's authority is lifelong, regardless of his nephew's age (Lingenfelter 1975, 113). That is, generational seniority trumps lineal seniority.

A similar situation is presented in detail by Alkire, who initially explains that on Lamotrek "the political affairs of the clans and of the island are organized" such that the chief "is the oldest male of the most senior lineage and the appropriate subclan" (1989, 32). Yet in providing us with the genealogy of the Saufalacheg, the second of the island's three chiefly clans, he demonstrates something quite different. The Saufalacheg's previous chief, Ochimal, was a member of the most junior lineage of the chiefly subclan, and the man who succeeded him, Ligiol, was a member of the second ranking lineage. The two genealogically senior males, Sahop and Taromai, members of two branches of the most senior lineage, were boys at the time of Ochimal's death and Ligiol's elevation to the chief's title (Alkire

1989, 44). Thus neither of the two Saufalacheg chiefs recorded by Alkire was in fact a member of the senior lineage. This discrepancy is problematic only if we take at face value the clearly articulated notion that the chief is the oldest male in the most senior lineage. It is precisely because chiefs are important leaders that they must also be fully mature, if not elderly, men able to discharge their duties capably.

This stipulation does have its limits. Lamotrek's paramount chief at that same time was a disabled woman named Lefaioup, the sole survivor of the appropriate lineage and subclan of the clan traditionally supplying the island's paramount chief. Rather than allowing the paramount chieftainship to cross subclan boundaries and thus throw its genealogical legitimacy entirely into question, Lefaioup bore the title, but most of her responsibilities were in fact discharged by the oldest man in the second-ranking subclan (Alkire 1989, 40–41).

The Chuukese resolve this recurring dilemma in slightly different fashion. When a lineage's genealogically senior male is younger than a genealogically junior lineage mate, the younger but senior man serves as the lineage's "symbolic head" while the older but junior man becomes the "executive head" of the lineage, or as Goodenough explains, the "executive headship was in the hands of the oldest competent male member, whether he was in the senior female line or not" (2002, 33, 37).

On Pohnpei, where competitive feasting is both a major pastime and central to the accumulation of prestige, the relative ranks of men working their individual ways upward through the hierarchical sequences of chiefly titles only sometimes coincide with their genealogical positions. Here the tension between genealogical rules of succession, which hinge on strict primogeniture, and equally well-articulated notions that the holder of the second-ranked title is successor to the chieftainship upon the chief's demise drives the entire political system (Petersen 1982a; 1999b). It is lifelong political participation—demonstrated most effectively in competitive feasting—that reveals the relative strengths and abilities of rivals for a chiefly title.

In northern Kiribati—Butaritari and Makin—the rules of succession are complicated, variable, and flexible, and there are usually several claimants to a chiefly title. Almost every heir to a title is challenged by a younger brother or cousin, and as a consequence a successful aspirant must be able to marshal the support of the community's people (Lambert 1978, 80–81, 86).

This dynamic process probably reaches its apogee in the Marshalls, where, as Mason has observed, people look to their chiefs for the leadership necessary to survive the precarious conditions that prevail on these atolls (1986, 5). Although it is commonly stipulated that succession should pass through a set of brothers (or sometimes siblings) before passing on to the next generation via the eldest sister's children, nearly every writer on Marshallese succession notes the intense rivalry for chiefly titles that ends up in highly contested interpretations of the rules.

Rynkiewich (1972) explains that the multiple principles governing succession, including age, birth order within a sibling set, and generational standing create enough ambiguity to make any particular case of succession "indeterminate." But this ambiguity in turn creates the space necessary for flexibility, which underpins the system of chieftainship.

People on Arno recognize that it is this dynamic that requires rival claimants to seek support. Rival contestants for an *iroij* title must marshal enough people *(kajur)* to make a show of force (also *kajur*). That is, the claimant to a chiefly title who is able to muster the most support among the people is the one likely to become chief. And people are of course inclined to support the individual they think will most effectively lead them. Successors to chiefly office are not elected, but the process entails markedly similar principles of securing support (Rynkiewich 1972, 67–52; 1974, 144–149), and it appears that in the Marshalls there has often been more political violence within lineages—between rival candidates for a title—than between groups.

In general, the more authority that accrues to the chief's role (as opposed to the authority he has achieved with his own character and skills), the more loosely are genealogical rules interpreted. Where a chief does little more than preside over a community of several hundred people, personal qualities are less important to his performance, and genealogy and seniority can play a greater part in his selection. Where chiefs—especially paramounts—have authority over significantly larger populations and are thus responsible for mobilizing more people and resources, there are more possible routes to the title, and freer interpretations of just what is necessary for succession.

On the larger islands, with their larger populations (including the southern Marshalls), where chiefs often exercise greater authority than on the smaller atolls, the dynamics of succession are necessarily complicated. But as the Lamotrek case shows, even on the small atolls succession is by no means a given. Nor in the case of the paramount chief is it necessarily a concern only of the senior lineage. In northern Kiribati not only are the rules of succession flexible, but there are also intense disagreements about whether chiefly titles belong solely to the descent group that fills them or in a larger sense to the community as a whole (Lambert 1978, 80–82). On Ulithi the elders of all the clans have a say in the senior lineage's choice of who is to be its leader and thus the island's paramount chief (Figirliyong 1977, 10).

Finally, it should be noted that the ambiguities and contradictions inherent in these systems of succession offer Micronesian communities several other benefits. Because of leeway available in the selection of its leader, a lineage has the option of attracting to it particularly competent individuals who might otherwise choose to settle elsewhere, by offering them the possibility of succeeding to the chief's title. And by adroitly parceling out titles to junior lines, a lineage can promote solidarity, keeping younger or junior males from directing their energies in other directions. It is precisely the ambiguities of succession to chiefly titles that contribute to the flexibility and responsiveness that have allowed these political systems to survive for millennia.

It is worth asking why Micronesians are so eager to establish and maintain chiefly forms of social influence, authority, and power when they so clearly recognize the threats that these hierarchical forces pose to them. Mana and the various forms of hierarchy that accompany it are, in the end, things people believe themselves sorely in need of in order to survive the exigencies of life in their vulnerable islands. Many scholars, particularly those who study social evolution, tend to conceive of political power as a necessarily negative force that inherently threatens people's well-being. But seen through Micronesian eyes, it appears as something well worth cultivating, a dynamic that, kept effectively in check, is capable of preserving patterns of communal behavior that guarantee survival. With this in mind, I now turn to some of the adaptive qualities of Micronesian politics.

Adaptive Qualities of Micronesian Sociopolitical Organization

Most mature Micronesians are aware not only of the precariousness of their place on the islands but also of the absolutely necessary interdependence of island communities that makes life on them possible. They understand the adaptive character of their political systems—that without many of these traditional forms of organization they simply could not survive. I believe the tremendous similarities among Micronesian political systems can be appreciated only within this context. The initial adaptive patterns their ancestors carried with them have proved so successful that people continue to recognize the practicality of retaining and refining them. Useful innovations were readily diffused from one place to another. The Marianas, Palau, and Yap were settled by peoples not directly related to those who descend from Nuclear Micronesian stock, but sociopolitical organization among these societies is nonetheless organized around the same basic principles. And throughout Micronesia we find a general willingness to adopt and adapt new ideas and practices (including understandings of the supernatural realm, dance steps, and breadfruit varieties). This reflects a common perception that innovations can confer advantages. At the same time, there is recognition that changes may have dangerous consequences if they entice people away from practices that have proved themselves advantageous over the long haul. I have heard Pohnpeians say, "Sohte me kin kapara inen Katau," which translates roughly as "Beware of the mother of foreign things"—that is, be careful of changes that appear advantageous in the short term but are likely to have severe consequences in the long term.[7] This notion reflects an outlook that is not simply receptive to innovation but equally recognizes that many older customs have long proved themselves invaluable.

Since the times of Aristotle and Confucius, at least, philosophers have been writing about what people want and expect from their political systems. People do not always, of course, actually get from their governments that which they seek. In chieftainship, though, Micronesians have found a basic political system capable of providing them with what they need.[8]

It is worth stopping for a moment here to consider what Micronesia's people do want and/or expect from their governments. By definition, localized lineages have their own internal organizations. The people and institutions governing Micronesian communities are charged with coordinating relations among these resident lineages. Because island governments are presided over by descent groups that are thought to be senior but in no other way ostensibly different from or superior to the rest of the community's lineages, they are able to lead only by fostering participation, not by commanding obedience. The senior lineage and its leaders coordinate rather than threaten.

In a community's domestic or internal sphere, chiefly leadership is especially responsible for seeing that ritual cycle and life-crisis ceremonies—e.g., first fruits and funerals—are properly observed. Chiefs represent the intersection and integration of both their lineages' ancestral spirits and the spirits of the place. The community's chief is head of the lineage whose spirits are strongest or most efficacious, and his mana promotes, though it cannot guarantee, the community's survival.

But the chief is equally expected to serve as the focus of his community's organizational efforts and strength, as it is observed by other communities. These derive in part from the community's successes in its domestic subsistence activities and thus reflect the chief's mana, but more to the point, others perceive a community's strength in terms of the image it projects of effective organization, enabling it to protect itself from outside attack. Many Micronesian communities have war leaders who are distinct from chiefs and who constitute part of the systems of political checks and balances, but it is the chiefs who are expected to assure that the community as a whole manifests an image of well-being, strength, and coordination.

Micronesian governments—in a nutshell, chieftainship—are charged with multiple responsibilities and it is difficult to say that any one of these in particular is markedly more important than the others. But together, the tasks promoting productivity, coordinating ritual and feast cycles, and projecting an image of strength and organization, entail considerable participatory activity. Chiefs must get people into motion and goods into circulation. They can most effectively do so by example, and for this reason generosity lies at the heart of what people expect from them. Not only do they manifest their lineage's mana and their own personal abilities, but they truly provide leadership, exercised through their comportment rather than coercion.

I have already raised the matter of differences between high- and low-island sociopolitical systems in several different contexts, emphasizing the commonalities while exploring the differences. The principles underlying these local systems are essentially the same everywhere in Micronesia. On low islands chiefs derive their status from the same notions of clan and lineage priority and seniority as their high-island peers, and the fundamental nature of Micronesian chieftainship itself cannot be attributed to conditions peculiar to any specific sort of island. What does differ is the absolute size of island populations and, as a consequence, the degree of social stratification encountered. The highest chiefs on the larger islands generally wield considerably more political influence than do their counterparts on smaller islands, and the key factor in determining the degree of stratification in these societies is simply population size—a phenomenon many Micronesians recognize.

To reprise, I largely agree with Orans' observation that the larger the island and its population, the larger its economy and thus the greater the extent of the roles its leaders undertake (1966, 31). Mason's conclusion that on the atolls leadership is most elaborated where there is the greatest economic abundance and that chieftainship and authority are "directly related to the production of surplus food" (1968, 328) would seem for the most part to apply to comparisons between high and low islands as well. Lessa, too, remarked that "the social systems of one type of island as compared with the other were functions of population concentration as much as anything else" (1962, 376; cf. Peoples 1993). The pioneer missionary Luther Gulick made a similar observation ten years after he arrived in the region. Though he was writing specifically of Kiribati, his point was in the context of an overview of all Micronesia. He concluded that political centralization—in his phrase, "the tendency to monarchism"—"is greater in the more productive, and consequently more luxurious, islands" (1862, 412).

There are within ethnological theory long-standing debates about the origins of social stratification in general and of chieftainship in particular. While I will not sidetrack into rehashing this history, it would be an oversight to consider differences in the varieties of Micronesian social stratification without reference to it. In its simplest form, the argument is between those who hold that stratification grows out of what are essentially management functions assumed by leaders who in time come to occupy positions at the top of formalized hierarchies, and theorists who maintain that these hierarchies are, instead, imposed by force and maintained by those who are able to harness the surplus labor of the general populace and then put it to use in continuing their domination over them.[9] I cannot say how Micronesian chieftainship first evolved, but it is clear that its origins do not lie in Micronesia. Patterns of language and social behavior throughout the island Pacific tell us that the basic principles of stratification were present among the peoples who left island Southeast Asia several millennia before the more distant islands were ever settled.[10] What is crucial is that Micronesians steadfastly retain nearly identical forms of chieftainship everywhere, and my interest here is in examining why it is that they continue to flourish.

Micronesians have chiefs because they want them—because they see them as fundamentally important to their continued survival—and not because the chiefs have imposed themselves upon the people. Micronesian thinkers recognize that leadership roles can be abused and that in endowing a degree of authority and/or power upon certain roles and the people who occupy them they simultaneously create the potential for its misuse. They understand that there are those who would use that authority primarily in pursuit of their own ends or benefit rather than the community. Goodenough describes this recognition in Chuuk:

> The power that came from bravery, knowledge, and property made it possible and tempting for those who enjoyed it to be arrogant in their dealings with others and to use their power in the service of their own interests at the expense of the interests of those who were dependent upon them and for whose welfare they were responsible. There was reason for emphasizing the importance of respectfulness in those who had power and authority. These ideals were especially important in the case of those who were firstborn sons and daughters, lineage heads, district chiefs, and those who commanded more potent forms of specialized knowledge (2002, 73).

Thus Micronesians have created and maintained ample checks and balances, and these in turn result in the seeming contradictions that abound in Micronesian politics. Too many descriptions have focused on only a single aspect, portraying it as peculiar to only one island rather than seeing the full compass. But these checks and balances are common to all Micronesian societies.

We should recognize that Micronesians play active roles in constructing their own polities; these systems did not evolve in simple unwitting response to natural and demographic pressures. Micronesians do not seem mystified by their leaders—they are too ready to ignore or even defy chiefs, even while showing the utmost respect for them—to be seen as naïve or credulous. This is not to suggest that some leaders in some places at some times do not abuse or exploit, but is instead a perspective that portrays Micronesians as fully aware of this potential and prepared to deal with it, even if they are not always successful. There is far too much local theory regarding the importance of keeping control over leaders and of preventing abuses to imagine that Micronesians are incapable of protecting themselves.

My point is simple. The people of these islands engage continually in exchange of goods and services—both within and between communities. On the smaller islands chiefs do many things and serve many purposes, but among the most salient are coordinating the ritual and social activities that organize exchange within the community; keeping people productive; preventing them from engaging in overproduction that might harm the environment; and overseeing interactions with other islands, interactions that serve to keep social relationships open and patterns of exchange flowing. On the larger islands, where there is greater potential for abundance, production for exchange is not merely a basis for survival but also a means for personal development and expression. While the politics of chieftainship on the smaller islands promote survival, it is the survival aspects of chieftainship—entailed in exchange—that serve as the arena for politics on the larger islands: chiefs manage competitive activities that define much of political life. Recognizing the insistent competition for status, as Goldman saw in Polynesia, is a key to understanding chieftainship on Micronesian high islands. There are many exceptions to this general theme, but in no way do these exceptions provide evidence to support the notion that Micronesian chiefs exist primarily as a consequence of their abilities to strip off the surplus labor of the "common" people. In short, the demands on Micronesian chiefs are such that many of them spend more time producing, organizing, and exchanging than do their subjects. The benefits to chiefs lie far more in the realm of prestige than in material acquisition.

Because institutions that are, in their essence, the same play such different roles and fulfill such different functions in large- and small-island societies, it is impossible to be certain how or why they first developed. They are successful because they are so malleable and adaptable. A few basic principles lend themselves either to maintaining an almost bare-bones survival under relatively difficult if not harsh conditions or to being put to use in harnessing the energies and competitive capacities of people in ways that enhance their lives under conditions of abundance. Micronesians put these principles to use, sometimes with quite contradictory ends in mind. They preserve customary principles and practices precisely because such customs promote flexibility and enhance survival, not because they are subservient to the tyranny of custom. Useem said of Palauans that in some cases they select particular customs they think likely to advance desired outcomes and then claim that they are merely following universal principles (1946, 57). In northern Kiribati there are ordinarily several claimants to a vacant political title, and each stresses the particular criteria that apply to his own case (Lambert 1978, 80). This is hardly peculiar to these particular societies: Micronesians honor their traditions because they work, but they see them as means to ends and manipulate them—use them wisely, if you will—in order to enhance their lives.

A part of what defines Micronesia as a coherent region, and not just as scholarly organizing device, is this shared format. From Palau to the Marshalls, high islands and low all draw on basically identical principles—matriliny, the interweaving of lineage and land, and the structure and ideology of chieftainship—to organize and preserve their societies.

Patrick Kirch (2000) has been trying to reconstruct what an original (or Proto-Oceanic) social structure might have been like for the Pacific islands, based on shared linguistic and social structural traits recorded by modern ethnographers. But in the same way that we cannot be sure whether the earliest Micronesian practices were more like those of the larger or the smaller islands, we cannot know whether the people who first brought these principles with them into the western Pacific were actually employing elaborate or spare, or both, aspects of them. I am not suggesting that attempts should not be made to reconstruct the characters of these ancient societies, but my own reading of the data tells me there is too much variation in the ways principles and structures are actually put to use for us to infer confidently what they were like originally, why they developed in the ways they did, and what was retained and what was discarded or lost. It seems worthwhile, instead, to focus on the contradictory dynamics of these principles and practices, and the ways in which people make conscious use of centralization and decentralization, hierarchy and equality, shared knowledge and concealment, people and place, and tribute and redistribution.

CHAPTER 8

Aesthetics, Beliefs, Values, and Behavior

THUS FAR I have focused almost entirely on institutions and processes—that is, on social organization—because my primary interest has been to show how Micronesian social groups, in particular the clans and lineages, provide the adaptive framework for survival in the islands. I have largely ignored other aspects of Micronesian culture. But there is a great more to life in the islands than the politics of descent groups, the organization of labor, and the management of land. Now I turn my attention to some of these aspects.

In this chapter I focus on art, religion and magic, and some of the values and behaviors that shape interpersonal relationships. Were I writing a book devoted to all aspects of Micronesian peoples' lives and cultures, I would give much more space to aesthetics, beliefs, and values. But this work is meant to explore only a limited portion of Micronesian life, and my consideration of these topics is largely limited to how they intersect with or enhance the social dynamics I have been writing about. While I try to provide a broader picture of these important parts of human lives, my primary goal is to show how art, religion, magic, and interpersonal relations manifest in one way or another basic Micronesian concerns with individual participation in social processes and with the constant interplay between equality and hierarchy that is so profoundly characteristic of all that is Micronesian.

Social Aspects of Micronesian Art and Aesthetics

In considering the place of art in Micronesian social life, I make a simple distinction between aesthetics and art. I speak of aesthetics in referring to ideas, values, or principles about what is good and/or beautiful; by art, I simply mean performances staged or items crafted with aesthetic notions or goals in mind. My approach here has been influenced by Peter Steager's account of art on Puluwat, in which he employs the concept of aesthetic locus—that is, the areas where artistic attention and interest are especially directed or more highly developed. Steager points out that the obvious practicality of so much of what Puluwat's people produce tends to obscure the aesthetic components in their work, but he insists as well that a consistent emphasis on "simplicity of line" can be seen in the care and skill devoted to carving wooden objects, plaiting and weaving, and the crafting of items meant to adorn the human body (1979, 342–346).[1]

Art is entwined as an element that runs through basic utilitarian activities, common social events, ritual and symbolic contexts, political considerations, and even economic dynamics. Among the most conspicuous forms that art takes in Micronesia are dance performance, architecture, textile weaving, mat plaiting, woodcarving, and tattooing. The artists and craftspeople who create these rely on an underlying perspective that emphasizes a merging of efficient design with elegance of form. Commonplace items are often transformed into works of art, while losing none of their utility (Steager 1979).

As in nearly every aspect of Micronesian social life, there are important commonalities across the breadth of the region, although there are significant differences as well. Both the similarities and the differences are consequences of fundamental aspects of Micronesian history: the extraordinary mobility made possible by the voyaging tradition, the disparate entry points of the original settlers, and adaptations to local environments and circumstances. Traditions carried by the settlers from the Southeast Solomons–Santa Cruz Islands represent one trend, predominant in the east, while Indonesian elements are evident in Palau; influences that arrived directly from New Guinea can be found in Yap and Palau as well (Mason 1964).

Song and dance performances are among the most striking Micronesian art forms. Karen Nero calls attention to

Micronesians' multisensory emphasis on the ephemeral arts of integrated chants, scents, and meditative movement—the composite line of dancers moving and chanting in unison, wearing hibiscus fiber skirts or geometrically woven *tur* cloths, their skin glistening with turmeric-spiced coconut oil, accented by garlands of rare shells and rustling coconut leaf decorations, crowned by richly scented floral wreathes. Many Micronesian artistic endeavors are transitory; their aesthetic emphasis is on the perfection of the performance rather than the creation of the lasting object. When perfection is achieved, the thrill of recognition in the audience fulfills local sensibilities, but translates poorly into academic discourse. (Nero 1999, 256–257; cf. Burrows 1963)

These performances are not only sources of entertainment for those who watch them but also sources of solidarity for those who perform them together and sources of competitive pride for the lineages and communities that present them.

While music, song, and dance take many forms, the most widely encountered form is probably the so-called stick dance, in which lines of dancers execute complex figures that include the striking together of long, thin poles in styles simulating combat (on Pohnpei, dancers often manipulate paddles). Dancers sometimes seem to enter near-trance states that enable them to give vent to aggressive, belligerent emotions normally repressed in everyday life. The martial character of much Micronesian dancing is so pervasive that when European ships began traversing the area, local choreographers immediately began copying Western military formations and contributed their own variations on close-order marching drills to the common Micronesian repertory. In much the same way that the stately, hierarchical nature of ceremonial feasting allows Micronesians to communicate to outsiders the well-organized character of their chiefdoms, this emphasis on the martial aspects of dance performances enables communities to announce both to themselves and others that they are prepared to defend themselves from unwanted intrusions (Petersen 1992).

At the same time, it should be kept in mind that Micronesian aesthetics emphasize simple and pure natural beauty. Edwin Burrows' study of Ifaluk song and poetry, *Flower in My Ear* (1963), acknowledges the overwhelming significance of flowers in expressing many aspects of emotions and desires. On Puluwat, as virtually everywhere else in Micronesia, "lavish use is made of flowers as body adornment"—they are worn as garlands around the head or neck or tucked into earlobes and are grown around homes for their beauty and especially for their fragrant aromas (Steager 1979, 352).

Textile weaving was first introduced into Micronesia from Indonesia via the atolls southwest of Palau and then spread to all the Carolines, with the notable exception of Palau (Riesenberg and Gayton 1952). The most commonly used thread is processed from the trunks of banana plants (known also as manila hemp); fibers processed from hibiscus bark are sometimes used as well. The threads are colored with natural dyes. Weavers, for the most part women (though on Yap men do some of the weaving), do their work on backstrap looms: one end of the loom is fastened to a stationary object while the other is strapped around the weaver's waist. Wider fabrics, used as women's skirts or folded into men's loincloths, are produced in most of the region, whereas narrower widths, referred to as sashes or belts, are particularly characteristic of Pohnpei and Kosrae and are considered to be the epitome of the weaver's art in Micronesia, in particular the examples richly brocaded with shell beads. Most woven designs are geometric or striped and bear important symbolic meanings. Cloth fashioned from pounded breadfruit bark—famous in Polynesia as tapa—is also manufactured in the Carolines.

Although most fabrics are used simply as items of apparel, some feature prominently in religious and political rituals, serving as "instruments of sacred

Yap. A young woman weaving on a backstrap loom, during the 1910 German ethnographic expedition. Cloth for women's skirts is woven on looms such as this one throughout the Caroline Islands. Courtesy of the Micronesian Seminar.

power," and "symbolically transform the wearer, tangibly imbuing him or her with spiritual force" (Rubinstein 1986, 60). They are critical to exchange relations among descent groups and larger communities (Petersen 1982b). Among the atolls of the central Carolines in particular, textiles play a critical role in the various interisland systems of both trade and social status. "A currency system of fairly fixed equivalents existed among woven skirts and loincloths, plaited mats, hanks of sennit twine, lengths of sennit rope, sticks of turmeric, and other goods such as tobacco, canoes, and shell belts," according to Rubinstein (1986, 62), while Steager observes that "chiefs, navigators, carpenters, and one class of ritual specialists could be identified by the colors and patterns of their loincloths" (1979, 349).

Although the peoples of the Marshalls, Kiribati, and Nauru are not weavers, obvious influences from and connections with the rest of Micronesia can be seen in their plaited mats, which employ many of the same sorts of designs. Throughout Micronesia similar design elements and motifs inform every aspect and genre of arts and crafts production. Most of these reflect traditional Micronesian tattoo designs.

Tattooing—the art of permanent bodily decoration—is one of the most striking features of Micronesian aesthetics. In traditional Micronesians societies virtually every adult, male and female, is tattooed; the bodies of mature Pohnpeian men are nearly covered with permanent designs. These serve cosmetic, religious, social, and psychological purposes, sometimes indicating clan and lineage affiliations and also manifesting the fortitude of those who endure the painful processes of having them inscribed into their flesh.

Wood carving is important throughout the region but is more highly developed and appreciated in some areas than others: "Wood-working is a major skill on Puluwat. It is evident in the marvelous symmetry of wooden objects; in their smooth, evenly curving surfaces combined with sharp edges and flat planes; and in the elegance of so complex an object as a canoe. This matching of great skill with aesthetic sensitivity is the essence of what we call art" (Steager 1979, 347). In some ways the social character of Micronesian art is at its most meaningful in the construction of canoes. Master canoe builders are among the most honored individuals in these communities, especially on islands with long-distance voyaging traditions. Canoe design incorporates concerns with maximizing both speed and stability. On Puluwat, where a new oceangoing canoe is a major source of pride to the entire community, "a large sailing canoe is regarded as a masterpiece of Puluwatan know-how, and its appearance and maneuverability are regarded as beautiful" (Steager 1979, 344). The workmanship a canoe builder puts into his canoes is matched by the knowledge and skills of the master navigators; together, their abilities and dedication make it possible for Micronesians to maintain the extraordinary degree of integration that characterizes relations across the vast expanses of ocean that their islands occupy.

Kosrae. A group of tattooed men, as sketched during Louis Duperrey's 1824 visit. These are typical Caroline tattoo designs. Courtesy of the Micronesian Seminar.

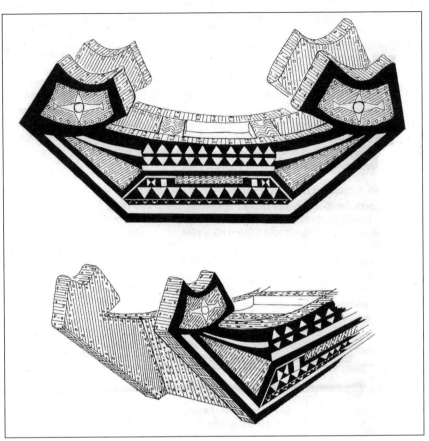

From Romonum island, Chuuk Lagoon. A receptacle for spirit offerings, from a model made in 1947 for the Yale Peabody Museum. Beautifully crafted by a skilled woodworker, this object is characteristic of art of the central Caroline Islands. From Frank LeBar, *The Material culture of Truk;* courtesy of the Peabody Museum, Yale University.

While dance performances, weaving, tattoos, and woodworking are examples of artistic endeavors on a relatively modest scale, architecture represents the manifestation of Micronesian artistic impulses and abilities on a much grander scale. Palauan community houses or meetinghouses—*bai*—are considered by some to represent the highest achievement of Micronesian material art. The elaborate wood carvings that decorate their exteriors are the most prominent aspects of these buildings, but as Mason also notes, "[Palauans] achieved an unusual strength of construction by utilizing their consummate skill in carpentry. The lofty gabled ends of the 50-foot-long meeting houses represented a composition of carefully hewn planks fitted horizontally behind framing batten boards" (1964, 922). Yapese meetinghouses can be favorably compared to those of Palau. For sheer grandeur of size in single structures, however, the Kiribati *maneaba* is the most telling. One such example on Butaritari was said to measure 114 by 250 feet (nearly 30,000 square feet).

The Chamorros erect many of their buildings on rows of massive, carved stone piers, called *latte*. It appears that competitive aspects are entailed in determining just how large to make the *latte,* which were still increasing in size at the time that Spanish occupation of the Marianas destroyed much of indigenous society there. *Latte* have sometimes been characterized as being without precedent in the region, but stone bases for the wooden uprights of large communal buildings are common throughout much of Micronesia, and *latte* may in fact be no more than a local efflorescence of a technique that diffused into the Marianas along with other Carolinian cultural forms and themes.

Construction on the greatest scale in Micronesia, however, is found in the vast complex of artificial islets and channels at Nan Madol, raised on the fringing reef at Pohnpei's easternmost point, facing the sunrise. A similar but much less extensive complex is located at Lelu, in Kosrae. Extending over approximately two hundred acres, Nan Madol's ninety-two islets were constructed over a period of centuries. On some of these islets, imposing stoneworks have been erected, culminating with the massive, soaring bulk of Nan Dowas. This structure covers an area of 208 by 235 feet; at points its walls, built with loglike basalt prisms transported from points far across the island, rise as high as twenty-five feet (Morgan 1988, 62–78). There is nothing else quite like it in the insular Pacific, and it represents the fruit of enormous human efforts. Although archaeologists have insisted that this labor was coerced by powerful rulers, it is at least as plausible that Nan Madol was raised as a consequence of the voluntary public works competitions that characterize Pohnpeian society. Its grandeur should not distract us from a telling aspect of Micronesian artistic life: people's nearly universal participation in it (Petersen 1995b).

The widespread participation of individual Micronesians in artistic endeavors is evidence of what might be called their democratic outlook. This is particularly obvious in Ifaluk, where virtually everyone engages in the creation of artistic works or pursues aspects of aesthetic expression—especially in the realms of song and dance, which represent the greatest flowering of the artistic ethos there. Gods or spirits may enter into anyone's body and possess them long enough to transmit new songs through them, and everyone sings and dances as means of pleasing the gods. While the people of industrialized societies may surpass Micronesians in sophistication, Burrows argues that islanders "excel us in participation" and that when it comes to "expressing the sentiments of ordinary people, their art serves much better than ours." As he observes, "In this respect, they have the advantages of democracy; we have those of aristocracy" (Burrows 1963, 431).

Social Aspects of Micronesian Religion, Magic, and Belief

In the same way that art cannot be separated from the rest of Micronesians' lives, religion is thoroughly woven into the fabric of their existence. For my purposes here, I distinguish between religion and beliefs (or, expressed another way, philosophy) largely in terms of religion's engagement with the supernatural. Rank, one of the central organizing principles of Micronesian social life, hinges to a great extent on primogeniture and settlement priority, which are, in turn, rooted in notions about privileged access to ancestral lineage spirits and, through them, to the gods and spirits who inhabit and oversee specific locales. This direct involvement of spirits and gods in chieftainship and politics means that religion permeates social life in general.

William Lessa has said of Micronesian religion, "[It] is a mélange of many elements: celestial and terrestrial deities, nature spirits, demons, and ancestral ghosts, with a strong infusion of magic, taboo, and divination. No one trait dominates the system" (1968, 498). Alkire, on the other hand, has explicitly disputed this notion, arguing instead that this apparent "mélange" of spirits, ghosts, and gods is "more easily classified and understood when viewed from the perspective of such key structural principles as land/people and brother/sister unity and the complementary distribution of power between land and sea, internal and external domains, and males and females" (1989, 90).

In his extraordinarily comprehensive study of "pre-Christian religious tradition" in Chuuk, Goodenough explores the many ways in which these traditions serve in both personal and social realms. As he notes, "The meanings and functions of customary beliefs and practices are often not easily determined. They can and usually do mean different things to different individuals," and thus "all members of a society do not share an emotional attachment to the same beliefs and practices" (2002, 9). Much of what he describes on Chuuk applies equally well throughout the eastern and central Carolines.

Consideration of traditional Micronesian religious beliefs can reasonably begin with widely shared notions of the human soul and an afterlife. Spirits of the dead serve as intermediaries between the world of the living and a supernatural realm that is inhabited by these spirits, by local "demons," and by gods associated with the sky. Spirits remain intimately involved in the lives of their lineages and loved ones but also gain supernatural powers that enable them to intervene with demons and gods when properly invoked or propitiated. The social aspects of Micronesian religion are entwined with rituals and rites intended to honor and propitiate these spirits and thus convince them to help secure relatively benevolent treatment of the living from nature, which is, in turn, largely under the oversight of the gods. In most Micronesian societies these ghosts, spirits, and gods—there is not a clear distinction between entirely supernatural beings and the spirits of the deceased—are known by some variant of the term *eni* or *ani*.

Micronesians tend to be ambivalent about the spirits of their recently departed kin. In most of their belief systems, the period shortly after death "is a time of tension" in which "steps are taken to encourage the soul, which can be dangerous, to leave the vicinity of the body and move on to its ultimate destination in the afterworld." Funeral practices are "in large part designed to placate the souls of the recently deceased and speed them" on this journey, "lest they endanger the living" (Lessa 1968, 498–499). On the other hand, skulls of loved ones are preserved and revered in a number of Micronesian societies, including those of Kiribati (Wilkes 1845, 86) and the Marianas (Driver 1983, 214), and in Chuuk the remains of a loved one might be wrapped in a bundle and suspended from the rafters of the surviving kin's house (Goodenough 2002, 138). On Ifaluk, burial at sea is thought to make it easier for the bereaved to forget lost loved ones (Lutz 1988, 126). In whatever way the remains of the deceased are disposed of, though, their spirits are assumed to sustain their deep concern with the living and to continue interacting with them, sometimes in benign ways, sometimes malevolently. Across Micronesia there are spirit mediums—individuals through whom the spirits of the dead are able to speak to the living, while the living are, in turn, able to petition ancestral spirits for information and assistance.

Much of Micronesian religious life is focused, then, on the conjunction of spirits' ongoing involvement with their lineages, lineage ties to land, and the spirits' links to gods. As we have seen, chiefs are typically among the more senior members of their lineages, in terms of either chronological age or genealogical reckoning. Those chiefs who are not older or genealogically senior are likely to be especially adept in their interpersonal relations or at warfare or else to possess other highly valued qualities, and they too appear to be blessed with close ties to their ancestors. Likewise, the senior status of leading or chiefly lineages is typically based on claims that their ancestors were the first to settle the island or community, and the chiefs of senior lineages serve as principal leaders of their entire communities. Thus a community's leading chief is among the individuals within his or her own lineage thought to have the closest connections to that lineage's ancestors, and by the act of recognizing someone as chief, both the lineage and the community endow him or her with the authority to act as their link with these ancestors. These are, of course, the ancestors thought to have the closest connections to the supernatural spirits of the island or the particular locale the community occupies. Paramount and community chiefs embody the spiritual power of both the community's leading lineage and the place itself and are consequently able to serve as intermediaries with precisely those spirits and/or gods of nature who have the most influence on the quality of life in any particular spot.

The most extensive, conspicuous, and consequential of all Micronesian religious practices are the first-fruits rituals. Although known by a wide variety of names—for example, Lamotrek *maulmei* (Alkire 1974), Chuuk *wumwusomwoon* (Goodenough 2002, 262–265), Marshalls' *ekan* (Carucci 1997, 168), Pohnpei *nohpwei*, and Kiribati *inagu* (Lundsgaarde 1978, 71)—they are nearly identical throughout the region (and throughout much of Oceania as well).[2] Like nearly all Micronesian rituals, first fruits are organized around chiefs, but whereas chiefs often simply preside at events such as funerals and dedication feasts for houses and canoes, first-fruits presentations and feasts are directed specifically toward the chiefs themselves. And while first-fruits rituals of one sort or another occur at the beginning of the harvest in traditional agrarian societies around the world, in Micronesian societies these are especially marked by an ongoing series of feasts held at sequential stages throughout a staple food crop's entire season.

First fruits are often portrayed as being primarily of political importance or, as in Goodenough's analysis of Chuuk's property system (1951), as statements about the ultimate ownership of land. These are certainly crucial aspects of first fruits, but I want to emphasize that the rituals are at their root religious in character. Because chiefs are, for all their political and secular qualities, fundamentally religious figures, they serve as channels between lineages and communities on the one hand, and ancestral spirits and nature spirits and gods on the other. Pohnpeians, for instance, when addressing a paramount chief or speaking about him, at least in formal circumstances, employ third-person plural forms ("they," "them") because they are ultimately speaking to or about a set of ancestral spirits. Still, it should be kept in mind that however much Micronesians honor and respect their leaders, they know that chiefs can, if they become problematic or abusive, be replaced.

Nature, on the other hand, must be placated. The force of storms and droughts is far too great, too unpredictable, and too likely to recur. In Chuuk, as elsewhere, "an arrogant failure to offer first fruits to a chief can lead to ghost [spirit] sickness in which the offender's land becomes barren" (Caughey 1977, 89). In treating their leaders properly, then, Micronesians are conscious that they are demonstrating their respect for the supernatural world that makes life either bearable or impossible for them. Because these rites are performed in stages throughout the seasons for most staple food crops, Micronesians continually engage in paying homage to these spirits and remain ever mindful of their dependence on them.

There are additional sorts of religious rites. Major rituals were once performed in the artificial island complex at Nan Madol (though most of these seem to have been truncated or abandoned even before the arrival of Europeans), and mythohistorical accounts on Pohnpei invariably describe its origins as a center for ritual activities (J. Fischer 1964; Petersen 1995b). Similar sorts of activities were undertaken by cults in other parts of Pohnpei, though on a much smaller scale (McCormick 1982); some of these spread westward to Chuuk and possibly beyond, and the ritual importance of large basalt stones in some of the Marshall atolls suggests that aspects of these beliefs diffused eastward as well (Goodenough 1986). "Spirit houses" and effigies are common in the central and western Carolines and are used in the performance of various rites, while on Kosrae and Pohnpei, preparation and consumption of kava *(sakau)*, a mildly intoxicating beverage squeezed from the roots of a species of pepper plant *(Piper methysticum)* that is considered to provide a particularly potent connecting link to the spirit realm, is central to all ritual activities.

Spirit mediums, who channel interactions with the spirits of the recently (and sometimes not-so-recently) departed, practice throughout Micronesia and represent a notably different aspect of religious activity. While most rituals are organized around pervasive hierarchical principles focused on lineage and community leaders, mediums allow individuals and families to establish direct personal contact with the spirit world. In doing so, they provide counterbalance to the political sway of the chiefs. In Chuuk, spirits communicate through mediums *(waatawa)* to teach special knowledge and spells associated with "the entire range of arts and crafts, such as healing, weaving, house building, and canoe making" (Goodenough 2002, 156). Even more striking and significant, however, is the prevalence of magic and sorcery in Micronesian societies.

I use "magic" to refer to practices and techniques (usually in the form of spells) employed by individuals to achieve one sort or another of relatively benign control over either the supernatural realm, nature (especially to enhance the growth of crops or manage local weather), or other people (particularly in the form of "love magic" meant to cause one person to become enamored of another). Such magic is usually performed by specialists, although most Micronesians possess knowledge of, if not any particular expertise in using, certain general formulas. By "sorcery," on the other hand, I mean the use of basically similar techniques in the service of negative or malevolent ends, either to inflict damage on the possessions, crops, or health of others or, in some cases, to kill them.

Because it is easy to misunderstand or misinterpret them, these are difficult topics to discuss without at least a few qualifications, but any description of Micronesian life that ignores them would be incomplete. As an exchange in a professional journal between Lessa (1961) and Spiro (1961) demonstrated, it is possible for a competent anthropologist to entirely miss the presence of magic and sorcery in a community—in this case, Ifaluk. But it is also true that some Micronesian societies emphasize and even publicize the practice of magic and sorcery while others minimize it. The people of Romonum island in Chuuk Lagoon, for example, are known for actively suppressing their aggressive feelings or tendencies, and anthropologists have reported that little or no sorcery is practiced

Lamotrek. A spirit medium performing a curing ceremony, during the 1910 German ethnographic expedition. Mediums provide the living with important connections to the spirit world. Courtesy of the Micronesian Seminar.

there. On Uman island, just a few miles across the lagoon, on the other hand, people are reportedly quite open and frank about both their aggressive relations with one another and their readiness to resort to sorcery to further this aggression (Caughey 1977, 170). My own experience on Pohnpei tells me that although magic and sorcery are practiced there, they do not concern people nearly so much as chiefly politics, competitive feasting, and kava do, although Martha Ward (1989) suggests that they play a much more dramatic part in Pohnpeian life than I have myself observed. I conclude that the impact of conversion to Christianity, and of their colonial experiences in general, have led most Micronesians to be quite circumspect in what they say to outsiders (and in many cases to one another) about magical practices, in much the same way that they are reticent about other topics, including sexual activities and family tensions.

There is a particularly Micronesian style of self-disparagement, often employed when speaking to outsiders, that lends itself to the exaggeration of traits that are likely to be perceived as unattractive or problematic; this can result in comments to the effect, "Look how bad we are—we engage in these unsavory practices." But there is also a common, counterposing tendency to attribute to neighboring lineages, communities, or island societies a wide variety of disreputable behavior, including unappealing dietary habits (e.g., eating rats or cats), domestic violence, and sorcery. And there is, paradoxically, yet another tendency to avoid speaking at all about certain sensitive topics. It is quite difficult, if not impossible, to know in advance just which of these mind-sets concerning life in their communities is shaping any given Micronesian's commentary to outsiders.

Based on years of experience listening to Pohnpeians speaking with one another in a wide range of contexts, but especially in lengthy conversations as they prepare and consume kava, it is my sense that while they take the implications of magical practices quite seriously, they do not spend much of their time actually fretting about them. Pohnpeian life lends itself to active, practical political participation, and while personal disputes and antagonisms sometimes call forth sorcerers' attacks, only occasionally do these spill over into the wider public domain. It would be a mistake for me to try to draw wider conclusions for all of Micronesia based on my Pohnpeian experiences, though, and my reading of differences of opinion and interpretation, such as those between Lessa and Spiro regarding Ifaluk or between the anthropologists who have worked in Chuuk Lagoon, suggests to me that we would have to know a great deal more about the contexts in which the outsiders have worked if we wish to draw any broad generalizations from their reports.

I am, however, willing to formulate several limited conclusions. First and foremost, the practice of magic and sorcery must be placed in the context of overall Micronesian life. For the most part these practices represent largely individual interests and drives. It is of the utmost importance to recognize this. Life in Micronesian societies is overwhelmingly communal and communitarian, hierarchical, and courteous. Sorcery and magic provide useful outlets for aggression that is otherwise habitually suppressed.

Magic and sorcery also reflect the general complexity of Micronesian sociopolitical attitudes and propensities. While the most visible sorts of religious activities are public rituals, almost all of which are focused on chiefs and chiefly hierarchy, anyone who wishes to can learn at least a few simple magical spells or other techniques and practice them privately.[3] At the same time, detailed knowledge of truly esoteric practices is closely held by individuals and lineages, is revealed only to a few aspirants, and must be purchased through payments of goods or services. Even more telling is what this reveals to us about underlying attitudes toward the gods and the supernatural realm that shape the vagaries of the natural world Micronesians inhabit. While spirits and gods are normally invoked through the offices of the chiefs, magic allows anyone to attempt to do so. That is, these practices reflect the deep-seated sense that if an individual learns and invokes certain techniques, he or she can exercise a degree of influence or control over supernatural forces and thereby gain a degree of influence or control over natural and social phenomena, be it a storm, a conflict, a competition, a disease, or even a romance. Moreover, chiefs themselves must constantly be on guard; their status and authority often provoke enmity or jealousy, and sorcery is an indirect but not entirely subtle means of resisting them.

As I have stressed throughout my consideration of virtually every aspect of Micronesian social and cultural life, the nature of social relations in the islands can be understood only as complex, contradictory, and nuanced. For every point at which hierarchy is in one way or another emphasized, we can find variant contexts and alternative ways in which a belief in or commitment to equality is also manifested. A leader who fails to redistribute or to give away at least as much as he or she receives has little chance of becoming or remaining a well-respected and therefore effective chief. And strong, forceful leaders are no more admired than those who are quiet, modest, and capable of promoting compromise and cooperation. Individual initiative and aspirations are not only recognized in aesthetic pursuits; although chiefs serve as focal points in religious ritual contexts, individuals are able to engage directly with the spirit world via magic and sorcery.

Values

It is difficult to separate out values from behavior. But in order to describe both distinct Micronesian cultures and the nature of what it is they have in common, I will try first to present some of the underlying values and then to consider some of the different sorts of behaviors that are shaped by them as Micronesians deal with specific circumstances. As I discuss in more depth below, in Micronesian cultures social behavior (and not just assumptions about what is appropriate) is the crucial determinant of how individuals and lineages create and maintain ties with one another.

Nowhere do generalizations about Micronesian societies and cultures seem as problematic as in terms of values, personal styles, and character dimensions. For anyone who has not lived in Micronesia, it might at first glance seem absurd to believe that the two communities of Ifaluk and Uman, as described by Catherine Lutz and John Caughey, respectively, have much in common, but in fact the people of Ifaluk (in the central Carolines) consciously strive to avoid what they consider dangerous traits or behaviors of precisely the sort that people on Uman (in Chuuk Lagoon) celebrate.[4] And Uman's people themselves recognize the potential for abuse in these behaviors and traits and seek to keep them in check. What is essentially the same array of attitudes and behaviors exists in both societies, but the tendencies and emphases differ. Because these two accounts are among the few thoroughgoing analyses of Micronesian value systems available, and because juxtaposition of the two communities provides us with an opportunity to examine rather contradictory facets of Micronesian value systems, I focus quite closely on them in this discussion.

Much of what is characteristic of Ifaluk lies at the core of Micronesian cultural values in general, especially the intertwined relationship between sociopolitical rank and notions about "taking care of" people. To hold high rank, or at least to be deemed worthy of holding it, an individual must care for others, either within a lineage or within a community, and demonstrate continuing concern for their welfare. In practice this entails acts of real generosity, the consistent giving away of one's goods, efforts, time, thoughts—in a word, of oneself. The converse, or corollary, of this is a recognition of a certain neediness on the part of most people, a willingness or desire to be taken care of.

People on Ifaluk value and try to exhibit personal behaviors characterized by *maluwelu*, which Lutz translates as, among other things, "gentleness" (1988, 112).[5] The same cluster of behaviors and values in Chuuk is known as *mosonoson* (humility, kindness) and is deemed "a good, admirable style of behavior" (Caughey 1977, 25–26). A crucial difference between the societies of Ifaluk and Uman is that on Ifaluk other traits that are especially admired include compassion *(fago)* and nurturance *(gamwelar)*, while on Uman the character dimensions that are valued in tandem with kindness are *pwara* (bravery, power) and *ekiyek pechekkun* (strong thought, competitive thought). These qualities are all known and esteemed in both societies, but the emphasis placed on each differ, and the traits stressed on Ifaluk buttress and augment one another, while on Uman they tend to offset and contrast with one another. Important aspects of both sets of these traits characterize life in all Micronesian societies.

In some places, such as Palau, greater emphasis tends to be placed on more assertive aspects of interpersonal style, although people there recognize and appreciate both styles of chiefly leadership behavior (see chapter 7). In the atolls of the central Carolines, low-key styles are more often the rule, although the peoples of adjacent islands, including Puluwat, Pulusuk, and Pulap, point to what they consider to be quite telling differences among them (Flinn 1992). And within what is usually taken to be a single cultural realm, such as Chuuk Lagoon, notable differences exist among nearby islands (Caughey 1977; cf. Marshall 1989).

Some individuals possess personality traits that enable them to occupy leadership roles successfully, while others are unable or do not desire to wield authority.[6] Micronesians also identify human frailties readily and are keenly aware that their leaders do not always measure up to the standards set for them. There is a Pohnpeian phrase, for instance, *sakanan en soupeidi*, "the misbehavior of chiefs," that refers to the supposedly irresponsible predilections of those accustomed to privilege.[7] And because of the multiple sorts of chiefly positions woven into Micronesian political systems, there are in fact quite different leadership styles.

Micronesians expect their chiefs, whether they are heads of lineages or communities, to be able to do two somewhat contrary things simultaneously. They should be strong and forceful enough to protect their people from both outside threats and internal strife. But they must at the same time be gentle and nurturing enough to take good care of them. For a variety of reasons, some having to do with historical and environmental circumstances and some with simple vagaries of chance, societies that otherwise closely resemble one another may differ significantly when it comes to which aspects of these sets of traits they emphasize.

Various Micronesian value systems, which are in most ways quite similar to one another, thus tend to emphasize somewhat different behaviors, styles, and attitudes. People on Ifaluk, like all Micronesians, stress the absolute necessity of sharing, yet "any great show of magnanimity in sharing is, however, frowned upon, as this putting forward of self is seen as denigrating of the other" (Lutz 1988, 89). On the other hand, Caughey describes how generosity is viewed on Uman: "Some of the most dramatic acts of generosity occur when an individual makes an outright gift of land or food to someone he has little obligation to help, but on whom he takes pity. These grand gestures are characteristic of the man of true bravery" (1977, 58). And as a particularly philosophical Pohnpeian once said to me in describing a great show of generosity, "Ah, to give away all that one possesses—*Ih soaren ohl*. That reveals the substance of a real man."

On Uman, a reputation for great "anger" is associated with "the ideals of strong thought and bravery." As Caughey notes, "Such a person is pictured as holding himself under control, in trying situations, only with difficulty and as being ready to explode in destructive rage if seriously crossed." When people describe situations in which an individual has exploded in anger, "their admiration is evident" (Caughey 1977, 39). On Ifaluk there is, on the other hand, "an absolute sanction against physical expression of inner events in violence or, to an important but lesser extent, in loud or impolite words." People there recognize that "a person may not look angry or irritated, but may still have angry thoughts/emotions." The act of suppressing anger is *goli*, "to hide." Lutz observes, "The object of keeping a state an internal one is not to conceal the fact that one is experiencing a particular emotion, but rather to avoid conflict or other unpleasant social consequences" (1988, 97). On Pohnpei, however, the ability to conceal one's emotions is itself a highly valued character trait. While *kanengamah* (literally, mature contents) serves the same purpose as Ifaluk *goli* (to hide), the object of the former is not simply to avoid conflict but to demonstrate one's self-control and strength in his or her own right. To act spontaneously out of anger or other violent emotion is to show that one is not mature enough to control oneself; even to reveal that one is experiencing such an emotion is to admit to lacking the self-control expected of a competent adult (Petersen 1993). This a point to which I shall return.

While such differences in emphasis mean that values and behaviors typical (or stereotypical) of people in given communities or societies vary, the entire cluster of expectations together define the broad sweep of a common Micronesian culture. Micronesians expect their leaders to be (or at least hope that they will be) strong, but this strength is measured at least as much in their ability to care for others as it is in any other dimension. While physical and personal power are admired, they are not ordinarily deemed effective unless they are accompanied by continual demonstrations of nurturing behavior by those who would wield them. Although generosity is a universal theme in all Micronesian social relations, leaders are expected to be more generous than everyone else. A corollary, or consequence, of this is that to show signs of need or neediness openly is to acknowledge that one is subordinate. Leaders commonly receive gifts of many sorts, but most leaders hesitate to demand or even request others' generosity. To do so might be taken as a sign of weakness. But it is equally important to recognize that even though individuals in any society are socialized into certain behavior styles, every society in fact encompasses multiple behavior styles. These can best be seen in contradictory expectations about leadership.

Micronesians in general (like most peoples) want leaders who are both hardheaded and kindhearted, tough and compassionate. Occasionally, these qualities may be found in the same person, but more often than not individual leaders tend more toward one style than another and are subject to both praise and disparagement for their accomplishments and shortcomings, depending on who is judging their qualities and performances.[8]

The great respect Micronesians show their leaders can easily be misinterpreted, since Micronesians demonstrate respect behavior toward a great many other people as well, including their elders, their siblings, and foreigners. And in Micronesian value systems the way to assure that one remains worthy of respect is to show reciprocal respect. Effective leaders are for the most part modest men and women. This is not to say that arrogance and hauteur are not occasionally encountered, but that most people strive to avoid them, socialize their children to avoid them, and are likely to chastise those who display them. With such role models in place, virtually everyone is respectful, polite, modest, and generous, traits that have always been identified with Micronesian culture.

In the same way that Micronesians understand that in order to be deemed worthy of respect it is necessary to act respectfully toward others, exchanges of food and other valued goods must be reasonably reciprocal. People frequently bestow various kinds of goods, sometimes in a form that appears to be tribute, on lineage heads and chiefs, among others. But the most effective elements of leaders' status derive from their ability and willingness to respond in kind. This is not to deny or diminish the importance of primogeniture and seniority of descent but only to reemphasize that these factors are not, by themselves, very good guides to understanding just who exercises authority in Micronesian communities or how they do it. "Rank is so highly valued and respected that it stands out as one of the master-values of this culture," as Burrows and Spiro (1970, 179) said of Ifaluk, but they equally stressed that chiefs must speak respectfully and act generously. This is true for all of Micronesia, and Micronesian culture and society cannot be fully understood except from this perspective.

Patterns and Styles of Social Behavior

Because Micronesian societies are organized around the two complementary principles of lineage and community, they possess enormous flexibility. Depending upon circumstances, individuals and lineages are free to rely on kin from distant islands (or communities) or to act together with the distinct and separate lineages that reside within their own communities. In her account of Pulap society, Juliana Flinn demonstrates that social behavior—the ways in which individuals act toward others—is the crucial determinant of how individuals and lineages activate and maintain their links with one another. "Behavior can take precedence over genetic substance," she explains, because "birth is not determinate. Even clan identity, seemingly tied to descent, is not exclusive but situational." Simply by behaving as kin, she says, people can emphasize new personal and group linkages, even while retaining existing ties. "Pulapese see no contradiction" between newer and older relationships, "and these multiple ties supply them with a variety of relatives to turn to when necessary." Individuals thus possess "a variety of ties and identities to choose from, and selecting one does not preclude activating another, depending on circumstance and inclination." This means, ultimately, that "Pulapese see their social world as historically far wider than their own tiny atoll" (Flinn 1992, 51, 53–54, 58).

The same principles apply to Pulap notions of rank. "Genealogical position is not the single, overriding determinant in descent group leadership. Personal ability and behavior allow someone to perform at least aspects of a leadership role, even if he or she is not born to the most senior position." Thus behavior, once again, can take precedence over genetic substance" (Flinn 1992, 51).

It can be said, then, that ambiguity drives Micronesian social systems, or at least makes Micronesian life possible. That is why this emphasis on behavior—that is, the notion that one's kin connections and one's rank are to a certain extent determined by how one acts—makes it possible for individuals to tie themselves to multiple kin groups and for entire communities to establish linkages with other islands. Thus an appreciation of individual and group behavior, and not simply genealogy or abstract principles and values, is critical to understanding the character of Micronesian societies.

I turn now to a consideration of what I call behavior styles. Although there is no common Micronesian personality or type, nor even a type common to any island community, the conditions of Micronesian social life, along with some elementary cultural precepts, shape the basic patterns of people's interactions with one another as they go about their daily lives. There are shared tendencies and expectations, and while some of these are specific to particular communities, others are more generally Micronesian.[9]

I have heard it said of the populations on tiny Micronesian atoll communities that there are no personality types, only individual personalities. And it is equally true that the population of each Micronesian island or community encompasses an entire range of human possibilities—that differences among individuals are as pronounced within these small societies as they are anywhere else. Micronesians certainly speak of one another in ways that make clear that in their experience, as in that of other peoples, "it takes all kinds," or as Pohnpeians sometimes say of themselves, "Pohnpei sohte ehu" (Pohnpei is not all of one kind).

As a general rule, Micronesians expect people to be engaged with one another rather than withdrawn. Most of life is lived in the open, communally, and people talk together in groups as a primary form of social activity. In some sorts of public discussions, the people present will on one occasion largely voice agreement with one another while in a later gathering the same people, discussing the same topic, may for the most part agree on an entirely opposite conclusion. It is just as likely, however, that lively disagreement will be the case. Alkire, for instance, describes the give-and-take at an island-wide meeting on Lamotrek (1989, 36–38), while Cheyne described Pohnpeians as almost coming to blows at public meetings (1971, 183). And although Micronesian politics depend to a great extent on consensus, it can be quite difficult to observe just how real accord is arrived at, since apparent agreement in any given situation is not a very good indicator of what people will be likely to agree upon on the next occasion they take up the issue.

On Pohnpei, where people gather in groups of ten to thirty in the evenings to prepare and drink kava, there is ordinarily banter and conversation, usually low-key but sometimes quite animated, for an hour or two until the participants gradually drift into song and then into shared silence. This continuum of talk, song, and silence promotes consensus, I believe, but I am not sure even Pohnpeians understand exactly what transpires on these occasions (Petersen 1995a). Much the same happens wherever men come together to drink palm toddy (mildly fermented coconut-palm sap), as in the central Caroline atolls.

I noted in chapter 6 that the trader Cheyne found the explorer Wilkes' description of a council meeting in Kiribati so apt that he modified it only slightly before including it in his own very observant account of Pohnpeian life. Although Kiribati communities are among the more egalitarian Micronesian societies, whereas Pohnpei's are among the more stratified, an essentially identical process is typical of both. It seems worth adding here that the process of talking until agreement is achieved implies the presence of differing views and therefore the existence of political opposition, a point the political philosopher Kwame Gyekye (1997, 118) uses to illustrate the dynamics of democratic processes in traditional African societies. The Micronesian tradition of achieving consensus, then, hardly implies underlying agreement—rather, a great deal of effort goes into achieving it. As a Palauan observed, things there are not settled "with arguments and counterarguments." He added, "It's not who has the last word. It's the feelings *after* the last word" (Kluge 1991, 223).

Precisely because it is the feelings that follow discussions that determine how any given decision is going to be received and implemented, at issue is the complex mix of nonconfrontational speaking and respectful listening styles that intersect with a shared recognition that people are being deliberately agreeable. No one can assume that overt or apparent agreement in any particular case actually represents underlying agreement; people know it is likely that they are going to have to come back and discuss the matter at hand multiple times, and they recognize the importance of leaving one meeting emotionally prepared to return for another. But then that is the essence of Micronesian social and political process: people coming together to speak and discuss over and over again.

Ironically, this awareness of the importance of shared goodwill actually encourages a good deal of teasing and ragging. It is intended, Micronesians have told me, to make people continually practice holding resentments, dislikes, and hurts inside, rather than openly expressing them. Many Micronesians seem to have a deep-seated sense that society itself depends upon their abilities to overcome irritation, even as they strive to avoid causing it.

Although Micronesian personal style and interpersonal relations are characterized by quiet calm, politeness, respect, and modesty, one does occasionally hear loud outbursts, public arguments, chastising harangues, and encounters between confrontational or boastful individuals. The exceptions to expected or acceptable comportment can indeed be glaringly obvious, precisely because they stand out so starkly against the gentle character of most Micronesian behavior patterns. Among the most notable aspects of this is the relationship between respect and humility or modesty. In public (and, in my experience, private) interactions, most mature Micronesians treat other adults with careful respect and display circumspect modesty. Even a high-ranking chief performing at the focal point of ritual ceremonies acts with restraint and humility. In all but a few circumstances, Micronesians speak quietly: Lutz found everyone on Ifaluk speaking in whispers (1988, 158), and as I noted in an earlier chapter, Lütke said of Kosraeans that their "usual custom is to speak softly" (1982, 125). Micronesians rarely call attention to themselves, and as a general rule they do not like to say no. As a consequence they are often mistakenly thought to be too compliant and deceptive. They value nonconfrontational styles and an ability to behave politely and considerately under all circumstances, but these traits are offset by other temperamental tendencies.

Their general emphasis on quiet calm notwithstanding, Micronesians, especially males, also stress the importance of a certain martial bearing. Living in societies with nothing remotely resembling organized military establishments or armies, virtually all able-bodied men are expected to serve their lineages and communities as warriors. In the atoll societies particularly, where seafaring is of such great importance, boldness is also expected of navigators and those who accompany them; squarely facing the elements and all the hazards of long-distance voyaging is a defining aspect of these roles.

More pervasive than these aspects, at least in everyday life, however, is the underlying, nearly ubiquitous emphasis placed on stoic bravery. Micronesians do not interpret quiet calm as timidity; it is instead an indication that one's emotions are kept firmly under control. But precisely because one cannot know what is going on behind another's placid exterior, it is easy to imagine that turmoil, agitation, or even violence lie just below the surface. On Ifaluk there is "an absolute sanction against physical expression of inner events in violence or, to an important but lesser extent, in loud or impolite words." People there are thus quite aware that someone can be angry without appearing to be. Men in particular are expected to and in fact do suppress anger. As Lutz notes, "The object of keeping a state an internal one"—that is, *goli* (to hide or suppress)—"is not to conceal the fact that one is experiencing a specific emotion, but rather to avoid conflict or other unpleasant social consequences." But there is little emphasis on the outright masking of emotion; indeed, it is frequently observed that one can always tell what the internal state of the other person is from facial, gestural, or situational cues (Lutz 1988, 97).

As I have explained, Pohnpeians, on the other hand, practice *kanengamah*, which entails, among other things, a habit of constraint, of concealing or suppressing one's feelings; masking one's emotions is behavior, at least under some circumstances, that is entirely expected of mature adults (Petersen 1993). A Pohnpeian aphorism—*Nennen sarau kommwad*, which might be translated either as "the quiet of the fierce barracuda" or "the fierceness of the quiet barracuda"—functions as a reminder. Pohnpeians say that while they respect sharks, they fear barracudas, which are given to hanging motionless in the water and then striking suddenly, without warning. Quiet persons should not be taken lightly—there may be much more to them than meets the eye.

There is, though, another, quite different aspect to this constraint. In the course of her research on Pohnpeian mothering, Maureen Fitzgerald was told by some women, "For Pohnpeian women it is a sign of honor not to cry or make a noise during labor and delivery; other women may cry out but not Pohnpeian women....If a Pohnpeian woman cries out it will bring great shame to the family" (2001, 77).[10]

On Uman a reputation for *song*, "great anger," is commonly associated with the ideal of bravery, and it is believed that it requires enormous restraint for a man to hold himself under control. Somewhat paradoxically, then, to appear strong and brave one must hint at great anger while keeping it under control. Caughey explains that Uman's people "want to be, and to be known by others as persons of bravery, respectfulness, and strong thought, and they very much wish to avoid being, or being regarded by others as, persons of cowardice, arrogance, or weak thought" (1977, 41).

Apprehension about the underlying potential for violence is quite fundamental to Micronesian social and political life. Micronesians respect peaceful, quiet demeanors and esteem humility and compassion not simply because these qualities have intrinsic value but because all these are understood to be essential in preventing outbreaks of violence. It is only by will and effort that thoughtful people ensure that they and their communities will be spared the consequences of violence. And outbreaks of cruelty and violence do occur. Within Chuuk's communities, Goodenough points out, disguised hostility can in time lead to physical assault (2002, 266). Some of the most potent—and useful—magical spells are used to control such outbreaks, and sometimes individuals and families simply move away in order to avoid them. Political assassinations occupy a significant place in mythohistorical accounts, and tales about them stand in rather stark contrast to the notions of quiet competence more generally expected of leaders.[11] In Pohnpei's mythohistory a dynasty of powerful leaders, the Sau Deleurs, were gradually transformed into cruel despots by the unchecked power they wielded until the last of them was defeated by a general uprising led by the culture hero Isokelekel.

When "justifiable anger" *(song)* is provoked in Ifaluk, it evokes the fear that it will be accompanied by aggression, even though "interpersonal violence is virtually nonexistent on the island." As Lutz observes, "Although the two expectations—of violence and of the lack of it—may appear contradictory, this approach to the angry person can instead be interpreted as the means by which the Ifaluk remind themselves of the possibility of violence while fully expecting that it will be prevented by the individual's maturity" (1988, 176). That is, a person liable to express justifiable anger is equally expected to be capable of suppressing it. Micronesians in general expect mature, socially competent adults to exercise a very high degree of self-control. A leader who threatened violence would have the perverse effect of demonstrating to his people that he was incapable of competent leadership.

Other personality traits and expectations about character are related to further aspects of this demeanor. Competent adults are more or less expected to show endurance, to be hardworking or industrious, to organize their labors efficiently, and to exhibit a degree of prowess in most of what they do. On the more fertile islands, where natural bounty is typical, it is theoretically possible for individuals and families to survive with very little expenditure of effort, but it is still understood that a good and decent, well-socialized person will strive to be a productive member of society. Along with this willingness and ability to exert oneself, it is also assumed that a mature individual possesses working knowledge of social, natural, and supernatural processes. A competent adult is expected to know a good deal of history and myth, to have a grasp of genealogies, and to have more than a passing familiarity with the techniques necessary to whatever fishing, farming, domestic, and craft activities are particular to his or her society. While much knowledge, of both the supernatural and natural worlds, is proprietary—possessed by specific individuals or lineages—everyone is expected to possess some knowledge relevant to his or her status and position in society. And adults and older children should be capable of local variants of what the people of Ifaluk call *repiy*, which Lutz translates as "social intelligence" (1988, 107). They must be able to function in communities that depend on cooperation and consensus for their survival.

Together, these fundamental qualities of respect, emotional strength, and productive abilities provide the basis for another cluster of attributes. Many Micronesian societies place roughly equal emphases on compassion and nurturing, on the one hand, and on vulnerability and dependency on the other. Individuals are embedded in a network of kinfolk and are both required to care for their relatives and expected to depend upon them, although they sometimes fear that they will not be able to depend on them. The ability to produce food is but a facet of a complex of skills and virtues that includes the obligation to provide it for others. A responsibility to nurture others inheres in the behavior appropriate for all adults but is especially expected, indeed required, of leaders. For this reason chiefs are commonly spoken of as fathers to their people, a fact that has caused some confusion among scholars.[12]

Although chiefs function as mothers' brothers to the members of their lineages in these matrilineal societies, in their communities at large they are almost invariably conceived of as nurturing fathers. In Chuuk a good deal of ritual recognizes "the chief as titular father of the district and custodian of the district's welfare" (Goodenough 2002, 261). In some of these societies, then, dependency is deemed a normal, admirable human quality. In others emphases on autonomy and personal strength are such that mature persons can be rather insistent on their abilities to care for themselves. Whatever the case, there is always a fundamental, underlying expectation that any well-socialized, competent person will be unfailingly generous and ready to share almost anything he or she possesses, particularly with kin but also with neighbors and even with strangers in need. And as Lutz points out (1988, 38–39), travelers are assumed to be in need and thus deserving of compassion and care. That is, the martial, defensive aspects of Micronesian social life are offset by an emphasis on being welcoming and hospitable.

Equality, Hierarchy, and Survival

Micronesian societies cannot be understood simply by describing them as either hierarchical or egalitarian, a point I explored at length in earlier chapters. Hierarchical relationships are woven into nearly every aspect of Micronesian social life, and chiefs invariably receive first-fruits gifts and noticeably larger portions of goods in the course of feasts and other redistributive activities. But they are also expected to be generous with whatever they receive and/or possess, so that in the end they are likely to wind up with little more than anyone else and sometimes with less. Always, then, we find equality of a sort. It is misleading to say merely that Micronesian societies are hierarchical or that they are egalitarian. They are both simultaneously. Lutz notes the contradiction inherent in the combination of a ranked social system with the general egalitarianism of wealth and an emphasis on exchange: "Despite the presence of a hierarchy of clans and lineages, Ifaluk is a relatively egalitarian society" (Lutz 1988, 189, 113).

Micronesians treat their leaders, and high-ranking individuals in general, with respect partly because they expect roughly equal treatment in return. This is what I have called the reciprocity of respect. It is not unusual to hear people speaking of their chiefs as being exploitative or greedy, yet one may also hear them insisting on their own rights to be treated with equality; the Micronesian experience is not so much one or the other of these extremes as it is that of living in contexts in which each of these presumptions complements and mitigates the other.

Together, all these qualities reflect the tangle of values and behaviors that characterize Micronesian societies. In part this complex grows out of the basic demands of survival, reflecting the environmental hazards—especially typhoons and droughts—particular to Micronesia's physical location. As Micronesians themselves understand their situation, they depend absolutely upon these carefully cultivated webs of relationships.

It is in this context, then, that we find that rank and status in Micronesian societies are not simply about prestige or privilege. Rather, they are about leaders' obligations to the members of their lineages and communities. Such great emphasis is placed on taking care of others that it is difficult, if not impossible, to possess social status without taking responsibility for and nurturing others; to fail to nourish one's lineage or one's community is to deny or negate one's status. Micronesians find it difficult to conceptualize power without compassion. A leader who fails in this regard is likely to be overthrown, at least according to most tenets of Micronesian mythohistory. Nevertheless, the notion of the monstrous person who somehow gains power but fails to act with compassion is an important one—it explains why Micronesians keep such close checks on their leaders and why those who would be leaders are carefully socialized into their responsibilities.

Whatever the circumstances of an individual's birth, his or her chances of becoming a leader are limited in the absence of personal qualities that include both productive abilities and reliable generosity. Yet it is precisely because violence is imaginable that chiefs must be effective leaders. If they are not themselves warriors, they must create and preserve contexts in which competent warriors hold leadership positions of considerable prestige and status. Inequality does exist in Micronesia: it ensures a great deal of both nurturing and military strength, two sets of qualities that Western societies tend to view as being opposite or at least mutually exclusive but that Micronesians see as complementary facets of what leadership is all about.

These multiple, crosscutting, and sometimes apparently contradictory principles allow for a great deal of flexibility. Competing individuals and groups employ them as justifications for their own right to ascendancy. Leaders' legitimacy can be challenged or resisted with assertions that they have failed to discharge their responsibilities or that they lack the attributes necessary for effective leadership, including claims to powerful ancestral spirits and effective performance in the contemporary political arena, especially in the realms of feasting, navigation, and military organization.

This web of values occurs in several levels or scales of interaction. Within communities it is most immediately visible at the interpersonal level, in interactions and expectations among individuals, but the full complex is essential to the existence, survival, and daily functioning of the basic building blocks of Micronesian society, the matrilineages. Lineage ties constitute the most basic web of relationships in which each Micronesian is enmeshed—people are most immediately and securely taken care of by their lineage mates. Yet all this applies equally to the meshwork that integrates entire communities. Each Micronesian community has its chiefs, who serve as focal points for these relationships. A community's various lineages relate to one another in much the same fashion as individuals within lineages, and issues of rank and equality, of compassion and nurturing, of calm and potential violence, shape these interrelationships. While some lineages and clans are higher-ranking than others and some possess more land or have a greater number of members, the members of all ranking lineages are responsible for seeing that their descent groups discharge their obligations to the community as a whole in the same way that individual leaders are expected to nurture their lineage mates.

The same holds for relations between communities and islands. As Alkire has pointed out, smaller clusters of atolls in the central Carolines are linked by ties framed in social, political, and economic terms that mirror the ways that all the islands are integrated together into the chain running from Yap and Ulithi nearly one thousand miles to the atolls just west of Chuuk (1989, 145–149). These islands are ranked relative to one another, with their status deriving primarily from their relative proximity to Yap. As Lutz notes, "The hierarchy of power that exists in the islands between Yap and Truk is also phrased in terms of the ability and duty of the higher-ranked islands to take care of the lower ranked." Because "rank does bring experience in nurturing," people on Ifaluk, for example, believe that higher-ranked island populations should be given more responsibility than those of lower-ranked atolls (Lutz 1988, 141–142). Elsewhere in Micronesia, where the chains of authority tend not to be spelled out in such detail, the larger islands and atolls with higher rainfall, all of which possess greater resources, are higher-ranked than adjacent smaller or drier islands and are thus charged with responsibilities to care for their lower-ranking neighbors. This geographical integration parallels and reinforces the much greater integration created by the dispersed clans that characterize all of Micronesia's social and cultural existence.

Whether it is a matter of aesthetic expression, religious belief, or interpersonal relations, Micronesian life exhibits both egalitarian and hierarchical aspects. Added to this complex of attitudes and attributes are complementary emphases on strength and a warrior ethos and on nurturance and compassion; Micronesians deal with the world beyond their immediate communities and beyond their own shores with somewhat contradictory perspectives. They are prepared simultaneously to defend themselves vigorously from invasion and to be welcoming and generous hosts. It is these qualities, which mark both individual personalities and social life in general, that have enabled Micronesians to survive as successfully as they have.

CHAPTER 9

Some Exceptions to
the Pan-Micronesian Patterns

I HAVE ORGANIZED this work around the many commonalities among Micronesian societies, and most of it focuses on similar traits and practices. The societies of the Marshalls, the eastern and central Carolines, and Palau are alike in so many ways that I have drawn on them for most of my generalizations. But I have tried not to overlook the many significant differences among the islands either. There are aspects of society and culture in Kiribati, Nauru, Yap, and the Marianas, in particular, that differ markedly from the rest of Micronesia, and in this brief chapter I examine some of these telling divergences.

Kiribati

Probably the greatest factor shaping the ways in which Kiribati differs from the rest of Micronesia is the impact of the Polynesian influences it has experienced. Unlike the rest of the region, it borders immediately on Polynesia, but of greater significance is the apparent migration of or conquest by a group of "Samoans" several hundred years before European contact. The classic meetinghouse *(maneaba)* system of sociopolitical organization is quite similar to the Samoans' *fono* system, and this in turn has shaped many other facets of life in the islands.

There remains in Kiribati, nevertheless, a quintessentially Micronesian emphasis on mobility; it can be most clearly seen in the nesting of localized lineages within dispersed clans and the coupling of provisional rights to land with overarching residual rights. In the northern islands this is manifest in the *utu* and *kainga;* in the rest of the islands it is especially apparent in the character of the *boti*. *Boti* are both seating places within the *maneaba* and descent groups. Localized groups occupy these seats in any given *maneaba;* when traveling, an individual can enter any *maneaba* and find the place the local segment of his *boti* occupies. *Utu* are localized kin groups, while *kainga* are the plots of land where homesites are established. And yet *kainga* also refers to the people who live at the site or have active claims to it, while *utu* are often thought of in terms of specifying just who has access to land. In Kiribati, as in the rest of Micronesia and in Polynesia, land and people, although sometimes distinguished from one another, are often conceptually merged.

What seem to be most typically Micronesian, however, are the ways in which localized groups of people are nested hierarchically into dispersed decent groups. In most of Kiribati the dispersed clans *(boti)* are composed of lineages *(kainga)* localized in each community. This pattern enables people to move relatively freely from place to place in order to gain access to resources in perilous times, in precisely the same way that it does in the rest of Micronesia. Maude wrote that according to tradition "the original inhabitants of the Gilberts possessed neither boti nor kainga"; these were, he suggested, introduced by the Samoans. But I interpret the evidence quite differently. The leader of a clan in a given community is the *atun te boti* (head of the clan). Within a *kainga* (that is, a localized group occupying and working a piece of land together), "the person known as *atun te kainga* (head of the kainga), or *te ikawai* (the old one), was the same individual who in the boti would be called *atun te boti,* for with the one title went the other" (Maude 1963, 33). The *kainga* is, then, among other things, a segment of a *boti;* it is a localized lineage of a dispersed clan.[1] Moreover, Kiribati custom "ensures that the visitor to any island, once proved to be a fellow clansman, will be looked after for the duration of his stay," while "a stranger landing without a local boti affiliation, and therefore kin protection, would almost certainly be stripped of all he possessed" (Maude 1963, 51). Kiribati descent groups also share the emblematic belief in clan totems characteristic of the rest of Micronesia: "A totem—the shark, turtle, stingray, black noddy or various other kinds of fish and birds—was recognized by each group of worshipers, who were forbidden to kill or eat their totem" (Tito et al. 1979, 18).

Clearly, Kiribati *boti* are in organization and practice the direct equivalent of the rest of Micronesia's dispersed clans, serving the identical purpose of enabling people not simply to travel but to be assured of hospitable welcome in what otherwise might be hostile territory; *kainga* are equivalent to the localized lineages. Together, this Kiribati pattern of *kainga*/localized lineages nested within *boti*/dispersed clans mirrors the rest of Micronesia's dispersed descent group organization. This pattern appears neither in adjacent Polynesia—Tuvalu—nor in Polynesia in general. Despite the Polynesian, patrilineal emphases now obvious in Kiribati social organization, the underlying pattern is rooted in Micronesian matriliny. These Micronesian roots are also hinted at in the great efforts Grimble undertook to explain them away.

In his discussion of Kiribati descent principles and practices, Grimble saw that there were significant matrilineal elements, but he tried to explain away the matrilineal aspects that appeared throughout his data.[2] Grimble recognized that children sometimes joined their mother's *boti* rather than their father's, especially when the father's *boti* was in "danger of overcrowding"; he noted that *te tabo ni kamawa botin tinam* (a place to make room, the *boti* of your mother) is "a well-known phrase throughout the Gilberts" (1989, 211). But, he explained, this "transfer of children from the paternal to maternal groups is therefore seen to be of only local effect"; that is, it was a lineage matter, concerned entirely with access to land. This exception was, he concluded, no more than "an extraneous influence," a "functional" intrusion on the daily operations of lineages: "Only in this indirect way has the matrilineal system interfered with the organization of the boti, of which the essentially patrilineal mould seems to contain hardly any relic of the customs of a folk who practiced mother-right" (1989, 212).

He does, however, go on to acknowledge "a fact of apparent significance." In his record of Kiribati "clans" (i.e., *boti*), he notes that six groups (approximately one-fifth of the clans listed) claim female ancestry and goes on to say: "At first sight this would seem to indicate that matrilineal ideas made themselves felt at some early period in the history of the boti organization, which I have supposed to be almost purely patrilineal" (Grimble 1989, 212). He immediately proceeds to hypothesize a range of explanations for why this was not likely to have been the case (1989, 212–215). In my opinion, however, he did himself a disservice. Grimble's data clearly demonstrate the importance of contingency on a local basis; individuals, households, and families take up residence, and thereby align themselves, with a particular localized lineage based on practical considerations of access to land, resources, and labor without in any significant way challenging or altering the overarching descent principles that link local lineages together as members of the dispersed clans providing them with ties to other communities and islands.

Variations among the individual island societies of the Kiribati archipelago reflect the exceptional degree to which they have been influenced by rainfall. Virtually everyone who tries to explain the marked differences between the societies of the northern and southern islands suggests that the higher rainfall on Butaritari and Makin, the northernmost islands, along with the lusher vegetation it supports, accounts for the greater degree of social stratification there, and that the lower rainfall and consequently more demanding environments of the southern islands are responsible for what is generally called their "democratic" political character. The development of the *maneaba* complex, which in this context is defined by the importance of the community and island councils that convene in these meeting-houses, in the central and southern islands is likewise used to explain differences in the organization of kin groups between north and south. So great is the emphasis placed on rights to sit in specific seats within the *maneaba* that these assigned sitting places, also called *boti,* have come to serve metaphorically for the clans that occupy the seats. In many of the islands these councils wield so much authority that although the Karongoa clan retains ritual precedence, there is effectively no chiefly clan or island high chief, a phenomenon nearly unknown in the rest of Micronesia.

Kiribati has long been known for the remarkable sennit or coconut-fiber armor Tabiteuea's warriors wore when the American Wilkes expedition stopped there in 1841; several examples were illustrated in the six-volume set of studies that chronicled the voyage. As Wilkes himself noted, however, the evidence clearly suggested that this armor was a recent development, apparently a consequence of turmoil stirred up by the visits of whaling ships and their crews in the immediately preceding years (Wilkes 1845, 93).[3] There are also numerous references to "slaves" in Grimble's account of Kiribati history, but the terms he translates as "slave" should more properly be rendered, he says, as "serf" because these persons retained "customary rights" on their land (1989, 343n1). These are people who were vanquished in war and thus lost a degree of authority over their lands but who could, by various acts of service as competent farmers, canoe builders, or healers, raise their station or acquire land and thereby reestablish their status (Grimble 1989, 154). That is, they are neither truly slaves nor constitute a true social class. Moreover, Grimble tells us, "There were very few real wars on democratic islands; and for several centuries, conquest and slavery were abolished" (1989, 153).

Opposing pulls between differing sociopolitical forms and values, which in other parts of Micronesia often manifest themselves in the dynamics within societies, can be seen in Kiribati to lead to differences between entire island communities. It is impossible at this point to hazard much of a guess about what Kiribati societies were like before the arrival of the Samoan influences, except to assume that they were quite similar to those of the Carolines and the Marshalls.

As I have already noted, I tend not to grant mythohistories a great deal of credibility, especially when they are highly detailed (which often indicates that they have been heavily embroidered). But when basic structural or organizational points are widely agreed upon, it does make sense to pay attention. Beru is commonly said to be the site of the initial Samoan entry into Kiribati. The *maneaba/boti* forms of sociopolitical organization are believed to have subsequently spread from Beru into the rest of the archipelago. Grimble reports that Beru went on to conquer every island as far north as Marakei and had at one time been preparing to attack Butaritari and Makin (1989, 87). Maude explains that the Beru pattern of *boti* and *maneaba* organization "is found to vary only in detail on the neighbouring islands from Nonouti to Onotoa"; that "on the more remote northern islands local political factors, such as the iconoclastic innovations of the Binoka dynasty on Kuria, Aranuka and Abemama, or centuries of endemic civil war on Tarawa, resulted in more material modifications"; and that "the small size of the two southernmost islands of Tamana and Arorae precluded the development of the full maneaba system" (1963, 10). He also excludes Butaritari, Makin, Banaba, and Nui as "culturally peripheral" and without the main characteristics of the *boti/maneaba* complex (1963, 9). It may be observed, then, that what Maude takes as prototypical Kiribati applies only to one-half of the archipelago's islands. The northern islands are spoken of as culturally marginal largely because they are so much lusher than the others, and the southern islands because of their sparse populations.

Mythohistorical accounts of Kiribati, the Marshalls, and Kosrae tell of interactions among all these islands, and a Pohnpeian clan, the Sounmaraki, traces its origins to Marakei. Much like the Marianas' location, to the north and outside of the east-west sweep of most of Micronesia, however, Kiribati's location to the south has kept its islands out of the main flow of Micronesian interaction, which is largely driven by the prevailing winds and currents. This perhaps explains in part why Polynesian influences (some of which reached Pohnpei as well) had significantly greater impact in Kiribati.[4]

Nauru

Nauru's differences seem to be primarily a consequence of the geographical isolation of the island and the strong equatorial countercurrent streaming past it, which makes ocean voyaging nearly impossible.

Nauruans live in dispersed homesteads and hamlets, which are only minimally organized into communities that might be called villages. As in the rest of Micronesia, the matriclans are dispersed throughout the island (Stephen 1936, 35). Primogeniture plays a key role in establishing rank within the clans; senior clan members are called *temonibe,* described by some as an upper class, while the rest are *amangame.* But Wedgwood observed that "often it is very difficult to determine very clearly whether an individual is temonibe or amangame for there is no hard and fast distinction between the two, and men and women whose position is on the borderline may be regarded as either, their personal character and popularity often helping to determine which" (1936, 377).

Although missionary influence may have skewed memories a bit, Nauruans claim always to have practiced individual inheritance of land through both male and female lines. Consequently, homesteads tend not to be closely associated with matrilineages.[5] Moreover, the composition of hamlets is fluid, with people frequently shifting residence (Wedgwood 1936, 371). Thus the shared Micronesian pattern of dispersed clans does not seem to be matched on Nauru by the pattern of localized matrilineages.

The significance of lineage organization is minimal, and local communities tend not to be defined geographically. Instead, Nauru's communities form around strong or popular leaders. Although senior members or leaders of clans are respected within their clans, communal leadership for the most part draws on individuals whose status derives from their personal prowess, wealth in land, and character rather than on primogeniture and seniority (Wedgwood 1936, 371; 1937, 4). According to Ernest Stephen, who lived on the island for most of the late nineteenth century, Nauru has "no chiefs proper," and it is the higher-status families that "have the chief say in transactions" (1936, 35), but as Wedgwood noted, public deliberations are open to the participation of landowners in general—that is, most of the adult population (1937, 2).

In a host of other ways Nauruan culture and society reflect common Micronesian themes and preoccupations. Ancestors in general, but those of influential leaders in particular, are honored; corpses of especially beloved or revered figures are sometimes kept near or within houses or buried beneath or immediately adjacent to the home, and skulls are kept as both mementos of and channels for communication with the departed. Mature adults do most of the subsistence work, while younger people, especially males, engage in athletic competitions and dancing and singing. A community may dispatch a group of performers to tour the island, visiting and feasting as they travel over the course of weeks.

Nauru land ownership is shaped by most of the same themes typifying the rest of Micronesia. In particular, there are multiple levels of rights to land and its fruits, and adoption provides individuals with multiple avenues of access to land, by enabling them to inherit through either their natal or their adoptive families.

The Marianas

Because of the massive disruptions caused by the Spanish conquest in the seventeenth and eighteenth centuries, and especially the forced relocation of the northern Chamorro populations to Guam, we lack any systematic ethnographic reporting on indigenous societies of the Marianas. The Marianas were almost certainly first settled from the Philippines, but societies there were deeply influenced by interactions with the Nuclear Micronesian–speaking peoples to the southeast.

The earliest Spanish accounts describe communities that sound virtually identical to those in the adjacent Caroline Islands, largely dependent on breadfruit, taro, and fish but also growing a small amount of rice (which was cultivated nowhere else in Micronesia) primarily for ceremonial purposes. Cunningham's reconstruction of traditional Chamorro life (1992, 157–190), which is the most comprehensive available, makes a number of inferences from Carolinian societies, but in the matter of basic clan and lineage organization these seem reasonable. There were dispersed matrilineal clans with localized matrilineages. The apparently high rate of interaction among the Marianas' communities and islands that archaeologists have documented through studies of local pottery styles and patterns of exchange seems to affirm the dispersed nature of the clans (Graves et al. 1990). Villages were composed of hamlets, which were generally coterminous with lineages. At least some of the clans residing within a given locality were status-ranked, and within a given clan at least some of the lineages were ranked in terms of seniority of descent. As in the rest of Micronesia, however, individuals' actual positions depended both on the seniority of their descent and their abilities and performances in the course of social life. Lineage chiefs constituted the village council, which was headed by the leader of the senior lineage of the village's senior clan, the *maga'lahi,* or paramount chief (his female counterpart was the *maga'haga*). Villages were in turn parts of districts that were apparently defined geographically rather than politically, and the missionary San Vitores reported in 1670 that "neither the islands in general, nor the villages in particular, have chiefs who govern more than their immediate vicinity" (Russell 1998, 141). Rogers has argued that the Chamorros' unwillingness to develop more centrally integrated political systems contributed to their undoing when they attempted, unsuccessfully, to resist Spanish conquest (1995, 40).

Much of the confusion regarding the nature of the Marianas' societies has to do with claims of a greater degree of stratification among the Chamorro than is found elsewhere in Micronesia, stratification so marked that differences in social status there have sometimes been referred to as "castes" (Spoehr 1954; Thompson 1945; Cunningham 1992). But a number of recent writers, including Cordy (1983), Butler (1988), Hunter-Anderson and Butler (1995), Rogers (1995), and Russell (1998) have maintained that the degree of stratification has been much exaggerated. While it may be true, for example, that there were three terms for different sociopolitical statuses, many societies in the central and eastern Carolines had equivalent terminologies; the simple existence of different words does not necessarily mean that there were significant differences in the actual status of the people to whom they referred.

While some individuals were treated with particular displays of respect, it appears that everyone was engaged in the work of making a living: the Spanish friar Juan Pobre, who spent time on Rota in 1602 and spoke with castaway Spaniards who had lived on other islands, noted that "every able-bodied person works" in the gardens and that "the men and women are hard workers, not lazy, and have little regard for those who do not work" (Driver 1983, 209–210). Juan Pobre reported that there were "one, two, or three leading citizens in each village to whom they show degrees of respect" and who were given places of honor at feasts and "receive the first and best food," but he went on to note that "this same respect is shown to the old people even though they may not hold as high status as the other leaders" (Driver 1983, 211–212). Another friar, Antonio de los

Angeles, who was on Guam in 1596–1597, observed that "they recognize no king but them[selves]" (Driver 1977, 21). Nothing about this would be out of place in the Carolines; neither would the general set of respect forms, including polite speech and bowing and crouching postures before people of high rank and elders and between brothers and sisters.

Juan Pobre also commented on the ways in which fish and agricultural products were freely given to relatives, friends, and neighbors both in casual exchanges and at feasts, on cooperative house-building projects, on their predilections for singing and dancing together, on the relative equality in gender relations, on the great care given to children, and the absence of quarrelling and physical punishments (Driver 1983, 210–215). De los Angeles also emphasized the importance of exchanges. In particular, he noted that the individual or group giving the biggest gift accrued the greatest prestige: "When they visit, it is their custom to take one another gifts; he who takes the best one is the most honored." De los Angeles commented in particular on competitive feasting: "Great preparation is made for their fiestas, especially for the contests which they customarily have to amuse themselves and to honor their idols." He noted as well that disputes were settled through the exchange of gifts (Driver 1977, 19, 21).

There is simply nothing in either of these accounts, nor in that of San Vitores, that would suggest significant economic or political stratification within communities. There may have been, however, some degree of imbalance between possibly lower-status inland communities and higher-status coastal communities on the largest islands (Driver 1983, 213), though Russell has raised doubts about even this distinction (1998, 142).[6]

Several other characteristics are worth noting here. In addition to the high rates of interaction among communities and islands within the archipelago, the archaeological record also indicates a fair amount of trade with the Carolines for turtle shell and shell disks, and perhaps ochre (Barratt 1988). Adoption was apparently a common phenomenon, and as in the Carolines, the adoption process allowed individuals to affiliate with either their natal or adoptive lineages, depending on personalities and circumstances (Thompson 1945, 18). Juan Pobre commented that while the people remained at peace, were "peace-loving," and never quarreled among themselves within their villages, they practiced a great deal with their weapons. What conflicts he did report took place between populations living far from one another (Driver 1983, 210). Most recent commentary affirms that warfare was rare and that what did occur was apt to be ritual in character (Hunter-Anderson and Butler 1995, 22; Cunningham 1992, 186; Rogers 1995, 39). The dancing that Juan Pobre and de los Angeles described may well have included the ubiquitous Micronesian stick dancing, which combines athleticism, aesthetics, and displays of martial skills. It is indeed a form of practicing for war, but more important, it displays a community's ability to defend itself against interlopers (Petersen 1992). That is, we find in the Marianas most of the classic Micronesian social adaptations: dispersed descent groups, a high rate of interaction among separate and often distant communities, patterns of adoption that provide individuals with multiple residence options, and regular displays of military prowess coupled with low rates of warfare, all indications of a way of life emphasizing successful responses to severe environmental disturbances.

Impressive stone house-support posts, known as *latte* stones, are sometimes described as unique evidence of significant differences between the Marianas and the rest of Micronesia. Archaeologists have convincingly demonstrated, however, that construction characterized by *latte* stones did not begin until perhaps as late as AD 900. This was a time when monumental stone architecture was being undertaken in Pohnpei and Kosrae. On Pohnpei, where basalt blocks are ubiquitous, virtually every edifice except cookhouses, where the ground ovens are built, is raised up on stone platforms; these are the *pehi* for which the island is named ("Pohnpei" simply means "upon a stone platform"). Residences and meetinghouses in some of the Caroline atolls, in Kiribati, and in other locales are also commonly built on coral posts, some as tall as four feet high. The posts characteristic of the earliest *latte* period tended to be no higher than four feet, and it was not until the latest stage of development, just before European contact, that the biggest stones, some as tall as sixteen feet, were carved out of the bedrock limestone. It appears that within the context of competitive social activities, characteristic of all Micronesian peoples, *latte* stones are no more than a local variation on a common theme: groups built with them in order to demonstrate their prowess, cohesiveness, and relative status.

Despite differences between the Marianas and the Carolines, traditional Chamorro social organization seems in most ways similar to that of the Carolinians. Some aspects of this similarity are attributable, to be sure, to common adaptations to oceanic environments. But all available evidence points to a Southeast Asian origin for the Marianas' population, rather than Eastern Oceanic roots, and these commonalities appear to have diffused from the Carolines to the Marianas, rather than to have arrived with the initial settlers. More tellingly, however, social organization in the Marianas is matrilineal in essence and pivots upon the system of localized matrilineages and dispersed matriclans that is diagnostic of social organization in the Carolines and the Marshalls.

As the descendants of the people who originally populated the Marianas adapted their societies to these islands, it seems that they found that a great many of the ideas, institutions, and practices in the adjacent Carolinian peoples offered significantly superior ways of surviving. While the Marianas differ geologically and topographically from the nearest atolls, they share several key environmental drawbacks with them. First and foremost, the Mariana islands are even more vulnerable to typhoon damage than most atolls, simply because of their location along the storm tracks. The southern Marianas experience significant typhoon destruction on an average of once every three years. The combination of the limestone geology and El Niño–induced shifts in rainfall make the largest islands particularly prone to drought. Food shortages are therefore substantially more common than might be expected on high islands. On the other hand, the worst impacts of even the larger storms tend to be localized—only rarely are more than two of the islands seriously affected simultaneously by the same storm (Butler 1988, 471). Consequently, patterns of social organization that have provided flexibility and security in the Caroline atolls prove equally adaptive in the Marianas.

Whatever their ultimate origins, over the course of the millennia in which the Chamorros have inhabited the Marianas, they became Micronesian in the sense of taking on several key Micronesian adaptations. They rely on the dispersed matrilineal clan and localized matrilineage pattern to ensure hospitable welcomes by kin residing at a distance. Emphasis on descent seniority and respect forms acknowledging the importance of their leaders and skilled martial performances make it clear that they are ready to defend themselves against those who do not come in peace. And prestige competition within communities and descent groups ensures that leadership roles are occupied by individuals and small groups fully competent to guide their communities, rather than by individuals selected by rigid genealogical principles. The simultaneous existence of status differences and the high level of interpersonal equality and individual autonomy reported by the earliest visitors can be understood only in terms of leadership systems encouraging competitive performances that socialize individuals into community responsibility, keep leaders focused upon their communal responsibilities, and draw on descent principles that focus on highly efficacious ancestral spirits who provide both grounds for social stability and some possibility of mitigating environmental threats.

Yap

As previously explained, Yap's language shows influences from the Nuclear Micronesian languages of the Carolines and from Palau, layered on top of what may well have been an initial settlement by a population with Melanesian origins. The prehistory of Yap is complex, and some aspects of life there appear to be unique within Micronesia. A closer look suggests that it may not be all that exceptional, however.

David Schneider's description of Yap's clans (*genung,* a cognate of Carolinian *kainang* and Pohnpeian *keinek*), which he refers to as sibs, makes it clear that they are virtually identical to the matriclans of the eastern Carolines. They are totemic, tracing a line of descent from a mythical ancestress (e.g., a person, spirit, fish, or animal) "whose living counterpart, if there is one, should not be eaten by members of that sib" (1949, 156). An adopted child belongs to the sib of the adopting mother but retains association with the totem of his real mother. The sibs are exogamous, and all members of a sib are considered to be brothers or sisters. Each sib has its own mythic place of origin (1949, 157, 161, 162). Sibs are not localized, and "although visiting distant parts of Yap is not a common practice, when it is necessary sib mates may be called on to provide hospitality" (1949, 161). Each sib has its chief, and each village has a man who acts as the head of his sib mates in the village: "To be eligible for the chieftainship of certain districts, the person must be a member of a certain sib" (1949, 160). While Yap is often spoken of as quite different from most of Micronesia, it shares the basic framework of dispersed matriclans with the rest of the region.

The term "caste" has been applied to aspects of Yapese social organization even more frequently than it has in the Marianas, but it is no more appropriate to Yap than to the Marianas. As in the rest of Micronesia, some descent groups are higher ranking than others. But only in Yap is land separated out from matrilineal kinship and transmitted primarily through patrilineally organized groups; land is also ranked, and much of an individual's or group's status derives from the rank of their land.[7] Thus there are, as in the rest of Micronesia, individuals and groups of higher and lower rank. But as perhaps nowhere else in Micronesia, there seem to be not only occasional individuals without land who occupy habitually subordinate roles, but also groups of people in this position:

> All chiefs in Yap have certain villages that provide services and goods without the competitive reciprocal obligations due to villages of the higher ranks. These rights were obtained during periods of severe population pressures in which land became extremely scarce and access to it limited to patrilineal inheritance and gift. Individuals who were disinherited became vagrants and beggars and gradually formed a landless class. These people eventually became organized into serf villages, working for wealthy land-owners in return for use of the land. (Lingenfelter 1975, 142–143)

Dependence on others for access to productive land and the occupation of child-like statuses because of their dependence upon chiefs were conditions that "served to solidify the poor group into a serf caste" (Lingenfelter 1975, 143). If Lingenfelter is correct in his conclusions, then some small portion of the Yapese population lies outside the general spectrum of Micronesian status ranking.

Yapese culture manifests a second anomaly in the matter of social status, its "eating classes" *(yogum).* These ranked categories are part of a broader system of ritual purity and pollution, however, and are paralleled by other pairs of opposing categories, including older/younger and chief/server. Young men are by definition ritually less clean; as they mature, they become increasingly charged with a certain sacred status. But membership in the uppermost levels of the eating classes requires enormous self-denial and personal isolation; these men must eat food grown and prepared under a host of ritual restrictions. Few men are willing to subject themselves to these demands, and it can be difficult to recruit those who are potentially qualified to actually undergo the necessary rigors. At the same time, however, villages need individuals to occupy these status positions in order to participate as full equals in intervillage politics. The titles and the food resources devoted to these high-status males do confer a certain amount of "political capital," as a means of both enticing individuals to pursue them and enabling those individuals to discharge their duties (Lingenfelter 1979, 418).[8]

These unusual aspects notwithstanding, the chief-server relationship and the eating classes are organized along lines that are basic to all Micronesian societies and cultures, and have to do with age, seniority, and the relative status of individuals and descent groups. They are highly influenced by competition and social mobility: Feast-making, warfare, political skill, and a variety of other factors cut across groups' and individuals' hereditary or ascribed statuses. And status itself, as a ritual or ideological phenomenon, provides no more than a few strands in a complex web of politics, economics, intelligence, personal charisma and skill, and group performance and cohesion (Lingenfelter 1975, 1977, 1979). For all the Yapese emphasis on the forms some ethnologists have referred to as castes or classes, their society functions in nearly every aspect in terms almost identical to the societies of the surrounding islands.

Late in the era before the Europeans' arrival, Yapese began to develop an exchange system organized around stone money *(fae')* that paralleled already existing exchanges of shell money *(yar)* and other valuables. Yap is famous for the large size of some of these stone disks (four to six feet in diameter), but more significant, at least in this context, are the voyages made to Palau and back to quarry the limestone and transport it to Yap. The desire to obtain this material and to be able to use the stone disks as status objects in elaborate patterns of exchange was great enough to mobilize these hazardous journeys on a frequent basis and required the cultivation of social ties in Palau. At the same time, the village of Gatchepar cultivated an extensive web of ties with the atolls to the east (often known as the Yap Empire); this is the system of interconnections I described earlier as the *sawei*.

What is perhaps most striking about Yap and its people, at least in the context of this comparative study of all Micronesia, is that its far-flung webs of ties to both the atolls in the east and to Palau in the west were not organized through the typical medium of Micronesia's dispersed matriclans. While Yapese traditionally represent themselves as figurative parents to the atoll peoples, these relations are not perceived as entailing the rough equality of shared descent. And while it seems that connections to Palau have probably been more complex than we now understand, what we do know about them suggests that they were not deeply embedded in notions of shared kinship or descent either—they were mostly about pure exchange. Despite—or perhaps because of—its central location among the nexus of Palau, the Marianas, and the Caroline atolls, and the basic similarity of its patterns of social organization notwithstanding, Yap is different. It is not, however, all that different.

CHAPTER 10

Epilogue

Traditional Micronesian Societies and Modern Micronesian History

THROUGHOUT this book I have emphasized both that traditional Micronesian societies have much in common and that each society has responded to historical conditions in its own way. Change has been frequent, if not continual, as communities learned new ways of doing things from their neighbors or pursued their own distinctive paths. Some of these changes have come about as consequences of conditions or forces over which islanders have no control, but the ways in which they have actually unfolded are for the most part the result of traditional patterns of social organization, cultural values, and behaviors.

I have focused in particular on the adaptive aspects of Micronesian social organization and culture and explained how the characteristic Micronesian matrilineal clans and lineages perform in a great variety of adaptive ways. These groups provide enormous flexibility when it comes to political leadership, creating what are in most circumstances pools of candidates (usually older men but sometimes women or younger men) eligible to hold chiefly titles, from among whom a competent leader may be chosen. And this system in turn supplies leaders for entire communities.

Although matriliny provides a basic framework for managing land almost everywhere, the existence of strong paternal ties, high rates of adoption, and the organization of lineages into overarching clans means there are always alternative means of distributing land. These alternative ways of gaining access to land allow individuals, groups, and communities to respond effectively to varying patterns of population growth and decline and, more often than not, preclude open hostilities over land. Most important, the ties every lineage has both to other groups within the community and to clan mates on other islands ensure that in a region subject to recurring natural disasters of awesome potency and destructive dimensions, everyone is thoroughly embedded in webs of connections that provide them with profoundly adaptive social insurance. The many threads of Micronesian social organization, woven together into something like a seamless web of culture, have shaped not only the flow of traditional Micronesian history but also the ways in which Micronesian societies have responded to the impact of European and American (and East Asian, for that matter) intrusions into their homeland.

In many parts of Micronesia, peoples of the low islands depend on high-island populations for sustenance of various sorts and interact often with them. They may seek to convince the high islanders that they are worthy of their attention and support by emulating them and hailing their superiority; and yet precisely because of this dependence they may also fear and dislike the high islanders and seek to demonstrate to themselves that they are different and, in fact, morally superior.[1] By the same token, over the long sweep of time, high-island populations have tended to lose many of their long-distance voyaging skills and become dependent on the atoll peoples' navigational skills to keep them in touch with the world beyond their reefs. Most Micronesian societies' mythohistorical accounts are filled with reports of new ideas, crops, and technologies being introduced from abroad. In a word, Micronesia has always experienced change.

Given the vagaries of ocean winds and currents, and the sailing patterns from Japan, China, and the Southeast Asian islands, it is likely that many of the islands in western Micronesia had experience with the occasional wandering vessel heaving to on their shores. And in the wake of storms, voyagers from the central Caroline atolls sometimes drifted to the Philippines, living there for a while before sailing back home via Palau. One group of early European explorers encountered a traveler from the central Carolines comfortably visiting in the Marshalls, and sailing directions to Melanesian islands off the north coast of New Guinea and to western Polynesia were well known among Micronesian navigators. Most Micronesians had long experience interacting with wayfarers coming from great distances and speaking unfamiliar idioms. (Indeed, an archaic name for what is now Sokehs chiefdom on Pohnpei was Pwapwalik—i.e., the place where "foreign languages" were spoken.) When the first European explorers and those who followed in their wake arrived in Micronesia, their appearance was no radical departure from what had happened in the past.

The Spanish explorer Ferdinand Magellan made landfall in the Marianas in 1521, coming ashore on Guam.[2] Over the course of the following century Guam evolved into a waymark for the Manila galleons plying the seas between the Philippines and Mexico, and Chamorros there had sporadic interactions with Spaniards. In 1638 a Catholic mission was established on Guam, and thus began the formal colonization of the Marianas and Micronesia. Epidemics, conquest, and forced relocations decimated the population, and only Guam remained inhabited. By the early 1700s no more than five thousand Chamorros survived (Rogers 1995). Spanish priests undertook several brief missions to the central Carolines but had little impact. The Carolinians were, however, interested in pursuing Spanish contacts, since they found some Spanish goods—especially iron for tools—to be extremely attractive.

Sporadic visits from Spanish vessels and a few others, including a shipwrecked English crew in Palau, took place in succeeding years, but it was not until the early nineteenth century that the region began to experience the full brunt of European and American contact. A mix of explorers, whalers, traders, beachcombers, missionaries, and, eventually, administrators and soldiers began coming ashore throughout Micronesia. The greatest harm that befell the Micronesians during this era was undoubtedly the ravaging of epidemic diseases, particularly smallpox and influenza, which nearly wiped out the populations of some islands and did overwhelming damage to the peoples of virtually every island at one point or other. "Blackbirding," a euphemism for enslavement, occurred on some Kiribati islands. Another major impact came from German policies in the Marshalls, where traditional chiefly leaders were transformed into feudal overseers of extensive coconut plantations. Christian missionaries worked assiduously to convert islanders and met with varying degrees of success, but by the end of the nineteenth century the peoples of almost all but the smallest, most isolated islands were practicing Protestants (mostly Congregationalists) or Catholics. Virtually all of Micronesia eventually entered into the world economy, as commercial planting of coconuts became the mainstay of trade relationships. Islanders cut up and dried the coconut and exchanged this copra for factory-made cloth, steel tools, alcohol, firearms, and a range of other items they were unable to produce themselves.

Two things in particular prevented the slow and erratic, but nonetheless relentless, penetration of outsiders into the islands from having greater impact than it did. First, because so many different sorts of foreigners were entering Micronesia, with quite divergent interests, there was no consistent pattern of exploitation or domination. And later, when colonial rule was established, the colonial powers themselves replaced one another and their policies with such frequency that few policies ever had enough time to take root. Second, the islanders already possessed a great many traditional means of placing checks on abuses of power in their own societies, and they readily used some of them to hinder the impact of colonial administration.

The Spanish maintained no more than a small garrison on Guam, and although they laid claim to the Carolines, they ignored them entirely. German trading firms gradually developed commercial interests in the islands, promoting coconut plantings and copra processing, and by the mid-1880s they convinced the imperial government that it should stake claims to the region. The German Reich annexed the Marshalls but ran into competition with Spain in the Carolines. This was resolved with a compromise that gave the Spanish nominal control while granting full trading rights to the Germans. The Spanish had little success administering the islands, and it can fairly be said that outside the Marshalls and the Marianas, Micronesia remained essentially autonomous until the end of the nineteenth century. With its loss of the Philippines and Guam to the United States in 1898, however, Spain abandoned whatever lingering interest it had in Micronesia and ceded its claims to the islands to Germany. Aside from the introduction of Roman Catholicism, the Spanish had little lasting impact on Micronesia outside the Marianas.

The Germans, on the other hand, established a colonial administration with substantial ambitions. They attempted to impose major changes in political organization, land tenure, and economic activities and met with varied success. The most visible aspect of the German presence in Micronesia, if perhaps not the most significant, was the rebellion of Sokehs chiefdom on Pohnpei. The rebels, fighting to reclaim control of their homeland from the interlopers, slew the governor and besieged the colony. The ferocity with which the Germans put down the uprising made it stunningly clear to all Micronesians that they were no longer self-governing peoples, and had Germany continued to rule the islands, it is likely that it would have wrought major changes in indigenous social life. With the advent of World War I, however, the Japanese occupied the islands and successfully maneuvered to have the islands assigned to them as a mandate under the League of Nations.

Unlike the Spanish and the Germans, who were interested primarily in administering the islands, Japan sought to populate them with its own people. In the course of the next two decades Micronesia was turned into an outpost of Japanese entrepreneurship and economic growth. While the Micronesian peoples themselves were not brutally or even particularly harshly oppressed by the Japanese (in contrast to their behavior in China and Korea), they were in effect shunted aside as their lands were put to use wherever possible for large-scale agricultural schemes. Again, if Japan had been able to continue its rule, traditional Micronesian life would largely have disappeared by the late twentieth century. As an element of its defeat in World War II, however, Japan was forced to turn the islands over to the United States, which took control of them under nominal United Nations supervision as the Trust Territory of the Pacific Islands.

By the time the Americans established themselves in Micronesia, the islanders had come to understand quite clearly both that they were subject to the whims of outside colonial powers and that their best hope for survival was to stand back quietly and wait until the next one came along. The postwar sweep of liberation and independence movements in Africa, Southeast Asia, and the Pacific, however, changed the context of American rule in Micronesia. The United States, after initially ignoring most of Micronesia (although Bikini and Eniwetok were the sites of numerous nuclear weapon tests, Kwajalein was transformed into a vast missile tracking and testing range, and Saipan was used by the CIA for training Chinese spies), undertook a massive economic, political, and social buildup in the 1960s in hopes of forestalling any Micronesian interest in self-government and independence. Times had changed, though, and most Micronesian peoples and their leaders concluded that their interests would be better served if they ruled themselves. Between 1965, when the Congress of Micronesia was established, and 1975, when the Micronesian Constitutional Convention met, it became clear that most Micronesians had little or no interest in becoming a permanent part of the United States, which the United States had initially insisted upon (Petersen 2004). In the ensuing years, the various island groups steered their own separate courses, and by the late 1980s and early 1990s they had become, in effect, separate independent countries and members of the United Nations (except for the Marianas, which established a commonwealth relationship with the United States).[3]

Micronesia Perseveres

Recent history in Micronesia should be considered not simply through the perspective of the outside colonial forces that ruled the islands, but within the context of traditional Micronesian ideas about what constitutes appropriate government. At the center of this question, at least from the perspective of this book, is the fundamental phenomenon of Micronesia's dispersed matrilineal clans. Micronesian matrilineal descent has both shaped the ways in which change takes place and been affected by it. Perhaps the most obvious impacts have been in the realms of land tenure and intercommunity linkages. Local notions that land should be held and managed by lineages and primarily passed along through matrilineal lines were for the most part deemed inappropriate by both administrators and courts. German, Japanese, and American colonial regimes all tended to promote land tenure policies that placed property firmly in private, individual hands and ensured that it be passed on to children by their fathers. In much of Micronesia there has been resistance to attempts to modify land tenure practices, but it is equally true that lineage control is no longer viewed as the only possibility.

The German and subsequent colonial regimes put into place prohibitions against the great interisland *sawei* voyages from the Caroline atolls to Yap and generally disapproved of long-distance voyaging elsewhere. In the place of traditional voyaging came transport aboard government ships. Both people and goods could be moved more safely, if perhaps not as efficiently, on steamers and motor vessels. Furthermore, the colonial administrations (and now the new independent governments, using aid from the United States) strove to mitigate typhoon damage by delivering supplies or, more significantly, removing endangered atoll populations to high island homes. The most striking example of this came with the German program to move large numbers of peoples from the Mortlocks (and eventually peoples from most of the islands adjacent to Pohnpei) to the Sokehs chiefdom, in place of the exiled rebels. Over the course of recent generations, traditional forms of reliance on kin connections with the peoples of other islands, in the wake of storm damage, have been replaced by governmental policies and practices. On the other hand, the very fact that traditional life in Micronesia was shaped by the existence of these widely dispersed ties has made it possible for atoll peoples to resettle on islands where they could legitimately claim ties in culturally acceptable ways. That is, in what were once called district centers and now are national or state capitals, people from many different islands have settled, and there is, by Micronesian standards, a high degree of ethnic diversity. There are tensions in these places, to be sure, but nothing remotely resembling the conflicts that trouble most of the ethnically heterogeneous Melanesian nation-states. People from Pulap, for example, are well established in Chuuk proper and feel that they have every right to be there because of their traditional connections to it (Flinn 1992).

There are many other ways in which traditional Micronesian forms of social organization have facilitated adaptation to new conditions. As I have tried to show, despite Micronesian emphasis on the role of matrilineal descent in the organization of landholding lineages, there have always been well-established principles stressing the importance of paternal ties in the organization of land inheritance, and the high rate of adoption has facilitated this flexibility as well. Micronesians have long managed to avoid open hostilities over land because of these built-in mechanisms for responding to imbalances in population sizes and landholdings. The impact of epidemic diseases on Micronesian populations, coupled with policies of moving peoples to new islands, could well have led to large-scale hostilities over land and population disparities. But these traditional mechanisms have enabled communities to work out means of resolving such tensions that stop far short of open violence.

The policies of colonial regimes attempting to govern the lives of Micronesian communities might well have caused irreparable damage to traditional chiefly systems, were it not that succession to chiefly titles has always depended equally upon broadly construed notions of descent (which provide elements of legitimacy to chiefs) and quite flexible notions of just who might legitimately claim eligibility for these titles. As the conditions of colonial rule and now independence have changed, new skills have been required of chiefs, and lineages and communities have been able to place individuals with these skills into office. And the existence of multiple kinds of political titles has meant that communities have managed to assign titles to individuals skilled at dealings with outsiders, such as Lamotrek's *tamolnipusash,* "chief for the foreigners" (Alkire 1989, 163, 181).

In traditional Micronesian societies, wealth comes almost entirely from the direct labors of individuals and lineages. And although various sorts of tribute are given to chiefs, the overwhelming stress laid upon generosity and redistribution means that chiefs rarely ever accumulate much more wealth than anyone else. The flow of so much wealth into Micronesian communities from outside, via colonial administrations and now the national governments, has created enormous potential for abuses in the form of accumulation of great wealth by a handful of well-placed individuals. With the exception of the Marshalls, however, this has happened only on a small-scale basis.[4] Traditional emphases on generosity and feasting have ensured that goods and wealth flowing into Micronesian communities continue to be redistributed. I would not want to paint a picture of complete equality by any means, but disparities are far less than they might be if so much heed were not given to traditional forms of giving and sharing.

It is within this context that the entire structure of modern Micronesian government must be understood. Micronesian political culture has always been organized around the dual dimensions of hierarchical chieftainship and lineage autonomy. Micronesians speak of how formidable their chiefs are, even while insisting in practice on their individual and lineage rights to do as they see best. I have striven in this book to give equal consideration to both of these tendencies and to explain the ways in which they are mutually interdependent. Micronesian chieftainship has been affected in many different ways in the course of a century of foreign rule; different island communities, at different times, have variously seen their traditional patterns of leadership supported, threatened, and ignored. On the whole, however, Micronesian chieftainship has thrived. What is more, it provided a template for the unfolding of Micronesian political approaches to the problems of bringing colonial rule to an end and to the growth of new Micronesian governments performing the roles of modern nation-states. The structures of traditional Micronesian government have always been oriented simultaneously to both centralization and decentralization, in ways that are, in essence, federal. Federal systems have everywhere been intended to provide the strength of unity when it is required and the freedoms of local autonomy when it is not. Traditional Micronesian clan, lineage, and community organization does just this.

In all their dealings with the United States, as they pursued first self-government and eventually independence, Micronesian leaders worked back and forth between the poles of unity and division. This was difficult to comprehend at the time (at least for outsiders), and the process did not always work smoothly. But in simple fact, the Congress of Micronesia was able to present enough of a united front over a long enough period to convince the American government that the United States could not annex Micronesia outright, as it wished to do. Only as it was becoming quite clear that Micronesia was going to gain self-government, in the mid to late 1970s, did the desire to create smaller, more localized governments crystallize enough to result in the fragmentation of the Trust Territory into the separate republics of Palau, the Federated States of Micronesia, and the Marshalls, along with the Northern Marianas commonwealth. In the FSM, aspects of this process continue, as the separate states jockey in opposition to one another and the national government. Micronesians, or at least their political philosophers, recognize the threats inherent in strong central government, along with the necessity for strength when dealing with outsiders. They seek to maintain enough centralized organization to provide themselves with protections from external dangers, even while trying to place ample checks and balances in the way of potential abuses of power at home. They do not always succeed, but the traditional forms, values, and practices are there for them to draw upon as best they can.

Contemporary life in Micronesia, at the beginning of the twenty-first century, can be understood only in the context of the islands' place in the modern world, in their strategic location near the sea lanes of East and Southeast Asia, in their nation-states' close ties to the United States, and in the seats they hold at the United Nations. But the ways in which Micronesians deal with all these factors are as much the products of traditional Micronesian social organization and culture as they are the consequences of the ways in which these outside forces impinge upon them. Micronesia's peoples have a noble heritage of self-government, in ways that were well suited to the immense difficulties life in the central Pacific has confronted them with. There is every reason to believe that if they continue to draw upon these traditions, they will be able to find solutions to the enormous challenges that lie before them today; indeed, a number of younger Micronesians seek to reestablish aspects of the ancient voyaging traditions as a means of reclaiming their heritage (Metzgar 1996). Questions of population growth, economic stagnation, resource shortages, and political fragmentation do indeed challenge them, but their ancestors discovered a unique and vital set of solutions to the challenges of life on far-flung islands and atolls in an environment often hostile to human settlement, and they thrived. Today's Micronesians seem capable of doing so as well.

Notes

Chapter 1: Introduction

1. In keeping with my use of the English-language names of the Marianas, the Federated States of Micronesia, and the Marshalls, and because both Palauan and English are official languages of Palau, I have opted to call the islands Palau rather than Belau (as the islands are known in the Palauan language).

2. In anthropology in general, the practice of putting ethnographic descriptions into the present tense is known as writing in the "ethnographic present," and it is recognized as an inherently problematic form.

3. Details of Micronesia's physical geography can be found in Karolle 1993 and Bryan 1971.

Chapter 2: Micronesia and Micronesians

1. Nicholas Thomas has observed "that there is virtually no discussion now of what regions are, of what status they are supposed to have as entities." As a consequence, he says, widespread dissatisfaction with the existing areas has not led to any change in anthropologists' reliance upon them, and "old fashioned ethnological distinctions are more tenacious than overt contemporary argument would allow" (1989, 27–28).

2. Each of these is defined and named in terms of different sorts of categories: Maghreb, for its *location* in the west; Sahara, for its desert *nature* or composition; Sahel, for its *appearance* as a coastline at the desert's meeting with the savannas; Sudan, for the skin color of its *peoples*.

3. While there was considerable interaction among, say, Tonga and Samoa and among the atolls of the Tuamotu Archipelago, significant areas of Polynesia—Hawai'i, the Marquesas, Rapa Nui, Aotearoa, etc.—did not, several hundred years after their original settlement, have any sort of persistent or deliberate interaction with societies in other parts of the region.

4. The Chamorro people of the Marianas sometimes refer to themselves as Tao-tao Tano (People of the Land), as distinct from the Micronesian (usually Carolinian) settlers on their islands, but this seems to be a recent phenomenon (Diaz and Kauanui 2001, 319).

5. Two atolls, And and Pakin, lie a few miles off Pohnpei's western shore and are integral parts of Pohnpeian society. Many maps delineate the cluster of Pohnpei, And, and Pakin as the Senyavin Islands, but the term is without meaning or use in Micronesia.

6. Pohnpei's weatherman once told me he believes rainfall may be close to five hundred inches per year at several remote points.

7. Damas' account (1994) of Pingelap culture and society largely overlooks the degree to which its institutions are derived from Pohnpei's.

Chapter 3: The Prehistory of Micronesian Societies

1. Although I shall be rather systematically arguing with some of Patrick Kirch's conclusions about Micronesia, my perspectives on Micronesian prehistory have been deeply influenced by his work on Oceanic prehistory. Both in his broader syntheses (Kirch 2000; Kirch and Green 2001) and in some of his more specific explorations (1984), Kirch has consistently focused attention on the key questions that must be considered; I have simply arrived at somewhat different answers to a few of these questions. Rainbird (2004; cf. Hunter-Anderson 2005) has provided a comprehensive overview of Micronesian prehistory and archaeology.

2. A slowly increasing body of data on the human population genetics of Micronesia's settlement is becoming available, but I view it with considerable uncertainty; too many contradictions remain. Several consistent points have, nevertheless, been made, suggesting that eastern Micronesians share their origins with Polynesians in populations that migrated out of Southeast Asia via New Guinea. In western Micronesia, Palau, Yap, and the Marianas, populations exhibit independent origins, also deriving from both Southeast Asia and New Guinea. There is substantial genetic distance among these latter populations as well as between them and eastern Micronesia, although there is also evidence of significant influx from the east. If these data ultimately prove to be reliable, they would seem to confirm the notion of separate origins for the east and west but also to indicate a noteworthy degree of interaction between them (Lum and Cann 1998, 2000).

3. There is a problem with this point. The modern peoples of these islands speak languages that are either Polynesian or non-Austronesian—that is, current linguistic affinities of the Santa Cruz people do not make them likely predecessors of any of Remote Oceania's peoples. It is assumed, however, that these modern peoples replaced earlier Austronesian-speaking populations (Green 1997; McCoy and Cleghorn 1988).

4. Nauru, which is a raised coral island, was clear of the sea at that time, and linguists suggest that while Nauruan is a part of a greater Micronesian family of languages, the island was settled early and its language soon separated from what would become Nuclear Micronesian (Jackson 1986, 212; Lynch et al. 2002, 117). This could, however, simply be an artifact of its geographical isolation rather than a chronological date.

5. The famous seaborne trading routes of the Massim region off the southeastern tip of New Guinea *(kula)* entailed complex interactions among different types of islands, but this is a thousand miles or so west of the sea-lanes that led voyagers to Micronesia.

6. It seems likely that both the eastern Micronesian atolls and the coastal lowlands and reef flats of the high islands in the region were awash and probably uninhabitable until the time they were first settled (Dickinson 2003, 498).

7. The northern Marshalls and southern Kiribati are much drier, marginal environments and may have been permanently occupied only after a fuller development of Micronesian adaptations, both ecological and social, and rising populations.

8. Interactions with Melanesia and Polynesia never ceased entirely. Kiribati was highly influenced by Samoan immigration, and the Pohnpeian language evidences considerable Polynesian, probably Samoan, influence (Rehg 1997). It also appears that the kava plant, used to produce a mildly narcotic beverage that was at one time of enormous importance in Kosrae and remains central to social and cultural life on Pohnpei, was introduced from Vanuatu at a later date than the original settlement of eastern Micronesia (Lebot et al. 1992).

9. Compare this to Irwin's argument (1992, 129) that the early Micronesian homeland was not a closed system but a sphere of interaction.

10. Hage and Marck (2002) suggest that matrilineal institutions are largely absent in Kiribati and that this correlates with a relatively insignificant interisland voyaging tradition. As I demonstrate in later chapters, however, the dispersed clanship typical of Micronesian matriliny has remained vital in Kiribati and has been of central importance in the maintenance of interisland ties (Lambert 2002).

11. Hage and Marck (2002, 2003) and Hage (1998b, 1999a, 1999b) suggest that Proto-Oceanic society was matrilocal and matrilineal; they assume consistent, closely bound relationships among residence, descent, kin terms, and sociopolitical rank: "By Proto-Oceanic times residence (matrilocality), descent (matrilineality), and kinship terminology (bifurcate merging) were perfectly aligned" (Hage and Marck 2003, 124). This perspective presumes correspondences between descent ideology and practical human behavior that are not supported by the relevant ethnography from the region. While their arguments are thought-provoking and elegant, they rest on the assumption that Proto-Oceanic–speaking peoples were somehow less inclined than their modern descendants to manipulate and ignore descent ideology as circumstances and personalities dictate.

12. It is possible, though not likely, that some aspects of matrilineal institutions reached westernmost Micronesia before the Nuclear Micronesian peoples influenced them (discussed below in the text).

13. Most of these institutions are also basic to social life in, for instance, the Trobriand Islands, just off the eastern tip of New Guinea (Weiner 1988).

14. I am not suggesting that this archetypical Micronesian system developed simply because it was adaptive, but rather that once it got started, strong adaptive pressures worked to keep it in place.

15. In their respective considerations of Micronesian matriliny, Hage and Marck (2002) and Damas (1979) treat this phenomenon as solely an eastern Micronesian one. As I explain below, however, matriclanship diffused from eastern Micronesia into western Micronesia.

16. In this context, "agroforest" refers to mixed stands of food-bearing trees, and "arboriculture" to the cultivation of these trees. Because the peoples of the Santa Cruz group are not now Austronesian speakers, it is difficult to be certain that the subsistence systems of modern Santa Cruz societies are essentially the same as those of a different population from earlier times, but archaeological work there suggests that they were (McCoy and Cleghorn 1988).

17. Although there are ample data recording both Micronesian navigators' knowledge of the region and their voyaging among the archipelagoes, the situation in Polynesia is not so clear-cut. A version of a map prepared for Captain James Cook by Tupaia, a Tahitian navigator, has been the subject of a great deal of scholarship, but we still have no unambiguous understanding of what knowledge the Tahitians had of western Polynesia, and vice versa (Forster 1996, 429; Dening 1963; Howe 2003; Di Piazza and Pearthree 2007).

18. While linguists tend to exclude Palau and the Marianas from Remote Oceania, archaeologists are more likely to include them (Pawley and Ross 1995, 43; Green 1997, 6).

19. The term *unilineal* refers to the pattern of tracing an individual's descent principally through a single line, determined by sex—that is, either through men *(patrilineal)* or through women *(matrilineal).* Other common forms of tracing these connections are *ambilineal,* or *ambilateral* (through either one line or the other), and *cognatic,* or *bilateral* (equally through both male and female lines).

20. Wenkam and Baker entitled a pictorial survey of the contemporary islands *Micronesia: The Breadfruit Revolution* (1971), but I employ the phrase in a vastly different sense here.

21. The dense stands of coconut trees that typified Micronesian environments in the late nineteenth and twentieth centuries are artifacts of plantings made for commercial copra production, often stimulated or enforced by colonial governments. They are not representative of the aboriginal landscape.

22. Ragone (1997) provides a comprehensive account of the distribution, genetics, and uses of breadfruit in the Pacific islands.

23. Older studies (e.g., Fosberg 1960; Barrau 1961; and Coenen and Barrau 1961) pointed out the morphological evidence of this hybridization, but it is only the recent work of Ragone and Zerega that has established the genetics of the process.

24. In the early 1970s the author calculated that in Awak, which is a particularly fertile and densely populated area by Pohnpeian standards, representative mature trees had approximately 100 bearing branches, each bearing two or three fruits in the major season. While there are many breadfruit varieties, two and one-half pounds is about the average weight of a fruit. Conservatively estimating two fruits per each of 100 branches, the yield per tree is 500 pounds. Adding a fifth of this amount for yields during the minor seasons renders a total of 600 pounds per tree. The trees are planted close together. (Koronel Cantero, born at the beginning of the twentieth century, was in the early 1970s celebrated in Awak for his ability to move from tree to tree while harvesting by walking along the breadfruit-picking pole he had laid across the branches of adjacent trees.) There are 25 to 30 mature trees to an acre, potentially producing an aggregate of well over 15,000 pounds of breadfruit per year. Raynor's observations and measurements of breadfruit production from a random sample of plots and trees throughout the island yielded an estimated average of 6,877 kilograms of breadfruit produced annually per hectare (1989, 88–96). This is undoubtedly a much more accurate and representative figure for the entire island than my own.

25. Ragone (pers. comm., 2001) reports that breadfruit does not grow on Polynesian atolls other than in Tuvalu and Tokelau, where the hybridized forms have been established.

26. High rainfall is especially critical to breadfruit cultivation on atolls because it maintains the freshwater lens on which the roots draw. While temporary drought conditions on high islands may keep trees from bearing fruit, on coral islands significant drought conditions will kill trees outright.

27. There is often disagreement among Pohnpeian farmers over just which named variety an individual breadfruit or yam specimen represents, and there is often more than one vernacular name for a given variety, so it is difficult to say with any certainty precisely how many varieties of these crops actually exist. These numbers should be taken as indicating no more than a rough approximation of magnitude.

28. Breadfruit seasons are, of course, directly related to the cycling of the natural climate, but like the calendars of most peoples, those of Micronesia tend to focus more on the influence of labor patterns as they respond to the weather than on the weather itself (Petersen 1985).

29. While I have no specific reason to doubt these dates, I am always dubious about anything that seems exact when it comes to Micronesia.

30. Although Kosrae's and Pohnpei's political systems are quite centralized by many standards, there is effectively little economic centralization. Precisely because breadfruit production requires little labor and the trees produce for scores of years, little if any centralized labor management or decision making is entailed. Pohnpeian chiefs traditionally traveled a great deal, visiting local communities and feasting in situ, while on Kosrae food was transported by water to the chiefs living at Lelu. The eastern Carolines do not fit standard models for the evolution of chieftainship that rely on frameworks of economic centralization or coercion, a point to which I shall return in later chapters.

31. In the Pohnpeian orthography, this is spelled "Katau," but it is pronounced "Kachau," a spelling I employ for clarity's sake.

32. Although there is a remote possibility that *A. altilis* was introduced from New Guinea, these would have been seeded varieties, rather than the seedless forms that are typically Micronesian.

33. Variants of the term "Kachau" or "Achaw" occur throughout eastern and central Micronesia, referring to a legendary place in the east whence early Micronesians immigrated and powerful mythohistorical figures originated; it may also refer in some contexts to Kosrae (Goodenough 1986; Mauricio 1987).

34. I generally hesitate to put mythohistorical accounts, which are inevitably complex and subject to too many unreported factors, to use for comparative purposes, but because of its seeming consistency in this context, I note that Palauan legendary history portrays the matriclans as having come relatively late to Palau.

35. It is worth noting that in contrast to, e.g., the peoples of Palau and the Marshalls, Pohnpeians say they have no specific myth or oral tradition relating to the origins of breadfruit on their island (Lawrence et al. 1964, 57).

36. The societies of Tuvalu's atolls have been likened to Micronesian outliers within Polynesia (Irwin 1992, 188), and Nui in fact has a Micronesian-speaking (Kiribati) population, but as Koch (1965, 201) has detailed, there is in fact a rather sharp cultural and social demarcation between Micronesian Kiribati and Polynesian Tuvalu.

Chapter 4: Descent and Descent Groups

1. Goodenough (2002, 41–42) provides a masterful explanation of how lineages can and do grow into clans over a span of time. I do not follow his example here, however, because the principles involved were introduced into Chuuk from elsewhere—that is, the basic principles existed long before any specific Chuuk lineages or clans did.

2. Kiribati, which was deeply influenced by Polynesian emigration, is an exception to this. At the same time, however, Kiribati's proximity to Polynesia has resulted in a great deal of Polynesian, specifically Samoan, influence on its kinship institutions and principles—Kiribati seems to be simultaneously Micronesian and Polynesian in the same way that Fiji is both Melanesian and Polynesian.

3. I take up the concept of conical clans in chapter 7.

4. "Cross-sibling" refers specifically and solely to the relationship between a brother and a sister.

5. Kenneth Rehg and Jeff Marck provided invaluable assistance with this material.

6. Older Pohnpeian orthographies often write *j* for the modern *s*, reflecting a relatively recent change in pronunciation. The *c* in Kosraean *sucu* indicates a vowel shape or sound, not a consonant.

7. Kosraean *sr* is pronounced much the same as the Pohnpeian *s* and Marshallese *j* (and sounds much like English *sh*). The terms *dipw* and *sruf* may be cognates, though linguists point to irregularities. Goodenough reports that, in Chuuk Lagoon, *futuk* means something quite different; he glosses it as "family" and says that "it is similar to our own concept of consanguinity" (1951, 102).

8. Smith's discussion (1983, 59–60, 68–71) makes it clear that these glosses do not adequately represent the complexities of the Palauan concepts, but they will do for the present.

9. Some ethnographers have written of "superclans," or groups of clans called phratries in Kosrae and Palau *(klebliil)* (Ritter and Ritter 1982, 35; Smith 1983, 38). See the discussion below, in the section "Subclans."

10. Elsewhere Marshall (1976, 183) refers to the term *futuk* as signifying "subclan"; see the discussion below, in the section "Subclans."

11. I make note of this because it is entirely possible to interpret Alkire (1980) and Hunter-Andersen and Zan (1996) as assuming the origins of hierarchically ranked relations between the atolls and Yap to be almost entirely local.

12. In earlier periods, Polynesian voyaging networks were more extensive than in later eras (Collerson and Weisler 2007).

13. On Pohnpei the concept of changing one's lineage or clan membership does exist, though extremely rare. It is known as *kepin mehme,* which refers to an infant eating premasticated baby food and taking on a new clan identity with it.

14. I discuss the meaning of "virilocal" in the section "Social Conditions" in chapter 5.

15. See Pollock (1976, 89) for a discussion of whether or not this is the case in the Marshalls.

16. In chapters 5 through 7, we will see how local responses to local exigencies draw upon descent principles as well as actively shape the actual framework of lineages and clans.

Relationships between lineages and clans are not only driven from the top down, as Sahlins had it, but work upward from the local level as well. In chapters 6 and 7, I address some of the differences between genealogical rank and political authority, showing in general that when filling leadership positions, Micronesian lineages and communities tend to draw from a pool of eligible people.

Chapter 5: Household and Family, Land and Labor

1. In an overview of scholarship on similar topics in Africa, Jane Guyer explores alternative analyses formulated in terms of households and lineages. Her conclusions are relevant to a comparative study of Micronesia: "The concept of 'the lineage' implies a politico/jural unit with collective ownership of resources, collective responsibility in law, and collective representation in wider political arenas. The concept of 'the household' implies a domestic unit with decision-making autonomy about production and consumption. What has emerged over the last twenty years of scholarship on kinship is that the concept of lineage and typologies of lineage systems disguise far too much of the variability in ways things get done: children brought up, livings made, authority achieved and assigned, land distributed, bridewealth paid, residence determined, and all the myriad other activities which can be organized along genealogical lines. Scholarship on the household will, I think, go in the same direction, much more reluctantly however, because of the theoretical need for a simple unit of analysis" (Guyer 1981, 89–90). "'Lineage' and 'household' as concepts share the problem of designating complex collectivities as units. They also share the problem of implying a single explanatory context: in the case of the lineage local political structures, and in the case of the household, the international economic structure. The reality of African social organization is a challenge to both positions" (ibid., 104). "All this does not mean that lineage and household are now useless; one has to use descriptive terms. However, all the evidence suggests that they indicate problems to be explored and not analytical concepts to be applied in rigid fashion. Differences in kinship and domestic organization have to be an intrinsic part of explanations of the documented differences in patterns of work" (ibid., 104–105). It is precisely because I have found neither approach alone to be satisfactory that I have included in my own analysis separate chapters on households and lineages.

2. Menstrual houses are separate structures, built on household land, which the household's adult females may occupy during their menstrual periods. They do so partly for their own convenience and partly because menstrual blood is sometimes perceived of as spiritually dangerous or polluting to men.

3. I have occasionally had Pohnpeians tell me that exogamy proscribes only marriage and not sexual relations. Compare the situation on Bikini (Kiste and Rynkiewich 1976).

4. Hage asserts that on Pohnpei the fatherhood metaphor "is applied not to the relation between chiefs and their subjects" but to the relationship between types of chiefs (1998a, 787), and Mosko concurs (1998, 793; cf. Petersen 1999b). But Hughes (1969) makes it quite clear that the relationship between a paramount chief and his people is explicitly likened to that of father and children. I return to this point in chapter 7.

5. The small populations characteristic of atolls when they were studied in the mid-twentieth century do not necessarily reflect the numbers of people who lived on them in

earlier times. For example, the populations of Lamotrek and Tobi, now minuscule, were previously much larger (Alkire 1989, 25; Buschmann 1996, 324–336).

6. I am using these terms in Goodenough's sense, described later in the text.

7. The term "fee" here derives from the same origins as the words "feudal" and "fief," not from a payment of money, and is historically connected to tenure and its attendant duties and responsibilities.

8. Experience tells me some will misinterpret this. I am not saying that Micronesians did not engage in warfare. There are aspects of warfare that are of real importance in Micronesian social and cultural life, and battles loom large in the mythohistories. But the historical evidence from the early contact years does not indicate that most Micronesians spent much time actually fighting or that obtaining and occupying land was the primary purpose for the fighting that did go on. I discuss warfare at length in chapter 6.

9. I stress that these contingencies are possible, not probable.

10. Indeed, conceptualization of land rights and the freedoms guaranteed by access to adequate land lie at the very core of Micronesian sociopolitical life. The opposition of Micronesians to American attempts to annex their islands permanently to the United States was fueled by the experiences of those who studied at the University of Hawai'i in the 1950s and 1960s. Every one of the leaders involved in political status negotiations with the United States who had spent time in Hawai'i has told me essentially the same story. The single most important lesson they learned there was that the native Hawaiian people had first been reduced to poverty and then marginalized in their own country because they lost control over their lands to Americans (Petersen 2004).

11. Some might argue that labor shortages or the need for additional labor are consequences of the postcontact epidemics that caused severe depopulation on so many of the islands, but the exigencies brought about by natural phenomena and the adaptations to them are too widespread for this pattern to have been a recent development.

12. The phrase "strange work" refers to a passage concerning God's "strange work" in the Old Testament's book of Isaiah (28:21).

13. The reference here is to Machiavelli's republican ideas (spelled out in *The Discourses on Livy*), and not to the more problematic program outlined in the much better-known *The Prince*.

Chapter 6: Chieftainship and Government

1. Douglas Oliver (2002, 269) has suggested terming these "clan senior" and "tribe chief," respectively. Because what I call lineage chiefs provide the underlying model for political leadership in Micronesia, however, I do not see the utility of calling them something other than chiefs.

2. "Reign" can mean either "to exercise sovereign power" or "to hold the title of monarch but with limited authority" (*American Heritage Dictionary*, 4th ed.). I use the term with a mixed connotation: Micronesian chiefs reign in the sense that they are recognized as sovereigns, but they exercise limited authority

3. Late nineteenth- and early twentieth-century German anthropologists were inclined to describe Micronesian sociopolitical systems in terms of German feudal pat-

terns and imputed to Micronesian chiefs powers that even German leaders did not possess (Petersen 2007).

4. Barnett maintains: "Some men who are clan leaders and consequently hold clan titles have additional titles which qualify them to sit on village or district councils and to exercise authority beyond the kin group. Only these men are properly called *rupaks*" (1960, 58–59). That is, only those leaders of lineages holding territorial authority are *rupaks*.

5. *Jefekyr* and *öföker* are variant spellings of the same word.

6. It is possible that in the Marshalls, however, *iroij* carried with it a little more clarity or concreteness.

7. Cheyne's description of Pohnpeian political process here is largely drawn from the American explorer Charles Wilkes' account of Kiribati published a few years earlier. In general, Cheyne seems to have been a reliable reporter. Dorothy Shineberg, who edited his work, describes it as "meticulous" (Cheyne 1971, 11). While acknowledging that he consulted the published accounts of others, she hails his qualities as an astute observer: "Not only is his record full and detailed, he is careful, on the whole, to describe only what he saw himself, or at least to distinguish carefully between what he saw and what he was told" (Cheyne 1971, 12, 27). Cheyne encountered the Wilkes Expedition in Manila in 1842, as it was sailing home, and spent time aboard the flagship in conversation with its officers. Shineberg notes that in comparing Cheyne's and Wilkes' accounts of Manila, "some of Cheyne's phrases are so similar to Wilkes's that it seems likely that either he used Wilkes's account as an aid to his own memory or that both used a common source." She suggests that the latter alternative is more likely and concludes, "There is, however, enough independence in Cheyne's own version to clear him of the charge of plagiarism" (Cheyne 1971, 70). The same cannot be said, unfortunately, about a passage concerning Pohnpei, which Cheyne clearly lifted from Wilkes. I hasten to point out, however, that given the overall scrupulous character of Cheyne's work, I assume he copied out this passage because it so clearly mirrored what he had himself observed, and I especially cite it because it demonstrates the great similarity between the political dynamics of the two different island societies. This is the relevant passage as it appears in Wilkes: "When a meeting is deemed necessary, the oldest or presiding chief sends out his messengers, whose business is to summon the people, which is done by blowing conches in all directions. The council then assembles, when the head chief lays before them the business, and everyone is at liberty to speak, and if he be so disposed, delivers his opinion. The discussions are said to be at times very animated, and violent quarrels sometimes take place between different speakers, who are with difficulty prevented from coming to blows by those who are present. No regular vote is taken; but the opinion of the majority is very soon ascertained, and this decides the business" (Wilkes 1845, 85).

8. "Under Bow" is a translation of "Faayiro," which, depending on context, can refer either to the abode of divinities in the sky (i.e., heaven) or a body of *itang* lore and teaching. In this context it means the latter.

9. As I have pointed out, both federal and feudal systems can be either centralized or decentralized. I choose to emphasize the federal tendencies of Micronesian political systems, rather than the feudal, primarily because of the connotations of the term "federal," which implies a significant degree of procedural equality, while "feudalism" carries with it

suggestions of constrained domination. Former Federated States of Micronesia president John Haglelgam is especially uncomfortable seeing the federal concept applied to traditional Micronesian politics; as much as I would like to oblige him, I have opted, finally, to describe these systems as federal.

10. David Schneider, one of American anthropology's preeminent theorists and an ethnographer of Yap, once wrote to me that "the English word 'chief' is still a problem but just to talk we have to accept some words as understood" (pers. comm., 1985). Translating *pilung* as "chief" seems to have given him pause. Acknowledging that the term "chief" has its uses, he still doubted that it was truly meaningful, suggesting that there was, even within Micronesia, no indigenous category or concept that was consistent enough to be translated by a single English-language term. Subsequent to that conversation and to Schneider's death, I have had ample opportunity to work together with Micronesians on chieftainship as a constitutional issue (Petersen 1997). There is little doubt in my mind that Micronesian societies do share a common sense of chieftainship. The differences between views on the nature of chieftainship within any given Micronesian society seem to me to be as great as the differences among the various Micronesian societies. That is, there are contexts in which Micronesians concur on what it means to be chief in any Micronesian society, and contexts in which the nature of chieftainship is debated endlessly, within a single community or even a lineage.

11. The term O'Connell cites here, *aroche,* is no longer in use on Pohnpei. It is closely related to the Marshalls' *iroij,* "chief," and *aroche tikitik* is cognate to the Marshalls' *iroij erik,* "lesser chief."

12. I recognize that a little philosophy can be a dangerous thing, but I am trying here to explain my own assumptions, not explicate these thinkers' ideas.

13. Wilkes provides us with an ample illustration of what the Tabiteuean people were responding to. When one of his own crew disappeared, he notes that the "most humane manner of effecting their punishment was conceived to be at once to show them the power of our arms, and sacrifice some of the most prominent among the savages." After shooting one man and firing a rocket at a group of people, the Americans set fire to the *maneaba* (meetinghouse) and town, destroying them. He estimates that three hundred houses were destroyed, and twelve islanders killed, with no American casualties (1845, 59–60). If the Tabiteueans were engaged in an arms race, they were not achieving much success. Donald Rubinstein (pers. comm., 2007) points out that sharks' teeth are embedded in sennit armor found in museum collections and that sennit would have provided no protection from whalers' firearms, suggesting that these implements were developed and used for local purposes, rather than in defense from outsiders.

14. I am hardly suggesting that this is in any way peculiar to Micronesians. Sahlins says of tribal chiefdoms in general, "The chieftain is usually spokesman of his group and master of its ceremonies, with otherwise little influence, few functions, and no privilege. One word from him and everyone does as he pleases" (1968, 21).

15. I recognize that there are also situations where some may think that taking a dependent or supplicating role or position may work to their advantage.

16. For example, in Kiribati, according to Grimble, government under the high chiefs "was precisely feudal": "All land was held at will and by favour of the high chiefs, who com-

manded *absolute obedience* from the *blood royal*, the chiefs, and their underlings" (1989, 154, my emphasis; see also Petersen 2007).

17. I discuss these dances at length in chapter 7.

Chapter 7: Politics and Leadership

1. This might be compared to what is known in the United States as a "good cop/bad cop" approach.

2. Nicholas Thomas (1989) has argued that distinctions between Melanesia and Polynesia tend to be couched in terms of moral judgments regarding equality and hierarchy. He says that an older bias toward centralized authority and hierarchy, which tended to give preeminence to Polynesia, has been gradually replaced by a tilt toward favoring decentralization and equality, supposedly Melanesian characteristics. Hays (1991, xxvii) has also remarked on the ethnocentric and racist assumptions some associate with these groupings. Marshall Sahlins, whose classic paper on "political types in Polynesia and Melanesia" (1963) bears the brunt of Thomas' assault, finds in Thomas' work a "tortuous allegation that modern anthropologists who use the terms 'Melanesia' and 'Polynesia' are thereby purveying an unconscious racist nostalgia, a sublimated or 'suppressed' modality of an older bigotry" (Sahlins 1989, 37). I would prefer, however, to call attention to Thomas' focus on "the equation Melanesia:Polynesia::equality:hierarchy": "These crude categories have obstructed the understanding of aboriginal Pacific societies in a number of ways. They have obscured varieties of inequality and divergent social transformations which are not readily mapped onto the axis which links small-scale egalitarian systems to chiefly confederacies and states. By associating inequality with ascribed leadership and rank, they have diverted attention from local and domestic asymmetries" (1989, 32). Setting aside the lamentable omission of Micronesia in this discussion, I note the underlying assumption here that the existence of hierarchy and/or rank inherently precludes equality, a misapprehension I have been striving to correct in this work.

3. Or it may be that there is a tendency to overestimate its importance in Polynesia.

4. I cite only observations of behavior here. These writers speculated on the nature of the Micronesian societies they visited, but as Carucci (1988) has pointed out, their ideas were influenced at least as much by the currents of European social and political theory as they were by what they actually encountered in the island.

5. He employs a construct introduced to Pacific islands mythohistory by Sahlins.

6. I analyzed aspects of this ambiguity in detail in Petersen 1999b.

7. I heard this aphorism a number of times during the Federated States of Micronesia's political status negotiations with the United States. The willingness of the United States to acknowledge the FSM's right to self-government and autonomy was contingent on the Micronesians' readiness to constitute a government that suited American notions of democracy. Many Pohnpeians were not sure that American electoral politics would serve their own expectations, shaped by immersion in Pohnpei's chiefly politics, about how leaders should properly behave.

8. Lord argues that Aristotle deliberately excluded "the political arrangements of contemporary tribal societies or empires" from consideration in *Politics* (1987, 134–135), but

it seems to me this interpretation implies that a tribe is nothing more than an aggregation of people, rather than a genuinely political community (Aristotle 1958, 40–41, 1261a).

9. Important discussions and useful summaries of these ideas can be found in Service 1985; Fried 1967; Haas 1982; Bogucki 1999; and Earle 1997.

10. Use of linguistic reconstructions as a means of demonstrating the nature of prehistoric social organization is fraught with more difficulties than have been appreciated by, e.g., Pawley (1982) and Kirch (2000). Cf. Lichtenberk 1986.

Chapter 8: Aesthetics, Beliefs, Values, and Behavior

1. The most thoughtful, or at least helpful, considerations of Micronesian art can be found in Burrows 1963; Mason 1964; Steager 1979; Kaeppler et al. 1997; Morgan 1988; and Nero 1999.

2. I think it is worth noting that terms for first fruits vary widely, unlike, say, terms for kin groups and chiefs, but I do not know why this should be so.

3. Some of the basic spells can be learned simply by mentioning the topic publicly, be it protection from dog bites or a romantic interest.

4. Caughey refers to Uman by the pseudonym "Faanakkar" in his book; I use its real name with his permission.

5. Spiro called it "non-aggression," and Burrows termed it "kindliness" (Spiro 1952, 498; Burrows 1963, 77–78).

6. Burrows (1963, 426) described an Ifaluk man in line to succeed to a chiefly title who told him he didn't want to be chief, because it was "too much trouble."

7. One might compare the British expression "drunk as a lord."

8. In what follows I am portraying Micronesian leadership and the individual behavior styles entailed in it in a manner that runs entirely against the grain of Marshall Sahlins' conclusions about the nature of chieftainship. In his work on "political types" in Melanesia and Polynesia—which had an enormous impact on nearly all Pacific island ethnology for several subsequent generations of scholars—Sahlins focused both on political structures and on the behaviors expected of individual leaders. While intent upon distinguishing between Melanesian and Polynesian types as "broad patterns" or "abstracted sociological types," he readily acknowledged the existence of "important variants of the types" (1963, 285). But among his central points was an attempt to identify differences in "quality of leadership," i.e., "differences in bearing, character, appearance and manner—in a word, personality" (1963, 288). The archetypical Melanesian leader (the big man) possesses and exercises "personal power"; he achieves his status as "the outcome of a series of acts which elevate a person above the common herd" (1963, 289). In order to become a real leader, "a man must be prepared to demonstrate that he possesses the kinds of skills that command respect—magical powers, gardening prowess, mastery of oratorical style, perhaps bravery in war and feud," as well as amassing goods and "distributing them in ways which build a name for cavalier generosity" (1963, 291). In opposition to this Melanesian type, Sahlins described Polynesian chiefly leadership as essentially impersonal. Chiefs' status "did not refer to a standing in interpersonal relations," and chiefs "did not make their positions in

society—they were installed in societal positions." Sahlins asserted, "Power resided in the office; it was not made by the demonstration of personal superiority" (1963, 295). Leadership qualities also went with the office, rather than being demonstrated by the individual, and exercise of authority was detached from any necessity to demonstrate personal authority (Sahlins 1963, 295). As I have been attempting to show, this dichotomy is not especially helpful in grasping the nature of Micronesian sociopolitical life (and as Bronwen Douglas [1979] pointed out, it falls short even for Polynesia and Melanesia). Both aspects—individual aspirations and genealogical structure—are of approximately equal importance in determining who actually leads, and as a consequence no one political type is characteristic of Micronesian leadership.

9. Many are more widely Oceanic.

10. They do not all view this in an entirely positive light. I once drove a young member of the Pohnpeian family with whom I live to the Pohnpei hospital, where she gave birth just a few minutes after we arrived. When I later expressed to her my surprise at how quickly she delivered, since she had been so calm and collected during the drive, she replied that she wished she could have been screaming, the way American women do.

11. Some assassinations are between rival claimants to political titles, while others are meant to get rid of abusive leaders.

12. Hage (1998a) and Mosko (1998) maintain that chiefs do not stand as fathers to their people on Pohnpei, but as I pointed out in my discussion of families in chapter 5, on Pohnpei, as elsewhere in Micronesia, chiefs are commonly conceived of as fathers to all their people, the basic precepts of matrilineal descent notwithstanding.

Chapter 9: Some Exceptions to the Pan-Micronesian Patterns

1. Because a *kainga* was both a place and a group, *kainga* as groups/lineages included most individuals residing on the *kainga*'s land, whether they were born into the *boti* or not.

2. Because of his grounding in British social anthropology's formative generation and his expectation that his ethnographic work would ultimately earn him his doctorate in anthropology, Grimble's intent was to demonstrate the incontestably patrilineal basis of Kiribati descent (Maude in Grimble 1989, xxv).

3. See the section "Warfare" in chapter 6.

4. Rehg (1997) has demonstrated that there are a good many Polynesian influences on Pohnpei's language.

5. While all Micronesian societies recognize the importance of passing on at least some land from father to son, Nauru's emphasis on transmitting land equally through both lines, even while otherwise emphasizing matrilineal clanship, is probably an import from Kiribati.

6. On a large Carolinian island like Pohnpei there are traditions of status differences between some inland communities and those along the shore.

7. Schneider (1962) described this striking intersection of matridescent groups and patrilineal inheritance of land as "double descent."

8. These classes have significant parallels with the graded classes found in parts of Vanuatu.

Chapter 10: Epilogue

1. This is a phenomenon several authors describe, including Poyer (1993) and Flinn (1992), and that I have explored (Petersen 1995c).

2. The most comprehensive histories of Micronesia since the arrival of Europeans are by Francis Hezel (1983, 1985). Especially detailed coverage of local histories is available for Guam (Rogers 1995) and Pohnpei (Hanlon 1988).

3. Important aspects of recent Micronesian political, economic, and social history can be found in works by Norman Meller (1989), David Hanlon (1998), and Francis Hezel (2001).

4. Because of exceptionally large payments made by the United States in the Marshalls as compensation for the destructive nuclear weapons testing at Bikini and Eniwetok and the disruptive missile testing on Kwajalein, there have been many more opportunities for financial abuse and inequalities.

References Cited

Alkire, William

1960 "Cultural Adaptation in the Caroline Islands." *Journal of the Polynesian Society* 69 (2): 123–150.

1974 "Land Tenure in the Woleai." In H.Lundsgaarde, ed., *Land Tenure in Oceania,* 39–69. Honolulu: University of Hawai'i Press.

1977 *An Introduction to the Peoples and Cultures of Micronesia.* 2nd ed. Menlo Park, CA: Cummings.

1980 "Technical Knowledge and the Evolution of Political Systems in the Central and Western Caroline Islands of Micronesia." *Canadian Journal of Anthropology* 1 (2): 229–237.

1989 *Lamotrek Atoll and Inter-island Socioeconomic Ties.* Prospect Heights, IL: Waveland. (Orig. pub. 1965.)

Alkire, William, and Keiko Fujimura

1990 "Principles of Organization in the Outer Islands of Yap State and Their Implications for Archaeology." In R.Hunter-Anderson, ed., "Recent Advances in Micronesian Archaeology," *Micronesica* Suppl. no. 2:75–88.

Aoyagi, Machiko

1982 "The Geographical Recognition of Palauan People." In M.Aoyagi, ed., *Islanders and Their Outside World,* 3–34. Tokyo: Committee for Micronesian Research.

Aristotle

1958 *The Politics.* Ed. and trans. E.Barker. Oxford: Oxford University Press.

Athens, J. Stephen, J. Ward, and G. Murakami

1996 "Development of an Agroforest on a Micronesian High Island." *Antiquity* 70:834–846.

Athens, Stephen

1990 "Nan Madol Pottery, Pohnpei." *Micronesica* Suppl. no. 2:17–32.

1995 *Landscape Archaeology: Prehistoric Settlement, Subsistence, and Environment of Kosrae, Eastern Caroline Islands, Micronesia.* Honolulu: International Archaeological Research Institute.

2007 "Prehistoric Population Growth on Kosrae, Eastern Caroline Islands." In P.Kirch and J-L.Rallu, eds., *The Growth and Collapse of Pacific Island Societies,* 257–277. Honolulu: University of Hawai'i Press.

Ayres, W., A. Haun, and C. Severance

 1979 *Settlement and Subsistence on Ponape, Micronesia.* Interim Report 78-2, Ponape Archaeology Survey. Eugene: Department of Anthropology, University of Oregon.

Ayres, William, and Alan Haun

 1990 "Prehistoric Food Production in Micronesia." In D.Yen and J.Mummery, eds., *Pacific Production Systems*, 211–277. Canberra: Department of Prehistory, Research School of Pacific Studies, Australian National University.

Barnett, Homer

 1949 *Palauan Society.* Coordinated Investigation of Micronesian Anthropology Report no. 20. Washington, DC: Pacific Science Board. (Also pub. 1949, Department of Anthropology, University of Oregon, Eugene.)

 1960 *Being a Palauan.* New York: Holt, Rinehart and Winston.

Barratt, Glynn, ed.

 1984 *Russian Exploration in the Mariana Islands, 1817–1828.* Saipan: Micronesian Archaeological Survey.

 1988 *Carolinian Contacts with the Islands of the Marianas.* Micronesian Archaeological Survey Report no. 25. Saipan: Micronesian Archaeological Survey.

Barrau, Jacques

 1961 *Subsistence Agriculture in Polynesia and Micronesia.* B.P.Bishop Museum Bulletin 223. Honolulu: B.P.Bishop Museum.

Bascom, William

 1965 *Ponape: A Pacific Economy in Transition.* Anthropological Records 22. Berkeley: University of California Press.

Bath, Joyce, and J.Stephen Athens

 1990 "Prehistoric Social Complexity on Pohnpei." In R.Hunter-Anderson, ed., "Recent Advances in Micronesian Archaeology," *Micronesica* Suppl. no. 2:275–290.

Bellwood, Peter

 1985 *Prehistory of the Indo-Malaysian Archipelago.* Orlando: Academic Press.

Bender, Byron, and Judith Wang

 1985 "The Status of Proto-Micronesian. In A. Pawley and L. Carrington, eds., *Austronesian Linguistics at the 15th Pacific Science Congress*, Pacific Linguistics C-88, 53–92. Canberra: Australian National University.

Bogucki, Peter

 1999 *The Origins of Human Society.* Oxford: Blackwell.

Bradshaw, Michael

 2002 *World Regional Geography.* Boston: McGraw Hill.

Bryan, Edwin

 1971 *Guide to Place Names in the Trust Territory of the Pacific Islands.* Honolulu: Pacific Science Information Center, Bishop Museum.

Burrows, Edwin

 1963 *Flower in My Ear.* University of Washington Publications in Anthropology, vol. 14. Seattle: University of Washington Press.

Burrows, Edwin, and Melford Spiro

1970 *An Atoll Culture: Ethnography of Ifaluk in the Central Carolines.* Westport, CT: Greenwood. (Orig. pub. 1953.)

Burton, Michael, Carmella Moore, John Whiting, and A. Kimball Romney

1996 "Regions Based on Social Structure." *Current Anthropology* 37:87–122.

Buschmann, Rainer

1996 "Tobi Captured: Converging Ethnographic and Colonial Visions on a Caroline Island." *Isla, A Journal of Micronesian Studies* 4:317–340.

Butler, Brian

1988 *Archaeological Investigations on the North Coast of Rota, Mariana Islands.* Micronesian Archaeological Survey Report no. 23. Carbondale: Southern Illinois University Center for Archaeological Investigations.

Campbell, J. C.

1989 *A History of the Pacific Islands.* Berkeley: University of California Press.

Cantor, Norman

1991 *Inventing the Middle Ages.* New York: William Morrow.

Cantova, Fr. Juan Antonio

1722 "Letter of Fr. Juan Antonio Cantova, Agana, 20 March 1722." Published as *Edifying and Curious Letters Written about the Foreign Missions,* by "some Missionaries of the Society of Jesus," Collection 18, Paris, 1728; MS translation, copy in Micronesian Seminar collection. Pagination refers to 1728 ed.

Carucci, Laurence

1988 "Small Fish in a Big Sea." In J. Gledhill, B. Bender, and M. Larson, eds., *State and Society*, 33–42. London: Unwin Hyman.

1997 *Nuclear Nativity.* DeKalb: Northern Illinois University Press.

Caughey, John

1977 *Fáánakar: Cultural Values in a Micronesian Society.* University of Pennsylvania Publications in Anthropology no. 2. Philadelphia: Department of Anthropology, University of Pennsylvania.

Caviedes, César

2001 *El Niño.* Gainesville: University Press of Florida.

Cheyne, Andrew

1971 *The Trading Voyages of Andrew Cheyne, 1841–1844.* Ed. D. Shineberg. Honolulu: University Press of Hawai'i.

Coenen, Jan, and Jacques Barrau

1961 "The Breadfruit Tree in Micronesia." *South Pacific Bulletin* 11 (4): 37–39.

Collerson, Kenneth, and Marshall Weisler

2007 "Stone Adze Compositions and the Extent of Ancient Polynesian Voyaging and Trade." *Science* 317:1907–1911.

Cordy, Ross

1983 "Social Stratification in the Mariana Islands." *Oceania* 63:272–276.

1993 *The Lelu Stone Ruins.* Asian and Pacific Archaeology Series no. 10. Honolulu: Social Science Research Institute, University of Hawai'i.

Cunningham, Lawrence
1992   *Ancient Chamorro Society*. Honolulu: Bess Press.
Damas, David
1979   "Double Descent in the Eastern Carolines." *Journal of the Polynesian Society* 88 (2): 177–198.
1994   *Bountiful Island*. Waterloo, Ontario: Wilfrid Laurier University Press.
D'Arcy, Paul
2001   "Connected by the Sea." *Journal of Pacific History* 36:163–182.
Davenport, William
1964   "Social Structure of Santa Cruz Island." In W. Goodenough, ed., *Explorations in Cultural Anthropology*, 57–93. New York: McGraw-Hill.
Davidson, Janet
1988   "Archaeology in Micronesia." *New Zealand Journal of Archaeology* 10:83–100.
Dening, G. M.
1963   "The Geographical Knowledge of the Polynesians and the Nature of Inter-Island Contact." In J. Golson, ed., "Polynesian Navigation," *Journal of the Polynesian Society* Memoir no. 34, 102–153. Wellington: Polynesian Society.
de Rienzi, M. G. L. Domeny
1872   *Océanie*. Vols. 18–20 of *L'Univers*. Paris: Firmin Didot Freres, Fils, et Cie.
Diaz, Vicente, and J. Kehaulani Kauanui
2001   "Native Pacific Cultural Studies on the Edge." *Contemporary Pacific* 13:315–342.
Dickinson, W. R.
2003   "Impact of Mid-Holocene Hydro-Isostatic Highstand in Regional Sea Level Habitability of Islands in the Pacific Ocean." *Journal of Coastal Research* 19 (3): 489–502.
Di Piazza, Anne, and Erik Pearthree
2007   "A New Reading of Tupaia's Chart." *Journal of the Polynesian Society* 116:321–340.
Divale, William, and Marvin Harris
1976   "Population, Warfare, and the Male Supremacist Complex." *American Anthropologist* 78:521–538.
Douglas, Bronwen
1979   "Traditional Leadership in South Pacific Societies." *Journal of Pacific History* 14:2–27.
Douglas, Mary
1971   "Is Matriliny Doomed in Africa?" In M. Douglas and P. Kaberry, eds., *Man in Africa*, 123–137. Garden City, NY: Anchor.
d'Ozouville, Brigitte
1997   "F. H. Dufty in Fiji, 1871–1892: The Social Role of a Colonial Photographer." *History of Photography* 21 (1): 32–42.
Driver, Margery
1977   "Account of a Discalced Friar's Stay in the Islands of the Ladrones." *Guam Recorder* 7:19 21.
1983   "Fray Juan Pobre and His Account." *Journal of Pacific History* 18:198–216.

Duperrey, L. I.

1982   "Memoirs on the Geographical Operations." In L. Ritter and P. Ritter, trans. and eds., *The European Discovery of Kosrae Island*, 9–19. Micronesian Archaeological Survey Report no. 13. Saipan: Micronesian Archaeological Survey. (Orig. pub. 1828.)

d'Urville, J. S. C. Dumont

1832   "Sur les îles du Grand Océan." *Bulletin de la Societé de Géographie* 17:1–21.

Earle, Timothy

1997   *How Chiefs Come to Power*. Stanford: Stanford University Press.

Eilers, Anneliese

1936   "The Cultural Situation of the West Caroline Islands Songosor, Pur, Merir, Tobi and Ngulu." Trans. K. J. Dennison. In G. Thilenius, ed., *Ergebnisse der Sudsee Expedition, 1908–1910*, 9:245–249. Hamburg: Friedrichsen, De Gruyter and Co.

Ember, Carol

1974   "An Evaluation of Alternative Theories of Matrilocal versus Patrilocal Residence." *Behavior Science Research* 9:135–149.

Evans-Pritchard, E. E.

1940   *The Nuer*. Oxford: Oxford University Press.

Fagan, Brian

2000   *Floods, Famine, and Emperors: El Niño and the Fate of Civilization*. New York: Basic Books.

Figirliyong, Josede

1977   "The Contemporary Political System of Ulithi." M.A. thesis, California State University, Fullerton.

Firth, Raymond

1957   "A Note on Descent Groups." *Man* 57:4–8.

1967   "The Analysis of Mana." In *Tikopia Ritual and Belief*, 174–194. Boston: Beacon. (Orig. pub. 1940, *Journal of the Polynesian Society* 49 [4]: 483–510.)

Fischer, Ann

1957   "The Role of the Trukese Mother and Its Effects on Child Training." PhD dissertation, Harvard University.

Fischer, John

1958   "The Classification of Residence in Censuses." *American Anthropologist* 60 (3): 508–517.

1964   "The Abandonment of Nan Madol." *Micronesica* 1:49–54.

1966   *The Eastern Carolines*. New Haven: HRAF Press.

Fischer, John, Roger Ward, and Martha Ward

1976   "Ponapean Conceptions of Incest." *Journal of the Polynesian Society* 85 (2): 199–207.

Fitzgerald, Maureen

2001   *Whisper of the Mother*. Westport, CT: Bergin and Garvey.

Flinn, Juliana

1992   *Diplomas and Thatch Houses*. Ann Arbor: University of Michigan Press.

Force, Roland
1960 "Leadership and Cultural Change in Palau." *Fieldiana: Anthropology*, vol. 50. Chicago: Chicago Natural History Museum.

Forster, Johann Reinhold
1996 *Observations Made During a Voyage Round the World.* Ed. N. Thomas et al. Honolulu: University of Hawai'i Press.

Fosberg, F. Raymond
1960 "Introgression in Artocarpus in Micronesia." *Brittonia* 12:101–113.

Fox, James J.
1984 "Possible Models of Austronesian Social Organization." *Asian Perspectives* 26:35–43.
1992 "Origin and Order in a Micronesian Society." *Canberra Anthropology* 15:75–86.

Francis, Peter
2002 *Asia's Maritime Bead Trade.* Honolulu: University of Hawai'i Press.

Freeman, Derek
1964 "Some Observations on Kinship and Political Authority in Samoa." *American Anthropologist* 64:553–568.

Fried, Morton
1957 "The Classification of Corporate Unilineal Descent Groups." *Journal of the Royal Anthropological Institute* 87:1–29.
1967 *The Evolution of Political Society.* New York: Random House.

Fustel de Coulanges, Numa Denis
1864 *The Ancient City.* Garden City, NY: Doubleday Anchor

Geddes, W. H., Anne Chambers, Betsy Sewell, Roger Lawrence, and Ray Watters
1982 *Islands on the Line.* Atoll Economy Report no. 1. Canberra: Australian National University.

Gilbert, Felix
1986 "Machiavelli: The Renaissance of the Art of War." In P. Paret, ed., *The Makers of Modern Strategy,* 11–31. Princeton: Princeton University Press.

Gladwin, Thomas, and Seymour Sarason
1953 *Truk: Man in Paradise.* Viking Fund Publications in Anthropology no. 20. New York: Wenner-Gren Foundation.

Goldman, Irving
1970 *Ancient Polynesian Society.* Chicago: University of Chicago Press.

Goodenough, Ward
1951 *Property, Kin and Community on Truk.* Yale University Publications in Anthropology no. 46. New Haven, CT: Yale University Press.
1956 "Residence Rules." *Southwestern Journal of Anthropology* 12 (1): 22–37.
1986 "Sky World and This World: The Place of Kachaw in Micronesian Cosmology." *American Anthropologist* 88:551–568.
2002 *Under Heaven's Brow.* Philadelphia: American Philosophical Society.

Gough, Kathleen, and David Schneider
1961 *Matrilineal Kinship.* Berkeley: University of California Press.

Gould, Stephen Jay

2002   *The Structure of Evolutionary Theory.* Cambridge, MA: Belknap Press.

Gould, Stephen Jay, and Richard Lewontin

1979   "The Spandrels of San Marco and the Panglossian Paradigm." *Proceedings of the Royal Society of London* B 205:581–598.

Graves, Michael, Terry Hunt, and Darlene Moore

1990   "Ceramic Production in the Mariana Islands." *Asian Perspectives* 29:211–233.

Green, Roger

1997   "Linguistic, Biological, and Cultural Origins of the Initial Inhabitants of Remote Oceania." *New Zealand Journal of Archaeology* 17:5–27.

Grimble, Arthur

1989   *Tungaru Traditions.* Ed. H. E. Maude. Honolulu: University of Hawai'i Press.

Gulick, Luther

1862   "Micronesia." *Nautical Magazine and Naval Chronicle* 31:169–183, 237–245, 298–308, 358–363, 408–417.

Guyer, Jane

1981   "Household and Community in African Studies." *African Studies Review* 24 (2): 87–137.

Gyekye, Kwame

1997   *Tradition and Modernity.* New York: Oxford University Press.

Haas, Jonathan

1982   *Evolution of the Prehistoric State.* New York: Columbia University Press.

Hage, Per

1998a   "Austronesian Chiefs: Metaphorical or Fractal Fathers?" *Journal of the Royal Anthropological Institute,* n.s., 4:786–788.

1998b   "Was Proto-Oceanic Society Matrilineal?" *Journal of the Polynesian Society* 107:365–379.

1999a   "Linguistic Evidence of Primogeniture and Ranking in Proto-Oceanic Society." *Oceanic Linguistics* 38:366–375.

1999b   "Reconstructing Ancestral Oceanic Society." *Asian Perspectives* 38:200–228.

2000   "The Conical Clan in Micronesia." *Journal of the Polynesian Society* 109: 295–309.

Hage, Per, and Jeff Marck

2002   "Proto-Micronesian Kin Terms, Descent Groups, and Interisland Voyaging." *Oceanic Linguistics* 41:159–170.

2003   "Matrilineality and the Melanesian Origin of Polynesian Y-Chromosomes." *Current Anthropology* 44 (Suppl.): 121–127.

Hall, Edward, and Karl Pelzer

1946   *The Economy of the Truk Islands.* U.S. Commercial Company's Economic Survey of Micronesia, Report no. 17. Honolulu: U.S. Commercial Co.

Hambruch, Paul

1932   *Ponape: Ergebnisse der Südsee Expedition, 1908–1910.* Vol. 1. Hamburg: Friederichsen, De Gruyter.

Hanlon, David

1988 *Upon a Stone Altar.* Honolulu: University of Hawai'i Press.

1989 "Micronesia: Writing and Rewriting the History of a Non-entity." *Pacific Studies* 12 (1): 1–21.

1998 *Remaking Micronesia.* Honolulu: University of Hawai'i Press.

1999 "Magellan's Chroniclers? American Anthropology's History in Micronesia." In R. Kiste and Mac Marshall, eds., *American Anthropology in Micronesia,* 53–79. Honolulu: University of Hawai'i Press.

2009 "The 'Sea of Little Lands': Examining Micronesia's Place in 'Our Sea of Islands.'" *Contemporary Pacific* 21:91–110.

Harrington, James

1992 *The Commonwealth of Oceania.* Ed. J. G. A. Pocock. Cambridge: Cambridge University Press.

Hays, Terence

1991 "Introduction." In T. Hays, ed., *Encyclopedia of World Cultures,* vol. 2, *Oceania,* xxiii–xxxvii. Boston: G. K. Hall.

Herodotus

1998 *The Histories.* Trans. R. Waterfield. Oxford: Oxford University Press.

Hezel, Francis X.

1983 *The First Taint of Civilization.* Honolulu: University of Hawai'i Press.

1995 *Strangers in Their Own Land.* Honolulu: University of Hawai'i Press.

1999 "American Anthropology's Contribution to Social Problems Research in Micronesia." In R. Kiste and Mac Marshall, eds., *American Anthropology in Micronesia,* 301–326. Honolulu: University of Hawai'i Press.

2001 *New Shape of Old Island Cultures.* Honolulu: University of Hawai'i Press.

Howe, K. R.

2003 *The Quest for Origins.* Honolulu: University of Hawai'i Press.

Hughes, Daniel

1969 "Reciprocal Influence of Traditional and Democratic Leadership Roles on Ponape." *Ethnology* 8 (3): 278–291.

Hunter-Anderson, Rosalind

1991 "A Review of Traditional Micronesian High Island Horticulture in Belau, Yap, Chuuk, Pohnpei, and Kosrae." *Micronesica* 24:1–56.

2005 "Contextualizing Our Past: P-M Lite Comes to Micronesia." *Micronesian Journal of the Humanities and Social Sciences* 4 (1): 69–75.

Hunter-Anderson, Rosalind, and Brian Butler

1995 *An Overview of Northern Marianas Prehistory.* Micronesian Archaeological Survey Report no. 31. Saipan: Micronesian Archaeological Survey.

Hunter-Anderson, Rosalind, and Yigal Zan

1996 "Demystifying the *Sawei,* a Traditional Interisland Exchange System." *Isla* 4:1–45.

Intoh, Michiko

1981 "Reconnaissance Archaeological Research on Ngulu Atoll." *Asian Perspectives* 24:69–80.

1996　"Multi-Regional Contacts of Prehistoric Fais Islanders in Micronesia." *Bulletin of the Indo-Pacific Prehistory Association* 15:111–117.

Irwin, Geoffrey

1992　*The Prehistoric Exploration and Colonization of the Pacific.* Cambridge: Cambridge University Press.

Jackson, Frederick

1986　"On Determining the External Relationships of the Micronesian Languages." In P. Geraghty, L. Carrington, and S. Wurm, eds., *FOCAL II: Papers from the Fourth International Conference on Austronesian Linguistics,* Pacific Linguistics C-94, 201–238.

Kaeppler, Adrienne, Christian Kaufman, and Douglas Newton

1997　*Oceanic Art.* New York: Harry Abrams.

Karolle, Bruce

1993　*Atlas of Micronesia.* 2nd ed. Honolulu: Bess Press.

Kihleng, Kimberlee

1996　"Women in Exchange: Negotiated Relations, Practice, and the Constitution of Female Power in Processes of Cultural Reproduction and Change in Pohnpei, Micronesia." PhD diss., University of Hawai'i.

King, Thomas, and Patricia Parker

1984　*Pisekin Noon Tonaachaw.* Micronesian Archaeological Survey Report no. 18. Southern Illinois University at Carbondale Center for Archaeological Investigation, Occasional Paper no. 3.

Kintoki

1986　*Ekkoch Masowen Weeween Faayiro* (Some Aspects of the Meaning of Under Bow). Transcribed by P. L. Chapman; ed. W. H. Goodenough. Archives of the Micronesian Institute, Washington, DC.

Kirch, Patrick

1984　*The Evolution of the Polynesian Chiefdoms.* Cambridge: Cambridge University Press.

2000　*On the Road of the Winds.* Berkeley: University of California Press.

Kirch, Patrick, and Roger Green

2001　*Hawaiki, Ancestral Polynesia.* Cambridge: Cambridge University Press.

Kirkpatrick, John, and Charles Broder

1976　"Adoption and Parenthood on Yap." In I. Brady, ed., *Transactions in Kinship,* ASAO Monograph no. 4, 200–227. Honolulu: University of Hawai'i Press.

Kiste, Robert

1974　*The Bikinians.* Menlo Park, CA: Cummings.

Kiste, Robert, and Michael Rynkiewich

1976　"Incest and Exogamy: A Comparative Study of Two Marshall Islands Populations." *Journal of the Polynesian Society* 85 (2): 209–226.

Kluge, Fred

1991　*The Edge of Paradise.* New York: Random House.

Knudson, Kenneth

1970　"Resource Fluctuation, Productivity, and Social Organization on Micronesian Coral Islands." PhD diss., Department of Anthropology, University of Oregon.

Koch, Gerd

1965　*Materielle Kulture der Gilbert-Inseln.* Berlin: Museum für Volkerkunde.

Komatsu, Kazuhiko

1990　"A Sketch of Chieftainship on Pulap." In I. Ushijima, ed., *Anthropological Research on the Atoll Cultures of Micronesia,* 21–34. Tsukuba: Department of Anthropology, University of Tsukuba.

Kroeber, Alfred Louis

1948　*Anthropology.* New York: Harcourt Brace.

Kronenfeld, David

1992　"Goodenough vs. Fischer on Residence: A Generation Later." *Journal of Quantitative Anthropology* 4:1–21.

Labby, David

1976　*The Demystification of Yap.* Chicago: University of Chicago Press.

Lambert, Berndt

1966　"The Economic Activities of a Gilbertese Chief." In M. Swartz, V. Turner, and A. Tuden, eds., *Political Anthropology,* 155–172. Chicago: Aldine.

1978　"*Uean Abara*: The High Chiefs of Butaritari and Makin as Kinsmen and Office-holders." In Niel Gunson, ed., *The Changing Pacific: Essays in Honor of H. E. Maude,* 80–93. Melbourne: Oxford University Press.

1981　"Equivalence, Authority, and Complementarity in Butaritari-Makin Sibling Relationships." In M. Marshall, ed., *Siblingship in Oceania,* ASAO Monograph no. 8, 149–200. Ann Arbor: University of Michigan Press.

Lawrence, P., M. Hadley, and R. McKnight

1964　"Breadfruit Cultivation Practices and Beliefs in Ponape." In J. DeYoung, ed., *Breadfruit Cultivation Practices and Beliefs in the Trust Territory of the Pacific Islands,* 42–64. Saipan: Office of the High Commissioner, US Trust Territory of the Pacific Islands.

LeBar, Frank

1964　*The Material Culture of Truk.* Yale University Publications in Anthropology no. 68. New Haven, CT: Yale University Press.

1972　*Ethnic Groups of Insular Southeast Asia.* Vol. 1. New Haven, CT: Human Relations Area Files Press.

1975　*Ethnic Groups of Insular Southeast Asia.* Vol. 2. New Haven, CT: Human Relations Area Files Press.

Lebot, Vincent, Mark Merlin, and Lamont Lindstrom

1992　*Kava: The Pacific Drug.* New Haven, CT: Yale University Press.

Lessa, William

1950　"Ulithi and the Outer Native World." *American Anthropologist* 52 (1): 27–52.

1956　"Myth and Blackmail in the Western Carolines." *Journal of the Polynesian Society* 65 (1): 66–74.

1961　"Sorcery on Ifaluk." *American Anthropologist* 63:817–820.

1962　"An Evaluation of Early Descriptions of Carolinian Culture." *Ethnohistory* 9:313–403.

1964   "The Social Effects of Typhoon Ophelia (1960) on Ulithi." *Micronesica* 1:1–47.

1966   *Ulithi: A Micronesian Design for Living.* New York: Holt Rinehart Winston.

1968   "Micronesian Religions." In M. Eliade, *The Encyclopedia of Religion*, 9:498–505. New York: Macmillan.

1976   "The Apotheosis of Marespa." In A. Kaeppler and H. Nimmo, eds., *Directions in Pacific Traditional Literature*, 61–81. Honolulu: B. P. Bishop Museum.

Lesson, P.

1982   "Voyage around the World." In L. Ritter and P. Ritter, trans. and eds., *The European Discovery of Kosrae Island*, Micronesian Archaeological Survey Report no. 13, 38–79. Saipan: Micronesian Archaeological Survey. (Orig. pub. 1839.)

Lewis, James

1967   *Kusaien Acculturation, 1824–1948.* Saipan: Division of Land Management, Trust Territory of the Pacific Islands. (Orig. pub. as Coordinated Investigation of Micronesian Anthropology no. 17. Washington: Pacific Science Board.)

Lichtenberk, Frantisek

1986   "Leadership in Proto-Oceanic Society." *Journal of the Polynesian Society* 95:341–356.

Lingenfelter, Sherwood

1975   *Yap: Political Leadership and Culture Change in an Island Society.* Honolulu: University Press of Hawai'i.

1977   "Emic Structure and Decision-Making in Yap. *Ethnology* 16:331–352.

1979   "Yap Eating Classes." *Journal of the Polynesian Society* 88:415–432.

Locke, John

1960   *Two Treatises of Government.* Ed. Peter Laslett. New York: New American Library.

Lord, Carnes

1987   "Aristotle." In L. Strauss and J. Cropsey, eds., *History of Political Philosophy*, 118–154. Chicago: University of Chicago Press.

Lowie, Robert H.

1921   *Primitive Society.* London: Routledge and Kegan Paul.

Lum, J. Koji, and Rebecca Cann

1998   "mtDNA and Language Support a Common Origin of Micronesians and Polynesians in Island Southeast Asia." *American Journal of Physical Anthropology* 105:109–119.

2000   "mtDNA Lineage Analyses: Origins and Migrations of Micronesians and Polynesians." *American Journal of Physical Anthropology* 113:151–168.

Lundsgaarde, Henry

1978   "Post-contact Changes in Gilbertese *Maneaba* Organization." In N. Gunson, ed., *The Changing Pacific*, 67–89. Melbourne: Oxford University Press.

Lütke, Frederic

1982   "Voyage around the World." In L. Ritter and P. Ritter, trans. and eds., *The European Discovery of Kosrae Island*, Micronesian Archaeological Survey Report no. 13, 84–163. Saipan: Micronesian Archaeological Survey. (Orig. pub. 1835.)

Lutz, Catherine

1988   *Unnatural Emotions.* Chicago: University of Chicago Press.

Lynch, John, Malcolm Ross, and Terry Crowley

2002　*The Oceanic Languages.* Richmond, Surrey: Curzon.

Machiavelli, Niccolo

1966　*The Prince.* Trans. Daniel Donno. New York: Bantam Books.

1997　*The Discourses on Livy.* Trans. J.C. Bondanella and P. Bondanella. Oxford: Oxford University Press.

Mackenzie, J. Boyd

1960　"Breadfruit Cultivation Practices and Beliefs in the Marshall Islands." Anthropological Working Papers, no. 8. Guam: Trust Territory of the Pacific Islands.

Marck, Jeff

1986　"Micronesian Dialects and the Overnight Voyage." *Journal of the Polynesian Society* 95:253–258.

2004　"Some Ancient Clan Names of the Chuukic Speaking Peoples of Micronesia." http://rspas.anu.edu.au/linguistics/OceanicClanNames.pdf.

Marshall, Mac

1972　"The Structure of Solidarity and Alliance on Namoluk Atoll." PhD diss., University of Washington.

1976　"Incest and Endogamy on Namoluk Atoll." *Journal of the Polynesian Society* 85 (2): 181–197.

1979　"Sibling Sets as Building Blocks in Greater Trukese Society." In M. Marshall, ed., *Siblingship in Oceania,* ASAO Monograph no. 8, 201–224. Ann Arbor: University of Michigan Press.

1989　"Rashomon in Reverse: Ethnographic Agreement in Truk." In M. Marshall and J. Caughey, eds., *Cognition in Oceania,* American Anthropological Association Special Publication no. 25, 95–106. Washington, DC: American Anthropological Association.

1999　"'Partial Connections': Kinship and Social Organization in Micronesia." In R. Kiste and Mac Marshall, eds., *American Anthropology in Micronesia,* 107–143. Honolulu: University of Hawai'i Press.

Marston, Sallie, Paul Knox, and Diana Liverman

2002　*World Regions.* Upper Saddle River, NJ: Prentice Hall.

Mason, Leonard

1943　"Social Organization in the Marshall Islands." Typescript, Yale University, Institute of Human Relations. Copy at Micronesian Seminar.

1947　*The Economic Organization of the Marshall Islanders.* U.S. Commercial Company Economic Survey of Micronesia, Report no. 9. Honolulu: U.S. Commercial Co.

1964　"Micronesian Cultures." *Encyclopedia of World Art* 9:915–930.

1968　"Suprafamilial Authority and Economic Process in Micronesian Atolls." In A. P. Vayda, ed., *Peoples and Cultures of the Pacific,* 299–329. Garden City, NY: Natural History Press. (Orig. pub. 1959.)

1975　"The Many Faces of Micronesia." *Pacific Asian Studies* (University of Guam) 1·5–37.

1986　"Land Rights and Title Succession in the Ralik Chain, Marshall Islands." MS.

Mason, Leonard, and Alois Nagler

1943 "Social Organization in the Marshall Islands." MS prepared for the Cross-Cultural Survey, Yale University, Institute of Human Relations. Copy in the Pacific Collection, Hamilton Library, University of Hawai'i, Honolulu.

Maude, H. E.

1963 *Evolution of the Gilbertese Boti.* Memoir no. 35. Wellington: Polynesian Society.

Mauricio, Ruffino

1987 "Peopling of Pohnpei Island." *Man and Culture in Oceania* 3:47–72.

McCormick, Suzanne

1982 *Master Part of Heaven.* Prepared for the Historic Preservation Office, Trust Territory of the Pacific Islands, and the Pohnpei Historic Preservation Office.

McCoy, Patrick, and Paul Cleghorn

1988 "Archaeological Excavations on Santa Cruz (Nendo), Southeast Solomons Islands." *Archaeology in Oceania* 23:104–115.

McKnight, Robert

1960 "Breadfruit Cultivation Practices and Beliefs in Palau." Anthropological Working Papers, no. 7. Guam: Trust Territory of the Pacific Islands.

Meller, Norman

1989 *Micronesian Constitutionalism.* Laie, HI: Institute for Polynesian Studies.

Metzgar, Eric H.

1996. *Spirits of the Voyage* (motion picture). Camarillo, California: Triton Films.

Morgan, William

1988 *Prehistoric Architecture in Micronesia.* Austin: University of Texas Press.

Morgenthau, Robert

1993 *Politics among Nations.* Brief ed. New York: McGraw-Hill.

Mosko, Mark

1995 "Rethinking Trobriand Chieftainship." *Journal of the Royal Anthropological Institute*, n.s., 1:763–785.

1998 "Reply to Hage." *Journal of the Royal Anthropological Institute*, n.s., 4:789–795.

Murdock, George Peter

1948 "New Light on the Peoples of Micronesia." *Science* 108 (2808): 423–425.

1949 *Social Structure.* New York: Macmillan.

1965 "Anthropology in Micronesia." In G. P. Murdock, *Culture and Society*, 237–248. Pittsburgh: University of Pittsburgh Press. (Orig. pub. 1948.)

Murphy, Robert F.

1971 *The Dialectics of Social Life.* New York: Basic Books.

Nakayama, Masao, and Fred Ramp

1974 *Micronesian Navigation, Island Empires and Traditional Concepts of Ownership of the Sea.* Saipan: Congress of Micronesia.

Nason, James

1974 "Political Change: An Outer Island Perspective." In D. Hughes and S. Lingenfelter, eds., *Political Development in Micronesia*, 119–142. Columbus: Ohio State University Press.

Nenner, Howard

1995   *The Right to Be King*. Chapel Hill: University of North Carolina Press.

Nero, Karen

1992   "The Breadfruit Story: Mythological Transformations in Palauan Politics." *Pacific Studies* 15 (4): 235–260.

1999   "Missed Opportunities: American Anthropological Studies of Micronesian Arts." In R. Kiste and Mac Marshall, eds., *American Anthropology in Micronesia*, 255–299. Honolulu: University of Hawai'i Press.

Nimmo, H. Arlo

1972   *The Sea People of Sulu*. San Francisco: Chandler.

Nunn, Patrick

1994   "Environmental Change and the Early Settlement of Pacific Islands." East-West Center Working Papers, Environment Series, no. 39.

O'Connell, James

1972   *A Residence of Eleven Years in New Holland and the Caroline Islands*. Ed. S. Riesenberg. Honolulu: University Press of Hawai'i. (Orig. pub. 1836.)

Oliver, Douglas

1989   *Oceania*. Vol. 2. Honolulu: University of Hawai'i Press.

1993a   "Rivers (W. H. R.) Revisited: Matriliny in Southern Bougainville, Part 1." *Pacific Studies* 16 (3): 1–54.

1993b   "Rivers (W. H. R.) Revisited: Matriliny in Southern Bougainville, Part 2." *Pacific Studies* 16 (4): 1–40.

2002   *Polynesia in Early Historic Times*. Honolulu: Bess Press.

Orans, Martin

1966   "Surplus." *Human Organization* 25:24–33.

Palau Society of Historians

1997   *Rechuodel: Traditional Culture and Lifeways Long Ago in Palau*. Trans. DeVerne Reed Smith. Micronesian Resources Study, Palau Ethnography. San Francisco: Micronesian Endowment for Historic Preservation.

Parker, Patricia

1985   "Land Tenure in Trukese Society, 1850–1980." PhD diss., University of Pennsylvania.

Parmentier, Richard

1987   *The Sacred Remains*. Chicago: University of Chicago Press.

Pawley, Andrew

1982   "Rubbish Man Commoner, Big Man Chief?" In J. Siikala, ed., *Oceanic Studies*, 33–52. Helsinki: Finnish Anthropological Society.

Pawley, Andrew, and Roger Green

1984   "The Proto-Oceanic Language Community." *Journal of Pacific History* 19:123–146.

Pawley, Andrew, and Malcolm Ross

1995   "The Prehistory of Oceanic Languages." In P. Bellwood, J. Fox, and D. Tryon, eds., *The Austronesians: Historical and Comparative Perspectives*, 39–74. Canberra: Department of Anthropology, Research School of Pacific and Asian Studies, Australian National University.

Peoples, James

1993 "Political Evolution in Micronesia." *Ethnology* 32:1–17.

Petersen, Glenn

1975 "Yams, Kava, and Picking Off Breadfruit." Paper presented at the Association for Social Anthropology in Oceania annual meetings, Stuart, Florida.

1977 "Ponapean Agriculture and Economy." PhD diss., Department of Anthropology, Columbia University.

1982a *One Man Cannot Rule a Thousand.* Ann Arbor: University of Michigan Press.

1982b "Ponapean Matriliny: Production, Exchange, and the Ties That Bind." *American Ethnologist* 9:129–144.

1985 "Ritually Changing the Seasons." In Charles Bazerman, *The Informed Writer*, 2nd ed., 378–384. Boston: Houghton Mifflin.

1987 "Redistribution in a Micronesian Commercial Economy." *Oceania* 57: 83–96.

1990 *Lost in the Weeds: Theme and Variation in Pohnpei Political Mythology.* Center for Pacific Islands Studies Working Papers, no. 35. Honolulu: University of Hawai'i.

1992 "Dancing Defiance: The Politics of Pohnpeian Dance Performances." *Pacific Studies* 15 (4): 13–28.

1993 "*Kanengamah* and Pohnpei's Politics of Concealment." *American Anthropologist* 95:334–352.

1995a "The Complexity of Power, the Subtlety of Kava." In N. Pollock, ed., "The Power of Kava," special issue, *Canberra Anthropologist* 18 (1–2): 34–60.

1995b "Nan Madol's Contested Landscape: Topography and Tradition in the Eastern Caroline Islands." *Isla* 3:105–128.

1995c "Power Corrupts—Does Corruption Empower?" *Oceania* 65:355–360.

1997 "A Micronesian Chamber of Chiefs?" In G. White and L. Lindstrom, eds., *Chiefs Today*, 183–196. Stanford: Stanford University Press.

1999a "Politics in Post-War Micronesia." In R. Kiste and M. Marshall, eds., *Anthropology in American Micronesia*, 145–197. Honolulu: University of Hawai'i Press.

1999b "Sociopolitical Rank and Clanship in the Caroline Islands." *Journal of the Polynesian Society* 108 (4): 367–410.

2000 "Indigenous Island Empires: Yap and Tonga Considered." *Journal of Pacific History* 35:5–27.

2004 "Lessons Learned: The Micronesian Quest for Independence in the Context of American Imperial History." *Micronesian Journal of the Humanities and Social Sciences* 3:45–63.

2005 "Important to Whom? On Ethnographic Usefulness, Competence and Relevance." *Anthropological Forum* 15:307–317.

2007 "Hambruch's Colonial Narrative: Pohnpei, German Culture Theory, and Hamburg Expedition Ethnography of 1908–10." *Journal of Pacific History* 42:317–330.

Pocock, J. G. H.

1975 *The Machiavellian Moment.* Princeton: Princeton University Press.

Pollock, Nancy

1974 "Breadfruit or Rice." *Ecology of Food and Nutrition* 3:107–115.

1976 "The Origin of Clans on Namu, Marshall Islands." In A. Kaeppler and H. Nimmo, eds., *Pacific Traditional Literature*, B. P. Bishop Museum Special Publication no. 62, 83–98.

1992 *These Roots Remain*. Laie, HI: Institute of Polynesian Studies.

Poyer, Lin

1993 *The Ngatik Massacre*. Washington, DC: Smithsonian Institution Press.

Ragone, Diane

1988 *Breadfruit Varieties in the Pacific Atolls*. Suva: Integrated Atoll Development Project.

1997 *Breadfruit*. Rome: International Plant Genetic Resources Institute.

2001 "Chromosome Numbers and Pollen Stainability of Three Species of Pacific Island Breadfruit (*Artocarpus*, Moraceae)." *American Journal of Botany* 88:693–697.

Rainbird, Paul

1994 "Prehistory in the Northwest Tropical Pacific." *Journal of World Prehistory* 8:293–349.

2002 "Pohnpei Petroglyphs, Communication and Miscommunication." *Bulletin of the Indo-Pacific Prehistory Association* 22:141–145.

2004 *The Archaeology of Micronesia*. Cambridge: Cambridge University Press.

Ramp, F., and M. Nakayama

1974 *Micronesian Navigation, Island Empires, and Traditional Concepts of Ownership of the Sea*. Saipan: Congress of Micronesia.

Raynor, William

1989 "Structure, Production, and Seasonality in an Indigenous Pacific Island Agroforestry System." MS thesis, Agronomy and Soil Science, University of Hawai'i.

Rehg, Kenneth

1995 "The Significance of Linguistic Interaction Spheres in Reconstructing Micronesian Prehistory." *Oceanic Linguistics* 34 (2): 305–326.

1997 "The Linguistic Evidence for Prehistoric Contact between Western Polynesia and Pohnpei." Paper presented to the Society for Hawaiian Archaeology.

Rehg, Kenneth, and Bryan Bender

1990 "Lexical Transfer from Marshallese to Mokilese. *Oceanic Linguistics* 29:1–26.

Richards, Audrey

1950 "Some Types of Family Structure amongst the Central Bantu." In A. R. Radcliffe-Brown and D. Forde, eds., *African Systems of Kinship and Marriage*, 83–120. Oxford: Oxford University Press.

Riesenberg, Saul

1965 "Table of Voyages Affecting Micronesian Islands." *Oceania* 36:155–170.

1968 *The Native Polity of Ponape*. Washington, DC: Smithsonian Institution.

Riesenberg, Saul, and Anna Gayton

1952 "Caroline Island Belt Weaving." *Southwestern Journal of Anthropology* 8:342–375.

Ritter, L., and P. Ritter, trans. and eds.

1982 *The European Discovery of Kosrae Island*. Micronesian Archaeological Survey Report no. 13. Saipan: Micronesian Archaeological Survey.

Ritter, Phillip
1978 "The Repopulation of Kosrae." PhD diss., Stanford University.
Rogers, Robert
1995 *Destiny's Landfall*. Honolulu: University of Hawai'i Press.
Ross, Malcolm
1996 "Is Yapese Oceanic?" In B. Nothofer, ed., *Reconstruction, Classification, Description*, 121–165. Hamburg: Abera Verlag.
Rubinstein, Donald H.
1986 "Fabric Arts and Traditions." In J. Feldman and D. Rubinstein, eds., *The Art of Micronesia*, 45–69. Honolulu: University of Hawai'i Art Gallery.
Russell, Scott
1998 *Tiempon I Manmofo'na*. Saipan: Division of Historic Preservation.
Ryle, Gilbert
1949 *The Concept of Mind*. New York: Barnes and Noble.
Rynkiewich, Michael
1972 "Land Tenure among the Arno Marshallese." PhD diss., University of Minnesota.
1974 "The Ossification of Local Politics." In D. Hughes and S. Lingenfelter, eds., *Political Development in Micronesia*, 143–165. Columbus: Ohio State University Press.
1976 "Adoption and Land Tenure among Arno Marshallese." In I. Brady, ed., *Transactions in Kinship*, ASAO Monograph no. 4, 93–119. Honolulu: University of Hawai'i Press.
Sahlins, Marshall
1958 *Social Stratification in Polynesia*. Monograph of the American Ethnological Society. Seattle: University of Washington Press.
1963 "Poor Man, Rich Man, Big-Man, Chief." *Comparative Studies in Society and History* 5:205–303.
1968 *Tribesmen*. Englewood Cliffs, NJ: Prentice-Hall.
1981 *Historical Metaphors and Mythical Realities*. Ann Arbor: University of Michigan Press.
1989 "Comment." *Current Anthropology* 30:36–37.
Sarfert, E.
1920 *Kusaie*. Vol. 2, B, 4, part 1, of *Ergebnisse der Sudsee Expedition, 1908–1910*. Hamburg: Friederichsen, De Gruyter.
Schneider, David
1949 "The Kinship System and Village Organization of Yap." PhD diss., Department of Anthropology, Harvard University.
1957 "Typhoons on Yap." *Human Organization* 16 (2): 10–15.
1961 "The Distinctive Features of Matrilineal Groups." In D. Schneider and K. Gough, eds., *Matrilineal Kinship*, 1–29. Berkeley: University of California Press.
1962 "Double Descent on Yap." *Journal of the Polynesian Society* 71:1–24.
1965 "Some Muddles in the Models." In M. Banton, ed., *The Relevance of Models for Social Anthropology*, 25–85. London: Tavistock.

Service, Elman

1985 *A Century of Controversy.* Orlando: Academic Press.

Shimizu, Akitoshi

1987 "Kinship-Based Groups and Land Tenure on a Marshallese Atoll." In E. Ishikawa, ed., *Cultural Adaptation to Atolls in Micronesia and West Polynesia,* 19–41. Tokyo: Committee for Micronesian Research, Tokyo Metropolitan University.

Smith, DeVerne Reed

1979 "Palauan Siblingship." In M. Marshall, ed., *Siblingship in Oceania,* ASAO Monograph no. 8, 225–273. Ann Arbor: University of Michigan Press.

1983 *Palauan Social Structure.* New Brunswick, NJ: Rutgers University Press.

Spiro, Melford

1952 "Ghosts, Ifaluk, and Teleological Functionalism." *American Anthropologist* 54 (4): 497–503.

1961 "Sorcery, Evil Spirits, and Functional Analysis: A Rejoinder." *American Anthropologist* 63:820–824.

Spoehr, Alexander

1949 "Majuro: A Village in the Marshall Islands." *Fieldiana: Anthropology,* vol. 39. Chicago: Chicago Natural History Museum.

1954 "Saipan: The Ethnology of a War-Devastated Island." *Fieldiana: Anthropology,* vol. 41. Chicago: Chicago Natural History Museum.

Steager, Peter

1979 "Where Does Art Begin on Puluwat?" In S. Mead, ed., *Exploring the Visual Art of Oceania,* 342–353. Honolulu: University of Hawai'i Press.

Stephen, Ernest

1936 "Notes on Nauru." Ed. C. H. Wedgwood, *Oceania* 7:34–63.

Stone, E. L.

1951 *The Agriculture of Arno Atoll, Marshall Islands.* Atoll Research Bulletin 6. Washington, DC: Pacific Science Board.

Sturges, Albert

1873 Letter to Clark, 9 September 1873. American Board of Commissioners for the Foreign Mission, Micronesia, 19.4, vol. 5. Houghton Library, Harvard University.

Sudo, Ken-ichi

1996 "Rank, Hierarchy and Routes of Migration." In J. Fox and C. Sather, eds., *Origins, Ancestry and Alliance,* 55–69. Canberra: Department of Anthropology, Research School of Pacific and Asian Studies, Australian National University.

Takayama, Jun

1981 "A Brief Report on Archaeological Investigations on the Southern Part of Yap Island; and Nearby Ngulu Atoll." In M. Aoyagi, ed., *Islanders and Their Outside World,* 77–104. Tokyo: Committee for Micronesian Research.

Thomas, John

1978 "Adoption, Filiation, and Descent on Namonuito Atoll." PhD diss., University of Hawai'i.

1980 "The Namonuito Solution to the Matrilineal Puzzle." *American Ethnologist* 7:172–177.

Thomas, Nicholas

1989   "The Force of Ethnology." *Current Anthropology* 30:27–32.

Thomas, William

1967   "The Pacific Basin: An Introduction." In H. R. Friis, ed., *The Pacific Basin*, 1–17. New York: American Geographical Society.

Thompson, Laura

1945   *The Native Cultures of the Marianas Islands*. B. P. Bishop Museum Bulletin no. 185. Honolulu: B. P. Bishop Museum.

Tito, Keina, Tebaubwebwe Tiata, Baie Teanako, Uentabo Fakaofo, and Arobati Tautua

1979   "Tradition: Ancient Gilbertese Society." In Alaima Talu et al., eds., *Kiribati: Aspects of History*, 12–28. Suva: Institute of Pacific Studies and Extension Services, University of the South Pacific.

Tobin, Jack

1952   *Land Tenure in the Marshall Islands*. Atoll Research Bulletin no. 11. Washington, DC: Pacific Science Board, Smithsonian Institution.

1956   *Land Tenure in the Marshall Islands*. Atoll Research Bulletin no. 11, rev. ed. Pacific Science Board. Washington: National Research Council.

1967   "The Resettlement of the Eniwetok People." PhD diss., University of California, Berkeley.

Useem, John

1945   "The Changing Structure of a Micronesian Society." *American Anthropologist* 47 (4): 567–588.

1946   *Report on Palau*. Coordinated Investigation of Micronesian Anthropology Report no. 21. Washington, DC: Pacific Science Board.

1947   "Applied Anthropology in Oceania." *Applied Anthropology* 6 (4): 1–14.

1948   "Institutions of Micronesia." *Far Eastern Survey* 17 (2): 22–25.

1950   "Structure of Power in Palau." *Social Forces* 29 (2): 141–148.

1952   "Democracy in Process: The Development of Democratic Leadership in the Micronesian Islands." In E. H. Spicer, ed., *Human Problems in Technological Change*, 261–280. New York: Russell Sage Foundation.

Waltz, Kenneth

1979   *Theory of International Politics*. Boston: Addison-Wesley.

Ward, Martha

1989   *Nest in the Wind*. Prospect Heights, IL: Waveland.

Wedgwood, Camilla

1936   "Report on Research Work in Nauru Island, Central Pacific." Part 1. *Oceania* 6:359–391.

1937   "Report on Research Work in Nauru Island, Central Pacific." Part 2. *Oceania* 7:1–33.

Weiner, Annette

1988   *The Trobrianders of Papua New Guinea*. New York: Holt Rinehart Winston.

Wenkam, Robert, and Byron Baker

1971   *Micronesia: The Breadfruit Revolution*. Honolulu: East-West Center.

Wilkes, Charles

1845   *Narrative of the United States Exploring Expedition during the Years 1838–1842.* Vol. 5. Philadelphia: Lea and Blanchard.

Wilson, Walter Scott

1976   "Household, Land, and Adoption on Kusaie." In I. Brady, ed., *Transactions in Kinship*, ASAO Monograph no. 4, 81–92. Honolulu: University of Hawai'i Press.

Yanaihara, Tadao

1940   *Pacific Islands under Japanese Mandate.* London: Oxford University Press.

Yen, Douglas

1974   "Arboriculture in the Subsistence of Santa Cruz, Solomon Islands." *Economic Botany* 28:247–284.

1982   "Southeast Solomons Cultural History." *Bulletin of the Indo-Pacific Prehistory Association* 3:52–66.

Zerega, Nyree

2003   "The Breadfruit Trail." *Natural History* (December 2003–January 2004): 46–51.

Zerega, Nyree, Diane Ragone, and Timothy Motley

2004   "Complex Origins of Breadfruit." *American Journal of Botany* 91:760–766.

Index

Note: Page numbers in **boldface** type refer to illustrations.

clans: conical, 83; cult of Kachaw (cult of Achaw), 61–62; dispersed nature of, 2, 47–48, 76–77; founding or apical ancestress of, 69–70; in Kiribati, 214–215; moral claims to aid from, 23; rank and hierarchy of, 49, 62–63, 67, 82–83; relationship to households, 72; relationship to lineages, 66, 67, 72; relationship to subclans, 80–81; terms for, 73–75; on Yap, 222–223. *See also* matriliny/matrilineal clans

Cleghorn, Paul, 40

climate, 1–2, 9–10, 22, 26, 31, 47, 85–86, 91, 222

coconuts, 55, 228, 238n.21

colonial period, 151, 227–230

communities: and chiefs, 129–130, 131–132, 182; and deviant/aberrant members, 103; on Nauru, 217–218; web of relationships and, 66–67, 100–103, 212

conical clans, 83

continental islands, 7, 9

cookhouses, 87–89

copra, 128–129

coral islands, 9

Cordy, Ross, 58, 219

councils, 145–146, 162, 215–216

cultural areas: Micronesia as, 12–19; of the Pacific, 13–14, 18–19, 20–21 (map)

Cunningham, Lawrence, 218, 219, 220

Damas, David, 49, 165, 236n.7, 237n.15

dance performances, 153, **154,** 188–189, 220–221

D'Arcy, Paul, 62

Davenport, William, 40

Davidson, Janet, 52

deities, 173

de los Angeles, Antonio, 220

de Rienzi, M. G. L. Domeny, 13–14

descent, 66

descent groups, 66, 71–72, 214. *See also* clans; lineages

descent principles, 68–73

dialect chains, 39–40

Dickinson, W. R., 42

Divale, William, 94

dogs, 104

domesticated animals, 104

domestic cycles, 89–90

Douglas, Bronwen, 247n.8 (Chapter 8)

Douglas, Mary, 98

d'Ozouville, Brigitte, 150

Driver, Margery, 195, 219, 220

droughts, 2, 9–10, 22–23, 26, 174, 222

Duperrey, L. I., 172, 173

Durkheim, Emile, 174

d'Urville, Dumont, 13–14, **41**

Eastern Caroline Islands: breadfruit in, 54, 59, 63; chiefs, 239n.30; houses, **86;** introduction to, 28–30; matrilineal clanship in, 64, 67, 222–223. *See also* *specific islands*

eating classes, 223–224

El Niño–Southern Oscillation (ENSO), 9–10

Ember, Carol, 46

Eniwetok atoll, 173, 229

epidemics, 228

equality, 96–98, 164–167, 210–212, 232, 245n.2

Etal (Mortlock Islands), 141, 156

ethnography and ethnology, 6–7

Evans-Pritchard, E. E., 99

exogamy, 70, 90–91

Fais, 30–31, 34, 44, 49

families. *See* households

fatherhood, 97–98, 99

feasting, 158–161, 165, 173

federal systems, 139, 143, 232, 243n.9

feudal systems, 135, 139, 243n.9

Figirliyong, Josede, 156

filiation, 68, 110

Filmer, Robert, 121

first fruits offerings, 112–113, 158–159, 196

Firth, Raymond, 170

Fischer, Ann, 96, 133

Fischer, John, 74, 77, 88, 91, 92, 93, 132, 196

fishing, **27, 32** 104

Fitzgerald, Maureen, 208

Flinn, Juliana, 85, 201, 204, 205, 231

menstrual houses, 241n.2

Micronesia, introduction and prehistory: archipelagoes, 24; breadfruit revolution and cultural surge, 53–61; as coherent region, 185; colonial period, 151, 227–230; as cultural area, 12–19; discreet local cultures within, 17; early economy in, 50–51; early social organization, 45–50; interaction and interdependence between societies, 19, 22–24, 42, 44, 47, 51, 64, 227; introduction to, 7, 9–11; map, 8; origins of eastern Micronesians, 39–44; origins of western Micronesians, 51–53; Pacific island settlement, 37–39; self-government and independence, 230, 232–233, 245n.7; survival in (*see* survival); types of islands, 7, 9, 10–11; use of term, 1, 4

Milad, 63

missionaries, 5, 117–118, 227, 228

modesty, 176, 206–207

Morgan, William, 193

Mortlock Islands, 30, 44, 75, **79,** 141. *See also* Namoluk

Mosko, Mark, 247n.12

Murdock, George Peter, 94, 135

Murphy, Robert F., 99

Nagler, Alois, 142

Nahnken, 132, 144

Nahnmwarki, 132, 140, 144

Nakayama, Masao, 62, 140

Namoluk (Mortlock Islands), 75, 79, 110, 120

Namonuito, 98

Nan Madol (Pohnpei), 29, 58, 59, 149, 174, 193, 196

Nason, James, 141, 156

Nauru: differences from the rest of Micronesia, 217–218; introduction to, 26–27; and Kiribati, 44; land rights, 113, 217, 218; plaited mats, 190

Nenner, Howard, 176

Nero, Karen, 36, 63, 171, 188

New Guinea, 37–38

Nimmo, H. Arlo, 51

Nuclear Micronesia, 40, 43, 49, 61, 64

Nuclear Micronesian language group, 19, 23, 24, 40, 43, 44

Nui, 17, 25

Nunn, Patrick, 42

Oceania, 14, 15, 17–18. *See also* Remote Oceania

Oceanic language family, 38, 39–40, 43

O'Connell, James, 5–6, 143

Oliver, Douglas, 46, 242n.1

Orans, Martin, 106–107, 183

Pacific island settlement, 37–39

Palau: adherence to customs in, 185; adoption on, 119; architecture, 192; behavior styles, 206; *blolobel* practice, 91; breadfruit in, 60, 63; chiefs, 131, 133, 134, 137–138, 139–140, 142, 145–146, 162, 163, 166, 170, 171, 177–178; descent groups, 74–75, 80, 81, 82; descent principles, 68; and feasting, 160; gender roles, 96, 97; households, 88–89; introduction to, 24, 35–36; land rights, 110, 112, 116; origin of matriclan organization, 63; relations with Yap, 51, 61; respect postures and positioning, 171; settlement of, 51, 52; sibling relationships in, 73; taro usage, 108

Palau Society of Historians, 134, 145–146, 168

pandanus, 27, 28, 50, 57, 108

paramount chiefs, 127, 134, 139–140

Parker, Patricia, 55, 59–60, 77, 81, 111

Parmentier, Richard, 88, 91, 138, 140, 160, 163, 171

patriliny, 47, 48, 49, 68, 99, 110–111

Pawley, Andrew, 39

Pelzer, Karl, 134, 137, 159

personality. *See* values, personal styles and character dimensions

Petersen, Glenn, 6, 34, 56, 83, 96, 98, 140, 141, 147, 152, 164, 177, 179, 189, 190, 193, 196, 203, 206, 208, 221, 230

Philippines, 51, 53, 218

pigs, 104

Pingelap, 165

Pobre, Juan, 219, 220